SAFE INSIDE

A MEMOIR

by
LEE KINGSMILL

ECKHARTZ
PRESS

SAFE INSIDE
A Memoir

Copyright © 2017 by **Lee Kingsmill**
Trade Paperback

Published in the United States by **Eckhartz Press**
Chicago, Illinois
All Rights Reserved

Cover Design by **Dave Stern**
Interior Design by **Vasil Nazar**

No part of this book may be used or reproduced in any manner whatsoever without written permission except in the case of brief quotations embodied in critical articles and reviews.

ISBN: 978-0-9983315-3-9

For John Kruzan
With all there is…and then some more

Claimer

What follows is a memoir of my youth. To explain to myself the strange and distant events which shaped me, it was necessary to invade the minds of those around me at the time. Consequently, any resemblance in these pages to characters living or dead will be met by the author with gratitude and relief. Where names have been changed, it is to provide the innocent (whom I hope I have, in fact, celebrated) and the less so, with at least some skimpy cloak of privacy when raw episodes rear up. They are gone now, most of them. Without exception, I wish them well.

TABLE OF CONTENTS

Chapter 1	Bungalow Blues	*1*
Chapter 2	Safe Inside	*6*
Chapter 3	The Blue Leopard and the Caves of Sapphire	*107*
Chapter 4	Picture Perfect	*160*
Chapter 5	Route 66..	*186*
Chapter 6	A Saturday Matinee	*216*
Chapter 7	Hostile Witness...	*244*
Chapter 8	Jumping Ship	*261*
Chapter 9	The Return of the Blue Leopard	*273*
Chapter 10	Merry Widows on the Town......................................	*308*
Chapter 11	Candy From Home	*324*
Chapter 12	Dream Car	*338*
Chapter 13	At the Slammer	*364*
Chapter 14	Northern Belles	*383*
Chapter 15	The Fall	*389*
Chapter 16	Altered State...	*396*
Chapter 17	Femme Fatale..	*417*
Chapter 18	Prize Night	*425*
Chapter 19	A Looney Tune	*441*
Acknowledgements...		*456*

CHAPTER 1

BUNGALOW BLUES

Chicago, February 1945

Shorty curled up at their feet under the dining room table, hoping they'd forgotten about him and would speak freely. They were having coffee. He was lurking comfortably. He hadn't known what this activity was called until his Uncle Victor gave it a name. "Your kid's a professional lurker." It sounded swell, but his mother had taken offense, something she did easily and often these days. Shorty, however, couldn't let it go, and when his mother would call out from the kitchen, "What are you doing, sweetie?" he'd reply, "Just lurking."

Tonight, the bungalow was quiet, deliciously peaceful. No one was screaming. Even Baby Anthony had ceased whining and fallen asleep, but every part of Shorty was awake, alert, and seeking clues. Where did things stand this evening? He knew where he wanted them to stand – everyone calm and getting along. It was still that way sometimes. He yearned for the magic to keep it that way. Mandrake the Magician would know how, but Shorty had much to learn of such arts. He looked at his parents' legs, held himself impossibly still, and wished with all his might for this calm to continue.

"Good dinner, Frances." His father's voice was warm and quiet. "You've made me like liver. My mother never could."

"She doesn't use calves' liver." Her voice was musical and girlish. They had told her so at the telephone company and hadn't wanted her to leave and get married, but she'd fallen in love with Daddy. It was one of Shorty's favorite stories. "It has to be calves' liver. I haven't made Shorty like it yet."

"You will. He already likes the gravy."

"He just likes looking at it. It's so black, welled up in the potatoes.

He told me it looks like a lake in a black and white movie."

They laughed. They both laughed. He'd do anything to make them laugh. He'd been practicing cartwheels in his room but kept banging into things and wasn't ready to try it in public.

"I've got something for you," his father said, and Shorty heard paper slide across the table.

"A present?"

"Open it and see."

Shorty heard an envelope tearing. "Oh my, Ed!"

"I thought for once you'd like to see something before Sheila does." Shorty's aunt Sheila did everything before anybody else got to it. It made her interesting – and annoying.

"*Oklahoma!* I'm dying to go. This is marvelous!" She giggled. "I'll ask Sheila to baby sit."

"Oh please do."

"Weren't they hard to get?"

"I have to confess: it was Warren who got them."

"Warren Trumbaugh?"

"Yes, he thought they would –"

His mother cut him off. "Would what?"

Shorty hugged his knees. He knew this silence. It was not a good one.

"Why do you talk to Warren Trumbaugh about me? What do you tell him?" Her voice was harsh and shrill now. "Is his snotty wife there when you talk about me? I'll bet that bitch loves the gossip. Is she still going on about how I didn't know any better than to serve wine with pie? As if there were no such thing as a dessert wine – as if I need etiquette lessons from that dirty pig." The words spilled faster and louder, almost covering his father's voice.

"Frances, please. We don't talk about you. Warren can afford it and was being generous – doing something nice."

"Niiice?" she hissed. By now the voice seeping out of his mother was almost unrecognizable to him.

"Honey,... honey, he knows these are difficult times. He thought it would cheer us up."

"Are these difficult times for you, Ed? Do I make them difficult?" It was flung as a challenge.

"Only when you act this way, Frances."

"It's not an act! Can't you see that? It's not an act!" His mother was shrieking. She stood up suddenly, pushing the table, clattering dishes and knocking over her chair. She gasped for breath and seemed to be laughing and crying all at once. Shorty felt the drip of coffee on his head through the space where the table halves met. He didn't move.

"I guess I do need cheering up. Let's see if this will do it. If two tickets are good, four are twice as good." He heard a ripping sound. "Or eight. Eight will be wonderful."

"Frances, don't! Those are expensive!"

"Maybe you can patch them together and go with shit-face Trumbaugh. Or maybe you can't."

"Oh my god! Don't swallow them!" His father stood up and moved toward her.

"Don't touch me!" she screamed, and ran from the room. Baby Anthony was awake again and crying. His father slumped back heavily into his chair. Two sets of tears echoed from the big bedroom, but the dining room was silent. After a moment, his father said, "Shorty? Are you under there?"

"No."

"Come out anyway."

Shorty crawled out and his father motioned him over. "Lurking's not always what it's cracked up to be, buddy." He frowned and stared at his son's head. "What's in your hair?"

"Coffee."

"Come up here," said his father, patting his leg. With his son in his lap, Edmond Sheffield senior took up a napkin and rubbed the boy's head vigorously. "It's all over you, dopey. Why didn't you move out of the way?"

"I didn't want to make noise – and I didn't want it to go on the rug."

"Don't you think you're worth more than the rug?"

Shorty found it an interesting question. Before he could form an answer, his father closed his arms around him. Shorty was almost eight – too old, he supposed, to sit on a lap, but he still liked it, and if his father didn't mind . . . for just tonight. . .

They sat without speaking, waiting, once again, for whatever would happen or not happen. His mother had quieted the baby, something only she could manage. They watched without moving as she left the bedroom and entered the bathroom. She was not likely to emerge for quite a while, so Shorty slid down and the two of them addressed the mess on the table. When his mother reappeared, she had lipstick on, and what Shorty thought of as her mask was in place. It was a look she got that closed her off from them. He knew she would go away again tonight, and he would be lonely in a deep, scary way that he never was when his father worked late. His father would always come back to them, but his mother might drift off to the moon and never be seen again. He couldn't stop her – there was no changing her mind once she wore the mask, but he had to let her know what it was costing him.

"Mama, don't put your coat on."

"I have to see if Grandma Foley's all right, and Aunt Nora."

"They're all right. They're fine. They've got a house full of people to look after them. What about us?"

His father squeezed his shoulder. Shorty was going too far. It was useless anyway.

"I'll be back late Sunday." Her coat was fully buttoned, locking them out. When a taxi arrived, Shorty knelt on the sofa and pulled the curtains apart to see every last bit of her. He turned back to his father.

"Is Mama mad at us?"

"She's upset."

"What's upsetting her?"

"I don't know."

His father was a smart man. This was a terrible answer. If Shorty wasn't careful, he'd soon be crying. His father came close to the sofa. "It's just us here for the weekend. What would you like to do? What would make you happy, buddy?"

Shorty burrowed his head into his father's chest, where his words were muffled by a sleeveless undershirt, "Could we go to the movies?"

CHAPTER 2

SAFE INSIDE

Chicago: November 1, 1945

1. The Road to Avalon

She took his hand, and he was happy to leave it in hers as they started down the steps. This wasn't something that either of them was always comfortable with anymore, but this afternoon, it struck him as a good investment. They weren't out of the building yet, there were lots of steps, and Shorty had learned to distrust the landings. It was there that his mother sometimes got a look as though something important, something bad, had just become clear to her, and she would turn around and go back up. No, he wouldn't let himself take anything for granted. A moment would come—that had not come yet—when he could feel certain enough to relax. Still, she was smiling. She was so pretty when she smiled. He wondered why, if you had a look like that, you would ever wear any other. He decided the odds were in his favor and abandoned himself to his mounting excitement.

A few more steps and they'd be in the tiny outer hallway with the flat metal mailboxes that you needed a key to open. He was developing a habit of looking to the left as he edged through what his mother called the foyer. It bothered him to see their name attached to a mailbox in this building that grew smaller each time he entered it. The first time he saw it, late at night after their things had been moved in, his heart sank. In the two months since, his opinion had not improved. He knew it never would.

This was not a building you could grow to like, no matter what his father had said that first night. He was dumbfounded that his father, of all people, could like it, or pretend to. There wasn't even room for the piano. They had left it behind in this messy rush to uproot themselves. The piano – the first thing he would have tried to save in a fire, before his toys, before anything. Shining and black as night, it was where the two of them would meet in the evening when his father came home. From the couch he could monitor the front steps and manage to be sitting on the piano bench as his father opened the door.

"Just let me wash my hands, Shorty," he would say, putting down his thermos bottle. But sometimes he would come directly to the piano. The hard bench was stuffed with sheets of songs whose covers made you want to hear the music right away – faces of singers in ties or necklaces gazing down at you from moons and stars that grew bigger in ripples to the edges of the page.

His father would settle in beside him. "What'll it be?" They both knew the answer: "Play 'Twelfth Street Rag'," and his father would, his fingers dashing up and down the keyboard, never making a mistake. Then they would sing something together.

"And then those flirty, flirty guys
With their flirty, flirty eyes,
Will have to flirt with dollies that are real."

How could there be no room for the piano where they were going – and if there wasn't, why was his father even considering it? Leaving it behind would be like leaving themselves. That first night, he had raced ahead up the stairs, frantic to prove there must be a mistake, there must be room. What he found startled and confused him. Their furniture looked ill at ease in the three tiny rooms, two of which were smaller than the smallest room in the bungalow they were leaving. The situation was not without hope. Across from the couch was an area of the floor on which nothing had been placed. He paced it off and ran back out into the hall.

"There *is* room! Let me show you."

"No, let me show *you* something you've never seen before."

He watched in open mouthed horror as his father stepped to the wall opposite the couch, and slowly let down what had been hiding behind it, a large, heavy, metal-framed bed. As the bulk of the bed thudded to the floor, his stomach felt as though he and the abandoned piano had been pinned beneath it.

"What do you think of that?"

Shorty thought it was the saddest, ugliest thing he had ever seen.

From that night on, he had contained himself, but barely, asking few of the questions with which his head felt ready to burst. Why were they doing it – even for the little while that everyone assured him it would be? If it were only for a little while, why did they need their name on the mailbox? And if someone actually sent them a letter here (which he fiercely hoped they wouldn't), they'd be gone by the time it arrived, wouldn't they? But it wasn't much use asking now, for he observed that both his parents, who before had always welcomed his questions with pleasure and interest, had lately become sort of—and it was not a word he like to connect with them—shifty.

He and his mother were outside at last. He took a deep and satisfying breath, wheeled around and felt himself inflating to normal size as he spun. There wasn't room enough for all of anything in the apartment, least of all for him. The building changed them into miniatures, squeezing the way they moved and talked to each other, and thought. Something had to be –

He caught himself from falling, ashamed at having banged his shins on the low iron pipe that guarded what should have been a lawn. Guarded it from what? Dogs could run under it. People could easily step over it – if they were paying attention. His right leg throbbed and he flushed with embarrassment.

"It's there to trip the drunks as they stagger out of Sonny's Tavern, a holding pen to keep them out of mischief till the sun comes up", that's what Aunt Sheila had said. And now he had almost fallen into it. She would have laughed at him in that startling way that made him feel not like her eight-year-old nephew, but like part of a large group of very stupid people put on earth for her amusement. His mother said Aunt Sheila spent too much time in New York.

This was not the first time he had staged this dance of freedom at the doorway, a ritual that he knew his mother wished would stop. She regarded it not with embarrassment or annoyance, either of which would have seemed reasonable to him, but with a sad dismay. It stung him to hurt her and this alone would normally put a quick end to anything, but these days he was possessed. She appeared to understand though she said nothing, but she refused to encourage him with an audience and moved to the corner.

"Did you hurt yourself?" His leg still throbbed, but he shook his head. Her sympathy threatened to magnify his embarrassment. They turned the corner.

Then he saw it.

There it rose, shimmering in the autumn sky, warm, ornate, beckoning and splendidly out of place in this most ordinary of neighborhoods – the plump exotic towers of the Avalon Theater. The dazzling graceful bulk of this bejeweled elephant dominated 79th Street and could be seen for miles in either direction. It was impossible for him to behold it without smiling, and now it was only three blocks away. Soon, it would envelop them in its comfortable strangeness – unless she changed her mind.

༺༻

The dark interior of Sonny's Tavern held a morbid fascination for Shorty, partly because he had been able to snatch only the most fleeting glances as he stood on tiptoe. The large windows were blackened except for a long oval just above his eye level, and he had to look quickly because his mother's disapproval was so pronounced.

"There's no one worth looking at sitting around in a saloon – no one but stumblebums and trashy women carrying on and drinking themselves under the table. You wouldn't be interested."

He was wild to see it. Once as he peeked in, a man at the bar spotted him and waved. Flustered, and knowing it was rude to spy, he looked away. The man had not seemed like a stumblebum, although part of Shorty's curiosity sprang from not knowing just what a stumblebum ought to look like.

As for the carrying on, however, he had actually witnessed a few seconds of that, last night on Halloween. He wanted to go trick or treating disguised, of course, as the Green Lantern, and his mother had offered to make his outfit. Her costumes had not been great successes over the years, and though he had provided her with several really helpful issues of *The Justice League of America*, he resigned himself once again to having more doors open in bewilderment than recognition. This year's attire seemed particularly unpromising: his green corduroys, a stiff green mask, a green blanket for a cape (none of these in anything near the right shade), one of his father's fedoras and a Crackerjack prize ring (these last two both wrapped in green cellophane). No matter how wide of the mark her efforts fell, he would always applaud them; in fact, the less distinguished they were, the harder he worked to protect her from his disappointment. It was discouraging, though, when at their first stop, Mrs. McManus across the hall exclaimed, "Oh it's a little leprechaun!"

After they had exhausted the opportunities on all three floors of the building, they tried the stores within a block or two, and his papier-mâché pumpkin on a wire was filling up nicely with candy corn, Maryjanes, Tootsie Rolls, and even some coins. They were almost back to Sonny's when he heard the loud burst of music, laughter, and rhythmic clapping. He lagged behind his mother to steal a glimpse of the mysterious festivities. What he saw was so bizarre that he couldn't look away, but his mother was about to round the corner. He had to take the chance that even she would find it remarkable. "Momma, it's a party with balloons and streamers, and there's a man running around in a circle taking his clothes—." He was whisked past the corner in mid-sentence.

The idea that they could neither enter nor leave the building without a reminder of public drinking was clearly upsetting to his mother. She seemed determined that this new familiarity with it should not make it seem more acceptable to him. "I would be very sorry to see you become a drinker." This was always said with a long direct look as though she were trying to cast a spell. Becoming a drinker couldn't mean taking a drink, because she had seen him do that at Grandma Sheffield's on Thanksgiving and hadn't objected. Maybe she knew he wouldn't enjoy it. Oh he had loved twisting the little ribbed glass on the long stem, holding it up to the light to watch the dark maroon liquid reflecting all the colors of spilled oil on a sunny street. He loved the toasting, the clinking, and the delicious sense of entering an adult world, but the deliciousness ended when the wine, Mogan David, crossed his lips. It seemed equal parts Karo syrup and Mercurochrome, and the assembled Sheffields enjoyed his grimaces as he swallowed.

He didn't think it was the Sheffields who had become the drinkers his mother worried about – certainly not his father. Liquor never seemed to be around, except on holidays. About the Foleys, he was less sure. Sometimes, when Uncle Brandon or Uncle Dennis came over, he could smell beer on their breath and his mother seemed impatient for them to go, but it was exactly at those times that they were the funniest and the most likely to play with him and pay attention. When Grandpa Foley had been drinking, the signs were easy to recognize. He would repeat himself – which Shorty actually found helpful since it let him know right away where things stood – and then the songs would begin, accompanied by the concertina, wonderful sad songs. You could depend on someone to die in every single one of them, leaving Irish ladies to weep each night by the sea for the rest of their lives. It gave him the shivers.

At none of these times, with his grandpa or his uncles, was there any raising of voices or disrespectfulness or cursing, so why... but he was forgetting Aunt Sheila. Aunt Sheila would be jolly enough when she arrived. His father would joke with her for a few minutes, then he would remember something he had to do and go out for hours and hours, usually not getting back until she had gone. During that time, it was as though not just Aunt Sheila but a whole crowd of people had come to the house. He had learned that it was helpful to be out of sight, under the dining room table when the last few of them arrived, like bitter town criers, shrieking and cursing. They had really nasty, shocking news to shout about everyone – even his mother, secrets so horrible (at least the ones he could understand), that they couldn't possibly be true, but insisted upon with such dreadful force that he feared some passerby might be convinced.

The ending was always the same: the high and mighty Sheffields were putting on airs and conspiring behind Aunt Sheila's back – even Shorty was showing signs of it. But she could see through them, and it wouldn't go on much longer. A terrible reckoning was coming, and they would all be exposed and brought low. Only after his mother called a cab and all the Aunt Sheilas had been safely piled into it would he crawl back out. This final outdoor phase of her departure was especially humiliating for him. So many loud and profane accusations still to be made as she threaded her way uncertainly down the front steps and out to the waiting taxi at the curb.

One excruciating night, he watched in anguish as the driver exercised a choice he didn't know they had and refused to let Aunt

Sheila into the cab. Shorty crawled back under the table as the entire process began a second time, and the woman his father had called "the cutest thing you ever saw as a young girl" reentered the house and slumped into a chair at the edge of his hiding place.

Well, if that was what his mother feared for him, she didn't need to worry. He meant it when he told her, "I won't become a drinker." Of course, what he meant was "I won't become an angry drinker who scares everybody and makes them feel bad." He didn't even want to become a happy drinker. All he wanted—and he didn't see why this couldn't work out every so often—was to wear a white tuxedo like Paul Henreid and toast people with a champagne cocktail in a wonderful glass. Paul Henreid never even got silly when he drank in the movies. Still, what if that, or something like it, was what Aunt Sheila wanted. What if you couldn't really know what kind of a drinker you were going to be? An unwelcome picture forced its way into his mind: Paul Henreid spilling the champagne cocktail, slurring his words, yelling and cursing at people. As Shorty struggled to expel the hideous image, he became aware of a change in the sky toward Stony Island. The giant vertical sign had come on for the evening, and the white bulbed letters were descending one at a time against the black background. A . . . V . . . A . . . L . . .

Soon.

Just beyond Sonny's was the Fensin lamp store, and his mother was drawn to something in the window that had not been there the night before. He liked to watch her examining things because it was so seldom that a piece of merchandise caught her interest, and when it did, her display of curiosity seemed especially graceful and attractive to him, as it did now. He hoped someone would come by while she stood at the window.

He remembered exactly when he first became aware of his

mother's appearance. One morning at kindergarten, he noticed that there were more adults than usual in the room, many more, and he didn't know any of them. They weren't teachers, but each of them knew someone in the class. Cups of Kool-Aid and pleated paper containers of nuts were being passed around. Did the other children know what was going on? Was he supposed to know? He hoped not, because he didn't, and he wasn't going to ask. If he kept quiet and paid close attention, maybe he could figure it out and pretend he had known all along.

Miss Sunburg was speaking to him, "Is your mother here, Edmond?" "No, ma'am." So these were mothers, and a couple of fathers. Was his mother supposed to be here, and was it somehow his fault that she wasn't? Well, that was okay. He wasn't sure he wanted strangers to know things about his family, and he didn't really approve of kindergarten. If they were never going to read anything (which he could) and if other children were going to push and be so hoggish about the toys—especially the wheelbarrow—kindergarten seemed a great waste of his time. He hadn't quite convinced his mother of that, though he knew she would never come to whatever it was that was going on here. But suddenly, there she was, in a red and white-striped blouse that he had never seen, talking to Miss Sunburg and smiling over at him. Somehow, she had figured out on her own that she was supposed to be here, and she was.

Jackie Carlson was at his elbow. "Izzat your mom?" "Mmmhmm" "She's pretty." Yes, she was. Why had it taken someone else to tell him this? He looked around the room with brand new eyes, and amid the general friendliness of the groups, he detected a stern look, a loud voice, fidgety hands, and several heads of messy hair. He looked back at his mother, tall and calm, her long, soft black hair all in place. No one had her large brown eyes and lashes, or her smooth complexion. No one had her smile. She wasn't only pretty, she was the prettiest mother in the room, and a classmate had just said so out loud. He began to smile uncontrollably.

This agreeable new subject, he decided, would give him something interesting to talk about with his father, and it turned out that Daddy shared Shorty and Jackie's opinion that Momma was good looking. He should have known that, he realized. It explained why so many of the movies his father took them to see, like *Sundown* and *China Girl*, were Gene Tierney pictures. Of all the ladies in the movies, it was she who most closely resembled his mother. But that had been when they all did things together. Since the move, or maybe because of it, he either did things, like yesterday and today, with Momma at the apartment, or with Daddy, at Grandma and Grandpa Sheffield's. It was like something had cracked in their lives, even though everyone broke into speedy smiles when they saw him looking at them, and Momma, if he asked how long they had to stay in the apartment before they could go back to the bungalow, would say, quite cheerfully, "It's just until Daddy and I sort things out."

If Daddy could see how she looked now, as she stood examining the table lamp with the green metal shade, things would get sorted out right away.

"Let's go in. I want to see what it costs." He couldn't have been more surprised if she had turned a somersault. She almost never bought things for herself, and lately he had begun to hear the exasperating but unanswerable "We can't afford it" regularly from both his parents. They had all the furniture they needed for the old house. It was safe somewhere, "in storage" they told him, and he believed them, even though it made him a little uneasy when they wouldn't let him go see it (if he could only take a quick look at the piano, he wouldn't mention it again). Now, he was getting very uneasy. His mother's curiosity about the lamp was beginning to alarm him. She wasn't thinking about it for the bungalow, he just knew it. She wanted something new, something permanent, for the wretched apartment that they should be leaving any day now. It must not be bought.

She opened the door and drew him inside.

The shop was small, crowding the lamps close together. Too close, he thought, but he had to admit that he liked the slim ones with the ribbed poles and the crisp, clean shades unbruised by heat marks. They were much more stylish looking than the ones they had at – at what? These days he had only to think the words "at home" to feel like he swallowed a cat. He forced his attention to the man in the gray suit pretending not to watch them from his desk at the back. He wasn't sure what he wanted the man to do. If he just kept sitting at the desk a little longer, maybe his mother would lose interest and they could leave. On the other hand, didn't the man think his mother was a real customer, with money to buy lamps?

There was another possibility, he knew, worse than anything he had considered so far. If his mother decided she was being ignored, she could become angry in that sudden, ferocious way that terrified him. It had never been directed at him, and he wasn't afraid that it would be. He knew that she loved him too much ever to be really angry with him. But he also knew that this gave him no protection from the scorching effect when she blazed out at others – their landlady, people waiting on them, his father, anyone she came to feel was taking advantage, being disrespectful…unjust…treacherous. He thought she was almost always mistaken about these people, but he had learned better than to try to change her mind. When it happened, it came in an instant, out of nowhere, caused by nothing he could put his finger on, or by something said in fun. It was like lightning from a sunny sky, or one second sitting in the back of the Buick at a stoplight and the next second going 90 miles an hour with the doors locked, the horn stuck, and nobody at the wheel. Watching it, listening to it, seeing the reaction of others to this sad, scary stranger who, a moment ago, had been your mother, was the worst thing that could ever happen to you. Then it wasn't a cat you had swallowed, but razor blades. Though he knew what it might lead to with the lamp, he considered going back to the man and asking him to wait on them.

"Do you like it, Shorty?"

"It's okay."

"This is a Tole lampshade. Isn't it a peaceful shade of green? They say that green is the most soothing of all the colors. Look at the tiny openings they've cut in the metal around the top. It's like a giant leaf in the jungle that a little monkey has been chewing on."

Maybe she just needed something pretty and new to look at while she sat in the dreariness of the apartment.

"It's nice."

"Do you think it would go, on the desk with the little lady feet?"

She was asking him to pick out colors for his coffin.

"Yes. If you really like it, I think we should get it."

As they stepped back out onto 79th Street, he turned to comfort himself with the sight of the marquee. AVALO was visible, but the N and the three-sided sign over the ticket booth were blocked from his view by a streetcar stopped for passengers. One more block and he'd be able to read the names of the movies and the actors the theater thought most important. He didn't always agree with their choices, or the order in which they named the movies. He also wished the sign could be much bigger so that really good people who had smaller parts, like Walter Slezak or S. Z. Sakall, could see their names on the sign too.

On this block between Constance and Cregier, the stores and the building above them took up only half the street on their side.

The rest was a vacant lot, bare ground that ended in a large billboard. The vacant lot had been praised and called to his attention before he had ever seen the apartment, on the first day of what he now thought of as "after." Most of his life had seemed to him a blissful, sunny, "before", and then there was this gray, confusing, and most unsatisfactory "after" that had started when he discovered they were moving.

They hadn't told him about it, let alone asked him about it, as they should have. He had stumbled upon the truth by accident. He was wedged into a corner of the front porch trying to draw Mr. Payne's yellow Plymouth when a shadow moved across his pad.

"Hello, Emmy."

It was Eileen Brennan's older sister. The Brennans lived next door, and there were so many of them that somebody was always outside, as though their house couldn't hold them all at once. Often, at lunchtime, one of them would hang around until his mother asked them in. He supposed it was the butter. Eileen, his most reliable playmate, couldn't get over his mother always spreading butter on the bread. Once he asked her what they used instead.

"Lard – or nuthin.'"

Emmy was too old to want to play with him.

"My mom's inside."

"Oh, that's okay. I just wanted to say goodbye and wish you good luck."

"Where are you going? Is Eileen going too?"

"No, we're not…, I mean, because you're moving and all."

"We're not moving."

"But you are. Everybody says so."

"Then everybody is silly. Why should we move?"

"Well, I wouldn't know about that."

"It's nice here, and I guess I would know if we're moving or not."

"I guess you would. Can I see that?"

He didn't like people looking at his drawings until he was completely finished with them, but Emmy was always nice to him and he was pleased with the grille.

"What do you think? I'm not through."

"You'll draw the ads one day, Edmond."

"I want to."

"Could I keep this?"

"Well it's not –"

"I know Eileen would like it too."

"Okay, but sometime I'll finish it for you or give you a better one. Packard is my best."

"Would you sign it?"

"Why?"

"You should always sign your drawings so if people like them, they know who did it."

"Where's Eileen?"

"She's home. She didn't want… she asked me to say good bye – just in case."

He stood up and pulled open the screen door.

"Mama, Emmy thinks we're moving. Isn't that –"

But it wasn't.

The word "shocked" took on an instant new reality for him. He was shocked into numbness, shocked out of throwing a tantrum, or whatever they had been afraid he would do if they didn't keep it from him and gave him time to think. He was shocked that they were leaving the house, the street, the people, the school, and every comforting, familiar thing that, until that second, he could take for granted. He was shocked that the entire neighborhood knew something so personal about him that he did not. He was shocked and he was ashamed.

His father's arrival that evening only confirmed and deepened his misery. He sat quiet and still as their sympathetic voices attacked him from what seemed a great distance with the many good and logical reasons why he should be happy they were moving. They assured him that nothing was going to change and everything was going to be different, only better. If they could just hear themselves. But he knew that no reasons of his own, or smiles or tears, would change their minds. Clearly, they had burned some bridge when he wasn't looking, and it was too late to fuss. Though he felt like screaming, he sat quietly, looking around the room at all the objects he wanted to throw his arms about and kiss.

At some point in that long night of sitting and listening, they had trotted out as a special attraction, the vacant lot that he and his mother were now passing. Did they think he was an utter ninny? Not only was there nothing interesting here, there was nothing here at all. He knew he had a reputation for being able to amuse himself alone, inside or outside, for long periods of time, but his imagination needed something to work with. Give him a pillar, an archway, some bushes to hide behind, and he could be in Arabia and in danger before you knew it. But this big, stupid space was impossible. If he so much as set foot on it, he might as well be in a fish bowl. All of 79th Street would know he had nothing to do and no one to play with.

It was a poor thing compared to the enormous prairie across from the bungalow. Filled with sand, weeds, and tall grasses, that was the perfect place to hide, to disappear. It went on forever. There could be twenty different games going on at once without anybody getting in your way – or even seeing you if you didn't want them to. And if you got tired of everything else, there would be a train roaring by on top of the hill at the end of the block. You didn't have to go very far into the prairie before you were out of sight of any parents standing on the front porches. It was perfect, and it seemed to him that all of the really interesting and unusual events in the neighborhood took place there. Once, Petie Iversen told him excitedly that Rudy Rutero and Margaret Cunningham had gone way out into the prairie, taken their clothes off, and put their things together. He tried to imagine it and pictured them back to back bumping their behinds. It made him giggle. "Why would they do that?" Petie didn't know but assured him that Rudy liked it a lot. It didn't sound like much.

The most fun he had ever had in the prairie had actually been his mother's doing. Halfway out, there was a clearing in which long ago someone had built a concrete pit with a grate. People said that hoboes from the trains sometimes cooked there. Petie and four other boys told him they were going to have a hobo fire and he could come if he brought marshmallows. He wanted to go, but even more he wanted an opportunity to redeem himself. He had not made a very good impression when they were playing red rover; in fact, the older kids aimed at him as a weak link in their line when they tried to crash through. The problem would be convincing his mother. Ever since the incident with the sparks and his leggings, the mere mention of fire provoked a lecture. He had come upon the embers of someone else's fire and decided he had better stamp it out and save the prairie. Luckily, Mrs. Schwendeman had been outside to hear him yelling, and the snow on his leggings made them slow to ignite, but he would never hear the end of it. This hobo roast would probably blaze on without him, but he had to try.

"Everybody is going to be there. Momma, I really need to do this."

"Who is everybody? How many are there?"

He gave her the names he knew.

"All right, you go ahead. I'll bring things out."

All right? She was letting him go, and alone! Well, almost alone. By bringing the marshmallows herself, she'd be able to check things out. That would make him look like a baby, but he wasn't going to complain and risk her changing her mind.

"Thanks a million!" He tore off into the prairie.

He was sitting on a log, facing away from the house when Petie said, "Here comes your mother." Shorty craned his neck and saw her swiftly nearing them with a grocery bag, gliding effortlessly around the holes and rocks that studded her path. "Man, that's a lot of marshmallows!" The bag was large indeed. Setting it beside the grate, she smiled and said, "Hoboes never eat just marshmallows, Petie." She acted as though she knew all kinds of hoboes. They stared as she pulled out enough Idaho potatoes to bake for all of them. She had brought salt, butter, milk, and a big pan to make cocoa.

The evening was cold, but they stayed out for at least two hours. She never left them, but far from embarrassing him, she raised his reputation in their eyes to a point he had never been able to manage on his own. She made them laugh, got the potatoes just right, and told them really scary stories about Irish ghosts and banshees. At the end, they fell all over themselves thanking her. As they left, they called him Eddie. He was delirious.

"Well, Mr. Eddie," asked his mother when they were alone, " do you think you can get by without butter until we get next month's ration coupons?"

"Oh yes!" He said dreamily.

They crossed Cregier and left the vacant lot behind. "I'm just going to step into Prendergast's to make a phone call, Shorty." This was never good news. The apartment had no phone, and since the move, his mother's link to the rest of her world was Prendergast's or whatever drugstore they passed in their rambles. He hated the waiting. At best it would be a tedious but quiet ten minutes if she called Grandma Foley, or one of his aunts. If she called Grandma

Sheffield, the conversation might be short, but before it was over it would grow loud enough to be heard well outside the booth and people would look at him. If it was his father on the other end of the line, the call could be so long and explosive that not even the farthest corners of the store could shelter him from the sound and the stares. He prayed it would not be his father.

He saw by the large Bulova clock above the soda fountain that it was seven minutes past four. His father was still at work, and Shorty had heard him beg her not to call him there anymore. "Are you trying to lose me my job? Is that what you want?" They used to wait until they thought he was asleep before they raised their voices and said such things, but 1945 was turning out to be the loudest year of his life so far. It was as if they had so many important things to say that there wasn't time to wait for him to fall asleep. He tried to be invisible, and sometimes, until one of them would remember him and stop, it seemed he was.

He wanted to seem invisible right now, just long enough to find out who she was calling. He followed as silently as he could, a few steps behind her, all the way to the back and watched as she sealed herself into the booth. On the rare occasions when he got to make a phone call in a booth, he would rub his fingers on the bumpy, brownish yellow metal that lined the walls. It felt like those red button candies on paper. He had noticed something almost magical about phone booths: while the phone was ringing, you were in a space so tiny that you could easily bang an elbow, but as soon as someone answered, the booth grew larger and you drew air and space from wherever they were.

There was no magic, however, when you stood outside the booth and watched. His mother held the receiver just beyond her ear and dropped a nickel in the slot. Ignoring the thick directories that sat on a shelf below the phone, she dialed the number from memory. When someone answered, she gave the numbers of an extension. She was calling his father.

Permitting the world to see him once again, Shorty strode toward the front of the store to lose himself in the teeming magazine racks. How he loved them. Left to himself, he could happily spend hours without moving from the spot. The problem was that once you actually opened a magazine and began to read, you would not be left to yourself very long. Some sort of meter started ticking in the head of whoever was minding that part of the store, and it wasn't long before you heard, "You gonna buy something kid? You can't just read all day," or "You think you're in the library kid? This ain't the library." How he wished it were, or that he could ignore such remarks as some children did, but it was no use. Once he had been spoken to, that was the end of it. No matter how rude their comments, it would be disrespectful to pretend he hadn't heard them. He would stop and move away. The trick was to anticipate when they were about to speak, and move away for a moment until they got busy with something else. Most important of all, was to stand back and survey the entire rack, so once the meter started ticking, you weren't wasting time on a hasty choice.

He stood amid the coin machines opposite the racks. For a penny, depending where you placed it, you could weigh yourself and read your fortune, get a piece of hard candy or a tiny metal toy, or, his favorite, a stiff card with an autographed photo of someone in the movies. Only about every fourth one was anybody you'd want at all, and there were far too many people in cowboy hats, but what fascinated him was that he'd never seen the same card come out twice. The machine looked as though it might hold a thousand or more. How he'd like to be alone in the store to open the back of the machine and spread all the cards on the floor.

He turned his attention to the racks for his preliminary survey.

At the very top, out of his reach, were the really cheesy looking magazines with the women on the covers looking either tough or terrified. A snarly looking man would be standing over them, and the titles would start with words like "True" or "Real" or "Authentic" and end with "Police" or "Detective." He liked mystery stories, even if they weren't true, but he was never tempted to read these. The covers made him sad. The men looked like they'd be yelling and cursing all the time, and the women looked like they needed somebody to be nice to them and buy them a better dress.

Just below these were *Esquire* and the sports magazines. Warren Trumbaugh, a man his father worked with at the steel mill, had given them a subscription to *Esquire* for Christmas in 1943. Everyone joked about it at the time, but Shorty didn't see what was so funny. It was a marvelous magazine, and so big. He couldn't wait for it to arrive each month so he could examine all the elegant advertisements. He liked the spiffy looking suits and ties. He would flip through the pages, hunting for the little cartoon man with a mustache who was there every month in a top hat and tuxedo with his big eyes popping out of his head. Best of all were the beautiful Vargas drawings of smiling ladies with really long legs. They were drawn in thin lines, which made it easy for him to copy them. The first time he did that his father seemed surprised and his mother disapproving. Then it became an accepted monthly event. Mr. Trumbaugh had asked him for one of the best ones to keep, and his father told Shorty he had seen it up in Mr. Trumbaugh's office. That was a long time ago, and Mr. Trumbaugh didn't come over any more. He missed *Esquire*, but it didn't look as though anybody was going to renew it.

The rest of that shelf held titles like *Field and Stream* and *Argossy* and covers with tigers, bears, and fish – lots of fish. They made him sleepy. He knew the stories were supposed to be exciting. He also sensed that some of his relatives, like Uncle Victor, would find him easier to like if he could at least pretend that they were exciting, but he couldn't fake it. In *Argossy*, a man would always be pitting himself against the deadly, giant something (which actually was not such a bad idea), but before the man ever got near the deadly giant something, he would describe all the equipment he was taking along to catch it. Each piece of equipment would have so many numbers attached to it that Shorty's eyelids would grow heavy. He didn't like to admit that there was anything he couldn't read, but in *Argossy*, he had met his match.

It was the bottom two shelves that held the real treasures, comic books and movie magazines. The choice was always difficult, but comic books seldom won, since you could count on running into them at anybody's house unless they had no children. Still, there were some tempting choices in front of him. *Little Lulu* never failed to amuse him, and he greatly admired the imagination of Marge, its creator. One of his daydreams was to tell her so when he became a well-known artist himself and they were pals. The friends he would have then! It stood to reason they would all want to get together and praise each other. He would tell Lee Falk how many times he had pretended to be Mandrake the Magician with his walking stick, having adventures with Lothar and Narda. And when a crisis arose? "Mandrake gestures hypnotically." What a wonderful phrase! He would tell… but what would they tell *him*?

What would they like about *his* stories, *his* drawings, *his* characters? His hero would be Manning Nugent: tall, really smart, good-looking, and polite. When Manning Nugent changed to his secret identity, it would happen very quietly, not with Shazam and a lightning bolt. He just knew it had to hurt each time poor Billy Batson had to stop being Captain Marvel and get blasted back to his newsstand and crutches. What a rotten other identity! No, Manning Nugent would just be sitting there, in the clutches of the crooks, and when they turned away for a second, they'd look back in amazement to see... to see... a big, powerful panther! No, a leopard! Sleek and cobalt blue like a Crayola, only savage and terrifying, biding his time, savoring their felonious hysteria, immobilizing them with the penetrating gaze of his blazing sapphire eyes and the low menacing rumble of his purr. At last, when he had spun out their panic to the breaking point and their nerves could bear no more, he would be upon them, ripping them to shreds with the celebrated talons against which no *Argossy* man could defend himself, no matter how much equipment he brought. Or, he might just scare them into changing their ways and let them go. You never knew with the unpredictable Blue Leopard.

Of course, Manning Nugent would only turn into a leopard under extreme provocation, or maybe sometimes if he were really bored. For run of the mill criminals, he would still be a man, but dressed in a cobalt blue outfit with a mask—no, a cowl—and a retractable cape which would only be used for his entrances and exits because sometimes a cape might get in your way and you wouldn't be sleek. His special power would be – no, he would need two: invisibility and flight. Armed with only those two powers, life would be perfect. He would roam the skies at night unseen, examining the tallest of trees, stroking the leaves, observing the birds. He would wander undetected through any store that struck his fancy, touching everything that caught his eye. He would fly to the Loop and glide up the surfaces of the Wrigley Building. He would perch like a gargoyle on the spires of the Tribune Tower and peer down at the nighttime crowds. He would soar to the top of the Beehive Building and examine the blue light undisturbed. He would suspend himself in mid air before each of the theater marquees: the State Lake, the Roosevelt, the Chicago, hovering unobserved as their radiance burst over him, showering his senses with color and light.

He would dip low above the waves of Lake Michigan and fly back south with the lights of the cars on the Outer Drive to guide him. The Blue Leopard would end his sky-borne evening atop the turrets of the Avalon, but before he sought sleep there in his secret lair, he would have one final chore to perform. Still unseen, he would pause, like a hummingbird at each letter of the sign as it blinked on, replacing from a bag of cobalt blue any bulb that had expired. In time, they would come to wonder, but they would never know whom they had to thank.

"Ed! Ed!" His father's name, cried out in his mother's voice, clutched at him across the length of the drugstore. Several pair of unwelcome eyes turned toward him. He realized that he and his mother were becoming pathetically familiar not only to the staff of Pendergast's, but to the customers as well. He could step outside and end it, or he could remain where he was, read, and hope that it would end by itself as it sometimes did. But even when it did, he felt as though something had spilled and spattered him so that even the new customers coming in would look at him. His mother didn't want him to go outside, and he felt that when he did he was in some way acting against her and justifying their stares. He would stay for a while.

The raspy buzz of the malted milk machine created a distraction; he stepped closer to the racks to explore the movie magazines. A row of joyful faces, Van Johnson, Deanna Durbin, and Maureen O'Hara, smiled their invitations to read about them for fifteen cents. *Modern Screen* was always good, although *Photoplay* was far and away the best. Their photographers seemed to take more time and never let anybody look old or tired like they sometimes did in other magazines. The pictures of nightclubs were bigger too, and more of them were in color so you could really tell what was sitting on the table, like those mysterious boxes of Sortilege. He wished somebody would open one, or tell what it was.

What intrigued him most of all were the movie ads, always more dramatic and detailed than the ones in the newspapers. He made his choice and reached for *Movie Story,* which doubled his chances of finding out about new movies because, in addition to the ads, they ran the stories of and pictures from seven new movies each month. He held Robert Walker and Hedy Lamarr in his hands. Robert Walker wore a hotel uniform. Hedy Lamarr's shoulders were bare, and in her hair was a jeweled crown. They both winked at him. It was a scene from *Her Highness and the Bellboy,* which was downtown right now at the Apollo. Very carefully he opened to the second page where he knew an ad for an MGM movie was waiting for him. MGM got special treatment, and he didn't think it was fair. Their ad was always first, no matter what the magazine, and on the opposite page would be the Leo the Lion column where Leo would brag about everybody in the latest MGM movies in a way that struck Shorty as most overdone and insincere. A quick scan of the table of contents revealed, just as he thought, *two* MGM movies, but nothing from Universal or Columbia. Something was going on.

The MGM ad was filled with three big faces: Edward G. Robinson, Margaret O'Brien, and Butch Jenkins in *Our Vines Have Tender Grapes.* This was the kind of movie he never had to ask to see. Someone would decide it would be good for him, which automatically reduced his interest. It might be OK, and since it had just opened at the United Artists, it would be another two months before it reached the neighborhood and he would have to deal with it. Maybe there would be a scene where Edward G. Robinson yelled at Margaret O'Brien. His face in the ad looked different though. That big bump was gone, and he looked almost younger and more wholesome than she did. Shorty's hopes were not high.

The Paramount ad on the following page was a lot more

interesting. In the bottom left-hand corner was a small picture of Jennifer Jones looking sad, mysterious, and beautiful. She was kneeling in front of a fire with a knife in her hand. The smoke from the fire billowed up to fill the entire page. The top half of the page held a much larger picture of Jennifer Jones lying sideways and being hugged by Joseph Cotton. They weren't looking at each other, but you could tell they were thinking very hard about the same thing – so hard that if you came up to them and spoke, they wouldn't even hear you. Then Shorty noticed something about the letters of their names. Instead of the plain typed letters of the MGM ad, their names and the title were written in a fancy, curly script, and the "f" in Jennifer looped down and became the "h" in Joseph. The artist was trying to tell you that they really loved each other. Alongside their heads were the words "Love Letters Leading to Murder . . . Hiding Exquisite Bliss." Now this was more like it.

The next ad gave him a shiver of pleasure. He didn't know why he liked the messy ads of Warner Brothers best of all, but he did. The letters would slant every which way on the page, and they often looked as though they had been scrawled by someone in a big hurry using lipstick or blood or a paint brush that was running out of paint. *Mildred Pierce* raced diagonally across the page, cutting in half the figure of Joan Crawford looking all smirky and holding a smoking gun. He could see that her face was a photograph attached to a drawing of her body that was a little too small for the head. That was careless, but boy did he want to see this movie. This was one they'd never take him to in a million years. Why couldn't they decide, just once, that something like *Mildred Pierce* would be good for him?

"Don't hang up on me!"

The magazine fell from his hands. He picked it up and returned it to the rack and moved quickly back toward the booth. When he was close enough to see that his mother was crying, he stopped and backed off a little, unable to turn his eyes away but knowing this was something he shouldn't see. Nobody should be watching this, certainly not the people sitting at the counter, or waiting at the cash register. He tried to position himself to obscure her from their view but not get so close that she became aware of him. She seemed aware of none of them. She held the receiver, but he didn't know if they were still talking.

"Ed? Ed?" She kept turning from side to side pressing her free hand to whichever wall she faced, as if to keep the booth from closing in on her. What he gaped at ceased to be a booth. It was now her cell, her cage. If only he could lead her out, calm her and comfort her. Mandrake gestured hypnotically, but his mother continued to cry.

2. Mr. Fix-it

He sat outside on the curb with his back against a mailbox. She would be able to see him as soon as she came out. The curb felt gritty. It was probably dirty. He would get up in a minute. He supposed they would just go back to the apartment now.

His mother stepped out of the drugstore and stood over him. "Here, I've got something for you." He reached up and took a long salted pretzel stick from her hand. She had another for herself. He ran his tongue over the nubs of salt and looked up at her. She had taken time to compose herself, and he saw no hint of the recent storm in her face.

"Stand up, Shorty."

She brushed the back of his corduroy pants and pushed his hair away from his forehead.

"I need you to do something before we have supper."

She started walking west with him.

They were still going!

His eyes devoured the marquee.

      B. STANWYCK D. MORGAN
      XMAS IN CONNECTICUT
      PLUS JOHN WAYNE IN
      BACK TO BATAAN

"Are you listening to me, Shorty?"

"Sure."

"I want you to take this envelope into Creighton's and give them the money for the rent. Make sure they give you a receipt. You mustn't forget. When you get through we'll have supper. Can you do that for me? I need to get a cup of coffee. I'll be in Miner-Dunn's, across the street."

He took the envelope.

"How long does this pay the rent for?"

"A month."

They would still be at the apartment in December with no room for a tree.

Against his will, he was getting to know this stretch of 79th Street quite well. To their right, just past the Chinese restaurant and The Ridgeland Tap, another tavern, was Zeinback's music store. Some of the other third graders at Our Lady of Peace took lessons there. Charles Melton, who played the accordion, had told him about the listening booth where you could take records and try them out. It sounded wonderful, but he didn't know if he would have the nerve to do it. Charles said they were nice in Zeinback's and didn't bother you, but Shorty was afraid that one look at him was all they'd need to know he wasn't really going to buy anything.

Spread out in the window were copies of *Hit Parader* and sheet music from several new songs. More than anything in these last two months, he missed sheet music and learning the words to a new song over his father's shoulder at the piano. He spotted one that, in the old days, his father would certainly have brought home. It had some of the best words he'd ever heard in a song. He had already memorized them from the radio and taught them to his father, although he wasn't sure he'd gotten everything in the right order.

"*I'm as busy as a spider spinning daydreams.*
I'm as jumpy as a puppet on a string."

"Don't forget about the receipt, Shorty."

They were at the corner of 79th and Ridgeland. He knew his mother's eyes were on him as he scooted across. It was unusual that she was sending him to pay the rent. His pleasure at being trusted with money was far outweighed by his discomfort at being the one to officially extend their stay at the apartment. For the first time, it crossed his mind that maybe she didn't want to do it any more than he did.

Aside from a church, Creighton's was the most serious building he had ever entered. There was nothing to poke through or shop for. No one chatted or smiled; they just stood writing things out at marble tables or lined up at the marble counter for one of the people behind bars. It was very formal, but it wasn't elegant – just serious. He didn't think it belonged jammed up against the Avalon.

The lines were long, and it was close to five o'clock. He wondered if they would close up with people still waiting. The rent was due today. What would happen if he couldn't pay it…or if he just didn't? Would that mean they had to get out of the apartment? What if he didn't move, just stood where he was, didn't get in line, and waited until they closed? He could be in a lot of trouble, but for once he wouldn't care. They might even believe him and not blame him. The Sheffields, of course, would blame his mother for letting it happen. Perhaps his father would too, and she had had enough trouble for today. Besides, where would they go? It might not be possible for them to move back into the bungalow right away. Whenever he thought of it now, he pictured it empty, but what if new people had gotten into it? He knew that staying with the Sheffields was out of the question. The thought of his mother there with them all together made him shudder. It would be like moving into an argument factory where no one could talk in a normal tone of voice, and only yelling or whispering behind backs was permitted. No, that was the only place that would truly be worse for them than the apartment. Then too, if his mother knew they were going to be thrown out on the street, would she still take him to the movies tonight? Well, actually, she might.

An inquisitive look from one of the men behind bars propelled him into the shortest line. How ridiculous he was to pretend he had any control over his life. What a baby's game. He smarted with embarrassment as sharp as if he had been caught thinking out loud. Why, when other people's thoughts were so mysterious to him, did his own seem so transparent to the rest of the world? He hoped in time this would change

⚜

The door of Miner-Dunn's opened into a reassuring world of cheerful smells and sounds. It was one of the most redeeming features of the neighborhood. He found his mother adding cream to an already light brown cup of coffee. Bouncing into the booth, he tossed the receipt towards her. Perhaps all the grizzly parts of this day were behind him.

"We're eating here, I hope."

"Mmmhmm. Take off your jacket."

He folded it neatly on the seat beside him and reached for a menu. They would both check out every possibility before ordering the only thing to have at Miner-Dunn, their splendid hamburger. If somebody told you they had been to Miner-Dunn for a hamburger, you automatically said "mmmm." You couldn't help it.

"Well, we could have the egg salad on toast," she began.

"Or we might try the cod fish cakes – with cod liver oil sauce."

"I don't see that on the menu."

"Neither do I."

"I guess we'll just have to have… um, hamburgers?"

"With everything?"

"Everything."

The waitress saw them fold their menus and approached them with a pad.

"Good evening folks, do you know what you're having yet?"

"Well, first, a little bit more coffee, and then two hamburgers with everything. Oh, and you do have cod liver oil?"

"Momma!"

"We don't get too many calls for that these days. Tastes change I guess."

"Well, we don't *want* any," bleated Shorty.

"No? Then what will you have to drink, sir?"

"Green River, please."

When the waitress left, his mother touched his hand. "I'm worried about Anthony, Shorty."

"Why? He's fine."

"Are you sure? I count on you to pay attention when I'm not there to look after him."

"I pay attention." How much attention could you pay to a two-year-old? He paid enough attention to notice that his brother was taking his own sweet time about becoming much of a conversationalist. To be fair, they both had less to say since leaving the bungalow, but Anthony seemed to be growing more shy, especially around Grandpa Sheffield, whose big voice could be startling. The night they arrived, it had made Anthony cry, and Shorty surprised himself by speaking up. "Don't, Grandpa, you're scaring him!" That's my job, he thought.

The pressure of his mother's fingers increased. "I was counting on seeing Anthony Sunday, but your father wouldn't say for sure that he was coming. Is he getting a cold? You know how easily— "

Uh oh. Had he said the wrong thing? What was the right thing? Had someone decided Anthony was not to see her this weekend? As always, he knew nothing about it, but he knew that only illness would strike her as a reasonable excuse for Anthony's being kept away. Anything else would make her angry, so it was better that she thought he was sick – but not too sick. He would have to be careful. And then what if they sent Anthony anyway? How was he to decide, and why should he have to? Didn't they realize she would question him? So often now, he felt like an actor pushed on stage without a script. Where he or Anthony, or both of them, were to go, and when, and for how long, and whether the results of the going had been good or bad took up most of the conversation these days. He had resented not being consulted about the move, but now when making choices only meant choosing who to disappoint, he wished they would just tell him where and when to report. If he told them the truth, which he did less and less now, he didn't want to be any of the places they were sending him. He would happily go anywhere that they were all together, but such a place seemed to have vanished from the planet.

"Well, his nose was running." That seemed safe to say about Anthony at any time.

Green River and fresh coffee arrived. She watched him drink.

"I'm going to the ladies room. I'll only be a moment."

She could still say that with a straight face, though they both knew that there were few of life's activities that could not be completed before she would return. By now, he thought grimly, he must have become the world champion at waiting. His photo should appear in the Inquiring Reporter column. "And what do you do, young man?" "I wait for people. I'm really, really good at it."

Ah, but this was a nicer place to wait than most. A Harry James record was playing, "It's Been a Long, Long Time." They should play it again when his mother came back. He liked Harry James a lot; in fact, he was probably his favorite musician, with Fats Waller right behind. He always knew when it was Harry James playing because there was something wild, almost naughty about his tone. It was as though he knew a secret, something wicked, that nobody playing or singing with him knew, especially the violinists. Even on a quiet, sweet song like "Sleepy Lagoon," you felt like he was only behaving himself while everybody else was there, and that if they all went out of the room, he and his trumpet would go crazy. Shorty heard music in colors, and trumpets were always yellow like something melting and spilling out of a vat at the steel mills. There were some sounds in music, like strings, that you wanted to reach out and pet, but this was a sound that you would no more try to touch that you would stick your finger in a socket. When the police, baffled by a crime wave, called Manning Nugent's penthouse to plead for his assistance, they would hear Harry James in the background.

Next to the napkin holder on their table was a box with pages that showed all the records you could hear if you put in a nickel. If you put in a quarter, you could hear six. He didn't have quarters often enough to spend them this way, but it always amused him to figure out which six he would have picked. He leaned over to examine the pages. "Till the End of Time" was good, and "If I Loved You." They had "The Atchison, Topeka, and the Santa Fe," but you heard that every time you turned around. Then he saw an old song listed, and the sight of its title made him pause and sit back. What was that still doing here? It was Anthony's song, though Anthony didn't know that.

He remembered exactly the circumstances under which he learned the words. It was the evening of July 26, 1943, and he was staying at the Sheffield's while Momma was at the hospital to get a new baby. He didn't especially see the need for one; as a matter of fact, he thought things were quite perfect as they were. They told him that things would be even more perfect when the baby came, and he would have company. Wouldn't he like company? Not necessarily. They told him he would have to be quiet around the baby. He was a quiet person; didn't they know that by now? And he would have a lot of new responsibilities. They were really on the wrong track with that. New responsibilities were even less intriguing than the idea of perpetual company. But they were both so excited about it that they were like children themselves, and you had to smile at them and go along with it. If a new baby was going to make them that happy, it must be a good idea, and he wouldn't be selfish about it.

He had already been at the Sheffield's for several days and was eager for the baby to come so he could see his parents again and get things back to normal. The change was interesting, and he had to admit that the Sheffield's house was tidier than the bungalow. You would never see newspapers lying about here. It was fun too, to have so many different things to touch and look at, like the painting of the horseshoe curve with pieces of mother-of-pearl for the rocks, and the beautiful cut glass vases in the dining room. Best of all were the songs at night. Grandma Sheffield sang him wonderful old songs that he had never heard before, as she tucked him in, like "The Sleepytown Express" and "Playmate, come out and play with me." Then there were the sad songs, like the one about the two brothers, Jack and Ned, whose lives went separate ways until – oh it was really sad. Grandma wasn't Irish, but the songs certainly could have been.

There were starting to be little hints however, that a long visit here would not be such a great idea. Grandpa Sheffield would give him a measuring look and say, "Now you do want us to have a good report for your father when he calls?"

Why wouldn't they?

Then there were things with Uncle Victor, who lived upstairs, that were not so little. Shorty would be minding his own business, and Uncle Victor would come down and say things like "Well, there's gonna be some changes made now. Ha ha ha," or "Well somebody's not gonna be king of the roost much longer. Ha ha ha." Even when he didn't actually say, "Ha ha ha," it sort of came built into all of Uncle Victor's snappy remarks.

So when the call came on the 26th that he had a baby brother, it was most welcome. The day became a holiday, with aunts and uncles dropping in, smiles all over the house, and an air of anything goes hilarity. As he headed for the door with his roller skates, to his utter astonishment, Uncle Victor flipped him a quarter. "Gonna need it kiddo, another mouth to feed!" He stuffed it in his pocket, thanked his uncle, and scrambled down the steps, a man with a mission. It was still light, and he had to find Simone Ryboviak. Only she could help him with his plan. If she was outside anywhere, he would find her, and the skates would help. In all his life, he had never known another girl like Simone Ryboviak. She was pretty, with long dark hair, and dark eyes, but that wasn't it. She had a swell smile, but that wasn't it either, because half the time she was laughing at him like she thought he was the funniest joke in the world. He wasn't even sure that he liked her, and he was glad she didn't live in his neighborhood because she seemed to be able to get him to do just about anything.

At the moment, she had something he needed, a copy of *Hit Parader* with the words to the song that was number one right now. He had gotten it into his head that this would be the perfect song to memorize and sing to the baby when it came home. Two days ago, she had told him she would let him see it, but she kept teasing him. There was always one more thing he had to do before he could see it. Now the baby was here and there was no more time. Obviously, he would be leaving tomorrow – maybe even tonight. He had to find her.

He didn't have to look far. Parked in front of the apartment building next to the Sheffield's was a gray De Soto, being swarmed over by seven or eight children, Simone among them. She waved him over. He came within a few feet of the car and stopped.

"Whose is it?"

"Oh, a man who lives in the building."

"Wouldn't he mind?"

"I guess not, or he wouldn't leave the doors unlocked."

"Maybe he forgot. They shouldn't be doing that."

"You're funny, Edmond."

"The Baby came. I'll be going home. I need the song."

"You've got skates. It's a good night for skating. I'll go get mine. Wait for me."

"Bring the magazine too."

Her hair flipped as she answered over her shoulder, "Sure."

He watched uncomfortably as children climbed in and out of the DeSoto, turning the steering wheel and slamming the doors. By the time Simone returned, the others had tired of the game and gone away. He didn't see the magazine.

"Get in the car, Edmond."

"No."

"You can pretend you're taking me for a drive."

"No."

"Don't you want to?"

"I'm not supposed to."

"You're not supposed to take me for a drive? When did your parents tell you that?" She laughed at him, but it was like music and made him smile just when he was trying to look his most serious.

"I'm not supposed to play in other people's cars."

She opened the door and slipped into the passenger seat.

"Don't you want to get behind the wheel?"

"No . . . I don't know"

"Get inside, Edmond."

He eased himself behind the steering wheel and gingerly ran his fingers around it. He folded his right hand over it, then his left. He began to turn the wheel back and forth, though there was not much give. He was in heaven. He reached down and touched the gearshift. He twirled the radio dial, and grinned at Simone.

"Do you like our new car, Edmond?"

"Yes, Simone."

"Then let me show you how to really make it yours."

She opened the door and skipped behind the car. He followed her. The trunk was dusty above the bumper. She took his index finger in her hand and pressed it to the car.

"But –"

She moved his finger to shape an 'E', then a 'D'. In less than a minute, he was looking at "EDMOND S" in the dust.

"Now it's yours. Let's go skate."

He wasn't very good, but she didn't mind. They ranged wide and free over an area of streets so vast that he almost lost his bearings about where the Sheffields lived. Whenever they came to an open space free of parked cars, she would take his hands and wheel him really fast in a circle with her hair whipping all around. Once when she let go of him, he skidded into the curb, lost his balance and skinned his knee when he fell. It was bloody but he was laughing. Had he ever had fun like this before?

The light had almost gone. Soon it would be too dark to read.

"Did you bring the magazine?'

"No."

"You promised me! And now it's too late."

"Don't worry. I know the words. I'll teach you, they're easy."

"Teach me – right now."

"What will you give me?"

"What do you want?"

"I might take a kiss . . . but I think I'll take a dime. Is it worth a dime to you?"

"You can have both, if you really teach me right now."

"Well, give me the dime first"

They just stood there in the street and she began.

"You'll never know just how much I miss you,

*You'll never know just how much, I car*e."

She really did know all the words. He made her go over them several times until he was sure he had it.

This was great. When they put the baby in the crib, he would stand at the railing and croon it to the little guy. It would welcome him into the family. It would let him know that in this house, things were done with style. It would signal the beginning of the "even more perfect times."

He leaned over and kissed Simone, then skated back like the wind. He ran up the stairs to see if his father was there to take him home. He burst into a living room full of people but eerily silent. He had last seen them as giddy revelers. Now they looked like a jury. Grandma and Grandpa Sheffield just stared at him, but Uncle Victor said "Been for a joyride, huh kiddo?"

"What?"

"This is a fine time to be coming home. You've had your grandmother worried sick." His grandfather had the lowest, deepest voice he had ever heard. It didn't quite fit when he was trying to be jolly, but when you wanted to let someone know how bad they had been, it was perfect.

"I'm sorry I'm late."

"Where have you been?"

"Playing….skating…I was learning a song … " Somebody please say something.

"Learning a song?" His grandfather's tone made it sound both naughty and feebleminded.

Uncle Victor piped up "Was that before or after you scratched up Old Man Neissler's car?"

"Scratched up?"

"Don't lie to us, son," said his grandfather. "It only makes things worse."

"Yeah, they've got the goods on you, sonny boy. Not too many Edmonds in this precinct. And when you throw in an "S", it doesn't take Sherlock Holmes. You better forget about a life of crime, till you get a few more smarts. We thought you were supposed to be such a hot shot in school."

He could have strangled Simone. He could have strangled himself for being such a dunderhead.

His grandmother finally spoke.

"Mr. Neissler was here this evening to see us about the car. There are scratches on the hood, and even on the roof. At first we didn't believe that you could have anything to do with it, and we told him so, but when he took as out to look at… "

"At the autograph," said Uncle Victor helpfully.

"There was nothing we could say. It was very embarrassing, especially after how we had defended you. Son, this is a time when the whole family should be pulling together, and instead, you've really let us down. It's quite a disappointment for us, Edmond."

His grandmother's voice was weary, kind, and sad all at the some time. This was harder to take than his grandfather barking at him.

"I'm sorry, Grandma. I feel terrible about this, but I didn't scratch anything. I wouldn't do that."

"Did you get in the car?"

"Yes, everybody did, but I just sat behind the steering wheel for a minute. I didn't climb on the car like the other kids."

"Other children were there?"

"Grandma, the whole neighborhood was crawling all over it, but I wasn't, honestly. I love cars. I think cars are beautiful. That's why I draw them. That's why I got into it, but I would never do anything to hurt a car. I mean it."

"I think he's telling the truth, Pa."

"Whether he is or he isn't, we may still have to give Neissler some money for a touch up."

"Yeah, kiddo. Too bad for you, the whole neighborhood didn't sign their masterpiece – only you. And now Grandma and Grandpa have to bail you out, when it's your mom and dad who should get stuck with the tab. You still got that quarter I gave you?"

Shorty nodded.

"Hand it back. You don't deserve it."

It was like a scene where the bad soldier is having his buttons ripped off. He couldn't stand having people displeased with him and the worst thing was that he knew it was his fault.

He was about to find out however, that that was not, in fact, the worst thing.

"This will never happen again, Grandma, I promise."

"Well then, we won't say anything about it when your father calls tonight. If they're going to take you back, a bad report wouldn't do you any good."

He was wide eyed and speechless, but his unspoken "If? If?" thundered around the room and set up camp.

"With a new baby at home, they can't have bad boys misbehaving and causing them worry."

For the next week and a half he edged on tiptoe around the giant, sullen "If?" Then his little case was packed, and his father bundled him into the Buick. "You're awfully quiet, Shorty. Did you miss me? You'll bite your lip if you chew it like that. Grandma and Grandpa said you were a good boy."

"Did they?"

"They certainly did. I'm proud of you."

"Am I coming home for good?"

"What are you talking about, honey?"

"Nothing."

"Now, when we get back, I have to ask you a special favor. Your mother has been very sick; that's why they didn't let her leave the hospital until today. I was going to let you relax at Grandma and Grandpa's for another day or two, but she wants to see you right away."

"She does?"

"Well yes, but she doesn't want to see you crying. Now here's the favor. She's going to have to rest a lot, so if we both keep from making a bunch of noise, it will help her get well faster."

"Does the baby make noise?"

"When he does, he can't help it, but we can. OK?"

"OK."

Back at the bungalow, his father led him over to the crib.

"Meet Anthony."

Now he had a name. Shorty peered over the bars at the smallest person he had ever seen. He decided the song of welcome for the "even more perfect times" would make too much noise, and it went unsung.

Now, more than two years later, Shorty realized that Anthony had never heard his song. The right moment had never presented itself. One day, if it did, he would sing it. He wondered what Anthony thought of these "even more perfect times," especially the last few months. Did he notice a difference? What went on in that little blond head?

"What are you thinking about?" His mother had returned.

"Old times."

The waitress wore an expression of concern as she approached the booth, and Shorty averted his eyes from what he feared was coming.

She would pose the innocent question often asked, but never welcomed, after one of his mother's extended disappearances. By asking it, she would exile herself to the enemy land of the intrusive, from which no one ever returned. The mildest "Is everything all right?" had a fifty-fifty chance of setting the process in motion. This unfortunate waitress chose a variation that Shorty knew removed all hope. "Is anything wrong?"

"We'd like our food."

In one stroke, the meal was transformed, like so many before it, from a simple pleasure to a complex problem. It needed to be managed and contained before it grew so big that it pushed their plans aside. They had come so close to entering the theater, but now the woman's remark had awakened some inner antenna of his mother's which, until they left the restaurant, would scan ceaselessly for further evidence of hostility, of judgment. Finding none, it might supply them on its own. If he had an instruction manual to thrust into the waitress's hand, it would read "There are only bad things to say. There are no good ones. Go quickly, hide, and when you must come back to us, keep your eyes down and say nothing, not even "yes Ma'am."

Their food, of course, had been ready for some time and was quickly set down. Biting through layers of warm bun, beef, onion, mustard, catsup and pickle relish, Shorty could wish for nothing more than to be quiet and do silent justice to these savory pleasures, but there wasn't time. The waitress had left them, but his mother's eyes followed her. She had to be soothed and distracted. He could do this. He had done it before. It should be easier with no one else here to say the wrong thing or break his rhythm.

"Grandpa Foley said the oddest thing to me."

Her eyes turned back to the table.

"I really didn't know whether to believe it."

"And what was that, Dear?" He snatched another mouthful.

Standing at the cash register, he tried not to fidget while his mother held out the dollar and waited for her change, but finally he could bear no more. He pulled at the door to admit the reassuring sounds of traffic. She snapped her pocket book shut, and he drew the door back for her. Once outside, he ran to the curb, but she caught his hand and held it until the traffic broke. At last they were crossing the street. They could be inside the Avalon in minutes. With each step it came closer, and he felt himself changing, a little dizzy, moving slower while everything around him blurred and sped up. He could no longer identify the make of each car as it whooshed by, nor could he be sure just what his mother was saying. Was this what it felt like as you transformed to your secret identity? He was going a little crazy as he knew he always did when they were about to get the tickets.

The block did not begin for him at East End; first, they had to get past the dark stone of Creighton's. From there on, everything was Avalon, the ancient Orient leaping to life on 79th Street! He always walked on the inside here, pressing as close to this beloved building as he could without looking ridiculous. Had he been alone, with no one on the street, he might have hugged it. Under the circumstances, he contented himself with trailing his hand along the yellow bricks. No structure in all Chicago teemed so magically with life. It demanded to be touched. He always obeyed, and was never unchanged by the touching.

The magic began with a false window topped with a pointed Arabian curve. Inside the curve, where the window glass would have been, was smooth stone painted a bluish green, and outlined in red, a strange design, a sort of bowling pin that became a star at the top. He knew it must mean something important to the Arabians since it appeared so many times on the outside of the building. Next, framed within the widest of the outside arches, came the doors of legend, the stage doors. He had never seen them open so much as a crack, but he knew from family stories that years ago whole orchestras in formal dress had swept through them carrying their instruments. Stars promoting their latest pictures had hidden behind them while ushers peeped out to make sure a limousine was at the curb. His mother had told him how offended Grandma Foley had been to see Harpo Marx chase ladies up the aisles, after which he must have emerged from these very doors.

Now they passed another false window and then a series of five more arches, each containing double doors emblazoned with the same mysterious bowling pin design. Through these doors, the ordinary people in the audience spilled out onto 79th Street on Friday and Saturday nights when the lobby was jammed tight with the crowd for the next show. Sometimes, when you came out this way, you would still have to edge your way along a velvet rope to the end of the block before you got past the lines waiting to get in. The night they had taken Shorty to see *The Song of Bernadette*, the line had wound around the corner and begun halfway down East End.

Straight ahead was the marquee, and he felt his breath coming faster. To his left, behind glass, he saw a large poster for *Christmas in Connecticut*, all blue and white, with the faces of Dennis Morgan and Barbara Stanwyck hugging inside a snowball. Behind another glass were shining black and white photographs of scenes from both movies. Shorty couldn't resist a quick glance, but he knew it was better to examine them when he came out. Otherwise, when people were arguing or acting friendly in the movie, he had to put it out of his mind that he had already seen them kissing or shooting each other. Then too, he loved to postpone leaving the theater by pointing to scenes and asking his parents, "Do you remember this?" and "Wasn't it good when this happened?"

Now they were under the marquee. The sidewalk blazed like noon. His head tipped back and he blinked at a ceiling of a thousand light bulbs. His mother's hand was on his shoulder, guiding him backwards like a drunkard to the ticket booth, a tiny castle in itself, encrusted with exotic tiles. He held his breath. They were seconds away from the safety zone of a bought ticket. Things had been known to change and go disastrously wrong before, but never after that. His mother extended the coins through the bottom of the glass. The girl in the Avalon uniform pushed several buttons, and the most beautiful sounds in the world ensued, bright metallic clinking as their change slid down a curving chute, and a fast, resonant explosion as their tickets shot up out of slits in a brass topped counter. It was done and would not be undone. Now it was he who guided, grabbing her hand and leading her inside to breathe an air of purest bliss.

3. Showtime

All traces of 79th Street, indeed, of America itself, fell away as they pushed into the outer lobby. Such was the power of this small room to suggest what awaited them. Crammed with extraordinary shapes and oddly painted tiles, it did not contain a familiar sight from one end to the other. It was nothing compared to the extravagance of the vast main lobby they were about to enter, which, in turn, paled in comparison with the staggering auditorium itself. Still, he knew it served an important function of its own, like the decompression chamber he had seen in a newsreel about submarines. Without this little room, you would step unprepared from the street to the main lobby and lose all reason. At least he felt *he* would.

A few steps ahead of them rose an array of golden doors, each hollowed out to frame its own tall window in a shape that suggested to Shorty a caped palace guard in a pointed hood. They had only to choose one to enter and present their tickets, but this was not a space to be hurried through.

Unsurprised, his mother let him crisscross the room, drawing her to the gallery of coming attractions that hung about the sidewalls. On the right, below the sign "Friday for One Week," was a large poster for *Anchors Aweigh*. The grinning faces of Frank Sinatra and Gene Kelly in sailor hats flanked Kathryn Grayson in a high white headdress, pursing her mouth into a pretty, smiling heart. "That looks good," he said aloud. He could tell that the people who ran the Avalon expected it to be popular because in the adjoining glass case was not a poster, but a plain white sheet lettered "Added Feature: *Hollywood Caravan*," whatever that was. Clearly, it was so short, or so crummy, that nobody bothered to make a poster of it. Shorty was annoyed. Movies (except when they first came out downtown) were meant to be seen in pairs, setting each other off.

The left wall, thankfully, presented the rightful order of things. Under the words "Week After Next", two posters in starkly contrasting moods confronted each other. Striding toward you from the *Pride of the Marines* poster were John Garfield, Eleanor Parker, and Dane Clark. Arm in arm and smiling their faces off, they looked like they were at the head of a victory parade because they had just won the war triple handedly. It looked too cheerful to be a war movie, and the lettering bragged that it was an inspiring true story, something that Shorty did not automatically consider a recommendation. No, this one could be skipped without pain. The second poster made him reconsider. It too showed three figures, but what a difference. George Sanders, who could usually be counted on to be in movies where people were up to no good, stood looking grim and troubled. At his feet, looking up with her arms around his legs, was Ella Raines. What was going on here? To make things even more interesting, a big Geraldine Fitzgerald was leaning back and looking like when she was through causing trouble for them, she might start in on you. The very title drew him in: *The Strange Affair of Uncle Harry*. For Shorty, "strange" was a spicy seasoning, certain to improve the flavor of whatever was being offered. The lettering heightened his enthusiasm. "The shocking play that stunned Broadway!" If "strange" was good, "shocking" was even better, and "stunned"! He had to see it. He hid his excitement from his mother. They wouldn't take him to this blindfolded unless he could think up a truly clever plan.

"Okay, Momma, let's go in."

As they neared a door, a uniformed arm on the other side drew it open for them, and once again, he felt pitched headlong into a kaleidoscope, beset from top to bottom and on all sides with dense layers of elaborate and richly colored designs that had no counterpart in the rest of his universe. No inch of this immense hall had been left undecorated. Nowhere could Shorty's eye escape, or penetrate the mysterious plan of the architect. Only in the sheer size and openness of this spectacular lobby was mercy to be found. In a smaller room, he could imagine such visual intensity driving people to cry out or flee.

The gentle splashing of a fountain drew his eyes to a tiled pool on their left. He felt his mother slipping the ticket stubs into his pocket, and they began to move easily across the length of a shimmering marble floor so reflective that its farthest edges seemed to lie under a thin film of water. On a weekend night, their swift progress would have been impossible. Then, they would have stood penned in long lanes, inching ahead only when an usher would emerge from the auditorium, unhook the velvet restraining rope at the front of one of the lanes, and call out "Two together on aisle four in the balcony," or whatever location had just been vacated. If you were at the head of the lane and the seats sounded good or you were just tired of waiting, you would follow him through the dark as he shined his flashlight on the floor and led you to the exact spot.

Even though they had just finished supper, his mother would know that he would want popcorn for his "separate popcorn stomach" as she called it. In their current circumstances, however, he wasn't sure it was right to ask. Shorty kept silent as they passed the silver machine whose eruptions filled the glass case with popcorn enough for the Blue Leopard to dive into and splash around. "Wait right here for me, Shorty." Parking him at a marble bench, she descended one of the wide, twisting staircases that led to the restrooms.

The sleek black and white bathrooms in the Avalon, and the lounges that surrounded them, were the worst places in the world for someone like his mother, given to chronic lolligagging, to be turned loose. Even a speedy washroom visitor would find interesting distractions there, like the pond with the jumbo goldfishes, the fountains, or the writing room. If you were watching a movie and suddenly realized you needed to write a letter, or send a secret message, you could do it here. A writing desk with pens, ink, envelopes, and special stationery waited for you, though he had never observed anyone using them. The management of the Avalon thought of everything! Luckily, for some reason, his mother never kept him waiting as long here as she did most places. Or if she did, he didn't notice; there was too much to see, and he would never be done examining it.

So few people were walking around in the lobby that, for once, he could get a really good look at the floor. It didn't seem like a floor at all, and it was certainly too pretty to be walked on. Tonight it looked to Shorty more like a giant board game, backgammon maybe, if people from another planet had designed it. His eyes rode the patterns to the far edge of the floor and moved upward. A dark border of busily splashed marble as high as his waist, and inset with squares and rectangles of contrasting colors, ran the length of the hall. Here and there, the wall receded and the border became a bench with room enough for him to scoot back and sit among the tall columns that rose from it to support stone walls bursting with carved and painted images that might be flowers, but weren't exactly. Cut into these walls were rows of the pointy hooded arches. Behind the pillars and under the arches were painted scenes of Arabians lounging about in an oasis or at a bazaar. Shorty could even see a naked lady from the back. She was stretched out relaxing and none of the Arabians were paying any attention to her. Enclosing each of these areas were borders studded with jewels as big as your fist. In between, and up above were jutting balconies and wonderful tall windows screened by stone arches with holes cut into them and so many curves and scrolls and zigzags that it made his head spin. If this was what Arabia was truly like, he would move there in a minute and say goodbye to everything he knew.

His head leaned back against a pillar and his eyes reached the ceiling. A gigantic oriental rug of stone spread out upon an even larger and more complicated stone carpet. This should have been the floor. It was though he were hanging upside down. He blinked his eyes but still felt dizzy.

"Are you ready?"

Through a side door, he followed his mother into the darkness.

He could make out only a few empty seats, no two of them together. The audience was completely silent. One of the pictures was already in progress. He knew it was *Christmas in Connecticut* because there was snow and no soldiers. People were inside a wonderful home with a fireplace so huge you could stand up in it, and the biggest window he had ever seen. It took up most of the wall and looked like they put about a dozen normal windows together. This was going to be a great house, and he couldn't wait to see the rest of it. The music, too, let him know that this couldn't be *Back to Bataan*. That was RKO, and this was definitely Warner Brothers music. In a Warner Brothers movie, the music didn't leave any empty spaces. It was louder and ran all over the place helping you figure out what the characters were really up to, and what was going to happen later on.

"Shorty," his mother whispered and tugged at his sleeve. It was always a big mistake for him to look at the screen before he got to his seat.

When they'd settled in, he looked back up and the softest of sounds escaped his lips. "Ohh...." It was his first glimpse of Barbara Stanwyck. He had seen her photograph and heard her voice on the radio, but here she was, twenty feet tall, moving about in front of him, wearing a checked aprony sort of dress with white sleeves and collar, her long dark hair bouncing around her shoulders and looking – well, absolutely perfect. She was so pretty, but friendly, and kind of flirty. She seemed to be keeping a really good joke to herself, but at the same time, you knew she needed your help and you wanted to give it. Her smile would make a cat purr, and at the moment he was feeling very catlike. There were some people you wanted to get to know the moment you saw them, and she was certainly one.

The help she needed involved flapjacks or "flip flops" as S.Z. Sakall, in a tall chef's hat, kept calling them. For some reason, which would be made clear when they saw the beginning of the movie, it was very important that she flip a pancake for Sidney Greenstreet; otherwise, he would find out that everybody had been telling him a pack of lies, and terrible things would happen. But she couldn't do it, not even with S. Z. Sakall helping her practice, and telling her how easy it was. It certainly didn't look easy, and she was making a terrible mess of the kitchen, flipping them on the stove, on the ceiling, and just about everywhere except the frying pan where they were supposed to go. Finally, Sidney Greenstreet arrived for the flap jack showdown, and Barbara Stanwyck tried all kinds of feeble excuses to get out of it, but nothing would work. Shorty wished he could be with her in the kitchen to try to help her out, but he knew he couldn't think of anything either. With a hopeless shrug she picked up the frying pan, closed her eyes, and flipped. Shorty couldn't stand it when people made fools of themselves in public, and he squirmed in his seat looking at the screen though the fingers of his right hand. But then, an amazing thing happened: the pancake came down out of the air and landed exactly where it was supposed to. People in the audience laughed, and some of them clapped. They were as relieved as he was. He felt glad to be part of this mass reaction. It was so good not to be peculiar for a little while, and here in the dark he was just like everybody else. It was a feeling he longed to carry back outside with him, but he knew it would evaporate before he could reach the sidewalk.

As the scenes moved from room to room in the Connecticut house, it proved to be everything he hoped and more. You could sit in one room, look through the window and see into an entirely different part of the house. What happy lives could be lived in so much space!

It seemed to Shorty that really good movies fell into one of two categories. There were the kind like *To Have and Have Not* where, even if you didn't want to be there yourself, you were excited every minute about what was going on. With others, it wasn't important what was happening, you just wanted to hang around in them. Once in a great while, there was a movie like *Casablanca* or *Ali Baba and the Forty Thieves* that fit into both categories, and he supposed they were the best of all. *Christmas in Connecticut* was clearly the second type. It didn't matter to him what particular mischief and nonsense the characters were up to, as long as he could hang around. Before it was over, he got to poke through the house from top to bottom trying out every chair and sofa, raid the icebox at night for a drumstick, go to a square dance, and then get taken on a swell sleighride. At the end, when Sidney Greenstreet finally calmed down, forgave everybody, and said "What a Christmas! What a Christmas!", Shorty wasn't ready to leave Connecticut.

But then the lights came up, and there was an even better place to be – Avalonland. You were inside the auditorium, but you were really outside at night, in the courtyard of an Arabian Palace. People were getting up and stepping past them to go out to the bathrooms, to get snacks, or, possibly, to write letters, but Shorty was rooted to the spot. When he absolutely had to go, he could slip out during the newsreel, or a travelogue, but he wasn't going to waste a second of what he could see before the lights went back down. Up in the ceiling, stars were twinkling in a dark blue sky, and all around, even in back of him, were gleaming golden jewel studded towers with the curious names his father had explained to him – minarets and parapets. Some of the towers were slender with windows near the top for men to call out prayers to the Arabians down below. Others were wider with fat domes and grills cut into the stone for the Sultans and princesses to look out at you. The screen was behind a deep red curtain under the widest of all the arches. It was guarded on both sides by large winged lions with round shields on their chests and by two more winged creatures at the top of tall swirly columns. Billowing out from a roof above the screen was a golden tent with red stripes, supported by spears with shields hanging from them. There were arches all around with the same pointy shapes as the ones in the lobby, but behind them, instead of paintings, were rooms hung with lamps of gold and colored glass and filled with fountains and statues. These arches remained softly lit when the other lights went out, so even if the worst movie in the world was playing, you would never be bored if you just looked around. Here he was smack in the middle of what he had imagined when his mother first read him stories of Sinbad, Scheherazade, and Aladdin. They would all feel right at home here. He didn't want to move, and at the same time he wanted to jump out of his seat, climb the towers and run around the rooftops, leaping from building to building.

"I didn't like the looks of that man who sat next to us. He's up to something. If he comes back, we'll change our seats."

Shorty shook himself back to reality. In his mother's view, the strangers who sat around them were often up to something. They came with no intention of seeing the movie but were bent instead on snatching their belongings or worse, though the worse had never been spelled out for him. He and his mother had been spectacularly successful at foiling this army of evildoers. Not once had so much as a mitten fallen into their clutches. This, of course, had involved considerable changing of seats over the years, something that he despised. It broke his concentration, he was sure it disturbed other people, and especially on those wretched occasions when multiple seat changes took place, it brought them a kind of attention that made him cringe.

"He didn't leave his coat, Momma. I don't think he's coming back."

She opened a shell shaped compact and studied her mouth.

Instead of applying the red lipstick directly, she massaged it with a finger and lightly stroked her upper lip, which she then pressed against the other. He never tired of watching this delicate procedure which made the slatherings of some other ladies seem quite crude.

The lights had begun to dim and people were drifting back in around them.

"Do you need to – ?"

"In a minute."

First he had to make sure that things would be shown in their proper order. Darkness descended and the majestic red curtain parted so slowly that, before it had gathered to the sides, glittery letters were swimming in a blur behind it: "Friday for one Week." Just as he had expected – previews first. He would have been a fool to have left his seat.

Anchors Aweigh was going to be in Technicolor, something they only used for musicals, pirate movies, and animal stories where you were outside all the time. You didn't need it for ordinary stories; in fact it could mess them up. You certainly wouldn't want color in a mystery. Even something like *Christmas in Connecticut* was prettier in black and white, and what if one of the horses had peed in the snow? No, Shorty thought, color should be saved for special occasions.

It was just the thing, though, for *Anchors Aweigh*, and what color it was! Everything and everybody looked as if they had been freshly painted. Kathryn Grayson was gorgeous and sang the most impossibly hard songs, really high and fast with a smiley look on her face like "Oh, it's nothing." Frank Sinatra was not as handsome as most people in the movies, in fact his face had a triangle shape, like Submariner, but when he sang, he could have looked like a Gila monster and you still would have been crazy about him. Jose Iturbi was in it too, and it was surprising to see him not wearing a tuxedo.

Behind him was an even bigger surprise, a stage full of more pianos than Shorty had ever seen in one place, all being played by kids. But the most unusual thing in this preview came when Jerry, the cartoon mouse, started dancing with Gene Kelly, and doing exactly the same steps. He had never seen anything like it, and neither had his mother. It was going to be easy to get taken to this one. More sparkly letters appeared: "Coming Soon." The scenes they showed from *Pride of the Marines* were less happy-sappy than the poster suggested. One of them was quite disturbing, when blind John Garfield knocked over a Christmas tree.

The *Strange Affair of Uncle Harry* preview wasn't giving away any secrets. Shorty could get no clue as to why everybody on Broadway had been so stunned, and some of it looked disappointingly normal. But there was still Geraldine Fitzgerald with that voice all fresh and sticky like lemon drops and those fiery eyes darting all around and a scary nervousness that made you think she'd been pushed to the limit, had nothing to lose, and was capable of absolutely anything. If they ever wanted to make a movie about his Aunt Sheila . . .

Suddenly, the plan that Shorty had been seeking came to him. He wouldn't say a word about *Uncle Harry*. Instead, he would act excited about seeing the true story of this brave patriotic marine and all the hardships he had overcome. Once they were sitting in the theater, especially if he could time their arrival so *Pride of the Marines* came last, they weren't likely to leave. It would be too late for them to do anything but sit there and be stunned and hope he wasn't noticing anything. Though shaken to his very core, he would show nothing and remain blameless. He knew his parents weren't stupid and he disliked being insincere, but drastic measures were called for. There was never enough in life to be stunned about.

The Pathe newsreel rooster was crowing. Shorty whispered, "I'll be right back." .

He returned to his seat in time for the end of a travelogue. People were in a big bowling alley and the narrator was explaining that even though you were halfway around the world, you could still bowl to your heart's content.

"Where are they?"

"Australia."

Shorty mentally crossed it off his list of places to visit.

Then, the most cheerful music in the world struck up and inside a circle with a rainbow of rings he read the welcome words "Looney Tunes and Merrie Melodies." He had never seen a bad Looney Tunes. He didn't think they had ever made one. This was not to say that he automatically liked every cartoon he saw, far from it. At those twenty-five cartoon matinees that adults seemed to think were every child's dream, most of what he had seen had been silly without being funny, and he would come out feeling groggy and depressed. But tonight it was Bugs Bunny, who Shorty admired and even envied. Bugs Bunny was an absolute genius at running his life. No one in the world had as much control over what happened to him as Bugs did. He never set out to harm other people, but when they came crashing into his affairs, he was brilliant at thinking up the perfect way to send them crashing back out.

After the cartoon, a familiar and most pleasurable beeping sound began. The RKO tower, atop a spinning world, sent out bolts of lightning. Shorty thought that all movies, even bad ones, began well because the studios had such good emblems, like the Universal letters reflecting in a mirrored globe or the beautiful Columbia lady in her white gown, holding up the torch with the glinting flames. RKO had one of the most exciting with letters that pulsed on one by one like jagged little pieces of lightning. The credits followed: thick two sided white letters, floating in front of a jungle: *Back to Bataan*.

John Wayne was the star, but mostly it was about Anthony Quinn who played a Filipino man whose grandfather had been a hero. For a true story, some of it made Shorty wonder, like when one minute Anthony Quinn is hurt and unconscious, and the next minute he's stomping around all pouty because he thinks his girlfriend is a traitor and he won't even eat the chicken broth that Beulah Bondi went to all kinds of trouble to make just for him in the middle of the jungle.

Really awful things kept happening to people, even the Japanese. Hundreds of them were trying to climb over a barbed wire fence to get at John Wayne, but they were all getting shot with machine guns and their bodies kept piling up on top of each other. Another one got stabbed through the neck with a bayonet that came out the other side. When the Japs took over a school and the principal refused to take down the American flag, they hanged him from the flagpole. The saddest thing of all was when a little boy died after saving John Wayne and everybody by crashing a Japanese truck, and just before he died, he apologized to Beulah Bondi for never having learned to spell "liberty." After he closed his eyes, she said, "Dear God, did anyone ever learn it so well?" and Shorty got snuffly.

By the end, when John Wayne had taught the Filipinos how to get rid of the Japs, Shorty's mind kept going back to the principal. Wouldn't it have been okay just to lower the flag and still be alive when things got better?

He would have to think about that later. *Christmas in Connecticut* was starting up again with his favorite studio sign, the big WB, squashed to fit inside a shield, and the deep horn music that, like the 20th Century Fox drums, seemed to say, "Stop talking! Sit up and pay attention! Something important is starting." The credits were the turning pages of a book, with snowy scenes, and the first page did something different to put you into the right mood. Under the names of the three stars were the words "wish you a very merry," and the next page, of course, was the title. "Who thought up these credits?" Shorty wondered. How lucky they were to have the job, and how eager they must be to get to work each day! It pleased him that they were in a playful mood. It pleased him even more that they had treated Sydney Greenstreet respectfully, with letters just as big as everybody else's.

He didn't know if they had missed much, but it turned out they had missed quite a lot, submarines, a shipwreck, a long stay in a hospital, and a terrific restaurant run by S.Z. Sakall that Shorty wanted to go to at once. The best scene they had missed was a very quiet one. Barbara Stanwyck was trimming a Christmas tree by the enormous window while Dennis Morgan played a romantic song on a grand piano. The tree had the same kind of lights and garland all dripping with tinsel that his family always had in the bungalow, but this tree was so high that she had to stand on a ladder to trim it. When she dropped a big glass ball and it broke, you knew it was because she was already in love with Dennis Morgan and she wasn't paying attention. Off in another part of the room, Reginald Gardiner and Sydney Greenstreet were talking quietly. Nobody was going anywhere, nothing was happening, and everybody was in a good mood.

He looked away from the screen and watched his mother watching. Her face was, as the announcer would say about Captain Midnight's foes, inscrutable. What was she thinking? Everything they had lost was going on around that tree. Could she see it? Did she miss it as he did? Would she do or undo whatever was needed to "sort things out" and get it back for them? She just kept looking straight ahead with no particular expression.

Too soon, he knew they had reached the part where they came in. His mother had completed the preliminary gathering of belongings, and was waiting for him to look at her. Finally, he did.

"Just until the pancakes?"

The flapjack made the same precise landing as before, provoking the same reaction from the audience. He and his mother stood up, and slowly, with several backward glances, he extracted himself from the darkness. Moving through the lobbies, he felt he needed a spare head. His own was swimming with images that were utterly useless on 79th Street, where, all too soon, he found himself.

4. In the Arms of the Dark

They stood near the curb where, if he leaned out a little he could see the viaduct across Stoney Island and tell if a streetcar was coming. His mother opened her purse to begin the inventory she seemed to find so reassuring. Not wanting to appear anxious to leave her, he stole only a quick glance down the street. If a trolley came soon, she wouldn't have time to persuade him to stay, but nothing was in sight.

"Which did you like better?" Maybe he could steer the conversation away from—

"Well, I don't really like war movies. It's getting late Shorty. Wouldn't you like to stay here tonight?"

There were so many reasons why he wouldn't, none of which he could tell her. He missed his father. He wanted to sleep in a real bed, not the narrow, fuzzy cushioned couch that felt itchy through the sheets. He wanted to get away from the apartment and – worst of all – he wanted to get away from her, at least for a little while. Not for long, but if he could just rest up from it tonight, he knew he could be better with her.

"There's some things I need to do."

"Can't you do them here?"

"Not really... I need to go pay attention to Anthony."

"My mother warned me that if I raised a house full of comedians, I'd regret it like she did."

"I don't have my catechism here, and on Fridays, Father Jordan comes around and asks us questions." That, he was sure, would settle the matter, but where was the streetcar?

"I'll write you a note about that. You won't get in trouble. I'll fix you a good breakfast, and this way, you can sleep later in the morning. You look tired, and it's just that I don't know if I'll be seeing either of you this weekend."

She must be lonesome. She really wanted him with her tonight, and coming from the woman who had just treated him to such a deliriously enjoyable experience, it didn't seem much to ask. He wasn't tired, he thought; he was selfish, and spoiled.

He had told her once that Uncle Victor thought he was spoiled. Her response had surprised him. "You are. We spoiled you terribly. That's because we love you. People who are loved are spoiled. When you meet someone who isn't, you should be kind to them because they have to spoil themselves and that doesn't always work out too well."

"Like Uncle Victor? Do I have to be kind to him?"

"Oh no, he's spoiled too."

"Who would love him? Even Aunt Rachel -"

"Shhh. Grandma and Grandpa Sheffield."

"But he's so…" Shorty screwed up his face.

"You make it sound as though they have a choice, and they don't. They love him just the way we love you and Anthony, and that has nothing – well very little – to do with being good or doing what you are supposed to. Now listen, it IS important to us that you are a good person – and I hope you always will be. You're more likely to be happy if you are, and it will certainly be easier on the people around you. But --." She corrected the misbuttoned top of his shirt. "We wouldn't stop loving you if you weren't."

"You wouldn't?"

"No, and you mustn't worry about that. You can't bribe someone into loving you by being good."

Well this was news.

"I guess you think that Daddy and I love you because you get on the honor roll and do what we tell you without arguing and make us laugh."

He stared at her without a clue as to what might come next.

"That's all icing on the cake. We just love you because we love you."

"But if I stole money – a lot of money?"

"We admire and respect and trust you, and we might stop feeling that way if you did terrible things, but we could never stop loving you."

What a perfect place to let things rest, but someone else had crawled inside him and wouldn't stop asking questions.

"What if I killed somebody?"

"There are things you could do that would break my heart, but all the pieces would go right on loving you. That doesn't change."

It comforted him enormously when she had said these things, but lately, he had begun to torment himself with the thought that they might not really be true. If they were, then no matter how strange things seemed right now, he could believe what they told him, that it was all temporary, like rationing. His parents could never stop loving each other and so, they could never stop loving him - but he was less and less sure of this as the weeks of temporary stretched into months.

Where was that streetcar? Had they stopped running entirely? He had only one card left to play. If it didn't end the discussion of his leaving, nothing would.

"Grandma wouldn't like it if I stayed over."

Instantly, he wanted the words back in his mouth, where they had seemed so logical and harmless. He had spat poison at her and he knew it, and it could not be taken back.

Her expression didn't change; it didn't need to. Just by continuing to look at him and without a word, she conveyed all that he needed to know of the undeserved pain he had inflicted. Why should his grandmother have power over their affairs? But she did, and it was clear in this moment that they both knew she did, and that knowing it gave him a kind of power. He didn't want it and would rather not defend himself than use it.

If there was nothing he could say to undo the wound he had delivered, was there at least something he could say to soften it, paper it over, and let them pretend it hadn't happened? They were both very good at pretending. There must be. He had to think.

He would not, however, be given the chance to atone, and his punishment would begin with the grinding screech of the streetcar that now bore down upon them with a shower of crackling sparks. "Well, you'd better catch this one then." His mother smiled at him.

If only – but he could find no words to reclaim his honor. Such cleverness as he might have was too slow to serve him now. Shrunken and cowardly, he fumbled up the steps of the trolley and turned back to face her.

"Goodbye, Mom. I had a really good time."

"Be careful, get inside."

The car lurched into motion and pulled him away from her. "Take care of yourself and look out for Anthony," she called to him.

"I will. I will."

She grew smaller and smaller, but he did not turn away while he thought she could still see him.

"Fare, please."

He dug out four pennies from his corduroys and showed the student streetcar pass they had given him at Our Lady of Peace.

Actually it was his second such pass. It had taken him less than a week to earn the mortifying distinction of "first to lose a pass." He had lost it even sooner than Sister Vallina knew. Rather than report it, he had paid double fare for days until he ran out of money.

You could, if you chose, spend the entire ride in the outer part of the car, standing clear of the curving iron steps, pretending to be the motorman. Tonight, however, he felt thoughtful and required the less stimulating surroundings of the inner car, although this area too, was not without its diversions. He loved the wet look of the woven bamboo seats, waxed to a high gloss, and the agreeable crunch they made as you seated yourself. He liked being surrounded by the advertisements that curved in at you on both sides from the top of the car. He spotted a new one. "Welcome him back with more than a pack," urged a smiling woman as she handed a carton of Pall Malls to an equally cheerful man in a Marine uniform.

At this time of night the car was not crowded, and he had his choice of seats. While his right hand fidgeted with the crisscrossed texture of the seat, he stared out a window to the west at a Jewish delicatessen and the Wee Folks clothing and toy store. They were not quite at Bennett. He could still jump up and get off. He could easily run back and be waiting for her outside the apartment. How surprised and glad to see him she would be. No decision was irreversible. How could you ever make one if they were? But instead, he sank back against the seat, drifting, as loud iron wheels propelled him firmly beyond whatever the night might hold for his mother.

The next stop was Jeffery, a major intersection, where he knew the car would make its longest pause of the trip. He also knew what he would be forced, inevitably, to consider as he waited for the lights to change and the traffic to clear. For once, he welcomed it. On both sides of the street were tin newsstands, hooded against the wind, and run by members of what must surely be the most unfortunate family he knew. The man, Emil, was confined to a wheel chair because of a dreadful but mysterious accident some years ago. His sister, whose name Shorty had never heard spoken, moved about on crutches and suffered the added misfortune of having very few teeth, the result, he supposed of the same horrible accident. Her mouth collapsed inward and her face seemed shortened, like Andy Gump in the funnies. No matter what the weather, the two of them wore stocking caps and many layers of clothing of no recognizable color. Their garments seemed to have absorbed every bit of grime the street had to offer.

Despite their disabilities, they ran their operation with incredible speed and efficiency, darting from one side of 79th Street to the other and dodging traffic so fearlessly that Shorty sometimes had to look away. He marveled particularly at their agility when the delivery truck arrived and heavy stacks of *The Sun*, *The Daily News* and *The Herald American* thudded to the curb. Heaven protect those who stood in their path, for they both could be quite brusque and gruff.

It was this, he guessed, that made them an object of mockery to some of his new schoolmates who found it endlessly hilarious to say whose blind date Emil's sister would be for a dance. The first time he had seen them, his mother made a point of talking about them when they got back to the apartment. He must never make fun of Emil and his sister because there was a dignity about what they were doing in very difficult circumstances. They worked hard for what they got and asked nothing of anyone. What would happen to him, she had asked, if he were in their place? He knew the answer to that one right away, though he chose not to share it with her. He would be flattened like a pancake the first time he hobbled into the street.

Even without her caution, he would never have ridiculed them. Confronted with lives so hard that he would find them unlivable, he could only back off in wonder and respect. He found himself thinking about them a lot. It bothered him that he never observed an action or a conversation between them that did not grow directly out of their job. Had the accident robbed them of their human natures as well? What would their Christmas be like? More of the same, but with a layer of ice to meet the point of her crutch?

He paused at their stands at times, trying to think of something to say to them that was not about newspapers, but they seemed to exist in a world that was not only feverishly busy, but closed to him, and the words would not come.

Through the streetcar window, he caught sight of Emil now, leaning against the north side stand, taking coins from his apron and filling the change maker that was strapped to his waist. What was his fascination with these people? Why did he study them so? For the first time, as he stared at Emil's nimble fingers, a reason suggested itself. He was trying to make out his future as foreseen for him by Uncle Victor. His father, his grandfather, and both his Sheffield uncles all worked at the steel mill, but it was rare that they all had the same shift. On one such recent occasion, Shorty had listened at the kitchen table as the four men grumbled about the injustices they continually suffered at their various posts at South Works. Finally, his father noticed him and extracted a promise that he would never apply for a job at the mill. It was an easy and a reasonable promise to make. In the many pictures he had conjured of himself as a grownup, never once had there been an image of The United States Steel Company. Afterward, however, Uncle Victor had drawn him aside. "Kiddo, I say this for your own good. Your dad means well, but he doesn't see you the way the rest of us do. I guess you've got some brains, but you're just not practical. You're no good at anything anybody would pay money for. Don't be so quick to rule out a job at the mill. You'd be lucky to get it, and luckier still to keep it. We don't want to see you on the dole."

There were times, he had to admit, when he believed Uncle Victor was a more realistic judge of his skills than his father. Shorty wasn't practical; there was just something missing in him, something that Uncle Victor, not blinded by his father's affection, could detect. It wouldn't matter for a while, but sooner or later these missing chunks could betray him. Would he wind up like Emil? Well no, actually. Someone had told him that certain jobs were set aside for people with physical handicaps, but no one had ever mentioned such jobs for people with something missing inside. No, if Uncle Victor was right, Shorty's future would not be the round-the-clock hardship, loneliness, and ridicule laid out for Emil and his sister. It would be something worse.

⚜

Screeching into gear, the car ground slowly across Jeffery, past the imposing structure that was now his parish church and school, Our Lady of Peace. If not for the Avalon, it would have been the most magnificent building on all 79th Street. Magnificent, but not especially likeable.

The church itself was the largest he had ever seen. The stone stairway alone took up half the block, and if you tried to run up, you would be out of breath before you got to the top. A dozen different groups of people could mill about talking at various levels without being in anyone's way. It didn't so much seem like the entrance to a church, but to a grand bank or an important government building. At the top of the stairs were three sets of green metal doors that you had to try hard to pull open, and shove to get back out again. Once inside, you passed through a dark hallway where smaller doors opened onto a great room whose height and distances and richness had made him gasp as he entered for the first time. Since then, even though he knew what was coming and wanted to appear casual about it, his eyes would still sweep involuntarily up the towering pillars, his neck would still crane back as he pondered the ornate ceiling, and he would still feel dwarfed by the ocean of cool marble, dark polished wood, glittering statues of saints, and the Blessed Virgin stepping on a snake.

Without question, it was a great and holy place. He could picture the Last Judgment being held there. But even as he admired it, he found it vaguely disturbing. Compared to Our Lady of Peace, Saint Felicitas had been cramped and puny, but it had never disturbed him and it too seemed a holy place. He could picture Jesus being born there. He missed Monsignor Walsh talking about Jesus as though he were a real baby and about the people in the Bible as though they lived on your block. You had to listen carefully to Monsignor Walsh because he had had a stroke and it made his mouth do odd things. But if you paid attention, he was extremely funny and convinced you that God liked you and looked out for you. One Sunday, he had given a fantastic sermon persuading Shorty that all kinds of angels were crowded around them in the little church and were going to follow them home and help them be good if only they listened to them. His father said it was like having Barry Fitzgerald in the pulpit.

It bothered Shorty that he didn't think Monsignor Walsh would fit in at Our Lady of Peace. The sermons were very different. Since September, he had been waiting for a good one. Mostly, they convinced you that it was going to be pretty tricky to stay out of Hell. Some of them didn't seem like sermons at all, just explanations of what the second collection would be spent for. Shorty's attention would wander, and as his eyes roamed about the enormous room bursting with treasures, he found it hard to understand why they even needed the first collection.

As for the school, he hadn't quite decided. "Welcome to OLP, the Old Ladies' Penitentiary," Vincent Kranz had said to him. Shorty had never seen a Chinaman, but at first sight, he wondered if that's what Vincent might be, with his slightly slanted eyes and smooth honey yellow skin. The face was unusual looking, rather long and narrow, unlike the Irish, Polish, and Swedish faces that Shorty was used to seeing at school. The eyes peered out from behind very long, dark lashes, and the expression was both sleepy and sly at the same time. Vincent was always trying to make him laugh when he wasn't supposed to. He couldn't make him talk during lessons. That was just rude, even if you didn't feel like listening, which, most of the time, he did. But Vincent had gotten him to respond in kind when he glared like a lunatic and shook his fist at him during the rosary. The rosary of all times! It was even more serious than lessons and he surprised himself, but this was the first real gesture of friendship anyone had extended him since he arrived and it needed to be acknowledged.

Sister Vallina had reprimanded them by name. "Edmond! Vincent! Control yourselves. Our Lord didn't suffer so that you two could mock the sorrowful mysteries. What you just did was part of his agony as he hung on the cross." Before Shorty had time to feel ashamed, he observed from the expression of other boys, who were still making up their minds about him, that the incident had done him no harm at all in their eyes.

Hoping to ride out the disruption of their moving until he could return to his old school, he had had no wish to set foot in a new one, and he had actually been able to stall his mother for the first two days. Any fear he might have had about falling behind had been dispelled by his experience in second grade. Saint Felicitas had seen very little of him this spring when he galloped through all of his childhood diseases in one great charge, dropping into class only long enough to pick up whatever was going around: first whooping cough and chicken pox, then measles, and finally scarlet fever. His mother was a splendid nurse, entertaining and cheerful, except when the Board of Health people came to check up on them. Then there would be loud discussions about moving him, but somehow she made them go away, for which he was most grateful. She was also a splendid teacher. When he had to be kept in the dark, she would drape a cloth over his eyes, read to him for hours, then hide the books and newspapers so he wouldn't be tempted.

Eventually, a notice arrived from Saint Felicitas that upset his father. Because of the time Shorty had missed, he would be kept back in second grade for another year. He was disappointed, but he supposed it made sense. His father, however, persuaded them to let him take the final examinations. Three days after he did, another notice arrived. His father read to him, in high excitement, that they were invited to an awards program at which Shorty would be given a pin for having the highest average in his class. His lack of reaction disappointed his father. Shorty had no excitement to contain and wasn't even sure he wanted the pin. He was relieved to be going to third grade, but it seemed odd to have a fuss made about being average, about winding up exactly in the middle of the class. Did they really want people to know that? After listening to Shorty's explanation in silence, his father called out, "Frances, come in here. You'll enjoy this."

Did his parents know then, as far back as June, that they were moving him away from Saint Felicitas? How long, he wondered, had the plot been hatching? And if it was so exciting to them that Saint Felicitas was prepared to keep handing him pins and praise and holy cards, then why did September find Our Lady of Peace looming up at him with all its marble and concrete? He had dug in his heels and kept it briefly at bay with an assortment of excuses, but on the third day of classes, his mother's indulgence expired and Shorty found himself enrolled.

Our Lady of Peace was so large that there were two third grades, and with no chance to examine them and make a choice, he was bustled to the Chappel Street side. The moment he entered the room, he realized that his breezy attitude about attendance had not been wise. Thirty pairs of eyes appraised him coolly. His delayed arrival only emphasized his status as an outsider. His skeptical audience was linked together by two years of shared experiences. He realized, too late, that they must have spent the last two days catching up with each other. Lounging in smug solitude at the apartment, he had missed the perfect opportunity to sneak in relatively unnoticed. Now, instead, he would bear the weight of their collective and undivided curiosity.

At Saint Felicitas, he had not been concerned with what his classmates thought of him. Why should it be different now? He didn't know, but it was. He had left a place where he was comfortably established as someone smart and funny and nice, and while this had not been important to him up to now, he found himself wishing that his new classmates had some sense of it. But for them to discover these things about him would take more time than he would be spending here. He would settle for their indifference.

He was aware, however, that in a few short weeks, without the slightest clue as to how it had happened, he had made at least one enemy. The white haired girl who sat behind him, Iris Rauch, to whom he had never been anything but pleasant and courteous, tricked him into turning around and then, as she hissed, "Goody, Goody, Two Shoes," jabbed her fingers into both of his eyes, making them tear up and smart. He was dumbfounded and wanted to know why, but Iris had been so emphatic and looked at him with such contempt that turning around again, maybe ever, seemed a poor idea. It was a very odd and uncomfortable feeling to be despised by someone who didn't know you, and it caused him, for the first time in his life, to think that he might need friends. It was only fair, if he were to have enemies.

He'd never had friends, he realized, but he had not especially missed them. He had playmates – at least he had at the bungalow. When he wanted company, he went outside and there they were. They accepted him as he accepted them, but that didn't mean you were friends. Like them, he just came with the street. You didn't know who was going to be there when you wanted to play; you just went out and took what came. If the choices were really impossible, you went back inside and nothing was simpler then amusing yourself. The house was filled with entertainments, quite apart from the obvious ones: the radio, his parents' books and magazines, his realistic little rubber cars, scratch paper. There were always rooms to be re-explored, and the contents of his own head to be rummaged through. None of these required friends.

A friend must be someone you made appointments to see, someone who would seek you out and get excited about spending time just with you, someone you could be completely honest with, share secrets about yourself with, and most important of all, someone who would keep those secrets. This he had never had. Well, there was Eileen. She might be looking at the drawing of the Plymouth and missing him at this very moment. But he would never share a secret about himself with Eileen. It would be all over the neighborhood like wildfire. Not that Eileen was any worse than the other kids, but kids just didn't keep secrets, especially good ones, news that would stop people in their tracks, even those who would otherwise ignore you, to listen in surprise and ask you questions. That was hard to resist, and he himself was no better than anybody else about it. He truly believed, however, that if a friend specifically asked him to, he would take a secret to the grave.

Easy to say, of course, when there was no friend to put him to the test. Could he keep Vincent's secrets? He knew he could and wondered what they would be. Of all the available prospects, Vincent seemed the most likely candidate for friendship. For one thing,

Shorty had observed enough to be confident that if Vincent had a friend, it was not one of his classmates. No one sought Vincent out or dealt with him in any special or familiar way. Shorty was convinced, in fact, despite Vincent's seemingly hostile attitude toward him, that in a peculiar and needlessly roundabout way, he was actually being invited to enter a friendship.

Coming from someone else, the insults, the punches, and the threats would have annoyed or even frightened him, but coming from Vincent they only pleased and amused him. Vincent's grin would follow and completely ruin the most bloodthirsty threats. His slanty eyes were soft and kind and let you know that whatever nonsense he was talking, he didn't have a mean bone in his body. The more he thought about it, the more it looked like Vincent's whole goofy bag of tricks only meant that he wanted Shorty to be his friend and didn't know how to ask. Well who did? Shorty certainly didn't. You couldn't just go up to people and say, "Will you be my friend?" It would be too embarrassing and probably send them running – though it shouldn't. No, you had to find the right way, and whatever he thought of Vincent's method, it did look like a friendship was Shorty's to accept or reject. It would be so much easier just to get from one day to the next, right now, if he had a friend. There were things he couldn't do for himself in this new situation, things that – well, he could use some help. It was as simple as that.

But there were problems. Vincent's loopy enemy act would probably get on Shorty's nerves after a while. Could he get him to drop it and have fun with him that wasn't so phony? Could he train him to be the kind of friend he needed? Could Vincent learn to be honest with him and—this was crucial—keep his secrets? Even if he could, where would they meet? He didn't care if Vincent lived in a broken down shack and his parents were werewolves, but what would Vincent think of him if he saw the apartment? Well, he would work it out somehow. He would create a friend, a good one. Suddenly, the possibility that he could trust Vincent, that he could at last let someone know what he couldn't tell even his family, that the present and the future were scaring him to death, seemed real. The prospect overwhelmed him, and he wanted it right now. A little moan escaped him. He shot his fist to his mouth and tried to turn the sound into a cough. He was not going to cry on this streetcar while strangers looked at him.

He turned his face to the window. He couldn't see the street sign, but he knew by the large corner shoe store and the elaborate scrolls and ornaments on a yellow brick apartment that they had come as far as Colfax. He knew what was across the street and swung around to enjoy it. This would be another site for the Blue Leopard's invisible rambling: White Castle. It was just the right size, not like a real store, but a toy. Everything was black and white and chrome, no colors anywhere except for catsup and mustard bottles. A sizzling, fragrant griddle, three stools at a counter, and a line of hungry, waiting people pressed back against the window – that was all, but it was all you needed. There was never enough room at White Castle. You were jostled and squashed until you felt like you'd pop through the wall if one more person came in. It was perfect. The waiting was a game, and no one complained because at the end of it came your reward, little wafers of succulent meat with holes punched out, draped with bits of onion and a pickle, encased in a steaming, miniature, pillow soft bun.

He could not contemplate the pleasures of White Castles without being reminded of Uncle Victor, who loved them as much as he did. Sometimes on Sunday mornings at Grandma and Grandpa Sheffield's, Uncle Victor would pile into the back seat of the Studebaker with him as they drove to mass at St. Bride's. He would always have been out all night, and Shorty suspected that if anyone on this side of the family knew about consorting with stumblebums, it was Uncle Victor. On the way back, instead of politely accepting Grandma Sheffield's offer to join them for a really good breakfast of toast with homemade apple butter, bacon, eggs, and paunhaus, he would say he was too tired and insist that Grandpa drive to White Castle and wait while he ordered a whole bag of them. At times like this, Shorty felt he knew true hatred for his uncle. Not only were all of their breakfasts delayed, but he had to endure the White Castle wait and the torment of the aroma all the way home with no reward. If Uncle Victor had at least shown the decency of keeping the bag closed and minimizing the scent, it might have been bearable, but no, he would sit there right next to Shorty eating one after another, their empty white cardboard shells spilling onto his legs and the floor until the last one was gone, never offering him so much as a bite.

After this had happened a few times, he mentioned it to his mother. While he had witnessed her criticize many people in an outburst of anger, it was not something she did in her calmer moments. When she was herself, she would try to explain and excuse the failings of others. For Uncle Victor, she made an exception. "I'll tell you what, Shorty. Years from now, when they cart Uncle Victor off to the Home for the Cranky and Snide, as we know in time they must, we'll go visit him. We'll wait until dinner time, when they're bringing in his mush, and then we'll sit down beside his bed with the most enormous sack of White Castles he has ever seen. We'll say 'Oh, Uncle Victor, we'd love to offer you some, but they'd be so bad for you, and we'd never be able to forgive ourselves.' And then we'll eat them, every one, very slowly." Watching her smile when she was in that mood was like getting your back scratched.

There were only two more stops, or three, depending which way he wanted to walk the block to Manistee. He would get back to the Sheffield's maybe a minute faster if he got off at Marquette, but he was in no hurry, so he waited until he neared Burnham before he braced himself to jump down. The streetcar groaned and slowed to a stop for a few seconds of pure silence. He felt the uneven bricks of 79th Street beneath his feet. The trolley rumbled away, and he was quite alone.

※

The stores were closed, and there were only a few cars in sight. He walked quickly toward the corner, not in fear, but the faster to reach Manistee and its comfortable darkness. There, unnoticed, he could slow down, pretend anything that came to mind, and maybe sing a little to himself, very quietly. The last lights and noises he would encounter were at Hil-jo, a mysterious place where Swedish people ate. He went close to the window and jumped up to peer over the dark half curtain. Two men and a woman with her hat on were talking in a booth, but he could not make out what they were eating. His mother had offered to take him there sometime for something called smörgåsbord. They would be able to eat as much as they wanted of lots of unusual things like herring, meatballs in cream, and fruit soup. It didn't sound very tempting, but she was keen on it. He knew that even if he couldn't find anything he liked, he could fill up on those big wheels of thin, hard, dented bread with holes in the middle. He loved to slather them with butter and crunch on them whenever she had been to a Swedish delicatessen. The door was open as he turned the corner, and the woman's laugh floated out at him.

"You're wicked, Ray, just wicked. I should have listened to June."

He was past the doorway and the woman's voice trailed off, but he would store her words away to be examined later. This was his favorite collection, better than marbles or oddly shaped stones – the conversational fragments of passing strangers. He liked to puzzle out what had led up to them and what would happen next. Why would you sit calmly eating Swedish food with a wicked person you had already been warned about? He wouldn't write it down in his tablet and put quotation marks around it like he used to. Uncle Victor had taken care of that. No, he would remember it for a while and then it would fade, perhaps even before he could fasten a story around it. It was better when he could write them down, but one day when he was sitting in his grandfather's overstuffed chair with the tablet open in his lap, Uncle Victor had come in unexpectedly. Like lightning, Shorty snapped it shut then realized his mistake.

"What's that?"

"It's nothing"

"I'll bet."

He was beside himself. It was too late to be casual about it, as he should have. There was nothing wrong with what he was writing, but in Uncle Victor's hands it would become one more piece of evidence that Shorty was peculiar and there was too much of that piling up already.

"Victor, is that you? I'm having trouble with the mangle." For once, he was in luck, but he wouldn't have long. His uncle's eyes made it clear that he would be back fast and get the tablet away from him. He knew there was no safe place in the whole house to hide anything. It was strange; at the bungalow there were hundreds of good hiding places and he had never felt the need for one. Here at the Sheffields' he was a guest or something, but he abandoned all privacy whenever he came inside. Uncle Victor would be back any minute. How he wished there were a cranny big enough to swallow not just the tablet but himself as well. Working like a demon, he ripped each page into vertical strips so that no complete words could be read. Then he tore each strip into tiny pieces and distributed them among three different wastebaskets. Uncle Victor's return was greeted with a blank and innocent gaze. Shorty would miss the tablet, and was comforted only slightly by the thought of the prolonged and useless hunt for it that his uncle would stage for the next few days.

As far as privacy went, Shorty knew he had more of it outside in the dark than he was likely to find anywhere else these days. The thought slowed his pace even more, and he crossed the street unnecessarily. He was in no hurry to lose such a prize.

It was not cold, but cool enough that people who, a month ago, would have watched him from gliders, porch chairs, and even the steps, were now listening to the radio inside, instead of through raised windows. They had gone and left him alone with stiff crunchable leaves, bare trees and, through spikey branches, a fat moon.

He knew a lot of moon songs, but the best one was from *The Road to Morocco*. He watched the moon move from tree to tree as he sang.

"Moonlight becomes you. It goes with your hair."

He moved his voice to the back of his throat, lowered it as deep as he could, and tried to sound like Bing Crosby.

"You certainly know the right thing to wear."

The result was so goofy it made him giggle.

Bing Crosby was his father's favorite. He had heard him say it more than once, but he would have figured it out anyway. The night they had gone to see *Holiday Inn* at the Hamilton, it was snowing when they came out. The three of them were going on and on about how perfect it was that that should happen. Then his father, who was a terrific whistler, started doing the exact whistles that Bing Crosby had done in the middle of singing "White Christmas." Nobody wanted to get in the Buick. They just stood around smiling and getting snowed on like figures in a glass ball. His father kept whistling and doing Crosby things with his pipe, and people who had just seen the movie would pass them and look at his father and smile at them because they knew what he was doing and he was doing it so well. Shorty could have stayed in that moment forever. He knew he was happy while it was going on, but at the time he thought it was just something nice – well, *really* nice, that happened and then you went home and waited for the next nice thing. Looking back on it now, though, he could see it was the happiest they had ever been together and maybe ever would be. You never knew when you were going through the last nice thing with somebody. It was important to pay attention, so you didn't miss it.

 He paused at the corner of 80th. A lone car was approaching, and it might not see him. He could tell by the grille it was a Nash, but it was too dark to make out the color. The taillights glowed bluish red, grew smaller, and disappeared before he crossed the street. In less than a block, he would be at the door of 8039.

 The mellow light of shaded lamps made the living rooms he passed seem warm and inviting. It was easier to imagine good things happening in a house when you didn't know who lived there. One day, if he had a house and a family of his own, another boy could peer through the window and see – Shorty tried, but the picture never came. He could erect a Persian palace in his head with speed and ease, but this simple image was beyond his reach and could not be forced.

 He had come to the last of the anonymous houses. From here to the end of the block lived people he had met or at least been told about. A few of them were famous in the neighborhood. Mrs. Bednarski had been a tennis star in Poland before the war, and the three Thompson girls, who lived directly across from his grandparents, had been known to put on plaid costumes and do a Scottish dance with swords on very special occasions. It sounded exciting, but Shorty had yet to see it. Since he and Anthony arrived, there had been no very special occasions.

 Now he had reached what was, for anyone under fifteen, the focal point of the entire block, the large stone slab in front of Tibby's, a small grocery right in the middle of all the houses. He could step to the curb, make a long diagonal across the street, and be at the foot of the Sheffields' front steps. Instead, he climbed the three steps of the slab, moved quickly to its darkest corner, and sank back in the shadows. "What are you doing?" he thought. Hadn't he practically fled from his mother and the prospect of another night in the apartment? Hadn't he yearned to be somewhere else? Well, he was about to be somewhere else; people were waiting there for him - and yet... He would go in soon. Here, he could still think in a way that would not be possible once he entered the Sheffield living room. But he must not be seen. Sometimes he pictured his relatives tallying up all of his "strange points" and dropping them like jellybeans into a jar. This would be worth too many "strange points," about fifty, he guessed. When they reached the top of the jar, he supposed he would be carted off to Dunning or Kankakee or one of the other places for crazy people that his grandmother spoke about. He scrunched farther back into the doorway where he would not be easily observed from across the street.

He, himself, had spent considerable time observing this slab from the windows of the Sheffield sun parlor. With stone steps on three sides, it was less of a porch than a stage where, at least twice a day, the children of Manistee assembled to play, or in the case of the older children, to make plans to play somewhere else. That was the morning session. The late afternoon session was devoted to long discussions of how well or badly the playing had gone, and whose reputations had been polished or dented by the day's events. Old Tibby was long dead, and his daughter, Grace Davis, generally tolerated the swarm of kids unless they blocked the doorway, trapping a customer. Then, snatching a pencil from her upswept permanent wave, she would rap sharply on the window and threaten to banish everyone from the stoop forever. Forever never lasted too long at Tibby's though, and sometimes when there was no business she would chat with them through the screen door.

Shorty saw more point to getting acquainted with people here than at Our Lady of Peace., He would always be visiting his grandparents from time to time. The unpredictability of his visits might make him seem a novelty and work to his advantage. People would be more likely to play with him if they couldn't take his being there for granted. He would meander over casually, remaining on the edges of the group until he had satisfied himself that there were no snakes present. Nicky McCann liked to tease girls with snakes, and Shorty was not going to be taken unaware if he could help it. As far as he knew, no one had guessed his mortal terror of them, but it took much effort and acting on his part. If kids could not be trusted with your secrets, they could never, ever be trusted with your fears. Nicky's snakes were usually small, and Shorty found that, if he saw them first and from a distance, he could force himself to be calm. The acid test had come one day when Nicky showed up late and sat down beside him. Nicky sneezed, and while his head was still turned aside, the leather band around Nicky's neck rippled and flicked its tongue at Shorty. By the time Nicky turned to look at him, Shorty had managed to get his eyes back inside their sockets, but he knew that his future serenity depended on not moving an inch and masking his tremors with nonchalance. He needed to say something. What would Paul Henreid do? "Do they come in other colors?" he inquired pleasantly. It earned him an odd look from Nicky but nothing worse. He had not been found out.

While he didn't want it to involve reptiles, he knew that he deserved to be teased – not because of anything he was but because of something he had done during the war, something bad that shamed him whenever he thought of it. Two doors from the bungalow was a large apartment building that was home to most of the kids on the block. One of them, a blond girl, slightly older than Shorty, had a German sounding name, Gretchen Besser. This was anything but a social advantage in those days since Japs and Germans were the villains in many of their games. At first, nobody would choose to be a Jap or a German; it was an unspoken rule that the Americans had to win. After a while, however, some of the kids realized that even if you would lose in the end, as a Jap or German you got to think up whatever horrible tortures you wanted and use them on your captives before they were untied. In 1944, all the really good games required rope.

Shorty wondered what Gretchen thought of these games, from which she was often excluded. He wondered too, what she thought when she saw posters with drawings of fierce and sneaky Germans in uniforms with Swastikas. Such posters had been up in store windows for several years. You saw them everywhere. And what did Gretchen think on the nights when the block warden came to everyone's door with a flashlight to herd them all down to the basement of the building for an air raid drill? The posters were there too. While they practiced keeping quiet, did people look at Gretchen and her father and wonder if they were spies?

Gretchen was quiet and kept mostly to herself, which led the kids to call her stuck-up. One day, when they knew she was home, Barbara Baldwin suggested they all go into the gangway below Gretchen's apartment and serenade her. No one had a better game to offer, and the older kids were all for it. It was decided. To the tune of "Mary" they would all sing:

"Oh it was Gretchen, Gretchen; Gretchen is a stinky name."

The little army of patriots stood up to get their marching orders. Barbara saw Shorty still sitting on the curb.

"Aren't you coming?"

He was never sure when they meant to include him and when

they didn't, but evidently Barbara wanted as big a parade as possible. He got in line, and they moved out giggling until she shushed them.

"No noise until we're under her window."

So many of them crowded into the narrow gangway that kids pressed against him on all sides. For once he really felt a part of things. As they began to sing, their voices echoed off the walls so loudly that he wondered what the other neighbors thought. Slowly, a lace curtain was pushed aside.

"There she is!"

He hadn't expected Gretchen to look out at them.

"She's crying."

He stopped singing and hoped she hadn't noticed him. As the voices and laughter swelled up around him, he elbowed his way out and went home.

That night, he discussed what had happened with his father.

"Did you know, Shorty, that Ireland refuses to side with the Allies."

"No."

"German ships could stop at Irish ports and get fuel and supplies to fight us."

"Hmmm."

"And you're Irish."

"But I'm American."

"They could still make up songs about you."

"I know."

"But they don't. You're safe because so many other Irishmen live here."

"I already feel bad, Daddy. What should I do?"

"Do you think you should go over and apologize to Gretchen?"

"No. Oh, it's not just that I don't want to. I'm not sure she saw me, and if she didn't know I was there, wouldn't it make her feel worse?"

"Hard to tell." His father drew on his pipe. "So you think it's best to do nothing?"

"Tomorrow, I'll go over and ask her if she'd like to play."

As it turned out the next day, Gretchen had already given considerable thought to playing with him, but Shorty was not prepared for the game she had in mind. She invited him in. No one else was home, and her idea was that they pretend they were married and she wanted to make him happy. For a couple of minutes, everything was fine. He enjoyed pretending he was coming home from work and telling her about his day at the office. When she spelled out the particulars of how she was going to make him happy, however, he grew extremely uncomfortable and wanted to get away. He couldn't stay, but how could he go without making things even worse for her than they had been before he came? What a crummy spy he would make; he was never ready for the things life threw at him. If he could just sit down and write her a letter, he knew he'd be able to manage it so her feelings wouldn't be hurt. But here and now – "Your family has a lot of nice things, those figurines – we don't have anything like that at our house."

"Don't you want to play?"

"I've got a stomach ache. I've got to go home."

"But you just - -"

"I'll come back sometime, when I can. You look really nice in that dress."

He tugged his belt from her hand and took the stairs two at a time. Back at the bungalow, his father broke off from a snappy rendition of "Ain't Misbehavin'" and looked at him in surprise.

"That was fast. How did it go?"

"I'd rather not talk about it." Part of the reason he couldn't discuss it was the knowledge that Gretchen's game might actually be interesting played with someone else. He didn't know who, but it wasn't Gretchen. What a monster he was!

The monster began to feel the chill of the slab through his corduroys and took a last look at the moon and the spidery shadows it cast on the pale bricks of the apartment building. Contentment flooded over him. Why were people afraid of the dark? It was just one more thing he didn't understand about the way he was supposed to be. They had it backwards. It was in broad daylight that the truly scary things took place. That was when you were judged and challenged and meddled with and found wanting. At night, you were beyond the reach of all that. In the dark, everyone was equal; no one competed or criticized. Darkness was a luxurious blanket of freedom and privacy, under which you could stretch out and be whatever your mind contained. While it spread over you, it kept everything bad at bay.

But it was time to go in.

5. Mrs. Fix-it

The Sheffield house was one of the oldest on the block, put up before his father was born. His grandfather had built it himself and, perhaps for that reason, the entrance looked like no other on Manistee. Because the basement was mostly above ground, the front door waited for you at the top of a huge stairway, at a height where you would expect the second floor to begin. Instead of banisters and railings, the stairs were guarded on each side by three big squared off steps covered in dark slate siding. The effect was like a black armchair for a giant, and Shorty had heard his uncles say to each other, "I'll wait for you out on Pa's throne."

This mighty porch was a source of great pride to his grandfather, but opinions among the rest of the family were divided. His grandmother cautioned him to hold to the edges on slippery days.

"You'll slide right off in a stiff wind," she'd say, shaking her head. Shorty himself went back and forth about it. That the porch was odd and dangerous were certainly nice qualities, but its homemade look didn't seem very fashionable. What finally tipped the balance in its favor was that it made such an imposing background for group photographs. The dining room buffet held an album pasted full of scallop edged snapshots that he loved to examine. You could find everybody in the family stacked on the sides of the porch like merchandise in a doll store, growing older from page to page.

Through the glass side panels at the top of the stairs, he could see that they had left the hallway lit for him. It was always a pleasure to pass through this outer hall; in fact, Shorty felt that once you had done so, you had seen the best the house had to offer. It seemed to him an oddly glamorous part of an otherwise no-nonsense house, and he particularly liked to play there. Beige paint had been splopped on the walls in such a way that it was full of pointy little lumps, and the lantern in the center of the ceiling held an orange flame-shaped bulb that cast the most cheerfully peculiar shadows. Whoever was responsible deserved his thanks, but it didn't seem likely it was one of the Sheffields.

Past the hallway, Shorty was met with almost total darkness in a chamber no bigger than a phone booth. To the right was the door that led upstairs to Uncle Victor's flat. To the left was the door to the Sheffield living room and whatever welcome the lateness of the hour and his dawdling walk had earned him. He took a breath and turned the knob.

He entered to mixed reviews. "High time," said his grandfather through the *Tribune*, but his grandmother smiled and chirped, "There's my honey bunch of garlic now." One of her warmest expressions, it was unclouded by any hint of disapproval. It was also an invitation for him to hug her, which he declined. To make the invitation more pointed, she set aside her embroidery, a handkerchief clamped between two metal rings, the only obstacle in his path. Except, of course, himself. He did not feel huggy – but so what? It was obviously what she wanted. It would please her and what would it cost him? Yet at times like these it was as though someone else, someone quite unreasonable, moved into his body and refused to take commands. He compromised and moved close enough for her to put her arms around him. A thimble bit into his shoulder.

"Hello, Gramma. Hello, Grampa."

She released him but not before her disappointment bled through the embrace.

"Did you have a good time?" she asked.

"Yes, we went to the movies and –"

"What was the sermon about this morning?" His grandfather had no interest in the sermon. They both knew it. This was merely a way to check up on his mother. Had she gotten him to mass? Actually, she had – at least she had awakened him in time in case he chose to go. She also said he looked sleepy and that neither she nor God would think less of him if he wanted to skip it and stay on the couch a while. He hadn't slept well and it was tempting, but even in his groggy state, he wasn't prepared to risk a mortal sin on a holy day of obligation. So he had gone, but she had not.

"Well, I wouldn't exactly call it a sermon."

"What *would* you call it?"

The folded *Tribune* had been deposited in a sheet metal magazine rack his grandfather had made at the mill, and his attention was now on the jigsaw puzzle before him. Shorty perched on a hassock and peered up over the card table that pinned his grandfather to the armchair.

"Go get a chair from the dining room; all I can see is your head."

"Father Jordan told us that tomorrow they're gonna give us all a book of subscriptions to *The New World*."

"What's that?"

"It's a paper that tells you who's being good and bad all over the world. They let us look at a copy, and there were lots of articles about things that if you do them or read them or think about them, you'll go to hell."

"Doesn't that sound inviting, Mama? Shall we take a copy? Think you want to go to the hot place?"

"We've never been. It's up to you, Pa."

"How much is it?"

"It's two dollars for a year's subscription, but we have to sell a lot of them. We're supposed to knock on people's doors and get them to take it."

"We'll see about that. Your father's not paying tuition for you to be a salesman."

This was unexpected good news. "Believe me, Grampa, I'm not looking forward to it."

His grandfather paused with a piece in midair and looked at him directly.

"No, I didn't think you would be." He snapped the piece into place.

"But they're going to keep track of how many everybody sells, and we get points. And if you have enough points you get a day off of school and if you don't, you'll have to go to school and do the hard problems from the back of the sums book."

"We'll see about that, too. They told you all this at the children's mass?"

"Mm-hmm."

"Did they tell you where the money is going?"

"It's for the propagation of the faith."

"Do you understand that?"

"It's to save the lost souls in poor countries and stuff."

Shorty could scarcely believe how much pleasure this conversation was giving him. It was most unusual for the two of them to have something to talk about that they could agree on, which he was beginning to suspect they did. He didn't want it to stop.

"Can I see a copy of this remarkable paper, Edmond?"

"I didn't bring one with me." This had been deliberate. He had discovered a most unwelcome column of reviews and ratings of movies. Those that were condemned had mostly foreign sounding names and were unfamiliar to him, but the "Morally Objectionable in Part for All" section was filled with pictures he dearly hoped to see. Shorty looked down at the blur of autumn colors jumbled on the card table. If he could help his grandfather find pieces to fit in, it would extend the conversation, but the edges had been done, the pieces were small, and few of them looked like they had anything to do with the picture on the box.

"Is this a hard one, Grandpa?"

"I wouldn't call it easy . . . but I wouldn't call it hard."

"What was the hardest puzzle you ever saw?"

His grandfather sat back and leaned his head against the armchair.

"That would have been the great two-sided puzzle with scenes of the North Pole." They both looked off in the distance.

"But that would be…" It almost gave him a headache to imagine it. "Did you finish it?"

"My finest hour." With his father, he would have been bold enough to say, "There's no such puzzle!" But he and his grandfather were not that way with each other.

"Time for sleepy town, Edmond," said his grandmother.

He dragged the chair to the dining room table and turned back to the parlor. "Goodnight, Grampa."

"Goodnight, son."

"There's no such puzzle… is there?"

"My finest hour."

※

The swinging door to the kitchen was propped open against the stove with a wooden wedge. This was so they could hear Anthony if he needed something. They didn't seem to realize they could lock the doors, go halfway down the block, and still hear Anthony when he needed something, but they would learn. To his right, just past the raised door to the bathroom, was the pantry. The pantry window, its only source of light, was useless at this hour, but he knew where to lay hands on graham crackers and a large glass with colored rings.

He set them on the oilcloth and pulled open the door of the ice box, which, like the stove, had been named to assist the feeble minded: "Cold Spot" and "Hot Point." One April Fool's Day, the Blue Leopard would enter the Sears store and unobtrusively switch such names around. People could be so dull, though; they might not ever notice. He set a bottle of milk beside the glass and raised the lid of the graham cracker box. It was just such a box that his mother had turned into a service station the year that he wanted a two-decker tin one they couldn't afford. In minutes, using his fathers' straight razor, she had cut and propped open two garage doors in front and in back, two side doors, windows all around, a chimney, and best of all, three standing gas pumps, Then she lettered the front to say "SHORTY'S SUPER SERVICE." He played it to tatters, and not just to please her.

His eyes roamed about the kitchen, his grandmother's kingdom. No other room in the house pointed out so sharply the difference between the two places, the two women. His mother woke up each morning a guest in her own home. Not that she expected others to work and wait on her, not at all, but she drifted from room to room with an air of unplanned discovery and never went to bed—or left it—with a schedule in mind. When she planned at all, she often consulted him, or pretended to, which pleased him just as much. "What if we beat the rugs today?" or "Suppose we get out the pin racks and stretch the curtains?" He never said, "Suppose we don't." because the next day she was just as likely to say, "Suppose we check the far end of Avalon Park for gypsies." At the bungalow, his mother's kitchen was a sort of study where the tea-stained glasses waited their turn in the sink as you pushed aside the papers and pondered what was the very best thing to be doing that day. Now, of course, in the apartment the papers were piled higher, the kitchen was standing room only, and in the tiny dining room, he and the glasses had much longer waits before she was ready to face them and the very best thing to be doing.

In his grandmother's kitchen, you always knew for certain what was going to happen, and you knew in advance. There were specific days for everything: baking, ironing, and cleaning on an exhaustive scale that Shorty though would only be necessary if battalions of muddy soldiers and their horses were trooping through the house on a regular basis. You could, in fact, tell the day of the week by observing his grandmother in action. In vast array, her tools stood clean, in place, and at the ready. Many of these devices were unfamiliar, even mysterious to Shorty: the long handled coffee grinder with its upended glass jar of beans, machines that clamped onto the table like the meat grinder with removable disks in case you changed your mind about the evening's chewing, and there, in a corner he liked to stay clear of, the dangerous mangle which left his grandmother's pale skin like the lampshades, seldom free of burn marks.

With one exception, his grandmother's bustling world was best viewed from a distance. Twice a week, she baked. If Shorty was at the Sheffield's on a Tuesday or Friday, he would find himself drawn from his own activities out to the kitchen to observe her routine with quiet admiration. Wearing a net on her hair and an apron of her own making with zigzaggy borders, she quickly churned up a storm of flour that dusted not only the tub of dough but the two of them as well. In the beginning, it was hard for him to guess where to stand out of her way, and he was truly startled the first time he heard, "One side or a leg off!" He learned to station himself near the icebox from which she had already removed what she needed to let it warm. Occasionally, she would ask him to hand her something, but this was a solo performance to which they both knew he was a useless observer. His only important function, one that pleased him considerably, was to guard her wedding ring when she removed it to slip her fingers into the lard and grease the sides of the baking pans.

He liked to see her punch and shape the dough and to hear the muffled thudding sounds that rippled through it as she slapped and kneaded. Watching her hands disappear under thickening white gloves, he would squeeze her ring tightly in the clean shelter of his own left hand. Behind her back, when she bent to place the first set of pans in the oven, he would reach out and rest his right hand on the remaining dough. It seemed to breathe and press back with a thrilling, forbidden sensation. Was this what babies felt like before they were born?

What went into the oven was often of more interest to Shorty than what came out. The pies and cakes were quite satisfactory, but the bread was not soft to begin with and after two days, became stiff without ever getting hard and crunchy. Sandwiches made of it had absolutely no trading value in the basement lunchroom of Our Lady of Peace. Homemade and unique, like his grandfather's stairway, it was for Shorty a source of both admiration and regret.

The empty glass in his hand was thoroughly speckled with graham cracker bits. He stepped to the sink to rinse it. Clearly, he thought, though others provided the money, his grandmother was the most necessary and important person in this house. The firm, predictable regularity of all the things she did was like the beat of a great orchestra, bringing order and a propelling rhythm to everything and everyone under this roof. It was just as well that he didn't really live here, for Shorty knew he would never be able to keep time.

He stood the glass on its rim to drain, crossed through open French doors, and entered a narrow room lined with windows. Normally a sun porch, it was pressed into service as a makeshift bedroom for him and Anthony. The Sheffields had gone to some trouble for such a temporary arrangement, fitting the doors with metal curtain rods at the top and bottom. Maybe his grandmother just didn't want to have to look at the only messy room in her house. The brown wicker furniture was pushed to one side to make room for a bed and piled with little stacks of their clothes. He pulled the doors shut behind him and undressed.

Emptying his pockets, he found the ticket stubs his mother had hidden away for him. Turning them over, he penciled in the date and abbreviated the names of the movies. Scanning the room for a cabinet, a drawer, or even a shelf, there was nothing to be found. While at the moment this was a nuisance, Shorty was pleased to take it as a sign that he and Anthony were not putting down roots and would soon be leaving. Lifting the base of a small table lamp, he slid the ticket stubs beneath it for safekeeping.

His pajamas, smartly pinstriped, waited under the pillow. He had picked them out himself. The bed was full of Anthony, sprawled out unconscious in light brown flannel on which horses bucked and reared amid six guns and hats as big as the horses themselves. In his hand was a squat leather dog of red and white, which Shorty knew better than to try to remove, but lurking lumpily under the covers were the rest of an extensive menagerie Shorty would have to extract carefully before anything like sleep could take place here.

First there must be prayers. He knelt, crossed himself, and began the nightly blessing and accounting session that seemed to grow ever longer and more tiresome. But what was he to do? If he left out any unfortunate person he had seen during the day or neglected someone he didn't like, he would only have to climb back out of bed again later to address his guilt. It seemed to Shorty that the less fond he was of someone, the more likely they were to appear in his prayers. There must be some reasonable limit he could set to this praying. After all, if prayers were said with impatience and resentment, how could they possibly count? He would soon have to award himself some strange points if the list kept expanding. How nice it would be, just once, to pop into bed and get to sleep without including Uncle Victor and an apology for his feelings. At length, he crossed himself and began tossing animals onto the wicker settee. Shorty was not used to sleeping with someone else and the bed was not wide, but there could be room for them both if he could shift Anthony toward the window. Lifting him slowly, he managed it without waking him. Groping under the pillow, he found a black sock, draped it over his eyes, and settled back to plan what he would say to Vincent at recess. Tomorrow would be a really good day.

But then the phone rang.

"Saginaw 3251." His grandmother had taken it on the third ring. "Yes, Frances. I recognize you. What is it?"

He sat up. Why was his mother calling? If his grandmother didn't lower her voice or close the dining room door, he could hear without difficulty.

"No, he's not here."

"Yes, I realize that, but he's not—"

"Well, I'm not exactly certain, but I'll tell—"

"Frances, if he were here I would tell you."

His grandmother's voice hardened and raised a pitch.

"I don't do that, Frances. I've never done that, though I've had plenty of reason."

" – because I know it upsets him, and he's already—"

"I understand you're upset too. We're all upset."

"Well, this sort of call for one thing, and that awful commotion outside Tuesday night."

Shorty winced in recollection.

"I'm sure you don't, but there are better ways – yes… yes, all of us only want what's best for – Frances, you've got to calm down".

Gasoline on a fire. Shorty braced himself.

"THERE'S NO CALL FOR SUCH HURTFUL LANGUAGE!"

His grandfather called out from the living room, "Hang it up, Mama, or I will."

"I'm going to get off now, Frances; there's nothing more I can tell you… If he were here, he would certainly know that by now."

"Along with all of our neighbors. Hang it up, Mama."

"The boys are already asleep, Frances. I'm not going to do that."

His mother wanted to talk to him. He slid out of bed and moved the curtain just enough to see without being seen.

"You heard me. What is the point of getting him up now?"

Though the telephone desk had a chair, his grandmother never used it when his mother called. She was pacing back and forth now.

"Yes, I know YOU'RE his mother. Who else would have sent him back this late alone in the dark?"

"He's NOT coming to the phone! Shame on you, Frances. You're trying to turn the child into a little spy. That's why you didn't keep him tonight, isn't it? You're trying to convince him that we're all liars!"

"Well, after a day with you, that wouldn't surprise me at all… Frances, I won't listen to this. Goodnight" His grandmother replaced the receiver and stood in the doorway, shaking.

It was all his fault. None of this would be happening if he had stayed at the apartment as his mother had practically begged him to do. He had been so clever in getting away by himself, and then he had taken forever to come in, making it look even worse for her. He could have calmed her and kept her indoors. Why hadn't he done it? If the scratchy apartment couch were a bed of nails, he couldn't be more uncomfortable on it than he was now, watching the results of his selfish trickery.

The phone rang again.

"Leave it be, for God's sake."

It continued to ring.

"It could be someone else, Pa."

"And pigs might fly."

It rang again, and he saw his grandmother reach for it.

"Jesus, Mama! How many hot sticks will you pick up before—"

"Saginaw – 32… I'm not positive, Frances, and he didn't leave a number."

"DAMMIT, tell her where he is, and hang it up!"

So they *did* know where his father had gone. But why did it matter? Someone was paying him to fix their radio, or the Tops were playing a night game at Bessemer Park. Why should his mother not be told? It wasn't as though she could call those places.

"Oh, Frances, please don't say things like that! Have you gone crazy? Are you trying to drive us all crazy?"

"Enough of this!" his grandfather roared, and Shorty heard the card table slam into the floor lamp.

"You've spilled the puzzle, Pa. Stay there."

But he was beside her, tearing the phone from her hand. Shorty let go of the curtain as his grandfather's voice surged out of the kitchen and surrounded him.

"Lady!" It came out like the worst thing you could be called. "You've got one helluva nerve. Luisa's crying. Another good night's work and I hope you're proud of yourself, but you've got me to deal with now. You'll not disturb this house any further if I have to swear out a peace bond!"

What was a peace bond?

"Well, maybe you should do just that. But before you do, I'd check with Father Walsh. Edmond has been with him all evening, and this merry-go-round is about to stop."

Monsignor Walsh! What did he have to do with any of this? Shorty pushed aside the curtain again and stood riveted to the spot.

"I'm warning you, don't call back."

His grandfather made his way to the kitchen table, and his grandmother, already seated, pushed a cup of coffee within his reach. The three of them stared at the phone in silence. *Where was she calling from?* Shorty wondered. Part of him wished he were there with her now. Part of him felt immense relief that he was not.

It rang again.

His grandfather sprang up, lifted the receiver without speaking, and banged it back down on the hook. His grandmother quickly swept the shattered cup into the dustpan and wiped its spilled contents from the floor.

It rang again. His grandmother stepped into the bathroom and emerged carrying a pillow and two blankets from the linen closet. Had she decided to sleep upstairs? The phone continued to ring as she approached it and raised the receiver without putting it to her ear. Instead, she set it on the desk, and for a few seconds, though he could not make out the words, he could actually hear his mother's voice: high, fast, and urgent. Then, as he watched, it was smothered under the pillow and blankets. Her final frantic attempt to penetrate the Sheffield fortress had been defeated.

He turned away and climbed back into bed, but the Sheffields had settled in at the kitchen table and were no longer silent.

"It has to stop, Pa."

"It has stopped. After tonight, things will be different."

"They've got to be. I just can't take any more."

"And you won't. One way or another. I'll see them out on the street before I'll have you put through any more of this."

"Don't say that. You don't mean it."

"I do. How many families are you expected to raise?"

"They're Edmond's boys, Pa."

"And hers."

Was he a piece of furniture? Did they imagine anyone was still asleep in this house? Were they so distracted they didn't realize he was hearing every word of this?

"Sometimes—" His grandmother's voice faltered. "Sometimes, I think little Edmond hates us."

"He doesn't hate us. He's eight years old, and he doesn't know who he hates. Even if he thinks he does. In time he'll learn which side is up."

"It makes me sick to think about him coming home by himself tonight."

"Then don't think about it. Would you rather she brought him and we had a repeat performance of the other night?"

"I was embarrassed to show my face the next day."

"He's old enough to survive a streetcar ride by himself. He's old enough for a lot of things he doesn't do, like helping you around the house."

"It's still new to him, Pa. Heaven knows he can't be used to it, considering… When he doesn't offer, and just sits around reading, I don't force it. No, that's not what bothers me."

"What then?"

"Well, you see how he is. Such a cold and undemonstrative boy. It's not natural."

"He comes by it honestly. He's her son and glued to her hip half the time. He'd sneer at us through a monocle if he had one."

The sneering Shorty could forego, but the monocle struck him as an interesting idea.

"You've put your finger right on it, Pa. She has a constant, powerful influence on him, and it's not a good one. As long as there's nothing to balance that out, he's never going to be healthy or manly, or even normal. For his sake, it's got to change, and I see now what I have to do."

Where was this going?

"When he leaves for school in the morning, I'll go with him. I'd already been planning to write a note for him to take to the nuns explaining what we're up against with Frances, but it's much better to do it face to face, in his classroom."

Shorty went rigid and his nails dug into the sheet.

"I know I can get their cooperation, if I can just make them see how important it is to take a strong hand before that woman makes a total sissy out of him. Perhaps they could arrange a boxing match at recess."

"You're going to say all this with him right there?"

"No, you're right, that might embarrass him in front of his classmates. The classes have cloakrooms, though. If they have him wait there, I'll be able to speak more freely."

Shorty's mouth went dry, and he felt his temperature dropping. She would do it. There was no stopping her. She would pour out her version of his life for the entire class to laugh at, and Vincent would never be his friend. No one would. If only he had hugged her tonight, but no, the thought now of ever hugging this woman again made him shudder.

He felt a stirring at his side and looked at Anthony, who was staring at him, wide eyed.

"Go back to sleep." And he thought, "It's not your turn yet."

"You've a great heart, Mama, and broad shoulders. This is more than you need to do. Are you going to tell Ed when he gets in?"

"No, he has enough on his mind tonight, and God knows what hellish tricks she has left to play!"

"Stop it! Stop it!" Shorty thought, jamming his ears to his head. He didn't want to hear another word. He wanted to be away from this, out of here, right now and forever. He wanted to go home.

But where was that? Now, the enormous, deathlike thought he had succeeded in keeping at bay for more than two months rose like a black wave and smashed over him, leaving him pinned to the sheets and struggling for breath. He had no home.

This was no temporary situation. Nothing was going to be "sorted out." This was his life from now on. What was gone was gone. The piano, the prairie, everyone happy at the same time, these had been swept away in dark, icy, dangerous waters, and he would be swept away too if he tried to clutch at them. He had to draw back, get used to this "after" life, and cling fiercely to whatever remained. From now on, he would shuffle back and forth between places where he loved people, but there no longer was, nor would there ever be again, a place where he was free to be himself, to relax and simply let words come without thinking of what was best for people to hear. When he had had a home, it had warmed and sheltered and delighted and welcomed him unconditionally. No place would ever do these things again.

He felt as trapped and tormented in this bed as his mother had seemed in the phone booth. He would lose his mind if he kept thinking in this dark new way for even one more minute. He squeezed his eyes tightly shut and conjured the guardian image of the Blue Leopard in his lair. There was still a place, he realized, though he could only go there now and then, that could do for him the things he had thought lost forever. He had been there tonight, and for several hours it had held him safe inside.

CHAPTER 3

THE BLUE LEOPARD AND THE CAVES OF SAPPHIRE

Baziffe, Arabia: November 1945

1. Desperate Night

In the cloudless kingdom of Baziffe, high in the hills of sunny Arabia, there dwelt a happy family of three foreigners. Now the natives of Baziffe seldom opened their hearts to outsiders for they were as suspicious as they were mysterious, but in the last three years, most of them had been won over by the wisdom, generosity, and personal charm of the strangers.

The Nugent family had come to Baziffe from America. They had traveled in constant danger because of the world war raging all around them. The father, Strapley, had been appointed ambassador to Baziffe by Franklin D. Roosevelt and given a perilous secret mission that was vital to the war effort. If this mission were discovered, it would mean instant ruin for all and disaster for the allied campaign. F.D.R. knew there was only one man in his tiny circle of trusted advisors who was both wise enough to succeed at this delicate task and brave enough to try.

Strapley Nugent accepted the risk without a moment's hesitation as a personal favor to the leader he so admired. The President was not at all surprised by Strapley's instinctive show of courage, but he was very much surprised that the Ambassador insisted on taking along his lovely wife, Magenta, and his small but clever son, Manning. F.D.R. could only conclude that Strapley loved them both so dearly he could not bear to part from either of them for a moment. Whatever fearful events awaited them, clearly the Ambassador felt the family must stay together at all costs. Sadly, the President did not live to see the brilliant success of the mission. It had taken several years to complete, and each member of the Nugent family had made essential contributions. At great personal risk, Strapley had braved the dark lairs of the fierce warring

Baziffi chieftains and persuaded them all to sit down together. A series of feasts was held, not at the American Embassy, but at the modest bungalow where the Nugent family made their home in this beautiful but perilous land. By welcoming the chiefs into his own home, Strapley convinced their proud, angry warlords that he trusted them to behave themselves and get along with each other. Once inside the house, they were calmed and soothed by the beautiful and exquisitely gowned Magenta, who had quickly learned to cook goat cakes in lemon sauce and deer pie with lattice crust, the favorite dishes of Baziffe. She also introduced them to unfamiliar American treats, such as lamb chops and mashed potatoes, which the chiefs gobbled up eagerly. During some especially difficult negotiations, on the advice of her son, Magenta had arranged, at considerable expense, for a supply of White Castle hamburgers to be flown to Baziffe. They arrived just in time to turn the tide at a critical moment.

Sometimes, the chiefs brought their wives to these feasts, but little Manning was the only child permitted to attend. This was partly because his silly jokes could break the tension and keep everyone entertained. It was also because he possessed a skill the children of Baziffe had yet to learn — he knew when to shut up.

The combined efforts of the Nugent family had restored peace and happiness to the troubled land of Baziffe. Their work done, it was time for the Nugents to return to America, a change that was much on the mind of eight-year-old Manning. He had spent a happy youth in Baziffe and was not eager to leave Arabia. He little knew that his wish to stay was about to be granted in a most disastrous and terrifying way.

Shorty felt a jab and sat up. Anthony had rolled over in his sleep and planted his knee in his brother's side. Shorty pushed him away and felt around for his black sock, which now protruded out from under Anthony like a snub tail. Retrieving it, Shorty lay back and draped it over his eyes. "Disastrous," he thought, "and terrifying."

While his parents made ready for the departure, Manning had been sent to spend a final afternoon at the hidden hilltop oasis of Vivator, his tutor and his family's closest friend among the Baziffes. While the wise and talented Vivator plucked melodies of eerie loveliness from the strings of his saroon, a harp-like instrument encrusted with jewels, Manning splashed about naked in the secret pool with his faithful pet, the mighty elephant, Taponto.

The thoughtless day had hurried by, and now it was time for Manning to dry off and begin his farewells. As was his custom, the sun would be his towel. He patted one of the kindly elephant's huge front legs and called, "Up, Ponto!" Taponto lowered his trunk, wrapped it around the child, carefully lifted him high in the air, and set him gently on the back of his massive head. This was Manning's favorite perch to survey the countryside. Wearing only a turban of cobalt blue, he lay on his stomach and cast his gaze down to the house in the valley below, where his mother was packing up their belongings. Her task would not be easy. In addition to everything they had brought from America, there were now the many unique and delightful gifts from the chieftains and their wives. His favorite was an ivory model of the royal palace with all its domes and towers complete with miniature soldiers and prominent members of the court. Manning shifted as Taponto sneezed, and he noticed smoke rising from the chimney of the bungalow. He knew what that meant. His father was burning secret papers in the fireplace.

Taponto's large right ear scraped ever so lightly over the boy's bare back, and Manning sighed with pleasure. "I'm going to miss all this,

Vivator." His voice echoed across the petal-strewn pool. "Are you going to miss me?"

"Not one bit," said his tutor. "Silly, chattering boys are easily replaced."

"Oh, I think you'll miss me very much, and even if you don't, I know Taponto will."

"Spank him, Taponto," Vivator called out. "He contradicts his elders."

"Ow!" said Manning as the elephant's ear flicked the boy's behind. "Well, I guess I won't miss that. Stop it, Taponto. Your master is a cruel old man who tortures innocent children."

Vivator smiled, and the little silver bells that hung from Taponto's blanket tinkled as if even the elephant shared their joke. The stately tutor put aside his sparkling saroon and crossed the courtyard to stand beside the enormous animal and its tiny rider. Gazing down into the valley, Vivator spoke quietly. "When your family departs, it will be a great loss to me and to all right-thinking people in Baziffe."

"But the wrong-thinking people will be happy?"

Though the boy joked, Vivator answered him most seriously. "They are few in number but dangerous. Yes, my brother and his followers will be happy to see the last of you." He referred to his evil brother, Vindictor, who was as different as it was possible to be from his brother in everything but appearance. Both men were tall and handsome, but even when Vindictor smiled, his sneaky eyes flashed with cruelty. He was the only chief who had opposed Strapley Nugent's peace proposal to the bitter end. When the agreement was finally signed and celebrated, Manning had watched with a shudder of fear as the ceremonial quill pen was passed to Vindictor. Instead of signing, the resentful chieftain rose to his full height, broke the pen in two, and threw the pieces at the startled boy's father. Fixing the family with a freezing stare, he cursed the day they had arrived and vowed to destroy them and the horrid treaty, just as they, he thundered, had worked to destroy his country. A lot of what he said was in Baziffian, and some of it was obviously so horrible that the other chiefs gasped, and the interpreter looked too ashamed to translate it all. Then, Vindictor stormed out and disappeared into the mountains with his ferocious band of henchmen.

His brother's outburst had deeply embarrassed Vivator at the time, and now, Manning was afraid his remark about the "wrong-thinking people" was an unkind reminder. The boy rolled over and sat up. "I'm sure everything will turn out for the best, Vivator. I'm going to tell everybody about you and your amazing country as soon as we get home."

Vivator smiled, but his wise eyes remained sad and serious. "It is time to dress," he said as he handed up a small pair of cool, cobalt blue satin pants that were perfect for fiery hot days in Arabia. As Manning pulled them on, he heard his friend say, "I do not like the look of that." The boy turned his head back toward the valley, expecting to see a rare storm cloud. Instead, he saw a thin line of men on camels, threading their way down from the hills. The only destination in sight for many miles was the Nugents' isolated bungalow. With a start, he recognized the colors of the men's costumes, purple and yellow, like a swarm of angry bees. It was Vindictor and his band.

"What are they up to, Vivator?" Manning asked anxiously.

"It may be nothing, my friend, but it would be wise to alert your parents." With the speed and grace of a much younger man, Vivator mounted the elephant in a flash. Manning gasped with pleasure and surprise as strong, brown arms reached around him to gather the reins, and a deep, stirring voice rang out, "Hai, Taponto!" Down they sped into the valley, to the little bungalow and its unsuspecting occupants.

The secret byways and shortcuts of these hills were well known to Vivator, and he steered Taponto swiftly through them, gaining precious minutes on Vindictor's menacing caravan. Manning's heart pounded against his ribs as the plucky trio of rescuers reached the rear of the bungalow still unseen. They had beaten the advancing troops but not by much. Vivator leaped down and dashed into the house. The Nugents would not be taken by surprise, but there was little time for explanation.

Manning scrambled through the door, yelling, "Mama! Daddy! They're after us. We've got to run!" The startled couple looked at Vivator with bewilderment and alarm. His manner was calm but serious, in contrast to the boy's wild state. "Vindictor's troops come this way," he explained. "It may not be as bad as the boy tells you, but it is certain they mean you no good. Taponto can carry you all to safety. Flee, I urge you, while there is still time to avoid these uninvited visitors." Manning gazed up at his tutor in admiration. He envied Vivator's magical gift of making dangers shrink by describing them in cool and quiet words. It was a skill the boy longed to master.

Strapley Nugent frowned as he spoke. "We thank you for the warning, my friend, but an ambassador of The United States of America does not flee." He gestured toward the fireplace and the files nearby. "I would be a sorry specimen indeed, if I let these fall into the wrong hands."

"You have never given me cause to doubt your bravery, sir," said Vivator, "and I do not mean to question it now, but time is short, and if Madame Nugent wishes –"

Before he could say more, Vivator was interrupted by Magenta Nugent, who proved that her courage was a match for her husband's. "I will not desert the ambassador, but if you would be so kind as to entertain my son until things are quieter …"

Manning was pleased to see his mother shared Vivator's gift, but he wanted to shout at her, "Run, run! These are horrible people. Don't be crazy." But his parents' brave example kept him from showing himself to be the only coward in the family, and he said nothing.

Vivator nodded, "It shall be as you wish. I pray your husband's skilled tongue can calm these troubled waters. The boy shall be well and safely entertained. You have my solemn pledge on that, but only if we leave at once."

Manning was embraced tightly but silently by each parent then whisked out the back door. As he clambered aboard Taponto, he heard his father call out, "Don't worry, son. I'm good at this. That's why I'm called a diplomat." Manning knew that if anyone could talk reason to Vindictor and his wild crew, it was his father, but the boy's heart was in his mouth as Vivator cried, "Hai, Taponto!" and they thundered away through the bushes.

They had not gone far before Vivator halted their tusked chariot, jumped to the ground, and raced to the edge of the dense thicket that hid their whereabouts.

"Can you see them?" called Manning.

"Hush! Do not get down," answered his tutor. "Yes, they have reached the house and are surrounding it. My accursed brother dismounts and goes into the house. He takes four others with him."

Manning was almost hysterical. "Let me see! Let me see!" Without turning around, Vivator thrust his palm toward the boy, forbidding him to move.

"I must be your eyes for the moment, little cat." The wise Baziffian had tried to teach the child patience and used this nickname to remind him of his shortcomings. "You will know all, I promise, but to see all is sometimes a danger to little cats."

Manning squeezed his eyes tightly shut, trying not even to think about what Vivator was afraid the boy might see. He rubbed the back of Taponto's head and wondered if his beloved giant could feel the friendly pats through his great, thick hide. The little bells shook softly. Perhaps he could.

Vivator continued to stare into the distance with his back to the boy, who could make out nothing beyond it. "What's happening now?"

"They are all still inside, but I have counted the camels, and two came unridden. This means they have come to take your parents away with them, but it also means they will not harm them here."

Manning knew that Vivator was trying to tell him all he could without scaring him too much, but the word "here" only opened up frightening new possibilities. "Where will Vindictor take them?"

"As yet, I cannot tell, but the working of my brother's mind will soon reveal itself. If he emerges from the house alone, then your father's skills have calmed his wrath. It will be safe for us to return at once. If your parents accompany him, then by the direction in which they strike out, I will learn not only their destination but the degree of my brother's anger."

A hundred questions jumped about in Manning's head. He wanted to ask them all at once, but Vivator continued to speak without turning around. "The best thing for your parents would be that the camels head further down into the valley. That would mean he is taking them into town, to raise a public rumpus and denounce the agreement before a crowd. It will be loud and unpleasant, but it will fail. Your father and his ideas are too popular with our people. In the end, no harm will come to your parents, and Vindictor will have to let them go. The other chiefs will see to that.

"But he might take them somewhere else?" Manning longed to see the expression on his tutor's face, but Vivator continued to peer into the distance.

"Yes. Two possibilities remain. If the camels climb to the top of the rise where we first saw them and turn left, your parents will be taken to Vindictor's secret camp, where he will attempt to frighten your father with no one there to see. The other chiefs would not permit this, but my brother has used stealth to keep the site of his camp unknown to them."

"And rescuing my parents will be hopeless," Manning wailed.

"Oh no, my friend, do not despair. I have seen the camp and could lead the others there quickly."

The boy sighed with relief but realized how completely his family now depended on the wisdom and daring of one man to save them. "You said there was a third way they might go?"

"Yes." Vivator stood motionless at his vigil, his eyes still fixed on the entrance to the house. "If the camels climb the rise and turn to the right, then I am afraid their unfortunate destination is the dark caves of the followers of the ancient religion, wherein lies the sacrificial temple of the goddess, Connipsha."

"Sacri—?"

"Hush, child. They come out now."

Manning quietly nudged Taponto forward and stood on top of the great beast's head. Rising on tiptoe and struggling to keep his balance, he could peer above the bushes and just make out the scene below. His parents sat on camels, their hands tied behind them, helplessly awaiting the evil whims of Vindictor. His father faced straight ahead, but his mother turned in every direction. She was looking for him! He wanted to wave and let her know he was all right and looking out for her, but he dared not risk being spotted by one of Vindictor's men. He also wasn't sure he could manage a wave without falling from Taponto's head. He lowered his heels to steady himself but bobbed back up when he heard Vivator say, "He gives the signal to move out. It is safe to come forward and watch." Vivator turned and saw the boy already just behind him, in spying position. He frowned but said only, "My reckless cat."

The pair watched in silence as the camels tramped through the yard and reached the road beyond the house. Vindictor halted and turned his head toward the thicket. His piercing eyes seemed to be looking directly at them. Manning gasped, but Vivator reached up, gently touched the boy's dangling leg, and said, "The sun sinks low to befriend us, little cat. It blinds Vindictor, and we cannot be seen."

Manning breathed out with relief, for his trust in Vivator's word was boundless.

They watched Vindictor raise his hand and gesture to the troops behind him. The camels started up the hill, away from town. It seemed an eternity before the last of the caravan climbed all the way to the top of the rise. There, after a moment's conversation, Vindictor led the group out of sight. They had turned to the right.

"Oh no!" cried Manning.

Taponto squatted down to let Vivator mount him more easily. As they rode off, the boy found himself encircled by his tutor's arms, but he would not be comforted. "We're going the wrong way!" he exclaimed. "And there's not a moment to lose!"

Vivator sighed and pressed his fingers to the child's temples, massaging them in little circles. "Yesterday," he said softly, "I could have made you slumber through this night of dangers, but now, my brother teaches you what evil man may do. That knowledge makes a wild thing of you and robs me of my powers. You must surrender to my judgment and trust that I can help."

The boy's head slumped back against his friend's chest. "I surrender, Vivator, but help us, please."

"Then take what comfort you can from my experience with the followers of Connipsha. Their beliefs are strange and sometimes savage, but their traditions are strong and followed to the letter. Nothing that is to happen will take place before midnight. I have more than enough time to drop you off safely at my encampment."

"I don't need to be safe there," Manning bristled, "and I don't want to be. I'm safe with you." His eyes grew large as he stared up at his companion and continued to plead, "Make Taponto turn around. Don't lose another second."

Vivator smiled at him sadly. "What a brief surrender that was, little cat, and how little you trust me."

"I'm sorry, Vivator. It's so hard – but, I do. I really mean it this time." The boy went limp. "But won't you at least tell me your plan?"

Vivator nudged Taponto, who increased his speed. "The wisest plan, I believe, is to sneak into the temple with a few of my best men. A larger force could attract attention and serve no purpose. A silent rescue is needed tonight, not a battle, which would only increase the danger for your parents."

Manning nodded and said, "Then you had to go back to your camp anyway."

"Yes, even if you were not with me, so let that ease your mind."

"It does," said the boy. As they rose higher into the hills, the Baziffian sky blazed out with stripes of intense colors Manning had never seen in an American sunset. Each of his Arabian days had departed with loud splashes of orange, purple, and scarlet, as though his adopted country wanted to send him to bed with a head full of jolly, spectacular sights. But tonight, the bright picture spread across the sky not in celebration but in warning. Manning shuddered as he beheld it, for this day's sun was leaving behind only eerie suggestions of fire and blood.

Now the hill path grew steeper, but even in the fading light Taponto climbed sure-footedly.

"Manning," Vivator said quietly, "when we reach the oasis, I must arrange things quickly. There will be little time to talk. It would be well to ask me now whatever you would know."

The boy hardly knew where to begin, but after a moment, he spoke up. "Why does Vindictor hate us so? My father was never unkind to him."

"Your father is a foreigner. Vindictor is steeped in the ancient ways of those who raised us." As they climbed ever higher and shadows swallowed the desert below them, Vivator began to unfold a tale that was strange indeed to the ears of the American boy. It told of twin brothers, left as children to perish in the wilds when their father was *set upon and slain by bandits. Though terrified, the boys stood guard over the body of their fallen father, shouting and waving their arms to drive away the circling vultures. When darkness fell, the twins were paralyzed by fear at the growls and screeches they heard on every side. Menacing shapes moved out of the shadows and crept closer. Shaking, the boys clutched at each other in silent panic, as moonlight betrayed the slow but steady advance of many glistening eyes. Suddenly, their father's body shot upward. They shrieked as rough hands fell upon them and dragged them off into the darkness.*

Manning listened with wide, staring eyes while Vivator described the Conniptions, a secret cult of masked cave dwellers who nearly frightened the twins to death in the very act of rescuing them. "They meant us well, that wild tribe. They took us in and raised us as their own. There was much kindness in that strange lot, but oh, I can tell you, Manning, they took some getting used to."

The tribe, Vivator explained, was named after Connipsha, their goddess of death. Their health, their safety, the very food they ate, all these, the cave dwellers believed, came directly from the dreaded and all powerful Connipsha. She favored them above all people on earth and had been generous because, like her, they were unexpected, mysterious, sudden to appear, and at home in the dark, secret places of the night.

For her delight, they masked their faces, painted their bodies, and danced themselves into fits of frenzy. To honor her they hollowed out the largest of their caves to create an enormous temple, whose walls were decorated with smiling images of Connipsha watching fierce scenes of destruction that rose almost higher than the eye could see. The floor of this temple covered a vast area, and in its exact center lay a huge, ragged, circular hole, gaping like a ravenous mouth, from which smoke and fumes arose. If you peered carefully over the rim of the hole, you could make out, at a depth of a mile or more below, a seething mass of molten scarlet. It was here, when the flames surged upward with overpowering waves of heat and smoke, that the cave dwellers believed Connipsha demanded payment for her favors.

"P-payment?" Manning stared up intently at Vivator.

"I see you understand me, little cat. Yes, her payment was death, in the form of human sacrifices, to be thrown over the edge into the pit. The first example Vindictor and I were to witness was the body of our father, that very night."

"But he was already dead," Manning observed.

"This we knew, but they did not. Our actions in protecting his body had convinced them otherwise. They threw into the fiery pit what they believed to be the body of a severely weakened, but still living man. This offering was greeted with a great hiss and crackle of sparks. They were impressed. Connipsha had been satisfied."

"That's horrible," cried Manning. "You said they were good people, but they're bloodthirsty."

In the dim light the boy could just make out a smile on his tutor's lips. "Only children are naturally bloodthirsty, Manning. I think you will find that most people are good enough unless they are swept away by some false idea. If the Conniptions were truly bloodthirsty, Vindictor and I would have followed our father into the pit."

"Hmmmm," said Manning. Then he fell silent, and Vivator continued his story. He spoke of how the two young brothers had been cared for and educated by the Conniptions. At first, the frightened twins were distrustful of their fearsome rescuers and became even closer and more dependent on each other than ever. But soon, they realized that the weird tribe was actually trying to teach them how to survive in a rugged and dangerous land. The boys learned how to find food and water where none seemed to exist and what could be eaten without making them sick. They learned to move about with stealth and to hunt without being seen by man or beast.

Manning interrupted. "But didn't you WANT someone to see you *and take you back to your real home?"*

"We wanted it badly," said Vivator, "but the bandits who killed our father had pretended to be friendly, only to get close enough to rob us. After that, we feared all strangers, no matter how innocent they appeared from a distance. We dared not take the risk, and of course the Conniptions, for their own purposes, encouraged us to be fearful."

The boy looked satisfied. He nodded, and the story continued. The twins gradually began to relax and feel safe among the Conniptions. Musicians in the tribe taught them to play and dance. Artists shared their skills at painting and showed them which desert plants could be used to make brilliant colors and dyes. Slowly they came to understand the Conniption language, and as they did, they realized it was not merely kindness that protected them and kept them alive. It was the very fact of their twin-ness.

On that first terrifying night, when little Vivator and Vindictor were dragged before the entire assembled tribe, the savage crowd grew excited as the boys were pushed into the torchlight and presented to them. Many jumped up to point at the children, clap their hands in glee, and shout, "Zar Zar!" At the time, the frightened boys assumed that 'zar zar' meant something like 'yum yum,' and they would soon be roasted and eaten. Later, they learned it meant "twins." Among the Conniptions, twins were such a rarity that they were thought to bring a powerful blessing to the tribe, so long as both of the pair remained in good health. Again and again, in their first year with the cave dwellers, somebody would take them aside and warn them never to push or strike each other, even in play. So important was their wellbeing to the tribe, that no one must harm them, not even each other.

Up to that point, Vivator had thought of Vindictor as an extension of himself, but curiously, it was just as they realized their power as twins that the boys began to grow apart and act as individuals. Vivator had laughed when he saw how foolish their fears had been. He remembered smiling and saying, "What silly babies we were." But Vindictor had frowned and remarked thoughtfully, "And when they made us afraid, it gave them power over us."

The power of the Conniptions to strike terror in the hearts of others was the very first of many things the brothers would disagree about. To Vivator, it was a cruel and unworthy side of their protectors. It showed them at their worst and made him embarrassed and ashamed for them. To Vindictor, it was the most interesting part of life with the Conniptions, and he studied it endlessly. There were plenty of opportunities for the boys to observe it in action. Since their arrival, the two little Zar Zar had witnessed every single capture and sacrifice that took place. Vivator, who was horrified, protested and tried to refuse attending the grisly ceremonies, but the presence of both twins was expected and commanded.

Grim as they were, the sacrifices were not random. The Conniptions believed them necessary to change the seasons. The tribe ranged no farther than needed to seek out their victims, and if a member of the tribe grew very sick with some condition the medicine woman was unable to cure, then that person became a willing sacrifice for the good of the tribe. But if no such volunteer were available when a season neared its end, then some unfortunate traveler, straying too near the caves, would find himself the unwilling object of Connipsha's lethal desire.

At such times it became clear the powers of the Conniptions were not limited to paralyzing their victims with fear. They also possessed an extraordinary power to cause transformation, though this could only be accomplished at the rim of the temple pit, when the flames blazed their brightest. To make an offering more acceptable to Connipsha, or sometimes just to entertain the crowd and make the ceremony of death even more thrilling, the high priest would fix the victim with a penetrating stare and weave a spell with rhythmic gestures and incantations. The helpless shape that dangled over the flaming pit would change into something completely different, stirring the crowd to wild applause and moans of appreciation. The startled boys had seen elderly cripples turn into antelopes before their eyes. Unlucky travelers became cows and zebras, who bellowed and thrashed about for a few seconds of confusion, then plummeted to a fiery doom.

It struck Vivator that it was never the fierce creatures that put in these sudden, amazing appearances, but even so, he chose to remain as far away from the spectacle as he could get. Vindictor, on the other hand, was fascinated by the transformations and crept closer and closer. He would imitate the movements of the high priest, and after several of these magical ceremonies had taken place, Vivator watched with disgust as his brother silently mouthed the incantations of the executioner. Vindictor was determined to master this power, and by the end of their second year with the Conniptions, Vivator was shaken to discover just how well his brother had succeeded.

The ghastly extent of his brother's achievement became clear one night as Vivator sat at the opposite side of the pit from Vindictor, who seemed to be smiling and waiving at him. Happy that his brother appeared, once again, to be showing the warm, open friendliness they used to share, Vivator raised his arm to wave back but found it moving in a peculiar, jerky manner. He felt stinging sensations in his head, accompanied by little popping and cracking noises. Then, for the first and only time, he saw his brother pulled up, slapped, and shaken by a Conniption. The stinging stopped, and Vivator found that he could move his arm quite normally again. Several elders immediately removed him to a solitary cave and kept there until they had taught him not only the secrets of transformation but the defenses against it.

Manning gasped, "Your own brother! And he was trying to change you into a... a—"

"A monkey, I believe. Vindictor had always fancied one as a pet."

Manning shuddered. He knew that they would soon reach the secret oasis, and there was still much he longed to know. "Did you ever use the power?"

"Only once," said Vivator, "and in a small way that attracted no attention."

"Who did you use it on?" Manning asked eagerly. "What did you turn them into?"

"It was a very minor business. You would not find it so interesting as all that."

"Oh, but I would!" Manning wriggled and squirmed so excitedly he almost fell out of Taponto's saddle.

"Very well, little cat. Once, when I wandered off by myself, I got lost. Trying to find my way back to the caves, I stumbled upon something that I knew would be unwise to share with my brother. Yet, concealing it would be difficult. He had an insatiable curiosity and had grown suspicious of me. To keep him from discovering what I had found, I used the power to blur the tiniest corner of his brain. By reversing the image of what I saw that day, and projecting it forcibly into his mind, I have forever blocked it from his vision. He would stand before its entrance as a blind man, and pass it by."

"I know," the boy exclaimed. "It's your oasis."

"Ah, no," said Vivator. "It served my purposes to let him spy that out long ago, though he supposes I am unaware of his watchfulness."

Manning was always impressed by deviousness, and this example only increased his admiration for his tutor. "Then—" but the question halted in his throat. "Then, I guess it will always be your secret place."

Vivator beamed. "I am proud of you. It was not the little cat who spoke just then, but the man you will become. Yes, of this other place, I have spoken to no one. One day, perhaps, but as yet, there is no need."

As they rode on, the man he would become deserted Manning, and the boy he was began to tremble and cry. Vivator pulled him close.

"What is it?" he whispered, though he knew full well.

"My parents," Manning sobbed, "My parents are still in the clutches of Vindictor and the Conniptions."

"Only for the moment," said Vivator. They had reached the oasis.

Putting a golden horn to his lips as they entered the camp, Vivator sounded a brief but stirring call, and they were surrounded at once by attendants. Manning was handed down to a grinning soldier whose right cheek bore a crescent scar. As Vivator snapped out a series of commands in Baziffian, the boy was led off through the swarm of warriors pressing about them.

A tempting meal was soon spread out before the child, but he neglected it to peer from the entrance of the tent where had been taken. He hoped to speak to Vivator before the rescue party rode off to the caves. Manning stood still, clutching the tent flap, but his eyes darted everywhere. He needed to search for his tutor, but the crowd had kept him from seeing which way the man had gone. The noise and activity swirling outside the tent confused and saddened Manning. No one looked his way, and he could make no sense of the excited conversations around him.

He realized with shame that after three years among Baziffians who spoke his language well, he could say little more in theirs than "Pleased to meet you," "Thank you," and the names of maybe a dozen objects. How often could you work "Hai, Taponto" into a sparkling conversation? He had been spoiled and lazy; he saw that now. He had always been a foreigner in Baziffe, but until this moment, he had never felt like one and it frightened him. He had to find Vivator, but he dared not move from the spot. The tent was where Vivator would expect him to be, and Manning had such a terrible sense of direction that, if he wandered off to look, he might never find his way back. His feet began to tap faster and faster. A voice came out of the darkness beside him.

"You act like you need to go to the bathroom."

The startled boy turned to see a figure all in black whose face was smeared with mud. Manning sucked in his breath. Had one of Vindictor's men snuck into camp to kidnap him?

The strange figure spoke again. "Did you think I intended to sneak into the temple wearing my golden robe, Little Cat?"

"It's you, Vivator! Thank heavens! Take me with you, please."

"I must leave in a moment. I came only to say goodbye and to ask you to pray for our success." Vivator turned to leave.

The boy clutched at his sleeve. "You know I will, but can't I do anything but pray? Isn't there something real?"

"Prayer is real, except from a mouth that lies." His tutor replied sternly, but his ghostly disguise could not mask the kindliness in his eyes as he looked at the boy. "But yes," he continued, "there is something I had forgotten, something important, and you can do it. Go to Taponto. He waits beside the largest of the tents. Remove the little bells he wears. We must give my brother no warning."

"I'll do it right now!"

"Then you must return to this tent and try very hard to sleep. If all goes as I intend, your parents will awaken you."

The boy hugged his tutor tightly and ran off to find Taponto. The height of the main tent made it possible for even Manning to find it without difficulty. When he reached the elephant, he saw that Taponto had already been strapped with equipment for the rescue mission. After a few friendly pats of greeting, the boy worked quickly to remove the skirt of bells, threading it through the many straps of the supply pouch.

"You've got to be very quiet tonight," he said, "and very swift, Taponto. How I wish I could go with you!"

The last of the bells slipped free of their bindings and dropped to the ground at Manning's feet. He bent to pick them up, and as his eyes came level with the great beast's belly, they widened, and his mouth fell open. The pouch underneath Taponto's stomach was empty!

"Maybe I CAN go with you, Taponto," Manning whispered, "If I'm smart enough and fast enough." He snatched up the bells and darted toward the big tent to deposit them. Over his shoulder, he called out, "and really, really practical." He was back in an instant, spreading his hands to measure the pouch. "I'll fit, but…" He tapped his foot and chewed on his lower lip. "How can I fasten it once I'm in it?" Vivator and his men would appear any minute, and then it would be too late. He would just have to hope for inspiration. Voices could be heard approaching as the boy undid the buckle at the top of the pouch. There was not a moment to lose. He was probably going to be caught, punished, and kept in camp, but he had to try it. Swinging himself up by the straps that held the pouch in place, he slid through the opening and reached down with his left hand to grab a long, dangling piece of leather.

"Don't give me away, Taponto," he whispered as his right hand poked from the opening and fumbled about for the buckle. His fingers hit metal, but it fell away. He tried again, and yearned to be Plastic Man, elongating strategically for even a few seconds. He felt metal again and this time managed to close his fingers around it, but now the voices had reached the elephant's side, and one of them was unmistakably Vivator's.

"Manoot. Darjeekta zimman manoot."

Had they seen him? Were these words about him? The voice continued, joined by mutters of agreement. What in the world was 'manoot?' but no hands seized his to pull him from hiding. He held the buckle and strap tightly against the pouch so nothing could move or dangle. He was still unseen. He dared not stir, but if the clasp was not secured before they moved out, he could be jostled from the pouch and trampled as they picked up speed. He had to become whatever it was that could move without seeming to. He pretended his hands were two clouds creeping towards each other across the sky, silent and unnoticed.

The Baziffian conversation continued, urgent but indecipherable. After what seemed an eternity to Manning, the strap entered the buckle and was secured. The two little cloud hands stole back to their secret lair undetected. "Hai, Taponto!" rang out through the night air, and the mighty elephant lurched forward.

"I've done it," thought Manning. And then he thought, "But what have I done? What if we go through water and I drown? What if they order Taponto to sit? Will he remember I'm here, or will I be crushed to death? I only wanted to be Plastic Man for a few seconds, not forever!" As the back of his head bounced roughly against the elephant's belly, the reckless cat began to fear that he had squandered all of his lives on a foolish gesture.

Manning's face slid back and forth against the bottom of the pouch with every step Taponto took. Long before the elephant slowed to a creep, (Manning estimated about half an hour) the boy had wedged his hands under his nose for fear it would be rubbed raw. By the change of pace, he guessed they were proceeding with caution because they were nearing the temple site. Manning knew that he would have to be crafty, and he knew that craftiness did not come naturally to someone as pampered and privileged as he had been up to now. He tried to think of what the wise Vivator would do in his place. If he jumped out of the pouch when they stopped, there was no guarantee they would let him go with them into the temple. It was much more likely that Vivator would make one of the men stay behind to keep Manning from following, and he would have taken this wild, bruising ride for nothing. If he waited too long though, they could get so far ahead of him that he would lose his way. That, unfortunately, was something that did come naturally to him. Suddenly, Taponto halted. The riders were dismounting in silence. They were there!

If a brilliant plan was going to leap into Manning's mind, it had better do so right now. There was not a sound to be heard. The men must be communicating by hand signals. It was so quiet that they might already have struck out for the temple. It would soon be too late to follow. Yet, something told him to wait, though he could not have said what it was. Something had not happened, something that needed to. The pouches! He would have felt them being opened and heard the weapons being removed. If the men had gone, they were scouting the situation and would be back. They would not enter the temple without the weapons. He had been right to wait.

In a few moments, just as he thought, he felt Taponto shifting, and he heard the jostle of metal blades and barrels as the supply packs were lowered to the ground. When silence returned, his hands were not clouds but meteors as they undid the buckle. Quickly, he squirmed out of the pouch and jumped down into the weird tangle of woods that surrounded the caves. Inside the pouch, there had been total darkness. Now there was moonlight to see by, but it did little to help him make sense of what he beheld. Strange trees, twisted and gnarly, looked almost like unhappy people ready to grab him. Heavy vines wound from tree to tree like chains. It was as though he had been dropped into the middle of a prison revolt, with angry convicts struggling on all sides of him to break free.

He clutched at Taponto, took a deep breath, and told himself these were only trees. "I can't see any real people, Ponto. I don't know which way to go." He felt his friend's rough trunk at his neck, pushing his head to the right. Squinting into the distance, he spied the glint of moonlight on a curved sword, and the movement of several dark figures. Barely pausing to thank Taponto, he sped after them, zigzagging to hide behind thick trees and peeking out to make sure he had not been spotted. It was a game his father had taught him to play, and he loved it, but now it was in earnest and he dared not stumble or snap a twig.

Manning gained on the shadowy figures but kept behind them the distance of about ten car lengths. To his relief, none of the men looked back in his direction. They advanced without hesitation. He could not see who led them, but he knew it must be Vivator. Manning took their speed as reassuring proof of just how well his tutor knew this eerie and forbidding landscape.

Now, he could see the entrance to a cave just ahead, but the men passed it by. For the next several minutes, he watched in puzzlement as the ghostly soldiers ignored a series of openings into the grim wall of rock, some large enough to ride a horse through, others barely visible until you were right upon them.

Behind him, the high shriek of a bird caught Manning by surprise and made him stumble. The woods had been so silent up to now that he had forgotten that the watchful animals of the night, whose home the rescue party had disturbed, were all around him. When he got to his feet, he gasped to see that what he dreaded had come to pass. Vivator's men had vanished. His little body flooded with fear. He wasn't even sure he could find his way back to Taponto. Maybe if he called out to his friend, - but no, that could give the mission away. It was better to be hopelessly lost, lost forever, than to risk being responsible for the death of his parents.

He pressed close to the rock and spread out his arms to feel for openings. Wherever the men had gone in, it couldn't be much further than the distance he had trailed behind them. He inched along as fast as he could, hugging the rock. It occurred to him that the Conniptions would make it harder for an intruder to find the entrance to their temple than any other part of their village because of the secret nature of the dreadful doings that went on there. But he would find it if it took him all night.

It didn't. He soon came to a large rock that seemed at first to be part of the wall but stood slightly out from it. He slipped behind the rock and said, "That's odd." A ray of moonlight had managed to pierce the high rock and was glowing dimly on the wall in front of him. But how could it be? He put his hand out, but it was not the wall that met it; it was empty space, and somewhere deep within was a light. He had found the entrance.

⚜

The beginning of the cave was as dark and grim as the outside wall and would not have encouraged an ordinary traveler to enter, but Manning was drawn on by the pale light. After groping his way straight ahead about thirty yards, he was stopped by what seemed to be the back wall of the cave. Refusing to give up without finding the source of the light, he edged along the wall to his right. After a few feet it gave way, and he fell into a corridor with so many openings it reminded him of the stadium where his father had taken him to see the circus. Torches hung from the walls, which were decorated with brightly colored symbols he could not understand. They did not flow, like Arabian writing, and they were more like pictures than words. In some of them he thought he could make out eyes and teeth, but they didn't look like people, or even any animals he had ever seen. Hmmm, he thought. Welcome to the land of the Conniptions.

Manning couldn't hope to guess which opening the rescue posse had gone through. He would just have to pick one after another. If this place were really laid out like the circus, he would be in luck, and all the entrances would lead to the same big space in the center. He chose the nearest opening and found at once that the circus had not come to Conniptiontown.

The room he entered was lit by two torches that cast a creepy greenish glow on the walls. Between the torches the giant painting of a woman's face stared down at him from the back wall. She was certainly beautiful and she was smiling, but there was an excitement in her eyes that didn't seem quite nice and made him uncomfortable.

The only other thing in the room was a kind of table below the face. It was an altar, he decided, and the face must be Connipsha. People must put things on the altar as offerings to thank her or to ask her for favors, sort of like in church. She didn't look mean, exactly, though she looked like her voice would be really, really loud. She just seemed happy in a sort of crazy way.

He could see now that something had been placed on the altar, and his curiosity was getting the best of him. Was it flowers? Or fruit? Or maybe cookies? He moved closer and squinted as the green light flickered on the mysterious gift. He reached the altar, looked closely, and stifled a scream of horror. The altar was smeared with fresh blood, and the offering was a human head with a crescent scar on its right cheek. This very head had grinned at him not two hours ago in Vivator's camp!

Manning fell to his knees, scrambled under the altar as far back as he could, and thrust his arms up in front of his face. They were doomed! If the enemy was this cruel, this smart, and this fast, the rescue could never succeed. He would probably never leave this room alive. He glued his eyes to the floor, unwilling to raise them and meet the gaze of whoever else might be present and ready to add his head to Connipsha's collection. No one in the world was better at waiting than Manning, but after several minutes without the slightest breath of sound or rustle of movement, he lifted his head, peered out from beneath the altar, and determined that he was quite alone. He would live to get at least as far as the door. In his frenzy to escape he skidded in something below the altar and fell to the floor. His hand felt wet, and he shuddered. It was the soldier's blood.

Manning took a deep breath and thought, "All right, good. He's warning me from his grave to slow down and be careful." Silently and deliberately, he edged out of the room into the corridor. The hallway was dim, but there was nothing to get behind or crawl under. Once spotted, he would be seized. He knew he should run like mad, get free of the cave, and try to find Taponto. Instead, he dropped to a crouch, scurried from shadow to shadow like a bug, and entered each of the next several rooms after pausing to listen at the doors. He had to know what had happened, not only to his parents, but to Vivator and whatever remained of his brave men. If all were really lost, perhaps he could still save himself, but did he even want to? He would think about that later.

The rooms turned out to be storage spaces. He found stacks of torches, rows of horrid masks, chests of strange but beautiful costumes, and finally, some clay pots of paint. An idea came to him, not a brilliant one, but useful. He took one of the pot lids, wrapped it in several layers of costume to muffle the sound, and threw it as hard as he could against the rough, hard wall. Quickly, he tore open his makeshift package, examined the broken pieces of clay, and smiled. One of them was jagged and sharp. He had a weapon.

As Manning crept along the corridor, he heard excited voices coming from an unseen source a long distance away. After passing many doors, he went back to the one where the sound seemed to be the strongest. Slowly, he inched the door open. The room was dark and empty, but just below the ceiling was a grating through which the voices and a pale light floated. The walls were rough and bumpy. Some of the bumps were just large enough that he might be able to use them to pull himself up to the grate which was set back in the wall on a sill. Climbing was a slippery job on the damp rock, and several times he fell back to the floor, skinning his bare legs, but at last he hoisted himself up to the sill where he perched and peered down.

Far below him, Manning saw a vast circular space. Crowds of Conniptions milled about the edges of the circle. Red smoke floated up from a crater in the center of the floor. He thought he must be looking at the sacrificial temple where his parents would be taken if the mission failed. He pressed his face against the bars of the grate and squinted intently, not wanting to miss a single detail. The light from the pit and from the torches on the wall was flickering and eerie, but bright enough to give him a clear view. The scene was calm at the moment, like a party, early on, before you knew if it was going to be any good or not. A tall old man in a black robe and headscarf seemed to be in charge. People kept going up to him, and it looked like he was answering their questions or telling them what to do. Some of the people wore masks, some were dressed in animal skins and heads, and some of them had nothing on at all. If Vivator hadn't told him his dreadful story, Manning might have thought he was watching a really good Halloween party.

Suddenly, there was a commotion and shouting. Part of the crowd surged toward one of the entrances but then pulled back. A fight was going on between Conniption guards and Vivator's men. Curved swords flashed and scraped each other and people scrambled to get out of the way. The rescue party was brave and quick, leaping and jumping to stay out of the grasp of all the arms that snatched at them. One of Vivator's men plucked a torch from the wall and swung the flame back and forth to keep the crowd at bay, but more Conniptions poured in from behind. The rescuers were surrounded. "Nooo," sighed Manning. He could bear to watch no more and turned away.

While he had watched the sorry spectacle in the arena, someone had crept silently into the room and stood below the sill with upstretched arms that couldn't quite reach him. The boy trembled as he looked down into the gloom and tried to make out the upturned face. It smiled at him. Could it really be --?

"It's you! You got away!" He pushed himself from the ledge, fell happily into the waiting arms, and pressed himself close to the shadowy figure whose arms closed around him. "I'm so glad you found me," the child whispered.

"Not half so glad as I am." But the voice was not quite right, and the face pressed to his was clean, not smeared with camouflage. Now he could make out a disturbing red moustache. The luckless boy had leaped into the embrace of his mortal enemy! It was Vindictor who held him.

Manning's hand slipped inside his blue satin pants and felt for the sharp shard of clay. Once he had grasped it firmly, he whipped the jagged blade up into the air and thrust it down into the arm of his captor. A cry of pain rang out, and he was free. He dashed to the door, but Vindictor moved like lightning to block his path.

"The cat has claws and spirit, for a fancy pants." Vindictor's voice was low and quiet. "It becomes you. But not the claws."

A strong hand seized Manning's arm and bent it back until he was forced to release the shard and heard it clatter to the floor and break.

"He calls you his little cat, doesn't he?" the sinister voice continued, with a laugh of contempt that Manning thought was meant more for Vivator than himself. It sounded dirty, and it disturbed the boy that Vindictor should know, or guess, such a private part of his relationship with his teacher. It disturbed him even more when Vindictor dipped his finger into the blood on his arm and smeared a design on the boy's bare chest, saying, "Then cat it shall be."

Manning's only satisfaction was that whatever terrible things were about to happen to him, at least he had drawn Vindictor's blood, and not even Vindictor could change that. It still ran down his arm. Manning shrank back as Vindictor took hold of the boy's trousers and tore a thin strip from the bottom of one leg. Tying it tightly about his arm above the wound, he said, "Don't worry child. If I meant to hurt you, these caves would now be ringing with your howls. Pull." The silent boy obediently helped tighten the knot on the cobalt tourniquet. "Come, cat," said Vindictor, dragging Manning from the room.

The boy struggled to stay upright as Vindictor hustled him along the hall, and he had no sense of what was in front of them. Suddenly, Vindictor stopped short and held Manning behind him. "It seems we are to have a family reunion," he muttered. Manning danced frantically from side to side, trying to peer around his captor, but Vindictor's steely grip kept him hidden from whoever stood before them. "Brother," Vindictor called out, "you embarrass me. You would remove my guests too soon from my hospitality. My entertainments have only begun."

His parents were here in the hall, still safe! If only he could see them. Now Vindictor raised his voice. "Wait! Are you certain they wish to leave?" He pushed Manning out in front of him. His parents could not contain their shock and dismay. Vivator, however, seemed unsurprised. His eyes widened only when he saw the bloody symbol on the boy's chest. He shot an angry look at Vindictor, who only shrugged his shoulders in reply. They exchanged a few words in Conniption, but no one moved. Neither brother would concede the upper hand and quit the field without what the other held.

Vivator held a hasty conference with Manning's father, which Manning could not hear but thought he understood. The two men had to rush Vindictor before he could summon his thugs. Vindictor seemed to understand it too, encircling the boy with one arm and patting his dagger with the other. The two groups moved slowly, trading walls, but keeping the same distance. They were moving the way Manning imagined a matador and a bull might do, never taking their eyes from each other. Down the corridor, behind his father, Manning saw a Conniption come out of a doorway, look in their direction, and run off. He needed to shout to his father, "Do it now! Someone has seen us," but he got no further than "Daddy!" when Vindictor's hand clapped his mouth shut. Now they had only to stand as they were, and Vindictor would win. Any moment, and they would be taken as Vivator's rescue party had been.

Manning kicked at Vindictor, bit down on his fingers, and broke free. "Run, Daddy, they're coming! They've seen us," he cried as he darted across the hall. His father grabbed his hand, but then there was a moment of indecision. If they ran directly toward the entrance of the cave, Vindictor stood, or rather crouched, blocking their path with drawn dagger. One of them could easily be wounded, or worse. If they turned and ran in the opposite direction, whoever had seen them could soon be back with reinforcements and capture them before they found another way out.

On a silent signal, Vivator and Strapley Nugent rushed Vindictor. Manning's mother held him close and patted his head as they stared, open-mouthed, at the life and death struggle raging just a few yards in front of them. The three men were now a thrashing pile of arms and legs, rolling about on the floor of the cave like angry boys or snapping dogs. Manning's mother wrapped her arms around him while he shook with tears at the sight. She had the good sense not to say, "Don't be frightened," which of course he was, but that was not why he cried. Somehow, the undignified spectacle of the three smartest men he knew (though he hated to admit that Vindictor was one of them) coming to violent blows was just too sad to bear. He knew he was no better. A moment ago, he too had been a wild animal, kicking and biting. It had been necessary and he would do it again, but he was a kid. These were adults, wise men and diplomats, and it was upsetting to watch them lose control, even when it could save their lives. He had learned the rules. He followed and respected them, but he needed them to apply to every situation in life, and it was discouraging to witness such clear proof that they didn't.

A gong rang out behind them. Manning and his mother turned to see the old man in black with his arms upraised, leading a host of Conniptions toward them. The fight stopped at once. The three men straightened up and backed away from each other. The old leader sadly shook his head and questioned the two brothers. There were many questions, but mostly, the old man listened. Finally, he clapped his hands. The brothers stayed at his side, while Manning and his family were nudged into the procession at spear point and led off to the *sacrificial temple.*

As they entered the room he had seen through the grate, Manning's heart beat wildly. The space seemed ten times larger and more terrifying than it had from the safety of his perch. Vivator was too far away to speak to them, but he tried to comfort them with gestures, pushing his hands downward, as if to say, "Be patient. Don't panic. I'll handle this." But if ever there was a room to panic in, Manning thought, this was it. Nothing good could happen here, with enormous Connipshas staring crazily down at you from all sides. Below her, thousands of painted people met their deaths, no two of them in the same way. He wondered if future Conniptions would frolic beneath a likeness of him meeting some unspeakable doom. Actually, they could just paint him looking at these walls and having a heart attack.

The old man mounted the steps in front of a big raised chair and sat down. His hands were on the armrests, which ended in -- no, they couldn't be! Manning squinted to make sure, and yes, they were indeed human skulls. He hoped his parents, who had been moved away from him, didn't notice.

Below the old man, the twin brothers stood, taking turns talking to him, frequently pointing to Manning's parents. The old man nodded and listened with as much respect to one as to the other, so Manning couldn't figure out if things were going their way or not. It occurred to him that what was going on was a sort of legal case, in a particularly spooky courtroom. Vivator was their lawyer, and the old man was the judge. It comforted him a little to think that even the Conniptions had to follow rules and couldn't just chop people's heads off whenever they felt like it.

They were lucky, Manning thought, to have such a good lawyer. It was starting to look like Vivator was persuading the old man to let them go. Vindictor looked boiling mad and shouted something. The old man nodded and spoke to the guards who surrounded his parents and brought them to the steps. They were going to testify. Manning wished that the old man understood English. His father would have persuaded him in no time.

His parents were strapped into chairs, and Vivator asked his father if he had come to the temple to spy on the Conniptions and harm them. His father replied that he had been kidnapped by Vindictor and brought to the cave by force. Vivator translated for the judge, who turned to see what Vindictor had to say to this, but he had disappeared.

Everyone looked around for him, and then one of the Conniptions pointed to a large wheel in a dark corner of the arena. Vindictor was turning the wheel as fast as he could. Manning gasped in horror as he saw that a stone bar attached to the chairs that held his parents was swinging them out over the fiery pit. Vivator streaked to the wheel and tore Vindictor away, but the fiend pulled a club from under his robe and struck Vivator on the head, knocking him to the ground, unconscious. A loud "Oooohh" went through the crowd, and many shouted, "No connip zar!"

Vindictor stood over his fallen brother and tried to calm the crowd. "No connip," he said again and again, lifting Vivator up so the crowd could hear him moan and see him move a little. Then Vindictor raised his voice and spoke really fast in Conniption. Manning could imagine the rubbish he was telling the crowd about his father to save his own evil neck. Without Vivator to speak the truth, this backward mob might believe him. Even the judge might be convinced.

His parents still dangled over the pit, but all eyes and ears were on Vindictor. Manning slipped unnoticed through the crowd and made his way to the large wheel. He tugged at it, but it was heavy and hard to move. Crawling up onto the spokes, he used all his weight to tug them down to the left. It worked. The wheel began to move. The witness chairs slowly edged their precious contents toward the safety of the rim. Vindictor's deep voice continued to ring out, whipping the crowd to a frenzy. No one watched the chairs. Just a few more inches and his parents would be able to unstrap themselves and step down to solid ground. Then came silence.

Manning knew what must have happened, but he continued to tug at the wheel until he was torn from it and held high in the air by two muscular arms, one of them encircled by a cobalt blue tourniquet. Vindictor strode to the edge of the pit and lowered the boy's body until their faces met. He regarded Manning with deadly calm as he spoke. "You sought my attention, boy, and now you have it." He flipped the child face downward, and dangled him over the flames, saying ominously, "It is time."

Manning felt a scream welling up. He stared as if from a mountaintop into the hellish, dizzying abyss below. Was Vindictor about to drop him? Were these his last seconds of life? Vindictor's hands released him and the scream broke from the boy's throat, but he slipped only an inch or two before the fiendish hands gripped him once more. Before his death, he was to be played with and tortured. He trembled as Vindictor chanted in Conniption and turned him upward to stare into eyes that now blazed with an irresistible force. His trembling turned into cramps in his arms and legs. The child's muscles tightened and twitched while Vindictor's eyes bore into him. Manning could feel himself changing, but into what? He desperately sought a look at himself, but Vindictor's eyes held his like a vise. The sound of the flames roared in his ears. From a distance he heard a cry that he knew was his mother's, but then he was pulled back from the pit and thrown to the ground. He landed unhurt on what should have been his hands and feet, but now were paws of cobalt blue, ending in razor sharp claws.

"What's happened to me?" he cried out, but he heard only a deep rumbling purr, which frightened the wits out of him. He was not a boy now, but some kind of freak blue cat. He sprang to his mother's chair, and she shrank back from him. He started to cry. Then he felt her hand on his back, petting him timidly. Whatever he looked like, his mother still recognized him as her son.

Vindictor stood above him, saying strange things that confused him and made him miserable. "Take what comfort you can for now, little blue one. You are hers no longer. Now you are mine, and must do my bidding. As you grow, you will prove useful to me. Crawl away. Go where you wish. Grow comfortable within your new cat self. But never think you can hide from me. Your color sets you apart from all other leopards. Even they, your new brothers, will find you strange."

"It isn't true!" thought Manning. "This is insane. I am a boy. I can't live my life as a leopard – a blue one!" This transformation must be an illusion, a trick of Vindictor's, like Mandrake's hypnotic gestures. It couldn't last, this cobalt blue fever. Out of Vindictor's presence, the spell would be broken. He must get away at once, but how, when his legs looked and felt like paws? He took a deep breath, sprang forward, and was amazed at how fast he covered the distance across the room to a darkened cluster of rocks. Vindictor could not see him now, no one could. But still the spell held fast.

He thought it best to hide in the darkness for a while. He could not bear to be seen in his present condition. At least he was out of Vindictor's reach and could not be forced to do his bidding. From such a distance, however, he could be of little use to his parents. They were too far away for him to even see them clearly – but no, the power of his vision had improved as much as his speed! He could make out the expressions on their faces as they dangled once more, far out over the edge of the sulfurous pit. He even felt their fear in a new way. He could smell it.

Vindictor denounced them furiously, working up the crowd; then, he seized a lever on the wall. If only Vivator would regain consciousness, but that was not to be. Manning saw his father grip his mother's hand, and then, in the most awful instant of his life, his claws dug into the rocks as he watched Vindictor pull the lever down, capsizing the chairs and pitching his parents headlong into the pit. If they screamed as they plunged toward the flames, the sound was mercifully drowned out by the savage roar of the bloodthirsty crowd. Now they whirled and danced dangerously near the edge of the pit, chanting over and over again, "Co-nip-sha! Co-nip-sha!" From the darkened rocks, only the widening eyes of the leopard child could be seen, glinting in the torchlight. They stared in sickened disbelief. His parents were no more. The last few minutes of this hideous evening had rendered him an orphan—and a beast.

He lowered his head, closed his eyes, and drew his paws over his ears. The sounds of this noisy celebration of death would drive him mad. There was nothing more to be seen, nothing he would ever want to see again, least of all the Conniptions. He already hated the sight of them, and now, with their demented party echoing all around him, he came to hate the sound of them. In leopard form, he even hated something the boy had missed: the smell of them. They were a smelly people and a stupid one. Trapped in hiding, he wondered, was it better to face a stupid enemy, or was it even more dangerous if your foes lacked good sense?

It was almost an hour before the murderous lunatics grew weary, and their voices trailed off. His nose told him that he was now alone with his misery in this great chamber of horrors. His eyes opened, and he hoped against hope that his old form had returned, but no, this spell was strong. He was still a leopard. He moaned in despair, but the sound that came out was a deep, rumbling growl. It startled him, but it thrilled him too. Some of his fear was leaving him to make room for a burning rage at the unholy tribe that had robbed him of all that he cared about. But maybe Vindictor wasn't as smart as he thought he was. He should have dropped Manning into the pit when he had the chance, or changed him into a bunny or a kangaroo. Instead, his fancy spell had set loose an angry blue leopard, seething with hatred for his creator. No mere boy could escape this cave, but a fierce, fleet leopard? Who could hold him back? He hoped some of them would try.

Leaping from the rocks, he prowled the floor boldly. Halfway across, he came upon a fallen human form. If it still held life, his revenge would now begin. The body was sprawled out face down. The leopard cub nudged it onto its back so his first victim could better appreciate the terror about to strike. Straddling his wounded foe, he prepared to try out the fearsome effect of his excellent new growl, but when he saw the face, he merely purred.

Vivator stirred and opened his eyes. "What has happened, my boy?" For once, Manning was relieved not to be called his little cat. Vivator strained to sit up and turned toward the pit. The two empty chairs still hung upside down. Slowly, he turned back to the leopard cub and said, "I have failed you miserably. It would be better if you had never known me." He lowered his head. "I cannot face you. Your family honored me with great trust, and now I am shamed."

The blue cat nuzzled the man's face, licking it gently. "You can forgive me then, boy? You have a great heart. It will serve you better than I have." The leopard pressed foreheads with the man until he looked up and met the cat's now friendly gaze. Vivator petted the animal for a moment then forced himself painfully up to a standing position. He turned and looked carefully in all directions before he spoke again. "What is done cannot be undone, Manning, and much is lost but perhaps not all. I can still be of use to you. I do not use these Conniption spells, but I know them as well as my brother does. They cannot be broken –" The little leopard whined, but Vivator put up his hand to silence him. "Do not despair. I have not finished. Though these spells cannot be broken, they can, for a short time after they are cast, be greatly modified, but only in the presence of the rising flames. Do you understand me, Manning? Do you see what we must do? There is little time left. I ask you to be brave and trust me one last time." He held out his hands. The cub looked fearfully at the pit, then leapt into Vivator's arms.

They approached the edge. "You tremble," said Vivator, "but this must be done now or not at all. The flames will flare up only a few more times tonight, and it is only in the height of their surge that a spell can be cast, or, as I shall do it, recast. You will still be the leopard, but only at times. If I do my work well, you, not Vindictor, shall choose those times."

The leopard cub arched its back with excitement at these words. Vivator stroked the cat's head and spoke close to its ear. "See how the red grows brighter, Manning? Do not fear it; we will harness its fury. When I saw the bloody symbol on your chest, I knew the exact spell Vindictor planned to cast. Though I cannot undo it, when the flames are at their highest, I can seize control for our purposes, not his." Vivator's face, lit from below with scarlet, looked unearthly. "Trust me now," he whispered, moving the cub out to arms length, and lowering him into the pit. "I will not drop you." For the second time this night, Manning stared into the blazing abyss and shook with fear.

Vivator spoke louder now. "The flames will blaze up twice. The first time will give us control, but the second time is just as important. Vindictor has chosen a powerful spell, but the strongest spells offer the strongest gifts to those who control them. At the very height of the second blaze, you may choose a special power man does not possess. Choose wisely, child. It is almost time."

Manning's claws dug into his tutor's robe and his mind raced. He had always dreamed of such powers and pretended, in his games, to possess them. But there were two that he longed for. Which should he choose? Which? His blue fur bristled as he watched the flames surge up at him from far below. The heat was searing, and he was almost engulfed by the fire. Mixed in with the roar of the blaze were the strange Conniption words chanted by Vivator. The flames fell away, and Vivator's fingers felt differently on his fur. It was not fur, but skin! "We have gained control of the spell!" cried Vivator in a triumphant voice. When the flames surge again, you shall snatch a reward for the indignity Vindictor has thrust upon you."

Regaining his human form, however, only increased Manning's terror. Suspended above the dizzying hell, the boy could not be as brave as the cat had been. He stared up at his tutor and pleaded, "Pull me up, Vivator, please! I can't stand it. I don't need any powers. I can't look down again. Get me out of here!"

Vivator smiled to encourage him. "You will not die. I will not let you. Only a moment more, Manning. See how red my face grows. I will tell you when to look down." The boy felt the heat racing up the shaft to scorch him. "Now, Manning, now!" cried Vivator. "Look, and choose!" The boy looked, shuddered, and chose.

The flames receded. Vivator swung him up and well away from the edge of the pit. Manning hugged the solid ground and panted. When the boy's chest stopped heaving, Vivator held him close and said," I am so proud of you." Manning thought the compliment undeserved but accepted it in silence. Vivator stood him on his feet and took his hand. "We must leave here at once. I have played and hidden in every inch of this cave. We will take the quickest and darkest way out." They seemed to walk through walls as Vivator led them outside, swift as an arrow.

Once outside, Vivator made a low trilling sound several times and waited. Manning knew better than to speak until they were safely away from the Conniptions. There was a noiseless movement in the bushes, and then, to his utter delight, he felt Taponto's trunk curl round him in the darkness. Stealthily, they glided back into the bushes, with Taponto moving as cautiously as a tightrope walker. Safe atop the mighty elephant's back, Manning nestled against the chest of his only remaining protector. They breathed as one. Vivator whispered, "I dare not take you back to my camp, but when we have put a little distance between us and these demons, we will pause and rest. We have much to tell each other before the end of this desperate night.

2. The Education of a Blue Leopard

The three friends slid into the night and away from the caves as if on wheels of velvet. Except for the gentle rocking motion of the saddle, Manning could not have been sure Taponto was really moving. A day earlier and he might easily have fallen asleep as they traveled, but now his old life was gone, and his new one must be thought about. His head tipped back into Vivator's shoulder, and he watched the stars multiply as they put the caves behind them.

"We won't be heard now," said Vivator. "No one has followed us." It was an invitation to talk, and Manning had a boxful of questions. "Do you think they died quickly?" he asked.

"Yes, almost at once. The heat and smoke made them faint long before they reached the flames. Your parents felt no pain. They didn't suffer." Vivator's hand pressed his wrist reassuringly.

The boy continued, "Why can't we go to your camp?"

"I want Vindictor to lose all track of you. It is too easy for him to monitor the activities of the camp. In time, if possible, I want him to think you have perished and forget about you completely. That would be the best thing and the safest." Pressed against his tutor's chest, the boy felt the words buzz through him in a rich, comforting baritone.

"I'm just a kid. I don't even have activities," said the boy. "Why does he need to monitor me?"

Vivator's chuckle vibrated between them. "He doesn't, for now. It is only when you grow older that he plans to use you. He thinks he still controls you, so he is content to let you wander as you please, but one single glimpse of you in human form and Vindictor will know that we control the spell. At my camp you would have to spend every moment as a blue leopard. Surely, that is not your wish."

Manning shuddered. "Ugh! Surely not."

"Ho, Taponto!" Vivator brought the elephant to a stop. "Let us get down and be comfortable. It is safe to pause here for a while." They dismounted, and Vivator spread a blanket of softest violet cashmere upon the sand. "Sit beside me. I have much to tell you, little – no; we have had enough of cats for now, haven't we?" Manning nodded vigorously. "Some of what I have to say is troubling. Do you agree that it is best to hear that first, and then move on to what may please you?" asked his tutor.

"Oh, yes," said the boy.

Vivator nodded. "Very well then. There is a danger to be avoided at all costs. If ever my brother sees you as you are now, you cease to be his pawn and become a mortal enemy who could take revenge as an adult. Vindictor would not wait to find out your intentions. He would deal with you now, without a moment's hesitation."

"Yikes!" Manning squeaked.

"Exactly," said Vivator, "and you would be no safer in your own country than you are in Baziffe. Vindictor's tentacles reach everywhere. That is why I must deny you even the comfort of your relatives in America. They could not shield you from his wrath, and would, themselves, be in danger. No, there is but one place of safety for you in human form."

"And where is that?" demanded Manning.

"Do you remember," asked Vivator, "when I spoke of a secret place to which I have forever blinded the eyes of Vindictor? I have never shared its location with another soul, but you have earned the right to know of it." He looked away and added, "In my failure to protect your family, I have forfeited the right to keep this secret from you."

Manning touched his tutor's shoulder. "Oh, Vivator. I don't blame *you. I never will. You were about to lead them to safety when I showed up and ruined everything."*

Vivator shook his head and said, "Child, did you really think I was surprised you smuggled yourself along to take part in the rescue? I would have been surprised if you had not. It is what I would have done myself in your place."

Manning gasped, "You knew?"

Vivator smiled sadly. "I suspected. I should have bound you hand and foot and posted guard. You had to try. The fault is mine." He squeezed Manning's hand. "Tell me that you understand that. Say the words!"

Manning said nothing, and Vivator sighed heavily. "You are stubborn, boy ... but you are kind." He changed the subject. "What power did you choose? Will you show me?"

The boy became animated. "I may not be able to. I'm not sure it worked."

"It worked if you chose in the blaze of the flames," said Vivator with conviction.

"Well," the boy's hands made vague circles in front of him. "The problem is, I had two powers in mind, and I really wanted both of them. When the flames came at me, I couldn't decide, and they probably cancelled each other out," he said, sheepishly.

Vivator massaged his chin and looked long and hard at Manning. "Greedy boy," he said at last. "You may have thrown away a miraculous opportunity that will never come again. Still, the spell is one of the strongest and never cast on one so young.... It is just possible that your error may prove a stroke of genius." He drew the child into a patch of moonlight, just ahead of the elephant, and stepped back. "Test one of the powers. Show me."

Manning squinted in concentration and clenched his little fists. A startled Taponto reared up and snorted as the boy vanished from sight without moving. "Good! Good!" cried Vivator. "All is not lost." Manning reappeared, causing Taponto to trumpet in terror.

"It's all right, Ponty," the boy said, laughing. "I even scared myself." Vivator took up the reins and patted the elephant. "Now, the other one," he commanded Manning. Taponto shrank back and tried to bolt when Manning slowly rose into the air, higher and higher, moving in awkward circles as if trying to swim. Finally, he landed on the amazed animals head, saying, "Now I can mount you all by myself, Ponty."

Vivator clapped his hands like a gleeful child and exclaimed, "Brilliant! Brilliant! Invisibility and flight! What could be more useful? Splendid choices, and you have them both. Fly to my arms and let me embrace my greedy, reckless, and ever-so-practical boy."

Manning did as he was told, which set Taponto stomping about again. Vivator squeezed the boy tightly. "You have done well. Much has been taken from you, but much has been given. You will survive. Yes, you will survive." The man was laughing and crying all at once. Never had Manning seen his dignified tutor behave in such a manner. Neither had the amazed Taponto who had had enough and charged off into the dunes.

"What can we do now?" asked the worried boy.

"Isn't it obvious, Manning? And isn't it wonderful? You will fly over the dunes, find Taponto, and bring him back!" After a moment's reflection, the boy nodded giddily, and his grin became as wide and idiotic as that on the face of his tutor. "When you return," said Vivator, "we will set out for your new home, the secret caves of sapphire." The caves of sapphire! The sound of it excited Manning's imagination, as did Vivator's next words: "Now fly! Fly!"

Finding Taponto was easy. Calming the astounded beast was more difficult, but Manning did it. When they returned to Vivator, the pride his tutor took in him seemed to the boy, for once, well justified. Before they set out for the Caves of Sapphire, Taponto rocked his mighty head and shoulders from side to side, gave them both a grumpy look, and grunted as if to say, "No more nonsense."

Manning was extremely curious about the exotic lair where he was to be hidden for the foreseeable future. Was it, for example, really made out of sparkling sapphires, or was it like a gloomy mine where you had to dig for them? Vivator did not encourage his questions. Instead, he massaged the boy's temples and softly chanted the Baziffian word for sleep. It was long and soothing and did not seem to contain any vowels. Manning grew drowsy and drifted into a pleasant dream about an enormous room in which all the objects around him were in lustrous shades of blue. When he awoke, he was indeed in just such a room. He was stretched out on the floor, with a soft, plump cushion beneath him and a pillow under his head. A deep blue dome rose high above him, twinkling with what might be stars. At first, he thought he was outside, but when he sat up and rubbed his eyes, he saw that he was in the center of a room whose dazzling walls shimmered with a magical blue light. It was the most beautiful room he had ever seen. A sigh of pleasure escaped him.

"Welcome," said Vivator, extending a tall blue chalice of zaleem, a refreshing Baziffian beverage made from blue plums, ginger, and honey. "Do you approve of my humble retreat?"

"I think it's splendid," said Manning, who had waited his whole life for a proper opportunity to use the word. Up until now, nothing had ever been splendid. "Is this where I'm to live?" he asked breathlessly. Vivator explained that the caves had many other rooms for the boy to explore, but this chamber was his tutor's personal favorite. It would be Manning's room, if that was agreeable.

"It'll be great for the daytime," Manning exclaimed. "It's like the sun is shining, even though there are no windows. What makes it so bright, Vivator?"

"Embedded in these walls are over a trillion azure sapphires, the greatest concentration anywhere in these caves. In their presence, a single candle creates the illusion of sunlight."

"It's the most cheerful place I've ever been," said Manning, "but...."

"But?"

"At night," said the boy. "How will I sleep?"

"Clap your hands together once, sharply," said Vivator. The boy did as he was told and gasped at the surprising effect of his action. Most of the sapphires ceased to reflect the candlelight, and those that remained illuminated created a design that encircled the chamber. It suggested a coast lined with palm trees and a sea dotted with Baziffian sailboats. Camels, leopards, tigers and elephants roamed the banks. Storks, bats, and pelicans soared above them in the sky. Manning was so charmed by the sparkling, joyous outline that he laughed out loud and began to applaud. He stopped in short order when his applause threw the room into an alarming cycle of split second changes from daylight to lightning bolts to utter darkness and back again.

"My goodness!" said Manning, "I think I'll just put a sock over my eyes when I want to go to sleep."

Vivator chuckled and said, "You shall do just as you wish, for this is now your home." Then he grew serious, adding, "Though I am but a poor substitute, I must now be father to you, and you must be my son." His words caused Manning to weep from grief, but also from gratitude to the man who now gathered the boy in his arms and embraced him tightly. "Sleep now," said Vivator. "Taponto and I will stay by your side this night. When you wake, you will see something familiar, the faces of those who love you."

Thus began Manning's new life, and when he awoke the next morning, his education began in earnest. The first lesson, because on it depended all the others, was that he was never to leave the caves as himself, only as the blue leopard. Taponto had to be trained as well, to witness the transformation from boy to leopard and back again *without becoming hysterical and dangerous. Manning decided that some signal was needed to let Taponto know that the transformation was about to take place. Both as boy and leopard, he would rub the tops of his ears as a warning to the anxious beast. The transformation had to be repeated so many times that Manning was near exhaustion and his ears were raw, but by the time Taponto finally understood and could watch the changes calmly, Manning had become so smooth and efficient at shifting his shape that it ceased to drain his energy.*

After a few days, Vivator stopped these sessions and said, "It is enough, Manning. You have mastered it well. Henceforward, you need only become the beast when you choose it, though it must take place at least once during each lunar cycle or it will come upon you unbidden. What I have done cannot be reversed by Vindictor. You will not lose control of the spell unless you lose control of yourself. Drunkenness or violent anger, for example, could bring the beast upon you unexpectedly, but—" he smiled at Manning, "we need not worry about that for now, do we?"

The boy looked very serious and said, "I don't think so."

"Do not be discouraged," said his tutor. "It is true that no boy has ever had to bear this strange burden, but it is also true that no boy was ever given such an opportunity. Accept it. Embrace it. You will find knowledge and pleasures unknown to any other human." And so it was to be.

At first, the little leopard left the cave only during the day and always in the company of Vivator or Taponto. Once he came to trust his new instincts, so different from the boy's, he was comfortable going alone and at night. In fact, he preferred it. In these solitary explorations, he learned the languages of all the animals and the secret meanings of their movements. He learned where they gathered to play, where they slept, and where they hid their babies. He learned who was feared and who was preyed upon. He learned that as the blue leopard, he was more important in the kingdom of animals than the boy Manning was in the world of men. No one preyed upon the leopard, and all feared him, even the snakes who made him shiver and caused his fur to rise. They didn't know that from this leopard they had nothing to fear. They didn't know he prowled only to observe and learn and not to hunt. He sensed, however, that it was best they never know these things, so he roared his fearsome growls each time he left the cave. He roared to say, "I am coming. Fear and respect me." He roared because it helped to calm his own fears. He roared because he liked the mighty sound it made buzzing through him.

One group of animals did not fear him or flee from his growls. The other leopards of the desert studied him as he studied them. They might easily have fought with him and harmed him, except for the two things that insured his safety. He was still a cub, and he was blue. His color puzzled and attracted the others. They had never seen it and found it mysteriously beautiful. They noticed his sudden arrivals and disappearances. They wondered how and why he had been separated from his tribe. Some thought there was no blue tribe, only this one. They wondered if he was meant to become their leader when he was fully grown. They tracked and studied him in silence, and he was protected by their confusion.

Safe inside the cave, the boy would remember what the leopard had seen. Often, at first, it disturbed him to think back on what his other self had watched with calmer eyes. It was hard for Manning to understand, for example, why, as the leopard, he had not intervened to save a small monkey from the jaws of a jackal. He knew he couldn't single-handedly civilize the world outside the caves, but it bothered him that his leopard self never felt the need to try.

The tiny group inside the caves could not have been more civilized. Vivator worried that Manning would be cut off so long from human society that when it was safe for him to rejoin it, he would no longer *know how to behave. To prevent this, his tutor regularly had him act out scenes in which Manning had to meet people of all ages and both sexes (all played by Vivator, of course) in every imaginable situation, with complications popping up at every turn. Vivator was so good at being cranky and demanding old ladies that Manning sometimes wished he could let the blue leopard take over for a few uncivilized minutes.*

Like it or not, the cave was now Manning's home. It was also his school, his library, his gymnasium, and his church. Vivator was determined to raise Manning to be a polished and accomplished gentleman of whom the boy's parents would have been proud. Since Vindictor must be kept ignorant that the spell had been altered and the boy was himself again, Vivator did not dare risk telling even his most trusted aides. This meant that he must instruct Manning entirely by himself, the boy's only link to the world he would one day enter as an adult.

Manning often asked Vivator when he thought it might be safe to leave the caves. The two had bonded more deeply than most flesh and blood relatives, but Vivator understood Manning's loneliness. "Perhaps it is not entirely bad that you must sometimes be the beast. At least, as the leopard, you are free to seek the company of others," he said one evening. He had read the boy's thoughts, for Manning was too grateful to his friend and protector to complain aloud. He was also keenly aware of the sacrifices Vivator had made for him. If the boy had lost a normal childhood, the man had put his life and affairs aside to become guard, cook, and baby-sitter.

As Manning grew into a strong and handsome young man, the leopard grew larger, sleeker, and more powerful. Now he feared no animal outside the cave, and all, even his fellow leopards, feared him. One night, returning to the caves, he found Vivator waiting up for him, observing him closely as his transformation took place. When he had completely achieved his human form, Vivator told him that at last he had taken steps to set him free. "Vindictor knows that by now the leopard is mature and dangerous enough to do his evil bidding. He has been seeking him out and watching me more closely than ever. He does not know you still exist as Manning, and the strapping, manly fellow you have become is a stranger who could go unrecognized by him." *Vivator went on to tell of the plan to convince his brother that the blue leopard had been killed.* "I am watched by fewer eyes now, which means the signs I have planted have been reported to him. He has taken the bait. Tomorrow night, you will leave for… Can you guess?"

"Not America?"

"Not at first, Manning, just as a precaution. First, you shall enjoy a brief vacation where you can blow off the dust of the cave, mingle with those your own age, and run a little bit wild. I have tried to teach you many things, but that one was beyond my powers. You will enjoy meeting people your own age including young ladies who do not resemble your old tutor. At least I hope they will not." *Vivator's mood had turned playful.* "Come now, guess."

Manning studied his tutor's face, but there were no clues. Still, there had been a change in emphasis in his lessons lately. He smiled and said confidently, "It's Paris."

"You are quick, Manning." *Vivator smiled.* "Of course it is Paris. For one who has been so serious as long as you have had to be, only Paris can restore the balance. Accounts have been set up for you through a contact unknown to Vindictor. You will stay with his family for a time. They know nothing of your background. For the safety of all, it is best they do not."

Excitement flooded through the young man's veins. His life was about to begin in earnest, and what a life it would be! Freed by Vivator's immense wealth from all ordinary needs, he would work only at what interested him. He would travel the world and reunite with his relatives. He would throw parties and make friends, dozens of them, crowds of them, throngs, mobs, hordes of them! He would be the friendliest man in the world, and his friendliness would only be exceeded by his kindness. He would follow Vivator's example and make his tutor proud. He would devote himself to fighting crime and righting injustice. With limitless riches and his mighty leopard powers behind him, he would not fail. And it would all be such fun. He was finally going to have fun! He could have whirled around the cave like a dervish in giddy anticipation of this brilliant new life, but he feared it would wound the feelings of the person who had made it possible. Instead, he said simply, "It sounds wonderful, Vivator, but I will miss my life here with you."

Vivator smiled. "Such diplomacy will serve you even better in Paris than your excellent French. I doubt that you will miss this half life we have shared here. It is enough that you remember it without pain. That would please me very much."

"Then be pleased," said Manning, crushing his tutor in a bear hug," for I will always, always remember you with delight."

Still smiling, Vivator disentangled himself. "You do not know your own strength, my son. Do you want to fracture my ribs?"

"I want to fold you flat and pack you in a suitcase. I want to kidnap you." Manning laughed, but then looked serious. "I know you're not coming with me."

Vivator shook his head. "You must make your own way. You know you want to."

Manning sighed, "I guess I do, but I won't know what to do when I get to America."

Now it was Vivator who laughed. "You will have adventures. You will get into danger. You will make a great difference in the lives of many people. You will make me proud – no, that you have already done." His eyes shone, and he smiled broadly with a look of great *satisfaction. In years to come, it would be this moment that Manning would conjure up to remember him. The way he was next to see him, he would bury at the bottom of his mind.*

The rest of that night was crammed with instructions for Manning's escape from Baziffe and details of the arrangements in Paris. For years, Manning had been instructed by Vivator, but now, he was being drilled. "Can't I sleep now?" he asked at last. "I've got it all down, and to go over it again will only make me nervous."

"It will make you careful. Your flight to freedom can only be attempted once. It is a final examination you must pass the first time, for your very life depends on it."

The young man squeezed his tutor's shoulder. "If I am not afraid," he lied, "why should you be? You have taught me well, and thought of everything."

A dark look passed over Vivator's face. "Not quite everything," he said. "There is still one thing I must be satisfied about before I set you loose. When I return tomorrow, you will go."

So little time remained to Manning in the Caves of Sapphire that he chose to spend it with the friend he would miss almost as much as Vivator. He washed and groomed Taponto, then dressed the mighty beast in his finest trappings. He brought him food instead of letting him forage and played the saroon, singing to him the elephant's favorite Baziffian melodies. Then, he climbed atop Taponto's back, scratched the enormous ears until he heard low grunts of pleasure and the jingling of tiny silver bells. Still aboard his tusked companion, Manning stretched out to sleep and said drowsily, "Ah, Taponto, what will life be without a warm elephant?"

The next day was uneventful. He waited patiently for Vivator's return, skipping even his nightly prowl for fear of missing his tutor. On the second day, he was restless, and on the third, he became so uneasy that he risked doing what had always been forbidden. He left the caves in human form, though disguised in native clothing. Half an hour's camel ride from the caves, his fears were confirmed. A trail of blood led him to a large boulder, behind which he found the body of his beloved tutor.

He dismounted and stood trembling above the crumpled form. "This can't be how it ends," he said aloud. Vivator stirred at the sound, opened his eyes, and spoke in a weak voice. "Allah be praised. You've reached me in time, though only just, I fear."

Manning bent down, held Vivator's head up, and brought a canteen to his lips. "Who has done this to you?" he demanded.

Vivator gulped at the water and then said, "In my foolishness, I have done it to myself. I had to be convinced that it was safe for you to leave. I had to see Vindictor at close range, and it is true – he suspects nothing. You are free to go, but you must do it at once."

"But you are wounded. How ...?" Manning stared in puzzlement.

Vivator spoke again. "A dark premonition sent me to him, but the safety I needed to fear for was my own. For the first time in many years, we were alone together, and he did what he would not have dared with others around. I thought that even after all that had passed between us, there was a bond of brotherhood that would not permit – but I am dying for my folly."

"No!" cried Manning. "I will get you to the caves and tend you myself until you can be taken to your camp for treatment. You will not die. It is he who will die, and I will see to it!"

Vivator pressed his hand to Manning's mouth. "That you will not do. You have pledged to me that you, who can kill so easily, will never do so except to prevent a killing. Anything else is base murder and unworthy of you. Get me to the caves, but do it quickly. My wound is mortal, and your saying otherwise cannot make it so. While I still have breath, there is one thing I must not leave undone if I can help it."

Manning cradled his tutor in his arms to cushion the ride as the camel lurched back to the caves. When they arrived, he placed Vivator on the softest of beds and began to examine his wounds, but Vivator interrupted him. "Bring me paper and pen, at once!"

Manning did as he was commanded. Then he tended to the wounds as best he could while Vivator scribbled with feverish speed in characters the young man recognized as the Conniption alphabet. Presently, the scribbling stopped, and the pen fell to the floor. "This is for you," Vivator whispered, pressing the scroll into Manning's hand. "Never let it out of your sight. It details my death at the hands of Vindictor. Presented to any Conniption, it will mean the end of my brother."

"I will take it to them tonight, after you are asleep, and you will be avenged."

Vivator smiled at him and whispered, "My champion. But no, you must swear to me that you will only use the scroll as a last resort if you, yourself, are in danger of harm. Swear it to me now because that sleep you speak of is my last."

"How can you ask me to spare him?" cried Manning. "How can you possibly ask such a thing? It is beyond all reason."

"It may indeed lie beyond the reason of an only child such as you. He is my brother, my twin, my other self. I cannot be the cause of his death."

"Not even," Manning choked out the words," when he is the cause of yours?"

"Not even then." Vivator's hand clutched at Manning's shoulder. "Promise me, or I cannot sleep."

"You ask too much." Manning could no longer fight back the tears that streamed down his face. "And I will do anything to keep you from that sleep." The sound of bells behind him meant Taponto was edging into the chamber. Manning motioned the animal to come closer.

Vivator breathed heavily and spoke with difficulty. "I go to join your parents. I will have such joyous things to tell them of you. Perhaps it will soften their hearts to me a little."

"You break mine when you speak this way, old man." *Manning dragged the back of his hand across his eyes.*

"Promise me you will spare him, little cat."

"I promise."

"Bury me, if you must, but do not linger here. It is time you began your adventures."

Manning lay down beside him, fearful of missing his tutor's faint words, but he had heard all that would be spoken.

In time, all that Vivator foresaw would come to pass, but for the moment, Manning Nugent's high adventures in America could wait. His grief was greater than human form could bear. And so, when at last Taponto emerged from the caves, it was not a young man he bore on his back, but a leopard of deepest cobalt blue. For many nights thereafter, had you strayed into the desert, a curious sight would have made you pause in wonderment. An oddly colored leopard perched upon the back of an elephant, and with upturned heads, the forlorn creatures bayed their sorrows to the great silent moon over Baziffe.

CHAPTER 4
PICTURE PERFECT
Fifteen months earlier: Chicago, June 1944

Victor Sheffield chewed his lip. "What perfect timing," he thought. "How in hell does Rae manage this stuff? It's like voodoo."

If the package had come in the morning mail, he might have gotten it aside, examined it, and mislaid it forever. If the afternoon delivery had come before Maude Weaver's arrival, his mother might have opened it in front of him and put it to rest on a closet shelf. But now, with her best friend comfortably settled in as an audience, it would have to be discussed, admired, and put on indefinite display.

The two women sat together on the wicker sofa as Louisa Sheffield sorted through the mail. The military character of the parcel immediately caught the attention of both Victor and his mother, who slid it casually under the July issue of *Redbook*. Maude drew it back out, their friendship being one of intimacy, long standing, and few boundaries. She spoke up excitedly, "Oh, it's from Rae, Louisa, all the way from Pensacola!" 'By way of Haiti,' Victor thought ruefully.

"Look, it's stamped 'glass' and 'fragile,'" Maude continued. "Do open it and let me snoop. Maybe there's a letter with it. Something told me this was going to be a good day to drop by."

"Any day you turn up is a good one, Maude. Pa will be sore that he missed you," said Louisa. Victor's father wouldn't have long to miss her. The women and their husbands had been close as long as Victor could remember, and it was a rare week that found them absent from each other's homes. Only Sunday, the four of them had gathered here in the sun porch on the same brown wicker chairs for pinochle. Their loud laughter and his father's scorn at hopeless hands had penetrated to Victor's flat upstairs. The Weavers' enthusiasm for life and genuine affection kept his parents in good spirits, and for that he welcomed their visits.

He was also by no means blind to the useful contacts and support that Daniel Weaver had at his fingertips. He was on the easiest of terms with most of the South Side's professional community. If Victor were ever to get a healthy start in local politics, Dan was the first person he'd want in his corner, and his wife the last he would want to offend.

"Yes, open it up, Ma. Let Mrs. Weaver have a look."

"All right then, although I'm sure it's really meant for you." His mother tugged at a knot in the twine. "Do you have something, Victor?" He opened and extended a mother-of-pearl pen knife. She beamed. "He still has that, Maude."

"I'm never without it."

"What do you think she's sent, Louisa?"

Mrs. Sheffield set aside the severed twine. "I can't wait to find out."

Victor was in no such suspense. From its shape and labeling, this was obviously a framed photograph of his wife, likely in her Wave uniform. As it emerged from the brown paper, his only surprise was at the delicacy of the frame, a series of curved indentations, edged in silver. It looked sharp to the touch. "Appropriate," he thought.

Maude drew in her breath. "It's lovely. Dan will want to see it when I tell him. Where will you put it?"

"Why, I don't know." Louisa placed it face down on the wrapping paper and looked at Victor.

"Was there a letter? a note?" asked Maude.

Louisa drew a sheet of Navy stationery from the wrapping and examined it closely.

"Well?" But if Maude hoped for a reading, she'd have to be content with Louisa's brisk summary.

"She's doing fine." Since Rachel's departure, Louisa had demoted her to pronoun referents, and refused to call her by name. "She misses everyone. She mentions you and Dan. There's nothing out of the – oh!"

"What is it?"

"She – she's taking lessons. She wants to fly a plane."

Silence and raised eyebrows all around.

Maude took up the photograph. "This must go in the living room." She nodded her head at the picture. "A good looking woman." She handed it to Victor. "Be careful, it looks like you could break it with a glance, but the edges are sharp." From the photograph, a frank, pretty face smiled up at him confidently. "You must miss her something fierce."

"Yes," he said. *Yes*, he thought.

"Come and help me rustle up a snack, Maude. I made a lemon pound cake Monday." The two women withdrew to the kitchen, and Victor heard the hoarse splintering of coffee beans as his mother vigorously worked the handle of the grinder.

Alone, he would have the next few minutes to explore, unobserved, the face beneath the glass. His index finger traced the outline of her lips, her nose, and finally, the large eyes, wide open as always. "They put me in mind of Ruth Etting," his father had said. "They don't miss a trick, but they're not likely to mislead you."

Victor had first felt their steady, unblinking gaze in the summer of 1938, at the Pla-Mor bowling lanes. Bowling had been one of Victor's lucky accidents. In one's youth, even one such accident can make the difference between an anxious slog through life and something far nicer and less effortful. Victor Sheffield was the beneficiary of several such lucky accidents, physical beauty, an easy personal charm, and of course, his almost spooky prowess at bowling. He was ridiculously good at it. Hardly an important skill, and as a sport, well, it wasn't football . . . and yet it continued to generate the steady stream of attention and goodwill that had begun in seventh grade. Captain of every team on which he had played, he was now manager of the South Works Phalanx, the bowling league of the local steel mill.

That first night, the Pla-Mor was crowded with amateurs. Victor was peripherally aware of a boisterous group of merry but untalented young women in the adjoining lane. A quick scan of the group disclosed no stunning beauties, and he turned back to the score sheet in front of him. He smoothed the slim red moustache that embellished his upper lip. It was an excellent moustache. Like the fingers which groomed it and like the man himself, it was small but perfectly proportioned. To compensate for his size, Victor had willed the moustache into being in his senior year in high school. It was documented in the sports page of the Bowen *Arrow*, in a photo captioned "Keggler captain, Vic Sheffield, our own bantam Errol Flynn." At the time, Victor feigned annoyance but didn't think the assessment unreasonable.

He chuckled briefly at the memory. Laughter continued behind him. He swung around and saw the best looking girl of the week examining him with interest. She was a compendium of visual treats, and his eyes darted from the soft, wavy, auburn hair to the large hazel eyes to the slim waist, cinched with a white patent leather belt, to the slender arms emerging from a pale green angora sweater, to the plaid skirt and the shapely legs beneath it. The sole problem with this stirring vision was that the girl was laughing at him.

"What's so funny, cookie?"

"I'm sorry." Her voice was as good as the rest of her, crinkly butterscotch. "It's just that you looked so enormously pleased with yourself."

An accurate rebuke, but instead of smarting, it warmed him. "What if I said I was more pleased with you?" He slid in beside her.

She laughed again. "Then I'd have to warn you, I'm not a cookie at all, more of a saltine."

He backed off slightly. This would take time. He had time. "Are you with that dotty crew next door?" She smiled and nodded. He went on, "They're pretty miserable." Another nod. "You don't care at all about bowling, do you?"

"I've never done it. This is just an evening out." A warm smile seemed to be the natural state of her face.

"Wanna see how it's done? I can show you a few things so you won't stink up the joint when you get back over there. I don't have time to make you queen of the lanes, but it won't take long to make you better than they are. Would you like that?"

"Yes. I would. Yes." And in those early days, there were nothing but yesses from her. Victor was used to easy yesses. He was not used to having to earn them. He would grow to like it with this girl. He was as good as his word about improving her game. She would not, indeed, be queen of the lanes, but he found her delight at the rudimentary techniques he passed on to her quite intoxicating.

Finally, he asked, "Who are you?"

She said it slowly. "Rachel Ann Shalifu."

"That's . . . that's like music."

She didn't rejoin her companions that night

Nor did Victor. Somewhere in their first five minutes together, he took her arm to demonstrate a release. He pulled it back slowly. He felt the soft wool of her sweater on his skin and knew he would ditch his chums and drive this girl home. It didn't matter when he left; this was not a league night. He lingered only long enough to be sure she'd leave with him. He didn't care what his friends would think, but he didn't want to embarrass her in front of hers. She seemed above embarrassment, or outside it. When her companions giggled or rolled their eyes at her, she smiled at them blandly and made no move to return to their lane. She watched him play, and he felt her eyes on him as he made each approach. He liked them there and couldn't wait to turn and see her again. He began to do something he had always scorned as show-offy and beneath him. When the ball left his hand, he would spin around to face her, with no regard to the pins. He couldn't read his score in her reactions, for each time she smiled directly at him. The only comment on his skill was the clatter at the end of his lane. He was the most polished and formidable bowler in any direction she cared to look. But she didn't care and she didn't look, and it didn't bother him a bit. She lit the room for him like bottled sunshine. He would have told her so, but this was a girl with prickly edges who might think him a sap. He almost told her anyway.

As they walked to his car, he wished he'd bought what he'd really wanted to, a light yellow '35 La Salle convertible. It was used, but expensive and magnificent. He'd have been paying on it forever, but he should simply have done it instead of dragging the family to the dealer. His father's face was a study. Victor knew there'd be a caution coming, but he could see the old man's pleasure at his son's nerve and ambition.

"It's a beauty all right, but –"

His sister Paulina let out a laugh and said, "Come on, Vic. It looks like a big stick of butter on wheels. Who are you trying to impress?"

Her baby brother regarded her coolly. She had lost the knack of needling him, but not the habit. "Polly," he sighed, "we know Dennis will never try to impress you this way, but that's no call to get snippy." Victor had recently discovered that "snippy" could be counted on to send Paulina into a silent pout.

The car that he and Rachel now approached was indeed a convertible, but a sensible black Ford. He opened the door for her, and she slid in as though she belonged there. "Little saltine," he thought, " if you'd been with me at the car lot, I'd be driving you off tonight in my snazzy stick of butter."

He took her home by way of Rainbow Beach, where they sat in the moonlight with the top down. The radio was on low, and Rachel hummed along with the last few bars of "Love Walked In." He snapped it off so they could talk, or not. "A dirty shame he died so young," she said.

"Kenny Baker? When did that –"

"No, Gershwin. Kenny Baker can die whenever he wants to. There's always another tenor, but there'll never be another George Gershwin." She told him she was a nurse at Jackson Park Hospital. She had an early shift, but if he wanted to walk down to the water for a few minutes, she was willing.

When they reached the low stone wall at the beginning of the sand, she sat down and took off her shoes and stockings. He hadn't considered this and just stood watching her. She looked up at him and said, "Get our toes wet at least?" He rolled up his pants cuffs and would have followed her halfway out into the lake. The sand was cool on their feet, but granular. At first, he picked his way gingerly, but when she noticed and said, "Well, you wouldn't want this in your shoe," he forced a more even stride. This being Lake Michigan, the water was even colder than the sand, and now and then robust wavelets wet the edges of his slacks, but he had no desire to be standing anywhere else. His left arm cradled their shoes. He put his right around her and thought, " Pa's gonna like you."

Pa did, of course, and he was not alone when, several weeks later, on their way to a dance, Rachel was presented for inspection. Victor assumed his brothers would approve, but it was gratifying and a little surprising to see how quickly she won over the women in the family. Rachel seemed cosmically unruffled, not just with his mother, but even with such prickly pears as Frances and Paulina. He never caught her working at it. He'd never seen a woman, or a man for that matter, with so little to prove.

His mother questioned Rachel at embarrassing length about her experiences at the hospital. When Louisa asked if she kept a first aid kit about her, Rachel smiled, took her hand and asked, "Will I need it? Does Victor have a lot of dancing accidents?" It brought down the house, and Louisa laughed as loud as anyone. Frances responded well to Rachel's curiosity about baby Edmond, and soon the two women were taking long, companionable walks with the child in the stroller. The longest holdout was Paulina, possibly because her husband, Dennis, had greeted Rachel's appearance with a whistle. Eventually, Paulina realized there was fun to be had at Victor's expense by dredging up childhood anecdotes. Some of them were so bizarre; he decided she must be making them up for the occasion. He didn't care. The whole pack of them went around smiling now, and he had caused it by bringing this quiet little dispenser of joy into their orbit. It wouldn't have changed his mind if they'd all hated her on sight, but this was nicer – a helluva lot nicer.

It went on like that, each day giving Victor a new reason to keep seeing her. Three months in, his father lumbered up the stairs to Victor's apartment, a major effort, and because of the older man's limp, a rare occurrence. He sank into the sofa and waved his son to a chair. His voice, always imposing, was even more so in the small rooms of this flat. "You gonna marry this girl?"

Victor smiled broadly. "Yeah."

"You're not just fooling around, like before."

Victor shook his head. "No, Pa."

"Good." His father looked around the room, as though the premises might have a bearing on his next question. "Will she have you?"

"Of course." Victor grinned. "Why not?"

His father regarded him, unsmiling. "Don't act like this when you ask her. And ask her soon. Rachel is a woman of substance. Mama and I have talked about this, and though it's your decision, of course, this is a woman we'd be proud to have as the mother of our grandchildren."

"Thank you, Pa. I'm glad. I'm going to ask her."

"Then ask her soon."

Victor laughed. "What's the hurry?"

His father stood up. "You are not the only fish. She's at the hospital all day, surrounded by doctors making ten times what you do. Night shifts too. You think you're the only fish, but you're not."

Oh yes I am, thought Victor, as his father turned and made his way carefully back downstairs. *I'm the only fish for her, and you know it too, you gruff old rascal.* Among siblings, perhaps only identical twins perceive a parent in the same way. Perhaps it doesn't even happen then. Whatever terms Paulina, Jack, or Ed would have used to describe their father, "gruff old rascal" would not have been among them. Victor neither feared nor resented his father's temper because he had never experienced it. His father's eyes reflected pleasure and doting approbation as a rule, and when they did not, Victor read only a mild and half-hearted exasperation. He supposed, when he thought about it at all, that such indulgence had been meted out to each of the others in turn, and because he was the baby and the last to appear, his favored tenure had just gone on and on. Besides, wasn't he more fun than the others? That had to count for something.

If there were a more impressive wedding at Saint Brides that season, it escaped Victor's notice. Certainly the Sheffield clan had never seen anything like it. Daniel Weaver had taken a personal interest in the Shalifu-Sheffield nuptials and could have filled the pews with his friends alone. His unspecified but well-received donation to the church building fund saw to it that Rachel's conversion from Dutch Reformed to Roman Catholicism was handled expeditiously and did not delay the wedding. There were those who whispered that Fire Commissioner Weaver's generous gift was also the reason the Archbishop officiated at the wedding. Never one to look a gift horse in the mouth, Victor was beside himself at that turn of events. When the wedding photo proofs were developed, he spread them out on the floor, exclaiming to everyone within earshot, "That hat! Will ya look at that hat!"

His bride's choice of headgear had also brought him pleasure. She had collapsed in his lap after a day of trousseau shopping with his mother and sister. "You won't believe the veil Paulina wanted me to wear for the wedding."

"Oh, I probably would."

"It was very Spanish. Actually, it would have gone well with the lace on my gown." She looked up at him mischievously. "To tell you the truth, I looked pretty smashing in it." "You should have taken it."

"Oh, I couldn't." She laughed. "It was a mantilla, and it came to a point. It was sooo high." She was shaking with laughter now. "I would have towered over you."

"That bitch just never stops," he said quietly.

"Come on." Rachel poked him. "It's funny."

The local paper ran a full-length photo of the couple in its rotogravure, and no one towered over anyone. As Maude clipped it out for a scrap book, she said to Louisa, "They could be the little dolls on a wedding cake."

∽∞∽

And so, for a time, they were. Pretty little dolls, in their tiny three-room dollhouse upstairs. Victor never intended it as a permanent residence for them, but Rachel was uncomplaining, so he dawdled about looking for something else. Where would he find cheaper rent or more agreeable landlords? Rachel didn't seem to mind the close proximity to his parents, and his mother had learned a bit about marital privacy since her legendary debacle with Frances and Ed. Louisa had paid the couple an early morning visit soon after the honeymoon weekend. Unbeknownst to Frances, Louisa was possessed of a key to their bungalow and didn't bother to knock. Frances awakened to find her mother-in-law at the foot of the bed brandishing a tray of muffins. Accounts of what followed vary, but most agree that Louisa was ordered to surrender the key and fled in a hail of muffins.

Now, when Victor recalled those easy times with Rachel, he winced, but it was a path his mind still loved to travel. If a singer crooned of paradise, it was not a biblical garden that flashed before him but the Aragon Ballroom, the rickety roller coasters at Riverview, Manistee Avenue on a sunny day or a rainy one, anywhere she'd been with him, even the dark narrow stairway up to the flat, where she'd be waiting. That was his paradise. But he'd been cast out of Eden. Cast himself out, he supposed. What had happened to it all? He knew what, but gripping this photograph of Rachel's new life, he couldn't bear to think of it. Not yet. He had to think of something good, something . . before. When was the last time she had kissed him and meant it?

His last really good time with her was eight months ago. He knew the precise date, October 23rd, his parents' anniversary. This year, there'd be a big blowout for their fortieth, but last year had just been family. Jack had suggested an evening on the town in the Loop and brought five different papers the night before for a planning session. The project had a charm on it right from the start. Frances was home with baby Anthony, but everyone else was gathered around the dining room table, all in a good mood at the same time. No one was at cross purposes, not even his father, though he kept hurling unhelpful ideas from behind *The Times*.

"Here's *Maid O' the Ozarks* at the Great Northern. This ad says it makes *Tobacco Road* blush."

"We want smiles tomorrow night," said Paulina, "not blushes."

"All righty then, how about Minsky's Rialto? They've got Taffy O'Toole, the Blond Venus."

"Daddy! Be serious." She consulted the *Herald American*. "What about a movie? *Wintertime* is at both the Garrick and the Apollo, so it must be good."

"Swell!" said her father. "We can see Sonja's little hieney."

"Dad, have you been drinking?"

"He's loved that joke for years." Louisa sighed. "Loved it to death, I'd say."

Ed had the *Sun*. "Gene Tierney's at the United Artists – *Heaven Can Wait*. It's a Lubitsch."

"Well, he's always funny," said Jack, " but maybe tomorrow should be more special than just a movie."

"Where'd the *Tribune* get to?" asked Victor. The answer came from beneath the table.

" I've got a good idea," said Shorty.

Victor rolled his eyes and muttered to Rachel, "You see? He hides 'till we forget about him. The kid spies on us all the time."

Rachel patted his hand. "Shhh, be nice."

Jack called down, "What's your idea, Shorty?"

"Well, if you really want to go to a nice night club, Gertrude Neissen is singing at the Chez Paree, and Grampa could see the Chez Paree Adorables."

When the laughter died down, Victor said, "You're the expert on night clubs, kiddo?"

A pause, then, "I can read now. I try to keep up."

"You think you're coming with us?"

Slowly, a head peered up over the table. "Maybe?"

"Think again," said Victor. Rachel pressed his arm.

Ed drew his son onto his lap and said, "Tomorrow night is just for grownups, Shorty."

"I'd be good."

"I know you would." He kissed the top of the child's head. "It's getting late. Just let me know what you all decide, and when to be here."

Louisa looked thoughtful, and when they heard the Buick pull away, she said, "You know, it really doesn't matter what we do, as long as we're all together. I'd rather you didn't all spend a lot of money on this. It's over so quickly."

"How about this, Ma?" Rachel had been urged to call her that. "If we went to a movie where there's a stage show in between, it would be a little like a night club, and we wouldn't go broke."

"What's at the Oriental?" asked Jack.

Rachel smoothed open the entertainment page of the *Daily News*. "Hmm, the Andrews Sisters in *Always a Bridesmaid,* and oh, I don't know any of these people."

"Doesn't sound like much," said Jack. "What about the Chicago?"

Rachel looked again. "Oh this is good, *"So Proudly We Hail."*

"What? WACs getting whacked?" said Victor. "That's too grim for a celebration."

"Well, the war is grim, Vic." Rachel sounded stung. "But it's patriotic, and everybody likes Claudette Colbert… at least, I do. Harry Cool is singing on stage. We've heard of him. There's a comedian from New York, and a ballet…" She trailed off.

Louisa spoke up, smiling at Rachel. "I like Claudette too, and I think that all sounds lovely."

"The queen has spoken," said Victor, "The Chicago it is. But where should we eat?"

His father lowered the paper and regarded them slyly. "It's been taken care of. I made a reservation to take my girl, and this whole raggedy bunch to the Empire Room." Amid cries of "Hooray!" and, "Well done, Pa!" Louisa sat beaming.

Later, upstairs, Victor sat in his pajamas, watching from the bed as his wife brushed her hair. "You're quiet," he said.

Rachel didn't turn from the mirror. "What goes on with you and Shorty?"

"Doesn't it bother you? He's exasperating."

"That's more or less his job. He's six."

"It's more than that. His parents have spoiled him blind. He doesn't know his place. He thinks everything revolves around him, like he's a little king."

Rachel turned to face him with an amused smile. "Hmmm."

"What?"

"Oh, I was just wondering who else around here fits that description."

"Don't be tiresome."

"All right." She put down her brush and crawled into bed beside him, where she was anything but tiresome.

∽∮∾

The next evening, the celebrants pulled up to the Palmer House in two cars. Despite the offers of all three of his sons to be chauffeur, Henry Sheffield arrived, as usual, behind the wheel of his black Studebaker. Victor and Rachel had come with Ed and Frances. They were all greeted by several smiling doormen. Two took charge of the cars, and a third, decked out like an admiral, ushered them into the great lobby. Once inside, Louisa halted them.

"Just a moment." She gazed around, trying to take it all in. Slipping her arm into Henry's, she said, very quietly, "It's grand, Pa."

"No more than you deserve."

They neared the high, grand staircase which led to the Empire Room. Victor called out, "You look like a Russian queen, on her way to the throne room." And, in her curly, black lamb coat with the peaked, matching hat, Louisa did look, if not royal, rather Russian.

Henry motioned Victor over and whispered, "You're to dance with everyone tonight."

"Yeah, sure, Dad."

At the foot of the staircase, Victor held back, watching the others ascend. His father and brothers, all unsteady of gait, limped determinedly toward the top. An odd and unpleasant notion crossed his mind. Was this the real source of his father's affection? – that he alone among the Sheffield men was whole and sure of foot, the only son who was not a walking reminder of his father's infirmity, the only son who could be urged to dance with the Sheffield women and spare the family embarrassment on the ballroom floor? He would think about this later – or never. Tonight, he would do as he was bidden. He strode the staircase and caught up with them before the top.

After they'd ordered, Henry slipped Victor a couple of dollars for the bandleader and told him to ask for "My Gal Sal." "First song we ever danced to. Rescue me after a chorus." When the band struck it up, at a slow, safe tempo, Henry led a shy, smiling Louisa onto the dance floor. They moved cautiously to the music, never breaking eye contact.

"They're still happy, after all this time," Victor thought, "but when did they get to be so frail?" What would he and Rachel look like in thirty-nine years? Younger, he thought. Life would be kinder to them, and they'd take care of themselves. He caught a signal from his father and cut in.

When they were back at the table, a pretty cigarette girl took a picture of the group. When it came back to them, everyone but Frances was smiling. Didn't the woman ever smile? Victor had to admit she still managed to look good – better than Paulina who was smiling her face off. But this was no time to be serious. What goes through Frances' head, he wondered? He supposed she was still mad at him for spanking Shorty last Christmas. Yes, it was Christmas, but the kid was on his hands and knees, about to drive a toy car through the snow-covered church under the tree. Victor had worked for days getting that display just right – and what the heck was the brat trying to do? Slaughter the dolls as they prayed at mass? Anyway, Shorty had survived. Frances had snatched him up before Victor could get in more than a few whacks. And then she had raised the roof – in front of everybody, on Christmas!

Henry looked at Victor and nodded in Frances' direction. This was going to be murder. Well, maybe she'd refuse to dance with him. He wouldn't put it past her, even at an anniversary party.

She didn't refuse him though, and it wasn't murder. The band played "All or Nothing at All," and Frances was doing a swell fox trot. Had he never danced with her before? He must have, but tonight, they were the smoothest couple on the floor. She was following, gracefully, even anticipating everything he was doing. He decided to risk getting a little fancier, and still she kept up. He was aware of smiles of admiration from dancers around them. Lordy! Did they think he and Frances were a couple? Who cared? His partner was a woman who loved to dance, and knew what she was doing. She couldn't get much opportunity to show it with Ed. Victor was beginning to think that was a pity. He was not at all anxious for the song to end, and even Frances was smiling. The music stopped, and he surprised himself by saying, "Care for another turn?"

She shook her head. "It's too bad for Paulina that Dennis isn't home on leave. Don't let your sister be a wallflower."

A huge banner draped below the marquee of the Chicago Theater. Rippling in the slight breeze were giant images of Claudette Colbert, Paulette Goddard, and Veronica Lake. They stared up at some unseen enemy, their faces smoldering with patriotic fervor. Victor rolled his eyes at Jack, but Ed said to Frances, "We should steal that for Shorty."

She laughed. "We could drape it over him. When he woke up, he'd think it was Christmas."

"S'pose he's asleep by now?"

"What do you think?"

"Oh, I don't know," said Ed. "Sheila's a pretty ruthless babysitter."

"She's got him in bed, but he's not asleep," said Frances. "I hope we have half as good a time as he thinks he's missing."

They moved inside and became part of the large Friday night crowd waiting for seats. Once inside the auditorium, they weren't all able to sit together, but Victor wound up exactly where he wanted to be, with Rachel on one side of him and his mother on the other. His eyes wandered frequently from the stage to observe their amusement. Jack Durant, the New York comic was being funny maybe every third gag or so. Victor didn't think it a terrible average, and this audience had come to laugh. As the act went on, Durant got a bit risqué, but Louisa wasn't fazed. He was followed by "Fandango Fiesta," a wild ballet with even wilder costumes. The dancer's skirts were a riot of color and flared out for miles when the women twirled. Their headdresses were so high the dancers looked at risk of toppling over. Victor's cheek was pelted with popcorn, and Rachel whispered, "Good thing Paulina didn't see this before the wedding." He liked her like this. He glanced at his mother. Her head was nodding to the music. All was well.

Rachel's playfulness disappeared with the start of the feature.

The plight of the military nurses engaged her rapt attention, and he had their bag of popcorn to himself. Her empathy with their courage and resourcefulness was palpable. Victor liked her like this too, but it surprised him. Clearly, they were watching two different movies. To him, the plot, and the characters, especially Veronica Lake's grim martyr, were so melodramatic and improbable, that he could barely suppress a snicker. Suppress it he did, though, because his wife was stirred and touched. It seemed wise not to tease her about her reaction.

When the lights went up, Rachel shook her head and said bitterly, "They shouldn't have been out there, like sitting ducks."

"I agree," Victor said, cautiously.

"They should have been up in those planes, shooting the hell out of the Jap devils."

Victor said nothing and helped her into her coat. Paulina, waving energetically from a few rows behind, called out, "Ooh hoo," and presently the festive Sheffield motorcade was on its way home.

The rumpled *Tribune* still lay where Shorty had left it, beneath Louisa's dining room table. Its presence would have offended her fastidious sensibilities. Its contents would have offended Victor. Colonel McCormick's editorial scolds were in high dudgeon over the ease of draft deferments in certain quarters. Military service was not a subject he had ever discussed with Rachel, but his father had made his views known bluntly, early in 1942.

"Don't leave the mill, son."

Victor raised an eyebrow and waited for more.

"It may not be where you want to wind up. Probably isn't. I know that, but you can't leave now."

"Can't?"

"It's defense work. It's important."

"I'm an accountant, Pa."

His father glared at him, and Victor thought, *I'm being a bastard, making him spell it out when he really wants not to.*

"I'm sorry, Pa. I understand." But it was too late.

"Do you? Do you understand that at the plant you're protected. You won't have to go. Ed and Jack won't be taken wherever they work, but you'll be snapped up in a second. Your mother and Rachel need you alive. I need you in one piece. You can't leave the mill yet. Promise me!"

"I'm not thinking of leaving, Dad."

"Good. This family doesn't need another hero. We've got Dennis for that, and Paulina is worried sick about him."

She's worried all right, thought Victor, *but it's less about torpedoes than Dennis off the leash in a sailor suit.*

"I mean it," he repeated. "I'm not leaving the mill."

He wasn't lying. Not exactly. He knew the value of being sheltered by defense work, however loosely that was construed. He had no heroic ambitions. His ambitions were political, though best kept under wraps while the war continued and he was out of uniform. Though they had never spoken of them, he felt that, on some level, Rachel must understand these things. He was biding his time.

Victor was a firm believer that you needed to prepare for each new phase of your life if you were to have a soft landing when it arrived. That was what led him to start scouting Sears Roebuck and Company. It was also what led to the end of the charmed life in the doll's house.

⚜

Daniel Weaver had friends in Sears' management. Victor had met them and found them receptive enough to a few of his ideas, but very receptive, doubtless thanks to Dan, to Vic himself. It appeared a good job awaited him unless the war dragged on indefinitely. He was encouraged to explore the 79th street store at his convenience and observe and mingle with the staff. His favorite minglee, after a visit or two, was a bold, dark-haired sales girl named Jeannine. She was playful from the start. They hadn't been speaking for five minutes when she grabbed his ring finger, twisted the wedding band and said, "What a shame."

He laughed at her bawdy sallies but made none of his own. She amused him and kept him sprayed with the sort of naughty flattery he'd been accustomed to before his marriage. If he encouraged her, it was only by not discouraging her, but that was enough. Whatever department he investigated, he had only to stop at the coffee shop and Jeannine would materialize. Without fail, she would coax him to meet elsewhere. Without fail, he would refuse. She developed the alarming habit of slipping her phone number into various pockets. When she left, he would retreat to the men's room and search his clothes carefully for fear of leaving a telltale note for Rachel to misconstrue.

It was an idiotic game, but it was fun and harmless. They were adults after all. What was he supposed to do? Tell her mother? One day, when the coffee counter was all but deserted, she surprised him by dropping onto his lap and putting her arms around his neck. It was ridiculous and dangerous and had to stop immediately. Or pretty soon. He looked down at her and said, "You crazy, reckless witch. Get up, now, and don't come back, ever." He meant it but he was laughing, and she was laughing too. And then she wasn't. Instead, she was looking across the counter, saying, "Who's that?" It was Rachel.

She was gone before he could disentangle himself. He ran through the store and out onto 79th Street. The streetcars were nowhere in sight so she was still here, unless someone else had driven her. His mother didn't drive; neither did Frances. That left only Paulina. God, he hoped Paulina was not going to be part of this mess. If she were here to prod him with her righteous two cents worth, he'd have to strangle her on the spot.

He raced out to the parking lot but saw no sign of Paulina's car. Rachel was still here, secreted somewhere in the store – the ladies room, obviously. He went near enough to keep an eye on the entrance to the restrooms. He couldn't go tearing in there, but he had to speak to her now, to keep what had happened in proportion before it could fester. He'd send a woman in to find out, but who? None of them had ever seen Rachel – except Jeannine, and she'd never come out alive. He needed someone discreet, a woman who wouldn't stink up his job prospects with gossip. Was there anybody? Even if there wasn't, he had to talk to Rachel.

The lingerie counter was closest to where he stood, and there were two clerks on duty. He stepped over, told them his wife had felt ill, and asked if one of them could please check the ladies room. They were quite sympathetic, and the younger of the two went off to find out. After what seemed an eternity, she came back and told him his wife wasn't there. Was she looking at him differently? She'd been gone too long. Rachel was in there all right, and she'd asked the girl to lie. She wasn't coming out. There was nothing to do but go home and wait.

Driving back, he envisioned Rachel coming home alone, on a slow trolley, with too much time to think and torment herself. He wished that she'd let him drive her home, even if that meant stony silence or screaming at him all the way.

Back at the flat, it was over two hours before he heard her footsteps. She reached the top of the stairs and was confronted by the contrite face he'd been sitting there working on. Her eyes slid away in disgust and she went out to the kitchen. She came back with a cup of coffee and stood there staring at him with an expression that caused him physical pain.

"Is her name like music too?"

"She's just a flirt."

"And what are you?" She went back out to the kitchen.

This was not going to be the prolonged shouting match for which he had braced himself. It was going to be quiet and intermittent – the death by a thousand cuts. The kitchen was now her research lab, to which she kept retreating in search of new aspects of his awfulness. It was as though she couldn't bear to talk it straight through in his presence.

"This isn't the first time, is it?"

"There's never been anyone else. There isn't now."

"She knows you pretty well. She was fiddling with your ring."

"She's nothing to me!" he said loudly, then lowered his voice, not knowing what his parents could hear downstairs. "The whole thing was stupid – and wrong – but it was nothing."

"Oh, it was something all right."

She went back to the kitchen, but this time he followed her. She slumped into a chair and said the worst thing of all.

"Thank God I'm not pregnant."

"Oh, don't say that," he pleaded. He was standing behind her and put out his hands to massage her shoulders. "You know you want kids, and they'll be lucky kids to have such a mother – even if they've got a jerk for a father. You know you still want kids." His words were like an incantation now. "You know you do."

"Maybe." Her voice was tight. "But do I want yours?"

"Go ahead," he said, still massaging her. "Get all the bad stuff out of your system. I deserve it. But when you think it all out, you'll see that we're going to have a swell life together. After the war, I've got a great future. We've got a great future. I'm going to get somewhere in politics, you'll see. And you're going to be right up there with me."

Like a wet dog just come inside, she shook herself free of him and spat out, "I'd rather clean dried spinach from a whisk." She got up, went into the bedroom, and closed the door. He could hear her crying at last, out of his sight.

Victor didn't think this was necessarily a bad sign, and he left her to herself for several hours. Then he tapped lightly at the door and went in. She was awake and seemed calmer now. He sat down on the bed but didn't touch her.

"Rae, I'm so sorry. I swear to you, nothing like this will ever happen again."

She sat up against the pillows, not saying anything.

He was begging now. "Honey, after a while it's still going to be okay with us, isn't it?"

"We'll just have to see, I guess," she said gently.

She stayed in the flat for another three weeks, saying nothing to the family of what had happened. He appreciated that, but he knew they knew by the way he tiptoed around her. They were gentle with each other but not easy.

And then she was gone – enlisted.

❧

Why had she judged him so harshly? You weren't born knowing how other people needed to be treated – or wanted to be. He had inflicted pain without meaning to, before he even knew he had the power to do so. And for what? For something so completely unimportant to him as Jeannine? Was this ridiculous non-event at a public lunch counter to make a painful and permanent shambles of their life together? Of his peace of mind? He shook his head and blew out his breath.

He understood now that Rachel needed to have him seal them off within a moat of conspicuous, round-the-clock fidelity, and he thought he could do that. He had flirted his way through life, and it was a bit surprising to be expected to stop, but he could. He would. She must know that, and it ought to count for something. He had given it a lot of thought in the months she'd been gone. It seemed to him that if he could just pretend she were around, whenever things threatened to get interesting, he really would be able to change. He had already tried it out a couple of times, and it helped. But what was the use of any of this, with her a thousand miles away? He was reforming in a vacuum while she refused to consider the possibility that he could. It was maddening that she couldn't see or hear what he was becoming for her.

He thought of her constantly, trying to figure out how she spent her days. Did she think of him at all? At least once an hour, her words snagged his spirit like an open pin. "We'll just have to see." Their tentativeness was illusory, and when he probed them for comfort, they rang with more finality than if she had told him to go to hell.

Well, she could go to hell if she planned to drag this out forever. If she couldn't forgive him, he would scale his heights with someone else, someone who didn't demand to live in a world of perfection – someone who realized it didn't exist.

But it almost had existed with Rae. They had lived in a charmed, perfect world – or as close to it as he was ever likely to come. He sat wracked with the conviction that whatever heights he scaled, and with whomever he scaled them, it would never amount to what it would have with Rae. He had to convince her. He had to bring her back. She hadn't absolutely slammed the door. She had said, "We'll just have to see."

❦

"Coconut bars or ginger snaps? There's not enough left of the pound cake."

"Oh let's just pile all three on the tray."

The voices and laughter from his mother's kitchen grew louder, but they came at him across the distance he had traveled into his private world. The scramble to get back to his public one was not only jarring, it was unimaginable. He looked down at his hand and only now saw the blood.

His mother and Mrs. Weaver would soon be upon him. Stand up. Cross the floor. Climb upstairs. Explain later. This was what he sorely needed to do, but none of it was happening. Now the women were in front of him, armed with treats, staring. He felt exposed beyond nakedness. They could see not just through his clothes, but his skin.

It was Maude who spoke. "Judas Priest, Victor! You've gripped that picture frame so tight you've cut yourself. You can't make it talk, you know. Louisa, get some cotton and adhesive tape. Is there any mercurochrome?"

Neither Sheffield spoke. His mother left the room, and Maude's tone softened.

"I shouldn't tease you." She set the tray aside and gently pried his hands from the frame.

His mother returned, knelt beside his chair, and set to work. Maude took a napkin from the tray and wiped the blood from the frame.

"Too tight?" asked Louisa. Victor shook his head.

Maude surveyed the living room. "I'll just put this out of harm's way, but somewhere everyone can enjoy it. What about here?"

Rachel Shalifu Sheffield smiled at them from atop a lace doily on the floor model radio.

"Sometimes," Maude said brightly, "it will be like she's singing to us."

It struck Victor that the photograph, like its subject, was taking on an independent life of its own, far removed from his influence. For a moment, they regarded it with a trio of quite different silences, broken at last by Maude.

"She looks at home in that uniform."

Victor stood, and saying only, "She's not," he crossed the room and went upstairs.

CHAPTER 5
ROUTE 66
Chicago: November, 1947

1. Wednesday

No longer dreaming but still closer to sleep than waking, Ed felt the first swell of the tide that would push him to the shore of consciousness. He knew, dimly, that he should resist it. He should fight to remain in this lovely, safe, dark velvet sea. But he couldn't remember why. Something unwelcome waited for him ashore. The next swell would make it clear, or the one after that. Whatever awaited him could not be avoided, but it was good to put it off as long as possible.

He shifted position, and as he turned he felt the unfamiliar touch of metal above his head. This was not his own bed. He bumped ashore on one last large wave of lucidity, and without opening his eyes, he knew exactly where he was and why delaying his arrival had been so important. He lay in the in-a-door bed at Frances's apartment.

Burrowing into the pillow, he kept his eyes shut while the fog of medication dispersed to permit the return of clarity and pain. Three days ago, at the bottom of the stairway to Our Lady of Peace, he had been startled and pulled to the ground by the electric grip of a vise inside his chest clamping his lungs together. Thrusting his arm out to break his fall, he had only succeeded in jamming it with his full weight against an iron banister. Confused and unable to raise himself, he had looked up at the wide-eyed face bending over him and managed to say only, "It's all right, Shorty." This was far from true. His son made several attempts to lift him, then turned to the crowd exiting around them.

"Be careful! Don't step on him! It's my father."

Ed realized with apprehension that, for the moment, his situation was not in his own control but that of his ten-year-old son. This would soon prove to be a mixed blessing. With pride and relief, he saw that Shorty was not about to panic and would in fact be able to make some arrangements without leaving his side. This was followed by a second and rather disquieting discovery – the perverse resourcefulness with which the child would exploit this turn of events.

"Can someone help us?" the young voice piped up. "Will somebody please see if there was a doctor at mass? It's my father." How sweetly that phrase resonated above Ed as he remained prostrate on the church steps, disoriented, throbbing with pain and fearful of where his body proposed to take him. "It's my father." Over and over it sang out to the strangers around him like a commanding bell: "This is a person of significance. You cannot pass him by. You must stop and help him."

And they did. This being Our Lady of Peace, there were not one but several physicians in the crowd. Had Ed's troubles been of a legal nature, those too might have been addressed.

"Get me home, Shorty," he whispered, "not to a hospital." A doctor bent to examine him, and several men stood ready to give assistance. Shorty dug into the pocket of his father's overcoat and withdrew the car keys. It was determined Ed would lie still until the doctor's wife could pull the Buick up to the curb. The doctor would drive them home with his wife following in another car. Ed felt dazed, and the passage of time seemed especially peculiar, as if he had tripped over some temporal wire, disconnecting it as he fell.

Shorty and the doctor hovered with concern as Ed was raised upright and steadied by a stranger at each arm. They moved to the car in slow motion, and Ed attempted to give directions. "What's that?" said the doctor. "Did he say Manistee?" But Shorty had other plans.

"No, that's my grandmother's house. It's too far away. We live just three blocks from here. It's really close. We'll take good care of him there."

Ed sought his son's eyes, but Shorty evaded his gaze. Things were quickly getting away from Ed, but he was too exhausted to protest. He and Frances were to be under the same roof once more.

Gently, inexorably, well-meaning strangers conveyed Ed up the long stairway to the third floor. At the first landing, he passed out, from pain of course, but also to flee the inevitable end of this involuntary journey. Nothing was clear to him for a good while afterward. He awoke, to the extent that he did, to a blur of hushed activity around him. Strangers spoke about him but not to him. Phantom Shortys and Franceses steadied his head to feed him liquids and place tablets on his tongue. Mostly he slept.

Late on the second day (or so they told him—he couldn't seem to grasp the passage of time) he recognized Dr. Burke and made an effort to focus his attention during the diagnosis. He had had a heart attack, and in his fall had bruised his head as well as his arm. Nothing was broken, and there was no concussion. He would recover but must have a great deal of rest and quiet. For the present, he was not to be moved from the apartment. He had too many jobs and was getting too little sleep. He must slow down and watch what he ate. Fruit and fish were good. Fat and coffee were bad. So were wild motorcycle escapades.

Good old Dr. Burke. That made it unanimous. Except for Ed's brother, Jack, the entire world was now in agreement that his motorcycle trip to California with Warren Trumbaugh had been the worst of all possible bad ideas. His infamous getaway had even managed for once to put his mother and Frances on the same side of an argument. What none of them could grasp was that the trip, however sophomoric, had saved his life and his sanity. Far from harming him, he fiercely believed it had kept him from arriving even sooner at this strange bed. Here in the apartment, it came to his aid as his most recurrent dream. But now he was awake.

Shorty sat nearby, watching him.

"Hello, Daddy."

A yawn took hold of Ed before he could speak. "Hello there." His own voice sounded strange and weak to him. "Is it morning?"

"No, it's late. It's dark out now." The child's voice was calm, intended to soothe. Ed started to turn to the side, but the pain in his arm and chest brought him up short. "I'm glad you woke up by yourself," said his son. "When you're sleeping good, I hate to wake you, and it's time for you to take another one of these." Ed did as he was told.

"I'm confused, Shorty. Help me get this straight. Where's your mother?"

"She's gone to Gramma and Grampa Foley's. She's sleeping there for now."

"So you're with me at night?"

"Uh huh." To the boy, it was a perfectly sensible arrangement.

"That's no good, Shorty. You'll be tired for school tomorrow." He frowned. "Or is it the weekend? I'm a little mixed up."

"It's Wednesday, but I'm not going to school this week. Maybe next week if you're better."

Ed sat up carefully. "This isn't right."

Shorty came to the bed and put his hand on Ed's arm. "Please try to relax, Daddy. It scares me when you get upset. Dr. Burke says it's really important that you don't get upset."

The boy's words conveyed several messages. Ed digested them all in silence and said at last, "Don't be scared. I'm not upset. I'm lucky to have you here. You're doing a man's job. Do you know that?"

Shorty said only, "I guess," but Ed could feel the warmth he had ignited in the boy. "Would you like something to eat?" the child asked.

"I would, yes, a little. What's on the menu at this hour?"

"You could have zwieback, or graham crackers and milk. Or I could make you some scrambled eggs. I'll beat them up good so you won't see any white. There's tomato soup—oh, and Uneeda biscuits."

"My stomach may have forgotten how it works," said Ed. "I'll test it on some Uneeda biscuits first."

Shorty padded to the kitchen in his bare feet and brought back a dish towel which he spread out on his father's chest. "Crumbs in bed are nasty," he advised. Then he produced a dish of airy crackers and a glass of ginger ale with a straw.

Ed munched and sipped and looked about the room. "Raise the shades, will you, Shorty?"

There was only darkness, with a bit of moon.

"Did you think I was kidding you?"

"No… I just wanted to look. It's odd here, so quiet with just the two of us. We could be anywhere."

Shorty smiled. "Maybe we're on Mars. This is what it looks like."

His son was teasing him. Somehow, after an episode of exotic behavior by his children, Ed had begun to refer to them as "my little Martian boys." "What did I do to deserve these little Martian boys?" he would ask, and they would giggle uproariously. They cherished the label, taking it exactly as Ed intended it, not "Why am I cursed with these aliens?" but "How have I managed to earn them?" They sensed, correctly, that however the rest of the world might view their ornate eccentricities, their father saw them as sheer perfection.

Ed handed the dish and the glass back to his son. "It wasn't much of a spot, but that hit it."

"Good," said Shorty. From the kitchen, he added, "Maybe you'll be hungry later. We're open all night."

"It's just like New York," Ed remarked contentedly.

When his son returned to the bedside, Ed asked him, "How do you keep yourself amused here these days?"

Shorty's eyes danced upward as if to say, *Where do I begin?* "Let me show you something." He went behind the bed, and Ed heard him rooting around in the closet. He came back bearing the empty exterior of a Philco table model radio.

"How did that get over here? I wondered where it went."

"When you gutted it for the tubes, I didn't think you wanted it anymore." Shorty seemed apologetic.

"No, no, you're welcome to it, but what...?"

Shorty climbed onto the bed, smiling. "It's my theater, the Shield. That's short for Sheffield, but it's also the logo for my movie studio, Shield Pictures."

Ed nodded. "Uh-huh."

Shorty produced a pack of index cards. "These are the credits for the movie I'm working on now. It's called *Shattered*."

"Hmmmm," said Ed.

"I've got the theme music pretty much worked out. I'll hum it while I do the credits. I hope it's not too close to what Franz Waxman did for *Cry Wolf*. Mom and I saw that on Halloween, and it sort of got stuck in my head."

"That happens," said Ed, smiling.

"Well, here goes." Shorty crouched down to disappear behind the Philco. "The first part, the Shield fanfare, is always the same." In the oblong window that once housed the station dial, Shorty placed a card showing a crown above a shield that read SHIELD PRODUCTIONS PRESENT." He hummed a few notes of soaring portent.

"Quite a fanfare."

"You've got to get their attention. I've seen people sleeping at the movies!" The next card, in thick, flowing cursive, read "DICK POWELL and NINA FOCH in..." More humming, less portentous.

"Nina Foch?"

"She's not getting anywhere at Columbia, Daddy, and she has a lot of potential. This is going to be a career-making picture for her."

"I see," said Ed. "She'll thank you one day."

"I think so. You never can tell, but she seems nice." On the next card, SHATTERED, the letters were blurry and seemed to be exploding, as did the theme music. "I didn't start out with the title because the actors feel important if their names come first."

Ed chewed his lip. "You're worried that actors won't feel important?"

"Well, not Dick Powell, but it's just courteous, and I want to show Nina Foch I have confidence in her."

Several cards followed with a long list of supporting players as Shorty rang subtle changes on the main theme. Ed recognized a few of the names but had to ask, "Are these all real people?"

Shorty's head popped up from behind the Philco with a startled and somewhat offended expression. "Who, for instance?"

Ed chose his words with care. "Uh, well ... Victor Francen?"

"Oh, Daddy, you'd know him in a minute. Nobody is more suave and civilized than Victor Francen. He's in a lot of my pictures. He's always cheerful, even in the middle of his evil doings. If he's caught and they're going to kill him, he just shrugs and chuckles."

"Sounds like quite a guy."

The cards continued until no one in front of, behind, or under the camera had gone unacknowledged. Shorty stopped humming and painstakingly rearranged the cards for the next showing. Ed spoke without thinking. "But then what?"

Shorty looked at him, crestfallen. "Well, you see, the rest is in my head."

"I'll bet it's a pip," Ed said warmly.

"It's a pip all right, very psychological. It's about this woman who –"

Ed put out his hand and squeezed his son's arm. "I think I need to sleep now, buddy."

2. Thursday

Ed coughed himself awake in wracking spasms. He fought to stifle the sound, which, of all the trappings of his illness, alarmed his son the most. For a parent, the worst thing about pain can be watching it reflected back at you in the distressed eyes of your child. Lacking an adult's gift for hearty dissembling around the sick, a child's expression is not only incapable of minimizing the seriousness of your condition, it is more likely to magnify it. So it was with Shorty's troubling gaze of concern. Kindly meant, it was doing neither of them any good.

Ed's mind trolled for the right words to refocus the boy to the safety of the ordinary, but he was tired. "How's school?" he offered, but he had chosen badly, unaware of the seismic shift this topic had undergone since last they spoke of it.

"I hate it!" the boy spat out. Ed was surprised and curious but doubted he had the energy to participate in the conversation that now threatened to take place.

"You're not having trouble with your studies?"

Shorty's many-syllabled "no" was crammed with subtext: "of course not, don't you know me anymore?"

"Well... what's wrong?" If the boy would only just talk, Ed could manage to lie there and listen.

"Sister Immaculate hates me."

Ed tried to outwait the silence that followed but feared he would fall asleep. Sleep would be sweet and he would prefer it, but you mustn't fall asleep when a child has just said something like that. He would make the effort.

"Nobody hates you, Shorty. Nobody ever will. Why do you use that word so much? You're ten years old. Hate is a little boy's word. It doesn't happen very much outside of movies and stories. Love is real. Hate is…" Shorty looked dubious, and Ed feared he'd begun to ramble to no purpose. Mercifully, Shorty was ready to take over.

"All right then, Sister Immaculate dislikes me intensely. That's not an exaggeration. It's a fact. She told me she thought I was positively pukey. She whispered it to me during a test, so no one else could hear her. She hissed it at me like a snake."

The conversation, though Ed hoped it would be mostly a monologue, was showing possibilities of keeping him awake without difficulty. "She did this during a *test?*"

"Yes." Shorty paused for effect, pleased that his father recognized that the situation added injury to the insult. "The more I think about it, she probably meant to throw me off. I didn't let her, but it still hurt."

Memories of Ed's days at St. Brides lent Shorty's tale plausibility. Ed recalled the hushed, apprehensive waits with his classmates each September. Whispers of possible candidates and the scars they had left on older siblings would circulate ominously around the recess yard. Tension mounted until at last one of the good ladies would emerge from the stone edifice and reveal herself as the mistress of their destinies for the coming year. The academic background of these women was seldom in question, but their fitness to be set loose among children ranged through the entire spectrum of human behavior, from Marmee to Medea.

"Tell me about Sister Immaculate." Ed had been sitting up, but now he settled back to let the child's words pour over him. He watched a warm look of gratitude come over his son's face for the license he'd been granted. Shorty paused and put his fingers together in a way that was familiar to Ed. The boy was taking time to organize his thoughts for the best possible presentation. The child nodded to himself, then leaned in close to his father and began.

"She's very clean. I think she's the cleanest person I've ever seen. Her face and her hands—that's all we can see of her in the habit—they always look like she's just scrubbed them a million times. Her skin is so pale you can almost see through it, like a fish, or I guess, an angel. But she's no angel. She's the wickedest person I can imagine." Shorty stopped for breath and to gauge his father's reaction. "Is wicked like hate?"

"A bit." Ed nodded. "But not as much." His hand pushed up from under the woolen blanket and beckoned the boy to go on.

"Well, what I mean by wicked is she knows how to make every single one of us cry, and she likes to do it. We're in fifth grade already so it's really embarrassing, but there's not one of us she hasn't gotten to cry. She spreads it around. I'll give her that. She doesn't have favorites. She let a couple of the girls think she did, but that was just so they'd feel even worse when she went for them. You never know who it's going to be. You just know it's going to be somebody, practically every day. Some days she does double headers." Shorty gave a grim little laugh and then went on. "Sometimes you start to think she's forgotten, if it gets near two o'clock and everybody is still in one piece. But then she'll do it. You don't think there's enough time left, but she's like a magician. You don't realize you're the victim for the day when she starts. She's so quiet and calm about it. She never raises her voice. She just pushes and pushes and it starts to get personal and scary and you realize it's going to be you and there's nothing you can do about it. Before the bell rings, you're going to be crying in front of everybody. Then when you do, she acts surprised and disgusted. When she says, "Get control of yourself!" that's how you know it's over."

Ed started to speak, but a coughing spasm took hold of him. Shorty stepped around the bed to the lady-legged table. He took up a tablespoon and a bottle of thick amber liquid and brought them to his father's side. He stood grimacing for a long moment before there were sufficient gaps between the coughs for him to feed his father the medicine without spilling it. That had happened twice, but now Shorty knew the level to which the coughing must ebb before the syrup could be administered.

"I'm sorry," he said. "I won't talk about that any more. It's upsetting you."

His father shook his head and motioned for a pad and pencil. The spasm had subsided, but trying to speak would only set it off again. He wrote quickly and held the pad up toward Shorty. The message read, "Cough just comes. Not upset. Need to know whole thing. Tell me."

Despite his father's gestures, Shorty wouldn't resume until the smallest cough was stilled. "Well," he said at last, "The funny thing is, we used to treat each other worse than we do now that we know all these things about each other that we shouldn't. We're kinder than when we had somebody nice in charge of us. I mean, we're relieved that somebody else is getting it, but nobody ever laughs or brings it up later to make fun of you… and they certainly could." Shorty shuddered. "It's not exactly that we're nicer; it's just it could be you the next day – or the next minute if you react to what's going on. Sister Immaculate likes nothing better than to catch one of us snickering about some other kid's private life. Charles Carmody did that, and in a flash, he's bawling and Renee Worth is off the hook.

None of us ever forgot that lesson, and nobody ever said a word to Charles about it either."

His father could talk again, but slowly and cautiously. "How does she know these things?"

"She keeps secret files."

Ed shook his head and smiled.

"I know it sounds stupid, Daddy, but I caught her at it once and she was furious."

It wasn't like Shorty to lie, but this was a little... "You caught her at her secret files?"

Shorty sprang up from his chair and wedged himself onto the bed, in the crook of his father's legs. He spoke quickly and with considerable animation. "Here's what happened. She has this stand next to her desk with a statue of the Blessed Virgin on it, and Mary's crying. Sister says it's there to remind us how much pain we gave our mothers when we came into the world."

Charming, thought Ed, but he reserved comment.

"So, anyway, this big marble thing appears in front of Mary one day. It looked like an ashtray but that didn't make sense, so I decided it must be for flower petals or something, like a May altar, only in November. Then Sister Immaculate tells us it's there to burn the secret messages we're going to write to the Blessed Virgin."

"Sounds like a lot of smoke in the classroom."

"I know." Shorty smiled, encouraged by his father's irreverence. "Well, now it gets to the good part."

"I've been waiting."

Shorty disliked sarcasm in most people, but his father's was of a warmer variety, not meant to hurt him. In fact, it made them seem like old chums. He lowered his voice conspiratorially and went on.

"She said that Mary would intercede for us with God and reduce our punishment if we were really honest and wrote down the worst things we had ever done on the slips of paper she was passing out. She said the messages would be secret and nobody would see them, not even her, only Mary."

Ed arched his eyebrows. Shorty nodded and said, "I knew you'd see where this was going. Then she tells us to put our name on the slip. I knew better than to ask why the Blessed Virgin, who knows everything, would need our names, but poor Charles Carmody didn't, so he asks her. You should have seen the look she gave him. He's a nasty kid, but sometimes I'm glad he's in the class. This time, I thought he had her dead to rights, and you could see she was thinking up something hideous to do to him later. But then, as cool as a cucumber, she says, "It's a sin to write anonymous notes.""

"I'm impressed," said Ed, shifting his position. The blanket slipped down as he moved, and Shorty reached out to cover his father's neck and shoulders.

"Well," the boy resumed, "I didn't know what anybody else was going to write, but after that I certainly wasn't going to give away any of *my* dark secrets for Sister Immaculate's reading pleasure."

Ed smiled at his son and asked, "Do you have a *lot* of dark secrets?"

Shorty looked uncomfortable and muttered, "I don't know. Maybe a couple."

"I won't ask what you wrote on your slip."

"Oh, I'll tell you that. It was nothing. I put down the most boring, harmless stuff I could think of. I said that once I thought of teasing Anthony. I almost laughed out loud when I wrote it. I knew how annoyed and disappointed Sister Immaculate would be."

"If she read it."

Shorty's eyes grew wide. "Oh, she read it all right. I left my speller in the room on purpose, and when I went back to get it, there she was, not only reading the slips but making notes about them in a ledger."

"The secret file!" Ed squinted and asked, "Does she know you saw her at it?"

"Yes," said Shorty quietly, "and it's been worse on me since then. Sometimes I can be as dumb as Charles."

"At least," said Ed, consolingly, "she doesn't know anything bad about you."

"She does though." Shorty was barely audible now.

"How?"

The boy looked down at the floor. "She gets help," he whispered, "from Grandma."

Ed stared at his son. The boy did not look up. Ed closed his eyes and lay back to digest what he had just been told. It was unwelcome news, and Shorty's demeanor suggested both that there was more to be told and that it would not be readily volunteered. The conversation was over. Now there would only be silence or, if he had the stomach for it, interrogation.

He swallowed once and lay motionless. With the boy's last words, a bill on which Ed had been granted many extensions was now presented. Ed had robbed from his time with the children to pay for the divorce and the move. The second job and the courses which made it possible had been absolutely necessary, and guilt about them would serve no purpose. The divorce had been his decision. Frances' moods had grown blacker and more destructive, and the intervals between them had shortened to the point where he no longer had time to recover from one before the next was upon him. She was like a sharp-bladed machine whose vibrations had torn it loose from its moorings.

As for the move, Frances had forced his hand on that. In quieter, happier times, he had approached Mrs. Neiderman about eventually buying the bungalow, and she was agreeable. Frances herself had seemed pleased at first, but then the idea took hold of her that Mrs. Neiderman was taking advantage, even spying on them. Nothing he said could dislodge this fantasy. There began to be cryptic, then insulting comments made in the presence of their landlady. These escalated to dramatic confrontations loud enough to be heard by the neighbors. Soon there was no longer any question of their remaining as tenants, let alone prospective buyers. Mrs. Neiderman refused to renew their lease, and they were unceremoniously asked to vacate the premises.

Up to that point, Frances' dark moods had been unpredictable but intermittent. In the final days at the bungalow they were constant and chilling. Equally so, for Ed, was the prospect of starting over with her somewhere else. He couldn't. Things might have dragged on indefinitely where they were, but to uproot and begin again with the same outcome, inevitable, accelerated… it was unimaginable. Frances had taken them all into a spooky hall of mirrors and unreality. He had to smash a way out of it for himself and the boys. Father Walsh was understanding and resourceful. Arrangements were made so quietly and discreetly that few outside the family (and not everyone within it), knew exactly what was taking place. There would be a divorce, but he and Frances would continue to receive the sacraments of the church. The price was a pledge never to remarry.

Ed snatched at the first spot he found to settle Frances. She and the boys must have somewhere to see each other as long as… unless.., He knew she'd never harm them, but if her deterioration continued, they could be neglected and frightened. In any case, the warm and happy reception awaiting them at his parents' would be a welcome contrast.

But that was then, before two years of hindsight. This conversation with Shorty was only the latest indication that he had picked the wrong household to worry about. His head felt heavy.

Whatever needed fixing would have to wait. The mere thought of it exhausted him. He closed his eyes and took once more to the road.

3. Thursday Night

Ed opened his eyes and was pleased to see absolutely nothing. He didn't know what time it was, but all the lights in the apartment were out. Frances would have gone to her parents by now, and at the foot of the bed, though Ed couldn't see him, Shorty would be curled up on the couch sound asleep. Well, no, not sound asleep. During these night watches, the boy slumbered tentatively, like a sentry dog, able to shake himself awake at the sound of a cough or a murmured request. Ed lay still. The faithful dog had earned his rest, and in these close quarters, it was luxurious to be unobserved. Cloaked in shadow, he could re-examine the trip at his leisure.

Warren Trumbaugh had proposed the getaway at precisely the point where Ed had come to wonder if any of his life were really his own. He'd almost gotten used to the scramble to keep afloat, and it helped that a few people had owned television sets long enough for them to start breaking down. He preferred it when the repairs were not simple. If he had to bring a set home and work on it in the basement, he was at least available to the boys, if not actually with them. But there was seldom any time unaccounted for. Then this spring, his father died, and his mother became more dependent on him. He understood, but the change in their relationship virtually erased the last scraps of his time that weren't committed to someone else's wellbeing.

He was about to go under when Warren showed up and threw him a gaudy life preserver. Frances had never been comfortable with Warren, and their evenings with Warren and Miriam had gone the way of so much else that Ed found agreeable: from frequent to seldom to never. He hadn't stopped thinking about them, however, and he was tickled when Warren deduced the coast was clear and breezed in with a lulu of a proposal.

"We'll just *go!* We'll see everything there is on Route 66 and then some. We'll go down the Grand Canyon. We'll ogle movie stars. My cousin in Los Angeles will be glad to put us up when we get there. I've got a motorcycle now. We'll travel light, and it won't cost that much. We can do it in a couple weeks. You're gonna love it!"

Ed had never been so tempted in his life. He just grinned and said nothing. As long as he didn't open his mouth, he hadn't refused, and it was still a possibility. All he intended was to keep it that way for a few more seconds. Warren threw him a playful jab. "You won't even need to go halves with me. I want the company. I've missed ya."

"Oh, I'll pay my way."

"Yeah, yeah." Warren waived his hand dismissively, but then his mouth dropped open. They smiled at each other like Katzenjammer Kids. Ed's tense had trapped him. He'd meant to use the conditional. Instead, he'd accepted on the spot. It was meant to be. It was crazy and self-indulgent, but he wouldn't go back on it now.

He kept mum as long as he dared, to minimize the time for objections, but when his intentions became known, all hell broke loose, even in outposts where it was nobody's business, like his sister Paulina's.

"Across the country! On a motorcycle! With *your* legs!"

"With my legs, my keester, and my baby blues. Good night, big sister." As he replaced the receiver, Ed reflected that, with her vocal charms and sense of delicacy, Paulina could have a busy career playing all those soon-to-be-murdered wives on *Suspense* and *The Whistler.*

His brother Jack told him to have a good time and bring back some pictures, but otherwise the outrage and condemnation were universal. He resented the righteous outcry, but though it disappointed him, it didn't move him, which further miffed his small army of critics.

He really went. He couldn't believe it any more than those he left behind. It was as exhilarating as Warren predicted, and as liberating as Ed had hoped. They darted across the country through sun and wind and rain, accumulating stories for a lifetime. They made good time but dawdled when it suited them, particularly at the Grand Canyon. Their combined driving skills failed them only once, on a rainy night in New Mexico when a swerving truck forced them off the road and they slid halfway down an embankment. Roughed up and shaken, they stayed where they landed until dawn. Warren had been at the wheel, but Ed assured him the result would have been the same either way.

Warren's luck was no better on the doorstep of his Los Angeles cousin. A party was in progress, and they weren't being asked in. "We thought you were coming later in the week," said the cousin, planted firmly in their path. Warren looked miserable.

"We made good time," he said.

The cousin continued his outstanding job of filling the doorway, but music and laughter spilled around his shoulders. A female voice called out, "What is it, Jay?"

"It's nothing, honey."

It was nothing. They were nothing. Warren, who couldn't look at Ed, was melting from embarrassment.

"I don't want to rush you, Warren," said Ed, "but now that you've let your cousin know you're in town, we've got to get going. We're expected for dinner."

"Yeah, sorry, Ed," said Warren, backing down the steps. "See you around, Jay."

"Yes, be sure to do that," said the disappearing Jay.

"Be sure to kiss my ass," muttered Warren. He shook his head and looked up at Ed. "Jeezus Christ!" When they reached the motorcycle, Warren asked, "So just who exactly is expecting us for dinner, Ace?"

Ed shrugged. "Beats me. Although… why don't you try to find us a phone booth."

As they took off, Warren yelled over his shoulder, "Thanks for back there, buddy."

"Skip it," yelled Ed. "Families are fun. I've got one too."

When they spotted a booth and pulled over, Warren said, "I didn't know you knew anybody in L.A."

"Frances's brother Brandon lives out here somewhere. We used to get along. It's just a chance."

A very good chance. Brandon was in and insisted they come over immediately. When they found the house, a knockout that he had designed himself, Brandon fell all over them. Frances was asked about, but Brandon was as tactful as a diplomat. He seemed genuinely hungry for news of home, though Ed got the feeling his brother-in-law would never return. He and his wife had eaten, but Martha put steaks on the grill and had two guest rooms made up for them. Brandon wouldn't hear of them staying anywhere else while they were in town, and he became their tour guide for the next several days.

Movie stars materialized as promised, the highlight being Rita Hayworth, a flaming vision at the Brown Derby. Ed had been told some years back that Brandon was doing well, but Frances' mother's boasts had a spiteful edge, and he took them with a grain of salt. The reality of Brandon's success took Ed by surprise. In the den were framed pages from a recent Sunday roto spread devoted to stunning homes Brandon had built in Carmel. The prominence of the owners' names was jaw-dropping.

On the second night, Brandon came out to the pool and told

them, "Dry off, fellas. You're going to a party."

Ed shot Warren a look then said, "That's good of you, Brandon, but you and Martha go ahead. We don't want to cramp your style, and we wouldn't be dressed for it."

Brandon swatted him with a towel. "Neither will anybody else, Ed. It's a party, not a ball."

Ed was quite out of the habit of parties, but he took to this one in short order. Dress was indeed casual, though some of the outfits looked like they had cost an arm and a leg. Ushered in by Brandon and Martha, he and Warren were accepted not as gawking Midwestern hicks but fresh faces to season a familiar crowd. Jinx Falkenburg was drawing Warren out about motorcycles when Frances Faye arrived and Brandon waved her over.

"Give your pinkies a rest tonight," he said. "I brought a piano man from Chicago you're gonna like."

The singer swept their group with a withering glance. "Nobody done told me this was amateur night."

"Don't be a witch," Martha cooed up at her. "He's our brother-in-law."

With a jolt, Ed realized he was the subject of this exchange.

"Oh, brother-in-law!" Faye rolled her eyes. "Come on," she said, wiggling a hand at Ed. "Let's get this over with." She dragged him to the piano shouting, "Somebody's gonna owe me a cantilevered beach house for this." Then, with Ed beside her on the piano bench, she said very quietly, "You got anything, or is this strictly for laughs?"

"I'm as surprised as you are. Let's make the best of it – something quick, and I'll be out of your hair."

She eyed him coolly and with non-existent expectations. Perhaps she owed Brandon a favor. "Take it away."

Ed noodled for a few seconds, then went into "Don't Get Around Much Anymore," giving it a gently rocking rhythm. Under his breath, he said, "This should be my theme song." She watched him approvingly and joined in the second time through. He made split second adjustments where she chose to shorten or draw out a phrase, and they finished at the same time, in the same key. There were smiles and a bit of applause from those nearby, and he grinned and wiggled his eyebrows at Brandon as if to say, "I made it out alive."

To Frances Faye, he said, "Thanks a bunch. I appreciate it," and stood up to leave. She grabbed his collar and pulled him back down. "Where ya goin'? Where ya goin'?" she said for the room to hear. "You got 'Frankie and Johnnie?'" He did, and they did it, then "Summertime," "Ain't Misbehavin'," "Anything Goes," and "Time on My Hands." She trusted him now and relaxed into a more rambunctious delivery. The response grew warmer with each number, as people drifted in from other rooms and gathered around the piano. Finally, in a long and hair-curlingly off-color version of "Love Me or Leave Me," she dedicated herself unsuccessfully to trying to make him blush and blunder. At the finish, she threw her arms around him and cried out, "Keep the beach house. I want this guy!"

And then it was over. All too soon, they were back in Chicago. For the next week and a half, there was another person in the world who had seen it all and done it all with him. They had only to look at each other to feel the splendor of their motley odyssey surge inside them. Ed thought they would have it for good. Then a signal gate failed to operate and a train slammed into the motorcycle, dragging Warren out of Ed's life forever.

Now it was only there in his head, and no one wanted him to speak of it. It was only to be taken out and examined, as now, by himself, in the dark.

4. Friday

Ed could tell Shorty knew when he was thinking about the trip. Since his father had come back, the boy had added a new look to his repertoire, an appraising tilt of the head combined with a searching stare and just enough of a squint and a contraction of the shoulders to suggest he was bracing to ward off a blow. It made Ed squirmy, all the more because he had yet to see it directed at anyone else. Children, like jurists, place great stock in precedent, and Ed's abrupt sojourn had been unprecedented.

Shorty had earned the right to give him such looks, Ed supposed, but their duration and frequency conveyed that his eldest son now saw him as someone unpredictable who, having tasted escape, was capable of committing an endless series of far flung disappearances upon the family. The force of the look at the moment, with its unasked and unbearable question "You're thinking of how to leave us right now, aren't you?" made Ed wonder if, had the child produced it in June, it could have forestalled the trip. He wasn't sure.

The look, as now, usually preceded an inquiry about Route 66, as though, by focusing on the past, Shorty hoped to circumvent the future.

"Tell me about Rolla."

"Again?" Ed asked, but he was not surprised.

"I like it. It's one of the best parts."

And Ed knew why. His son was incredulous that someone could go all the way to Hollywood without setting foot in a movie theater. It was clear that if he had had the foresight to return with details of the marquees and interiors of Grauman's Chinese or the Egyptian (how did his son even know of these places?), Ed might have bribed his way out of the look.

"Okay. Well, we took the St. Louis bypass into Missouri to make time, and we crossed the river on the Chain of Rocks Bridge – the longest bridge I've ever crossed, with a bend right in the middle and the Mississippi sprawling below it. I wish you could have seen that, Shorty."

"Me too," his inquisitor reproached.

It was best just to go on, and as Ed well knew, there was no other audience for this tale. "By the time we got to Rolla, we were hungry, and Warren knew a good place to eat."

"The Blackberry Patch!"

"Yes," said Ed, with complimentary enthusiasm.

"At the top of the hill."

"You're right." *This act is set*, thought Ed. *We could take it on the road with matching outfits. Shorty could sit on my knee.*

"What was it like?"

"It was a large white turn-of-the-century house, and the rooms had been stripped of furniture to make way for the tables and chairs. We ate in a bay room off to the side, and like all the rooms, it had pictures and prints of famous racehorses on every wall: Seabiscuit, Whirlaway, and even Dan Patch." Shorty's eyes slid to the side, consulting some internal checklist of detail. His father went on. "The cook, the woman who owns the place, raised horses with her husband, and she loves to talk about them."

"Was she a good cook?" With each telling, the story lengthened and spun off in new directions before reaching its predestined conclusion.

"She was a prize," said Ed. "Nothing out of the ordinary but everything exactly as you liked it. Juicy, crispy fried chicken, hot baking powder biscuits, mashed potatoes with a boat of terrific gravy."

"Lumps?" asked Shorty, leaning forward.

"Not a one. You'd have asked for seconds."

The look was gone, replaced with a contented smile. "Was there pie?"

"Homemade peach or rhubarb that night, served warm, with ice cream if you asked her nicely."

Shorty paused to savor it, then steered back into familiar territory. "You were all tired out by then," he said, coming over to the bed.

"Exhausted, both of us. We didn't want to go any farther." Ed shifted over so Shorty could sit beside him.

"But you didn't know where you were going to sleep." Shorty sidled in and plumped his father's pillow.

"No, we didn't. The motel was full, and it could have been the cold stony ground for us."

"The cold, stony ground," Shorty echoed with relish.

"We threw ourselves on the mercy of the horsewoman and asked if anyone took roomers for the night."

"But she eyed you with suspicion," interrupted Shorty, almost stepping on his father's line.

Ed raised his eyebrows and nodded solemnly. "She eyed us with considerable suspicion."

"She sized you up as shady characters," Shorty said eagerly, "because it was the 'show-me' state."

"Not only that," Ed amended. "We were covered with five hundred miles of road grime and sporting eight o'clock shadow. We *looked* like shady characters."

Shorty sang out with glee, "But then the little Martian boys saved your bacon, just in the nick of time!"

"You surely did," said his father. "Luckily, I had prepared for just such a turn of events by concealing about my person a photo of you and Anthony which I whipped out and thrust before her flinty gaze."

"And she couldn't resist us." Shorty nestled his head against his father's.

"She never had a chance… although I do believe it was Anthony who caught her fancy," Ed whispered.

"Hmmmm."

They both stared up at the apartment's crack-lined ceiling. Shorty lowered his voice because they were so close. "Then what?"

"She directed us to a friend of hers, a Mrs. Ina Raesdale, about eight blocks away."

Shorty contemplated a crack that resembled the head of a cougar. "And it was on the way that you saw it?"

"Yes," said Ed. "About halfway there, in a vacant lot full of benches. On one side of the lot was a big portable screen, and in back of the benches and some chairs was a projector on a table, with extension cords running into the building next door. Maybe forty people were sitting there, and some of them had popcorn and soda."

"Was it in color?" Shorty's upward gaze was beatific. "Who was on the screen?"

"It was in Technicolor. Yvonne de Carlo was in it and oh, . . . let me think, who is that guy? Um . . . Rod Cameron."

Shorty nodded and softly breathed out, "*Salome Where She Danced.*"

"If you say so," said Ed.

"I say so." The boy looked at his father earnestly. "So, in Rolla, they show movies on the street?"

Ed shrugged. "They have to. It's a little town, with no theater."

"Oh, sure, I know," said Shorty, and his father smiled as once again his son's voice grew louder and he sailed beyond a matter-of-fact statement of limitations to land at his home, the red planet Mars. "But if I were out walking in Rolla or lived in the house next door, I could look out at night and see movies!"

"Yes," Ed said gently. "Yes, you could."

They were staring up at the ceiling again, but Shorty was in Rolla. "What a nice town. Nice people too, I bet."

The scent of Emeraude stole into the room. There were no warning footsteps, only the delicate insertion of a key. Then Frances was in the room, smiling down at them.

"What funny people I always find here." Her voice was light and playful, a girl's voice, as it always was when Frances was calm. "You two look like conspirators. What did I interrupt?"

Shorty spoke up loudly. "You'll never tear it out of us." Ed smiled weakly.

Frances looked at Shorty and said, "Don't be Tiggery. You'll tire your father out." Shorty rose from the bed and retired to a nearby kitchen chair. Frances removed her scarf, shook her head, and smoothed her hair. Her movements were minimal and efficient, but Ed almost looked away for fear of feasting on them. From their first schooldays at St. Brides, she had seemed to him to be without vanity, innocent of the effect of her movements and gestures. Her powers were undiminished in repose. The planes of her body fell without plan or effort into compositions of exquisite stillness which alternately, sometimes simultaneously, soothed and disturbed him. There was one image in particular he hoped to avoid during his convalescence: Frances with her hands together in her lap, her legs tucked beneath her, her head cocked slightly to one side, leaning back in concentration. It could make him ache with pleasure, and he wished to be spared it now.

Frances unbuttoned her coat, slipped free of it, and stepped behind the bed into what served as both closet and hallway to the bath. She emerged with a small brown bag. She had stopped at Pendergast's.

"I thought you'd feel better if we smartened you up a little," she said, opening the bag. Ed felt like the very devil and knew he must look it too. He wondered what she had in mind. She set out the contents of the bag on the lady-legged table: a jar of Williams shave cream, a shaving brush, and a straight razor.

Ed eyed them wearily. "I don't feel up to shaving, Frances. I know I look like Wallace Beery, but can you put up with this grizzle for another day or two?"

"You won't have to do a thing but lie back and enjoy it. I'll shave you."

Ed's eyes widened. "Oh, I don't know . . ." His voice was tight.

Shorty leaned forward on his chair. "It'll be fun, Dad, like a barbershop. You do look like Barnacle Bill. You're scratching us to pieces like a porcupine."

He thinks I need to be coaxed, that I don't want to put her out. How do you tell a child that his mother once held a bread knife to your throat while you slept? That you woke up not daring to close your eyes for the rest of the night? You don't.

"It's a straight razor, Frances. You're not used to it," he said evenly.

"I am, you know," she contradicted. "When my father was so ill, they'd send for me to shave him. He preferred it."

Ed turned away from her and looked at his fidgeting son. Shorty, his face floodlit with hopefulness, could not contain himself. "I want to watch, Daddy. I'll hold the hot water."

I'm not in bed; I'm on location. This is the shaving scene from Shorty's dream movie of family life. He wants to direct it... and I'm going to let him. He's starving for it. He wants it so badly he's practically peeing in his pants. Victor Francen will pop in any minute now to suave things up for us. Frances won't hurt me in front of the boy. I'm doubly protected, by the presence of my son and by my own illness. Frances is always great in a crisis that isn't of her own making. Good Frances is in charge here and will remain so as long as I'm sick. It's utter madness, but I'm safe in her hands. Shorty needs this too much, and it's all there's going to be for him.

"All right, Frances," he said. "It's very nice of you."

And so it came to pass that Ed was treated to – subjected to – an elaborate and very clean shave. Frances heated a pan of water, and his face was swathed in a steaming towel to soften his beard. Shorty whisked the cream to a froth with the brush and had great sport lathering him up, making so bold as to dab his nose. Ed couldn't remember when he'd seen the boy this engaged in something. Frances wielded the razor in slow, deft strokes, first with, then against the grain, pulling his skin taut as she worked, probing for missed patches with her fingertips. Ed could neither distract himself from nor fully relax into the sensuousness of the experience.

Frances pressed the damp towel against his face with both hands, removing stray bits of cream. She opened her compact and encouraged him to judge the results in the mirror. She hadn't nicked him anywhere. "I should have thought to get an after shave. There's nothing," she said apologetically.

"It's fine. It doesn't matter." Ed drew his fingers under his chin. "Thank you, Frances... and Shorty."

"You need some lotion to tighten your skin," said the boy, "Then it would be a perfect shave."

"It was. It was."

"You know, "said Shorty, "there's alcohol in mama's perfume. We could use that."

Frances shook her head. "Daddy wouldn't care for that."

"It was just an idea. It could've been the perfect shave. It came so close..." Shorty trailed off forlornly.

Ed felt a surge of blind affection for the boy. "You could never tell a living soul about it."

It took a few seconds for Shorty to grasp the implications of his father's words. Then he raced off to the bathroom and returned with a small vial of cobalt blue.

Frances rolled her eyes at Ed as Shorty daubed his father's cheeks with Evening in Paris. "Not too much, " she cautioned.

Oh, brother, thought Ed. *I've died and gone to somebody else's idea of heaven.*

It occurred to Ed that his very skin had now joined the conspiracy to amplify Frances's presence. She packed up the shaving gear and said, "You need to eat. What would you like this morning?"

Ed was tiring again. His strength still came in short bursts. "If there's any oatmeal, I could have a little." He fought with a yawn.

"Are you thirsty, dear? I'll squeeze some oranges."

"Please, and you don't need to strain the pulp." It was sweet to be spoiled, just for a little while, especially when he hit rock bottom physically. But did she realize what she'd called him? That was sweet too, even if she'd just drifted unconsciously into an old habit. It was inappropriate though. He was no longer her "dear," nor anyone else's.

Shorty was glaring at his math book. Except for the occasional sucking sound as the boy peeled up the film on his magic slate, the apartment was quiet. Ed had almost drifted off when his nose detected a duel of perfumes—his and Frances's. She sat beside him on the bed. Between them she had placed a blue mirrored cocktail tray with handles and a raised rim, part of a wedding gift set from Frances's sister Sheila. The merry round of toasts and libations Sheila foresaw for them had yet to materialize. They were Ed and Frances, not Nick and Nora. The shaker had been put to use only once, by Shorty who agitated tomato juice with unfortunate projectile results.

This morning the tray held more helpful fare. Beside the oatmeal and juice, there was a slice of raisin bread toast and a forbidden cup of coffee. Ed eyed it with longing. "Dr. Burke thinks I shouldn't."

"He'd think again if he saw how cranky you get without it," said Frances. "It's a cup, not a pot. He shouldn't have cut you off completely. Sometimes it's important to have what you really want."

Ed took the cup from her hand and sipped deeply. Over the rim, he regarded his lovely nurse, mere inches away on the blanket. *And sometimes it's important not to,* he thought.

After breakfast, Frances sat for a while reading to him from the *Tribune,* some of the funnies and Arch Ward's "In the Wake of the News" from the sports section. He closed his eyes and listened to her light, rippling voice make lilting gibberish of combat among burly athletes with burly names.

Shorty had solved, or tired of solving, his arithmetic problems. He fiddled idly with an old musical toy, slowly moving the handle the wrong way. "Jingle Bells" tiptoed into the room backwards. Ed felt the pressure of Frances's body lift from the bed.

"Shhh," she whispered. She had moved to the sofa where now they both sat watching him. "Daddy's asleep."

Daddy was not asleep, but if he could will it, he soon would be. Fast asleep. Sleeping fast. Speeding away from these dangerous people who loved him and whom he loved. Speeding with Warren on the back of a motorcycle down Route 66 where, whatever pitfalls awaited them, they did not include schizophrenic sirens and sad-eyed, watchful Martian boys.

CHAPTER 6
A SATURDAY MATINEE
Chicago: August, 1952

Morning sun gave the drawn window shade the look of re-used postal wrapping. The effect on the boy's part of the bedroom would soon drive him from it. For the moment, however, he lay with his hands clasped behind his head, contemplating his one success in the past year.

Before setting foot in high school, he had performed a name-ectomy and made it stick. To his classmates at Our Lady of Peace, he would be – forever and inescapably – Edmond. They would greet him as Edmond if he met them at ninety, which was reason enough to avoid them. But they had gone on to Catholic high schools: Mount Carmel, Aquinas, and Leo. Few of them followed him to the tuition-free corridors of public education. It was a golden opportunity, and he had seized it, amputating the hopelessly stodgy "-mond" which had encumbered and embarrassed him for fourteen years. It was excess baggage, with musty associations, and there was no need to drag it with him through the halls of South Shore High. Lopping it off with one quick stroke on the first school form he was given, he never looked back. To his new teachers and classmates, if not to his family, he was now a very crisp "Ed."

Of course, if the right person ever came along to warm and pet it into Eddie, well, that would be all right too.

Such thoughts reminded him why his hands remained behind his head, out of harm's way. As always these days, he had been awakened by his body demanding attentions that, at the moment, he was struggling to deny it. His forbearance this morning was the result of scruples, not the lack of opportunity. He was absolutely alone in the silent house, and would be so for the rest of the day. Should he choose to, he could run amok from one end of the Sheffield household to the other, committing mortal sins in every single room. While he was at it, he could throw in the basement and the garage for good measure. At least that's what he would have been capable of only a short time ago. Now, after two weeks spent almost entirely by himself, with more solitary contemplation than he had ever dreamt of, he had achieved insights into life, and especially his own character, that threatened to overwhelm him.

For the past seven years, he might as well have been growing up in a department store window for all the privacy his life at the Sheffields' afforded, but now he had been thrust into privacy with a vengeance. The opportunity of a motor trip to Pennsylvania had presented itself to the family – or most of it. Aunt Viola, his grandmother's sister, had spent the month of July with them. Unpretentious and undemanding, Aunt Viola spun out irresistible tales of family embarrassments that stretched back beyond the turn of the century, and spared no one, including herself. Her contentment was infectious, and whenever she was under their roof, the collective Sheffield spirits and behavior were invariably spruced up. Far from outstaying her welcome, Aunt Viola had been begged by everyone, Ed included, to extend her visit. But now there had been long distance calls from each of her daughters in Altoona, and she declared it was absolutely, positively, time to return.

She was persuaded not to use her widow's railroad pass but instead to let the Sheffields drive her back. Ed had looked forward to the trip, despite the prospect of close quarters with Uncle Victor. He saw in Aunt Viola a protector and champion. Aside from his parents, she was the only relative he could make laugh, and she won his heart completely the first time she intoned the magic words, "Oh, Louisa, leave the boys alone." He had assumed, until the day before the trip, that he was included. Not until his grandmother saw him packing did she explain that what with her, Uncle Victor and his new wife, Milly, Aunt Viola, Anthony, and their combined luggage, there was simply no room for him. She had delayed bringing it up, she said, to minimize his disappointment.

As far as Ed was concerned, she had maximized it. He would never cease to be dismayed and insulted by the Sheffield tradition of withholding unpleasant news from him until the last possible second. Given the years he had spent under their microscope, he failed to see what imaginary outburst they were trying to forestall. Why would he carry on when he knew he couldn't change their minds—especially if a slight or disappointment could be stored away and turned to future advantage?

Though he wished the decision had been handed down sooner, he had to admit it made sense. The rest of them would all be more comfortable without him crowding in. There was some consolation, too, in hearing his grandmother forced to concede that he was old enough now to manage on his own for a bit. It was startling and delicious to hear his name and the word 'manage' linked in the same sentence. Technically, he wouldn't be completely on his own, but his father, other than at supper, was pretty much a ghostly presence these days – off to the mill before Ed awoke and away at night at television repair courses or out on house calls. Obviously, it was Ed, not nine-year-old Anthony, who could best be left to manage alone.

The results of this independence were mixed. What he managed was to have something hot and palatable waiting for his father each night. What he could not manage was to pry himself out of the house to seek company. To Ed, solitude was so unaccustomed that he wallowed in it. By the end of the first week, his thoughts had taken him to some new and disquieting places.

It now seemed clear to him that while the sins he had committed in the past could be confessed and forgiven, he could expect no such mercy in the future. To some extent, he had always been troubled by the words of Sister Vallina, that we retroactively increase the agony of Christ on the cross with each new sin we commit. Now, however, after a week of undisturbed contemplation, he felt he understood those words completely and believed in them without reservation. *Because* he understood, no sin, for him, could still be venial. He had been singled out for enhanced understanding. From this point on, whatever transgression he committed, however slight, would be a conscious, knowing, deliberate choice to torture the crucified and helpless body of Jesus and to torment that besieged spirit with willful, pitiless evil.

With this realization, the world around Ed became a spiritual minefield. The slightest misstep would damn him without hope of redemption. Nor was the threat limited to *his own* actions. Knowing what he did, if he said nothing when others sinned in his presence, his silence encouraged further sin. The implications of this reasoning were unbearable. The sinners around him, who lacked his newfound insight, would be punished lightly and could be forgiven, but he would not. He would be guiltier for their sins than they were themselves!

If he had stayed inside the first week for reflection, it was now the mortal terror of human interaction that kept him indoors. It was not in his nature to make people uncomfortable, even to save their souls and his own. He was thankful for his temporary isolation. His father, the most uncomplicatedly good person he knew, presented no problem. But what was he going to do when the rest of his family got back? His new aunt, Milly, was breezy and amusing, but she took nothing seriously and curses fell freely from her lips. Did God actually expect him to admonish her—and in front of Uncle Victor? And what about the whole question of divorce, a sin so great it was denounced at mass on a weekly basis? Uncle Victor kept taking new wives upstairs. Aunt Milly was the *third*. Was Ed supposed to address *that* with them too? He'd find out fast where his soul was going; Uncle Victor would see to that.

Yet, how could there be half measures in this new, lonely world, where his understanding of guilt and responsibility had been so dangerously sharpened? He knew that everything he had been taught to believe was either true, to the letter and beyond, or else it was all sham and nonsense – an accidental world, devoid of order, reason, or meaning. That was a prospect as terrifying to consider as his own impending damnation.

He had no answer, but even before the return of the prodigal Sheffields, he would be put to the test this very afternoon by someone else: his mother. He had not seen her all week, and she was going to take him to the movies. He had to talk her out of it. Few movies would be safe anymore, and what they had previously decided to see, in their innocent ignorance, was now unthinkable. The Chelten was showing *Macao,* with Jane Russell.

His arms grew uncomfortable and he lowered them to his sides, but his body had not been listening to the philosophical debate. If he didn't leave the bed and dress at once, any hope of salvation would be a distant memory.

Ed headed for the kitchen, accompanied by the edgy moral obsession that had followed him from room to room for two weeks. Like a child's imaginary playmate, it demanded accommodation, but it had ceased to be any fun and could not be ordered to leave. Its brooding presence was mitigated a little by the realization that, although it was Saturday morning, no one else's agenda would be imposed upon him. In his mind, Saturday – his least favorite day of the week – was the scuffed, bleary ochre of the bedroom shade. On Sunday, in Sheffieldland, there was at least the chance you might be left alone, but on Saturday, never.

He took a loaf of rye with caraway seeds from the breadbox and placed it on a cutting board. His grandfather, though dead five years, lived on in this kitchen. It teemed with homemade reminders of the man, like the serrated steel knife in Ed's hand and the matching board and breadbox that would never wear out. He cut a thick slice and opened one side of the toaster. Glancing at the clock, he smiled. It was nine twenty-five. Normally at this time, he'd be scanning the sky in hope of rain, straining to come up with just one more plausible excuse to avoid baseball school and his weekly dose of public humiliation.

His father's deep love of the game, intensified by forty years of having to watch it from the sidelines, had driven him to approach the powers that be at Bessemer Park. His dream was a free baseball clinic, where South Side boys could sharpen their skills and smooth away their mistakes under the watchful eyes of experienced professionals. Active and retired baseball figures would be persuaded to give demonstrations and oversee workshops. Boys would turn out in large numbers, drawn by the chance to be coached by experts and spotted by scouts. Everyone would benefit, as would the park itself, from the ensuing attention and goodwill.

The officials of Bessemer Park, however, had not been dreaming such epic dreams and were quick to point out the risks and expenses involved. Their dreams were of a more modest nature – a balanced budget, with insurance rates unchanged. Nor did they share his father's confidence that there were sports stars sitting around, eager to give something back and just waiting to be approached.

On the afternoon when his father came back from presenting the proposal, Ed was waiting on the front steps, and his grandmother watched from the sun parlor window. Ed started to get up, but instead of going inside, his father sat down beside him. "They didn't turn me down, Shorty. They think they said enough so I'll turn myself down. They're wrong though." He stared across the street at Tibbee's stoop. "They can't really be against it. They just need me to convince them it's possible." He fell silent, idly tapping his fingers on his son's knee. "What would convince them?"

Ed had no idea but, not realizing his father was thinking out loud, felt a serious answer was required. "You'd have to get somebody really good, I guess. I mean…. so they'd be too embarrassed to say no."

His father looked at him and laughed. "People are a lot harder to embarrass than you think, Shorty." He removed his fingers from the knee, where they had ceased to tap and begun to exert a vice-like pressure. "You're right, though. I've got to throw somebody really big at them or forget about it."

"Like Babe Ruth?" It was the one stellar baseball name Ed knew but, as he quickly remembered, an unhelpful choice. "Too bad he's dead, though."

His father smiled at him as though the comment had not been idiotic. "But Rogers Hornsby isn't, and I might as well start at the top." He happily explained to Ed who Rogers Hornsby was and why this *would* be starting at the top – a hall of famer with three seasons over .400 and a sweeter, more dependable way with the bat than anyone in the game had ever had.

They stood up, and Ed followed his father inside where he sensed magic was about to take place. On their way to the telephone desk, they passed Grandma Sheffield, and Ed enjoyed her questioning look. It wasn't often that he was ahead of her (or anyone else) on family developments. His father smiled at her. "Be with you in a few minutes, Steve." These pet names for people mystified Ed, but when his father attached one to you, it stuck. He was "Shorty," his grandmother was "Steve," and Aunt Viola was "Dutch." They never made sense, but if you were lucky enough to get one, you wore it proudly, as a badge of great affection. He found it interesting that Uncle Victor had never been anything but "Victor."

He and his grandmother sat at the dining room table and watched as his father picked up the receiver and began to cast a spell over a series of total strangers. Ed had witnessed this phenomenon before, and each time it filled him with pride and pleasure. His father never just called people, he established relationships. Effortlessly, he charmed and courted receptionists, executives, and everyone in between. He got their names, he got their attention, and – without wasting their time – he got them to laugh by saying the droll and the unexpected. He would weave a conspiracy of two, creating a partner not merely willing to help but eager to do more. If he met with resistance, hostility, or indifference, it only added spice to the game—unless, of course, it was his wife on the other end of the line. She alone was immune to the power of his easy-going persuasion.

And so it was that day with Rogers Hornsby. Beginning with the manager of the Tops, a local team sponsored by Barney's Grill and Tap, Ed's father quickly ascended a ladder of helpful contacts that led to the Cubs' front office and beyond. Hornsby never had a chance. His appearance at Bessemer Park made the papers, and the school was off and running. Other players followed suit, and donations of equipment poured in. It was great news for his father. It was great news for the South Side. It was great news for everybody. It just hadn't turned out to be great news for Ed.

He had known for some time that he wasn't very good at baseball. Neighborhood games in the empty lot on Eighty-first Street had left him few illusions. What he hadn't known, until the baseball school made it abundantly clear for miles around, was that he absolutely stunk at the game.

The opening day ceremonies involved considerable hoopla.

Folding chairs had been set up in front of a platform, but in addition to the boys, so many parents had turned out that several rows of people were left standing. A photographer from *The Daily Calumet* snapped pictures of the speakers as they came to the podium. The microphone cut in and out, but Ed was sitting close enough to hear everything. First, a park official spoke, then an alderman, and then, amid cheers and whistles, Rogers Hornsby himself. Then, people from Goldblatts, Mages Sporting Goods, and other stores that had donated equipment were invited to say a few words.

As the kids grew restless and the program dribbled to a close, the photographer packed up his camera and slipped through the crowd. Ed's father was waved to the mike without it being made clear what he had to do with any of this. He spoke very briefly and looked uncomfortable. There was none of the eloquence that had created this moment and brought them all here. "It's all been said, and we know why we're here. Let's play ball." He spotted Ed and winked at him.

Ed sat for a moment as the crowd dispersed. His father stood chatting with the other men on stage. "He's so different from the rest of them," Ed thought. "He's so different from me. He created something really good, but he doesn't need anything from it – except to see it work. He's the best person in this park, and I'm the only one who knows it." The shabbiness of the hand his father had been dealt seized hold of Ed. At every turn, it had been guaranteed to minimize his father's chances. He deserved a different pair of legs – healthy and strong enough for his sportsman's brain to produce an athlete. He deserved a different background – money enough to have sent him on to college, instead of off to work immediately at multiple jobs. He deserved a different wife – calm and predictable enough to keep from blowing his plans to smithereens at regular intervals. And of course, Ed had to admit, his father deserved a different son – normal enough to share his dreams and make use of all that he had to pass on. It was time to play ball.

The opening day's activities set the pattern for the Saturdays to follow. Young hopefuls could choose among workshops at all positions plus a batting clinic. Then there would be games at several spots around the park. Ed's goal was to be anywhere that his father wasn't, until they could go home. At that point, he would stage what he hoped would be a convincing display of having had a grand time. His father would be circulating from class to class, so Ed would have to keep a sharp eye out. What was to be avoided at all costs was having his father actually *see* him playing. Ed was determined not to embarrass him in front of his colleagues. This was a special day, and his father was going to remember it without a demonstration of his son's backwardness on the diamond.

Still, he had to be somewhere. The catcher's class was not a tempting prospect. It was as a catcher that Ed had played his farewell game on the vacant lot. Not knowing how far to back off from the plate, he was soon slammed in the head with a Louisville Slugger. It hurt like the devil and stopped the game for a while. He was so dizzy the Thompson girls had helped him home and poured him out on his grandfather's steps to breathe his last. Surely, that was what you did when you had been slammed in the head with a Louisville Slugger. Gazing up at the concerned faces of Mary and Margaret Thompson, he realized he had yet to see their celebrated sword dance, and now, unless they rendered it quickly there on the steps, he never would. After a bit, when he didn't die, the Thompson girls went back to the game without him. He would skip the catcher's workshop.

The pitching clinic was also out of the question. Nicky McCann's assessment of his hurling prowess still rang in Ed's ears. "You know how some people throw like a girl?" Nicky had asked him. "Well you don't throw like a girl." Before Ed could smile in appreciation, Nicky added, "You throw like a fish."

The batting workshop looked promising. Everybody wanted to go home and brag that they'd been taught by Rogers Hornsby, so the line was quite long. "The longer, the better," Ed thought. Waiting was a skill he *had* perfected. He could keep out of trouble for quite a while in this line, and he'd be able to spot his father and duck out, if necessary.

An interesting feature of this class was the "batting tee." This had been a brainstorm of his father's. He had adapted a floor lamp so it could hold a baseball at a height that could be adjusted for individual batters, or for whatever type of strike or ball you wanted to simulate. Hornsby was quite taken with its possibilities. At the moment, there was only one of these batting tees, but several more were to be made up. Hornsby was talking each batter through swings at several heights and critiquing the results. His father was nowhere in sight when Ed neared the front of the line. If he went through with this, he could be more specific when he spoke to him later. He took up a bat and stepped to the tee. Forty other boys, at least, were watching him. "Go ahead," said the .400 hitter. Ed drew back the bat, squinted at the ball, and swung as hard as he could. There was no sound, except for a few sniggers. The ball remained on the tee, serene and undisturbed. He had whiffed.

"Don't be nervous. You're used to a moving pitch. That's what threw you off." Ed wasn't used to anything of the sort, but he appreciated the hall-of-famer's kindness. Slowly he drew back the bat, bored a hole in the ball with his eyes, and swung again. This time, there was plenty of noise, as the tee went crashing down and the ball thudded at his feet. Ed's mouth fell open in disbelief, and he stared in horror at the carnage. *Merciful heavens!* he thought. *I've killed my father's prototype, and I've done it in front of Rogers Hornsby!* The sound of forty boys laughing pelted his ears. He didn't want to look up. Turning around to apologize, he saw Hornsby doubled over and shaking. The great star waved his hands as if to erase himself and said, "Sorry. Sorry. What's your name, young fella?"

Ed looked him straight in the eye and said, "Muggins. Mike Muggins."

"All right, Muggins, we're gonna lick this thing. Fellas, get that tee back together will ya?" As the corpse was resurrected with screwdrivers and swatches of duct tape, Hornsby reached around Ed and swung the boy's arms slowly through several repetitions of a semicircle. "Now, with this gizmo, you can't come up under the ball for power, but you don't want to come down at it either. Just clip it, head on. Push it, smooth and easy." Ed felt as smooth and easy as the Frankenstein monster. "Please, please," he prayed. "I don't ask You for much." He tried to mimic Hornsby's motions, as he drew back and swung. To his immense relief, he connected, and though the ball didn't go terribly far, the tee didn't go anywhere at all.

Later that afternoon, as he and his father were leaving the park, a hearty voice called out from a black Cadillac at the curb. "Thanks again, Ed. Take it easy."

"Thank *you*, Rog," said his father.

"Oh, and Muggins, is that you?"

"Yes, sir."

"Remember, Muggins, just push it. Smooth and easy."

Ed's father eyed him quizzically as the car pulled away. "Muggins? *You've* had an interesting day."

"Oh, he's like you, Dad. He gives people goofy names....if he likes 'em."

⁂

And that was that, or so Ed thought. His duties had been discharged, and from now on he would spend his Saturdays at home, applauding the school from a safe distance. But in Sheffieldland, that was seldom that, as he found out the very next Saturday. He was sitting on the edge of his bed, trying to impose order on a blizzard of note cards that covered the spread, when the bedroom door flew open.

"What are you doing still here!" His grandmother's look was memorable. It distilled years of disappointment, worry, and disapproval, stopping short of disgust but not by much. It was about to give way to anger, and it was all for him. "Your father's gone already. I thought you'd gone with him," she said, stepping in and shutting the door behind her. " But you're always so *quiet.*" She made the word sound creepy and reprehensible. "You sneak around this house like a ghost. What's the matter with you?"

What was the matter with *her*? She hadn't caught him cracking open a safe. "I'm not sneaking, Gramma. I've got to organize my term paper."

She sat down beside him, on top of the note cards, and clutched his wrist to stay it from sorting them. "Son, are you determined to break our hearts, once and for all?" Her anger receded, but the teary state that replaced it was more frightening to him. "Can't you understand? He's done all this for you." The bedroom shrank to mere inches around them. Ed felt clammy and claustrophobic and wanted to pull away before she could say more.

"He couldn't play, Edmond. You're his legs."

He bolted up, but she gripped his hand and continued to cry. Looking wildly at the closed window, he yearned to jump through it. If she wouldn't let go of his hand, she could keep it.

But he knew there was only one way this could end. "It's all right. I'll go on my bike." She patted his hand warmly, staring up at him with a look of gratitude he found misplaced and chilling. He knew his father too well to believe it was *his* needs that were sending his son to the rescue.

The patting would not stop. "Deep down, there's a good boy inside you."

If she said another word, they might indeed discover what was deep down inside of him. Ed didn't want to know and wrenched free of her. Pedaling away, he heard her call out, "Make sure he sees you!"

And so he did, Saturday after Saturday. They never spoke of it again, but on Saturday mornings, her eyes would follow him around the kitchen with raised brows and a look of anxious uncertainty, until he gave some sign that his sacred mission would be carried out. He'd glance at the clock and back at her or he'd place his bicycle lock on the table, and she'd turn off the look. In time, his meritorious attendance earned him a baseball school jersey of maroon and gold. He would tear it off by Eighty-second Street and never wore it in the park, but if he placed it on a kitchen chair, it stopped the look. His father knew nothing of these wordless conversations swirling around him. The silence was broken only once, on a morning when the look continued well after Ed felt his intentions had been made clear. "I'm *going*," he snapped. He regretted it as soon as he left the house and realized no other words had passed between them all morning.

If Ed's attendance at the school was above reproach, his performance remained beneath contempt. At first, because they knew nothing about him or knew only whose son he was, team captains would pick him fairly early in the choosing up. He knew enough to ask to play right field, where, with any luck, he'd have less to do and make fewer errors. As the weeks passed, however, and word of his exploits spread, he'd be chosen last, and grudgingly. He continually misjudged where the ball would come down and often found himself frantically backpedaling, or worse, turning his back on the ball and racing to get ahead of it. Even at the rare times when he and the ball were actually in the same quadrant of the field as it descended, his upturned eyes might involuntarily close just before it landed. Batters soon learned they had a free pass to home plate if they could hit the ball anywhere near him.

When he started to overhear comments beginning, "That's Sheffield's kid –," that he hoped would never reach his father's ears, he knew it was time to pull himself out of the games. He'd have to keep reporting to the park, of course. An army of his grandmother's acquaintances roamed the South Side on Saturday mornings, and it wouldn't do to be spotted anywhere else. But if he showed up, signed in, and disappeared into such wilds as Bessemer Park afforded, it all might just work out. He began to identify with creatures of the forest, desperate to blend in with their surroundings when the hunt was on. It made for some odd mornings, and he learned more about the inner textures of shrubbery than he had ever intended, but it was a vast improvement over his debacles on the diamond.

As it turned out, he didn't even have to be playing to make an ass of himself. One morning, as he sat against the trunk of a large oak, lost in the paperback he had hidden under his shirt before leaving the house, a group of boys surrounded him.

"Hey, you wanna help us out?"

More than anything in the world, he thought, if only he could. Ed smiled and shook his head. "Even if you're shorthanded, I'm not very good."

"We know," said their spokesman, a redhead with a brush haircut.

Ed squinted at them with curiosity.

"We got nobody to umpire. Will you do it?"

Ed squirmed and weighed the risk. It was better to be honest. "I'd like to help you out, but I wouldn't be any good at that."

"Didja ever do it?" The redhead played hard, judging by the rips in his attendance jersey.

"Never, so – "

"Then why do you say you can't? C'mon, *anybody* can ump. You'd be doin' us a favor."

How he longed to throw a switch and be the person they needed, the person they still thought he was. If they only knew how hard it was for him to turn anybody down about anything, they'd know he was telling the truth and leave. "You'd be better off with somebody else, honest."

"There isn't anybody else." The redhead was a clown. "On your knees, guys. Will ya pleeeez just do this for us?"

"I don't want to make a bad call and ruin the game."

"You *can't* make a bad call. You're the ump. What you say goes."

"Really?"

"Really."

Ed stuffed *Black Alibi* into his jeans and followed them onto the field. As umpire, what he said didn't manage to go as far as a single inning. It wasn't his pitching calls that did him in, though there was considerable rolling of eyes about them. It was the call he had to make about the runner at third, while he was still looking at first, pleased that he had been able to make sense of what had gone on at that location.

"Whaddabout Baugher?" someone kept yelling.

"Um....he's....out." Ed had called the runner at first safe, so maybe to be fair...

"You could tell that with your back turned? You jerk!"

"Um, well...maybe...uh..."

"Maybe you need your ass kicked." Players from both teams were converging on him. The redhead who hired him looked especially murderous. His feet found a speed they had never reached running bases, but the disgruntled players tore after him like a lynch mob and he had barely made it out of the park on his bike.

The early warning smells of burning rye bread brought his mind back to the present. He rescued the toast and applied a thick coat of peanut butter to its wounds. Biting off a large chunk, he smiled with satisfaction. For him, until the great Sheffield motorcade returned from Altoona, The Bessemer Park School of Baseball was out of session.

⁂

As the morning wore on, he thought of what he might say to his mother. She had to be talked out of taking them to the movies. Lunch would be safe enough, he guessed, but he was starting to feel peculiar and vulnerable about even leaving the house. With anyone else but her, he wouldn't have to; he could simply call and pretend to be sick or something, but after seven years, there was still no phone in the apartment. What had begun as a temporary economy in lean times had hardened into tradition. When you were alone in the apartment, you were truly alone. It was the one place you knew that silence could never be pierced by the ringing of a telephone. Most people would have found it a privation, but his mother seemed to prefer it. She was unreachable except on her own terms. She was seen and spoken to only when she chose it, unless you made the effort of a visit and risked finding no one there to receive you.

Perhaps her attitude was a pose to save face. Ed sometimes wondered if his father had extracted an agreement from his mother as a condition of renting the apartment. A phone at her fingertips would have placed the Sheffields at the mercy of her moody outbursts even in the middle of the night. Still, the real answer might lie in the uncertainty of his mother's income. Since leaving the bungalow, she had pieced together a patchwork of employment as housekeeper, cook, or companion to a small circle of wealthy families, some of whom Ed had met and all of whom seemed to like her and value her services. But the demand was unpredictable, and he didn't imagine any of it brought in very much. If she were forced to prioritize her spending, Ed knew that outings with him or with Anthony would win out over additions to her wardrobe or the installation of a telephone.

There had been a moment, however, in 1948, when he really thought a phone was about to appear. It was at the time of the death of his Aunt Nora. Of all the Foley sisters, Nora possessed the sunniest disposition. She was sweet and young and pretty. She was also diabetic and tragically undisciplined about it. When Ed was little, he had liked nothing better than hearing Aunt Nora break into song. When she did, which was often, her voice was soft with a little burr and absolutely lovely. She taught him the words to her favorite: "You Belong to My Heart." One day, the two of them found it on the jukebox in the Zanzibar ice cream parlor. She got him to sing it with her over their banana splits, and when they finished, the other customers broke out in applause. Later, when he told his mother, instead of sharing his excitement, she sat him down and explained very seriously why he must promise never to let Aunt Nora take him for ice cream again.

Over the next few years, her trips to the hospital and episodes of coma became more and more frequent. When she died, The Foleys had no way to contact his mother, and had to call Ed at the Sheffields'. Grandma Sheffield's reaction was not what he expected.

"Will your mother be at the apartment now?"

"I think so. She doesn't work today."

His grandmother went to her purse and returned with two ten-dollar bills, which she pressed into his hand. "You must let her know about this right away. I'm calling a taxi for you. When you get there, ask the driver to wait, in case your mother wants to go to the Foleys. If she asks you to go with her, you go. Just call us if you're going to be late. It's all right if you stay over. If she doesn't go to the Foleys', send the taxi away and leave the rest of the money with your mother."

"Yes, Gramma."

"Be careful how you tell her. Don't run in and blurt it out like Walter Winchell."

And then, a startled Louisa Sheffield submitted to the spontaneous and satisfying sort of embrace she had long ceased to expect from her grandson.

Despite the scramble to reach his mother with the news, the funeral passed without anyone but Ed feeling it was time she had a phone on the premises. And so, she had continued in her splendid isolation to this very Saturday, and their plans could not be changed unless he ventured out to meet her. At ten to one, he locked the door and made his way down the sunny street, feeling as exposed and unnatural as a bat at high noon. It was dark inside the Hil-Jo, but his mother looked quite summery as she smiled at him from a rear booth. Her dress was cool and crisp leaf green with white polka dots and a mandarin collar. The belt was a scarf of the same material, the colors reversed. With her white shoes and purse, the outfit looked smart and expensive. It was a gift from one of her employers, Mrs. Marshall, who had worn it once and tired of it. Ed had seen Mrs. Marshall and thought it a wise decision.

"You look great, Mom."

"Well then, we both do, Ed. Thank you." She passed him a menu and a hand-written list of specials. "I've been looking forward to this. I hope you're hungry."

"Always." He started to read but then looked up at her. "You know, I really appreciate that you haven't minded just calling me 'Ed.'"

"Why should I mind? You think you're too old to be 'Shorty' anymore, and I've never really liked 'Edmond.'"

His eyes grew wide, and he put down the menu. "What?"

"I've just never really cared for it."

"But… But you *named* me 'Edmond.' Why would you give me a name you didn't like?"

"Well, at the time, I thought I was naming you after your father."

"WHAT?" He was aware he was becoming a little loud.

"It was your grandmother. She always called him 'Edmond' and I was trying to please her, but as it turns out, that's not really his first name."

He gripped the table. "You got married, and you didn't know his *name!*"

"Ed, dear, people are staring."

And they were. "But – but – Pbbsshhh…" He was so flummoxed he could only sputter. On top of everything, he, the soul of decorum, was being stared at while she sat there demurely, looking like the calm voice of reason.

"I suppose it does sound silly now, but there she was, calling him Edmond every time we turned around, so I assumed….and somehow, it just never came up with your father. To tell you the truth, I don't think he's so crazy about it himself."

Ed stared at her, feeling the onset of apoplexy.

"So," she continued, "the joke was on me, after your christening, when I discovered your father is not 'Edmond James,' but 'James Edmond.'"

"What are you saying?" he blurted. "James? Jim? I could have been *Jim* Sheffield? Mommmm," he wailed, as visions of the life that should have been his danced before him. Jim Sheffield was a name to conjure with. Jim Sheffield wore flannel shirts that barely stretched over his broad shoulders. Jim Sheffield! Everybody's pal, team captain, class president, *prom king*! Aaarrrggghhh!

"You've never tried the fruit soup, Ed." His mother was moving on with life. "You really should. They have it today."

Aaarrrggghhh!

When it arrived, the fruit soup was every bit as sweet as he had feared.

"What do you think?" she asked brightly.

"It's okay... but they should put it on the dessert menu."

She put down her spoon and sat back against the booth. "You've been pretty exclusive these past two weeks."

"I know." He pushed his bowl aside.

"What's it like, rattling around that place by yourself?"

"Different... very different."

"I'll bet it was fun at first, roaming through the set, without the usual cast of characters." Normally, such an opening would have drawn him out and launched a rush of words, but Ed seemed lost in thought. "Has everything been all right?" she asked, quietly.

"Oh, sure. I've just been... sorting some things out."

"Have you been looking after your father?"

"Of course. He'll be fat as a pig when they come back."

She smiled. "What have you been feeding him? You're not just opening cans?"

"No. You should taste my spaghetti."

"You must make it for me. Is it at all like mine?"

He spoke with some care. "It's not better than yours, but it's thicker. It's got lots of stuff in it – black olives, mushrooms, green peppers, garlic, and ...stuff."

"Hmmm." She seemed to be picturing the 'stuff'. "Try fixing liver one night. It'll be good for both of you. You can do it. You've watched me make it."

"I will. I'll get some onions." They were drifting, he thought, and there was no smooth way to bring up what he must. He would just have to dump it out on the table. "Mom, I don't think we should go to the movies today."

She cocked her head and looked at him narrowly. "You don't?"

He squirmed and looked away. "I think...mmmm...I think it might be too suggestive."

"Suggestive?" She seemed amused.

"Well, it's Jane Russell, and it might be like *The Outlaw*."

"I knew a little boy, once, who tried to drag me to *The Outlaw*. As I recall, he was rather put out when he couldn't."

"I was a child then. I was wrong. What can I say? I see things differently now." He couldn't meet her eyes.

"You're just too interesting for words this afternoon, Ed. Is there another movie you'd rather see?"

He shook his head. "No, I don't think we should see any movie at all. We could just, I don't know, walk around. We could walk over to Kroger's. You must need some groceries."

She reached out and gently tugged his chin around so that he faced her again. "Whoever you are, I want my son back. I'll pay handsomely." He laughed, but now she sounded serious. "What's the matter, Ed?'

He could have answered his father more honestly, if not more easily. His mother's approach to organized religion was too practical to suit this occasion. It was better to evade. "It's nothing. I'm fine, really. Just standard teenage confusion. You know what they say – every morning you wake up and you're a different person. You probably remember all that."

"It's odd, you know, but I don't. I grew up before they invented teenagers…before they labeled them, anyway. There were just people of all ages, and you started out confused and pretty much stayed that way for the rest of your life." She smiled at him warmly. "But I don't mean to be unsympathetic. Who were you when you woke up today?"

"Bishop Sheen." They both laughed. *But that's not quite accurate,* he thought. Bishop Sheen would give him a break. It was more like a Spanish Inquisitor pulling his strings these days.

"I'll tell you what," she said, "I don't think we have another *Outlaw* on our hands. There hasn't been any hue and cry about *Macao*, and you told me it would be fun to see what the place looked like. Let's give Jane the benefit of the doubt and go on as we planned. If it turns out to be suggestive, well, we just won't take their suggestions. Let's go and have a good time. I think you could use one."

Would he ever have another good time in his entire life? But it was easier to drift than to oppose her and try to explain. She paid the check, and they drifted out the door, drifted down Seventy-ninth Street, drifted, *like leaves*, he thought, *out over the mouth of an active volcano*.

They turned the corner onto Exchange, where the Chelten waited at the end of the block. Of all the theaters Ed frequented, the Chelten was the least palatial. It was quite humble, in fact, even a bit shabby, but it had served him well. It was his time machine, a doorway to the world as it was before he existed. Like the Ray on Seventy-fifth Street, it had shown triple features of old movies and changed them three times a week. If you had the money, you could have seen *nine* movies a week that were not just *about* times before you were born but had actually been *made* before you were born. You could see the clothes people had worn, the cars they drove, and the rooms they had lived in. You could see the life they had lived and watch them living it at the Chelten.

He remembered vividly the first time he had done it. He was nine and by himself. For years, his father had praised *Top Hat* as the best musical ever made. Ed didn't see how a musical could be better than *Meet me in St. Louis* or *Holiday Inn*, but since he never expected to see it, the point could not be argued. Then, for two days only, the Chelten offered *Top Hat*. Flush with loot from Easter, he decided to satisfy his curiosity. It was immediately obvious that his father was absolutely right. With the strains of "The Piccolino" still ringing in his ears, Ed ran home to tell him so, and they discussed it for an hour.

After that, he went back as often as he could and soon found he preferred a triple dose of the thirties to most of the new movies that opened downtown. Within the scruffy darkness of the Chelten, he burrowed deeply into the strange worlds of *Beau Geste*, *The Invisible Man*, *Topper*, and that most bizarre of all exotic kingdoms, the land of Kor in *She*. It was there that Ed had lost himself so completely that he was almost put out of the theater. The Chelten had a policy of checking tickets now and then to prevent young evil-doers from opening the side doors to let their friends slip in without paying. After a showing of *She*, the lights went up, and a mortified Ed was forced to explain that when She-Who-Must-Be-Obeyed stepped into the Fires of Eternal Life, he had gotten so excited that he had eaten his ticket. Remarkably, they believed him.

It was this magical museum that Ed and his mother now approached. Limping along in the wake of television, the Chelten was now attempting to stay in the game by reupholstering ripped seats and showing double features of more recent fare – hence, *Macao*. Ed braced himself for what lewd assaults the poster might hurl at them and prepared to avert his eyes quickly if that proved to be necessary. That proved to be necessary, but he wasn't quick enough. To the left of the nicely oriental looking letters of the title was a large circle with a scorching image he would not soon forget. Robert Mitchum and Jane Russell were fondling each other as she lay back on a sofa, smiling behind two enormous breasts that threatened to burst through her tightly stretched gown at any second. Her smile seemed to say, "Look what I've brought us to play with." They were bigger than softballs. They were more like the egg headlights on an old Buick. If anything that size had dropped from the skies in Bessemer Park, Ed knew his fielding average would have been phenomenal.

The situation was even worse than he had thought, and he had only himself to blame. He had drifted and let it happen. His mother was buying the tickets. He watched in a trance of dread. As a child, how often he had been comforted by the security he found in a bought ticket! Now, the only thing being secured was his eternal damnation. Was that really preferable to public embarrassment? Evidently.

Even in a darkened theater, it isn't easy concealing a feverish case of the jitters from someone sitting beside you. It is, in fact, hard work. Ed was sweating and breathing heavily, but conceal it he must. His mother knew his every mood and was easily distracted. His agitation must not reach the point where he would have to attempt an explanation that was hopelessly beyond him. If only he could will himself into a coma for the next few hours. How often he'd watched in dismay as an unsuspecting detective fell prey to a Mickey Finn and thudded to the floor. He had always thought it unfair, but right now he would gladly have paid someone to slip him one at the concession stand.

He hurled himself into a marathon of rationalization. Perhaps the makers of *Macao* were unaware of the threat it posed. You couldn't expect practical businessmen to be spiritually enlightened, and if they intended no harm… but *Macao* had been made by Howard Hughes, and Howard Hughes had made *The Outlaw*. Howard Hughes was unaware of nothing, and nothing in *Macao* would be unintended. But that didn't mean the Chelten audience would take it that way. Perhaps, like his mother, they had merely come to see an exciting adventure and would emerge with their souls intact at the end. Most of the scenes would probably be exposition or fights or suspenseful situations, with nothing suggestive at all. Perhaps – but the scene in progress stopped him dead in his tracks.

William Bendix stood at the rail of a ship, with Jane Russell. The top of her dress looked as though Howard Hughes had cut away enough material to make a tablecloth. William Bendix was leering at her neckline and telling her he was a traveling salesman. Now he was offering her nylon stockings. She was accepting them eagerly, bending over and raising her skirt to peel off the ones she wore. Now Robert Mitchum appeared below them, catching the old nylons as she threw them away. Now he was looking up her skirt and commenting about the view. Little pockets of knowing laughter broke out in the theater. "Going to the washroom," Ed whispered as he stood up and raced from the auditorium.

The men's room was at the back of the lobby, but Ed reached it in nothing flat. He pushed open the door and, relieved to find it empty, leaned over the sink, panting. He splashed cold water on his face and thought, "I can't be the collective conscience of the entire audience. It's too much to ask." Yet it did seem that was exactly what was being asked of him by some internal, goading voice. His conscience had been replaced by an implacable, humorless Jiminy Cricket, who, for two weeks had chirped an incessant, "Not good enough, not good enough." It had been a mistake to leave the house. It would be a mistake to leave the men's room until he could collect his wits – but had he any wits left to collect?

In his present condition, he didn't trust himself to distinguish between what he was thinking and what he might say aloud, and someone might come in on him at any moment. He entered the single stall, which was shielded from the rest of the room by a wooden door that latched but did not extend to the ceiling or the floor. The stall was unlit, cramped, and dank, but now that he was inside it, he had no wish to leave it again, ever. He stood, touching the cool concrete wall with both hands, and tried to pray.

"Dear God, I need help. I don't know how to live anymore, not around other people. I'm so afraid. I'm terrified of making a mistake, but I just don't think I can be this good, this watchful, not every minute. I know you deserve better. I know this isn't enough, but I'm exhausted. Is this really what you want, or am I finally going crazy? Please help me. I don't…. I can't…."

It seemed less likely with each word that anyone was listening. He found himself thinking of his mother. Could this be how she spent all those mysterious hours behind the doors of the ladies' room? Praying, in fear, while he waited? He hoped not, for he wouldn't wish it on anyone. It wasn't working, but he wasn't ready to leave. He would never be ready to leave. He started to cry.

There was one prayer he had always loved and found comforting, as much for the poetic flow of the lines as for the words themselves. He would say it now. If even *The Memorare* failed, truly, he would be without hope. The floor looked none too clean, so he spread out a mat of toilet tissue and sank to his knees.

Remember, O Most Gracious Virgin Mary
That never was it known
That anyone who fled to Thy protection,
Implored Thy help, or sought Thy intercession
Was left unaided.
Inspired by this confidence, I fly unto Thee,
O Virgin of Virgins, My Mother.
To Thee do I come, Before Thee I stand,
Sinful and sorrowful --

A sharp rap at the door was followed by, "Is there an Edmond Sheffield in there?"

Ed sprang up and unlocked the stall door. "Yes, I'll be right out."

The restroom door opened. A young usher looked in at him with amused suspicion and said, with an unseemly degree of satisfaction, "Your *mother* is getting worried about you."

She had had him *paged*! He who had spent patient, uncomplaining years waiting for her reemergence from a thousand ladies' lounges. Well, at least he could wipe that smirk from the usher's face. "Yes, she worries so. I'm just back out of the hospital... again." He accomplished more than he bargained for. The chastened and solicitous usher remained glued to his side until he had been delivered safely back to his seat. His mother studied him anxiously. "It may have been the fruit soup," he whispered.

He sat beside her, taking in the enormity of what he had done. He had soiled them with the same creepy attention of which he lived in dread from *her* behavior. The Sheffields had it right; he and his mother were two of a kind. The only difference was that he knew what he was doing. He had frightened her, and that was inexcusable. He needed to tear himself at once from the lustrous, damning images flickering in front of them. The waning afternoon sun outside the theater would calm him, even if it couldn't cleanse him. But, to add anything more to his mother's fears was unthinkable. Yet how, in this agitated state, could he endure their remaining wait in the dark? The irony of how often he had schemed to prolong this wait was not wasted on him, but this was a different darkness, intolerable and unforgiving.

He moved his head slightly to the right, not so far that she would notice he was avoiding the screen, but far enough that she wouldn't see he'd closed his eyes. As casually and discreetly as he could, he wedged bits of popcorn into his ears. But there was still his mind. He could close his eyes and plug his ears, but dear God in heaven, was there nothing and no one to protect him from the relentless and infernal machinery of his own mind?

CHAPTER 7
HOSTILE WITNESS
Chicago: August 1956

The day of his mother's commitment hearing had been a long time coming, but Ed could not remember when it had not been at least a possibility. Lodged like nettles, in his rosiest memories of childhood, were his grandmother's allusions to Dunning or Kankakee as a more appropriate setting for Frances than Avalon Park or Cheltenham. Her behavior had always been unpredictable and sometimes alarming. To Ed, it seemed no more so now than it had ever been, but the Sheffields were of a different mind. Their forbearance, long chafed raw, had severed at last.

This morning, as he dressed for the proceedings, Ed realized that his mother's freedom had been for him an important buffer. He brooded now not only about her prospects but his own. If rough justice were finally to be meted out in such matters, could his own exposure and incarceration be far behind? Was he, if some probing, intrusive light were shone on his own dark corners, more stable and deserving of liberty than she? The boy in the mirror, knotting his tie, laughed gloomily back at him and shook his head.

Another face entered the mirror and asked him what was funny.

"Not very much this morning, Tony."

"Can you tie this better for me, Eddie?"

Anthony's lumpy collar had lost the battle with the bulging knot beneath it. Last night in bed, Ed had explained to his brother why, no matter what anyone else wore to the hearing, it was crucial that the two of them dress in their best.

"What we wear tomorrow will be the way she'll remember us."

"Why? Aren't we going to see her again?" Ed could almost feel

Anthony's eyes widening in the dark.

"I don't know. That's the thing. We can't take the chance. And we don't want her to think we didn't take this seriously." The conversation had lasted far into the night, resuming after long stretches of silence, for each boy knew the other was not sleeping. By daylight, though they had dozed a bit, both of them were quite tired and animated only by their collective nervousness and uncertainty.

Ed stepped behind his brother and reached around him to undo the swollen knot.

"It's supposed to be ninety-five again today," Anthony said glumly. "Will there be air conditioning?"

"I can't promise that," Ed replied. "You'd think the judges would want it though." He regarded his brother's image for a moment, then slid the tie out of the collar and set it on the chest of drawers below the mirror. "Your shirt is nice. It'll look okay without the tie. You can leave it unbuttoned when she's not around."

"Good!"

From the kitchen, their Uncle Jack's deep cough penetrated the closed door. He, like their father, had taken the day off, not something done lightly or often at South Works. Uncle Victor and Aunt Paulina had also volunteered their services, but, much to Ed's relief, their offers were declined. Did his father share his opinion that the event was becoming a circus? He hoped so, but these days his father's mind, once a favorite playground, was not a place Ed could bear to visit. He took comfort in the thought that there were, at least, no family pets to be trotted out in ribbons for this imposing show of Sheffield solidarity.

"Let's go," he said to Anthony and pulled open the bedroom door, admitting a fragrant wave of maple and buckwheat.

"Grandma's made pancakes," said Anthony.

"Wouldn't she just?" Ed muttered darkly.

It pleased Ed to see that Uncle Jack had declined to gorge himself on a stack of wheats and was making do with coffee alone. Among the Sheffields, he was Ed's favorite, though it was scarcely a contest. He was sharp and funny and full of good songs and stories that amused Ed, no matter how often he heard them. In that respect, Uncle Jack was less a Sheffield than a Foley. More than anyone on either side of the family, he had a trait Ed admired greatly and hoped he himself possessed: a healthy sense of situation. When the brothers entered the kitchen, Uncle Jack appraised them seriously and said, "You men look very presentable this morning." He knew exactly what was up. He always did.

Even better, he liked Ed. He didn't need to spell it out; Ed just knew it. With the others, Ed entered a room and felt like disreputable chopped liver, but with Uncle Jack, there was always a palpable welcome, whether or not a word was spoken.

Ed would have preferred that no one outside the immediate family attend the hearing, but he knew that Uncle Jack's presence was a comfort to his father that Ed couldn't begrudge. The two men had forged a bond so close that at times they seemed to be extensions of each other, requiring few words, if any, for mutual understanding. Ed had often observed and envied this bond, but he knew it was beyond his reach.

For Ed and Anthony, that ship had sailed before Ed knew such a vessel existed. There was a greater difference in their ages; his father and Uncle Jack were only a year apart, but Ed knew that the blame was mostly his. He would not have chosen himself as an older brother (though he might have had some prospects as an appreciative younger one). He had been agreeable enough at times, but generally when it suited him and on his own terms. He made sure Anthony never lacked for someone to read to him, but then he liked the sound of his own voice intoning *The House at Pooh Corner* with little Anthony on his lap. When their cousin, Elizabeth, Uncle Jack's daughter, came to visit, Anthony was always included in the plays Ed staged, but he was far more likely to be run through with a sword than to win Princess Elizabeth.

As far as the really important big brotherly functions: training in sports, defense against bullies, and unscrambling the mysteries of girls and sex, Anthony might as well have been an only child for all the help he had gotten from Ed. To be fair, this had not been a willful dereliction of duty on Ed's part. If he ever gained the least bit of expertise in any of those troublesome areas of life, he'd be more than happy to pass it along, but he knew it was too late. He would never be looked up to as an older brother, nor did he deserve to be.

The two of them got along well enough, enough of the time. Comparing notes on their relatives was always good for some unwholesome merriment. They shared an adolescent relish for ranking things and would spend hours on their hands and knees under the Christmas tree spreading out each year's crop of cards and eliminating them one by one until only the supreme winner remained. The worthy sender received a letter of congratulation – at least the first one did. Then their father got wind of it and, for reasons they never understood, forbade the practice.

For a while, it seemed to Ed that music might provide them with a strong common bond. Anthony had patience and a vivid imagination, so it was not difficult for Ed to get him to listen with enthusiasm to Sibelius and most of the Russians. Ed was particularly gratified when Anthony, after being primed with stories of the Niebelungen, asked for repeated helpings of "Siegfried's Rhine Journey" and "The Ride of the Valkeries." He and Anthony were also in complete agreement that the genius of Les Paul was beyond dispute and must be shared with the neighbors by taking the hi-fi into the back yard.

The shared obsessions of the Sheffield siblings progressed nicely until the arrival of Elvis, at which point Ed realized sadly that he and Anthony were on opposite sides of an unbridgeable gulf. To Ed, rock-and-roll in general and Elvis in particular were "freshman music" meant for people who knew no better. It was devoid of all that made music the nourishing, enticing, magical force that it was for him: wit, poetry, melodic beauty, and rhythmic surprise and complexity. It just wasn't good enough, and he assumed it wouldn't be good enough for Anthony once the novelty wore off.

But it didn't wear off. To Ed's increasing puzzlement, with each numbing and joyless new record Anthony dragged home, his excitement burned brighter. Anthony was not a clod or a dullard; yet, this zealously unsophisticated fare met some deeply felt need for him. He was spared the sarcasm and derision that once would have spewed freely from his older brother because Ed's buddy, Miles Teichman, had called him on those tendencies while they were still in high school. Since then, Ed had progressed at least to the point where he could think something was profoundly stupid without being compelled to say so to those who took great pleasure in it. Conscious of the keen satisfaction he felt introducing Anthony to his own musical favorites, Ed was reluctant to deny it to his brother now that the shoe was on the other foot. He sat on most of his opinions but felt increasingly dishonest. Music, the very thing he thought might bring about a true meeting of minds, now seemed to him a symbol of opacity and otherness. He suspected that, unlike his father and Uncle Jack, he and Anthony would spend their lives regarding each other respectfully but from the outside, each lacking the key to a brotherly enigma.

If that was how he felt in general, however, this morning was quite different. The blazing glare of impending calamity shed more than enough light for the brothers to decipher each other and act as one. The connection he felt with Anthony was the only tolerable element of this noxious day. He hoped it would linger for more than just emergency use. Perhaps it would if for once he could be the older brother Anthony should have. If Ed could hold himself together and show them both how to navigate the hearing without shaming themselves, this temporary bond might last. But if so, he was off to a shaky start. Without realizing it, he had just consumed a pancake.

He slid his plate aside and put a question to his father. "How will this work today?"

"They'll do the final interviews when we get there, Shorty, and this time they want to hear from you and Anthony."

"Hear from us?" Ed squinted at his father, frowning. "There'll just be some yes or no questions. Isn't that right?" No one had led him to believe anything of the kind, but it was a version his nerves and stomach could tolerate.

"There'll be questions, but I don't think many of them will be yes or no." His father's voice was higher now and unnaturally tight, as though he had just spotted an open microphone at the breakfast table. Shorty felt sorry for him. "They want to get all the information they can before making a decision. They'll ask you to talk about what things have been like with your mother. Just tell the truth and bring up anything you think would be helpful."

Jesus Christ! Ed thought. "I see," he said mildly.

His father could always read his eyes, and it was easier when they were enormous. "There's nothing to upset yourselves about. Think of it as an interview, not an interrogation. Everything's going to be fine if we all just do what's right."

Let's see, Ed thought, *for me, that would be gossiping about your wife and my mother so they can brand her a psycho and lock her up.* "I see," he said, nodding. The pity he felt for his father was fast evaporating. "Will they question us all together?" he asked. Listening to his voice, Ed felt detached from it, and thought, *How normal this boy sounds.*

"No," replied his father, and Ed thought, *Thank God!* though he hoped he would be with Anthony during the interrogation. His father continued, "They feel if you're questioned alone, you'll find it easier."

As easy as getting up and smashing your head and then mine to a bloody pulp against the sink, thought Ed, *and twice as much fun.* He looked at his father evenly and thought, *That was worthy of Mom when she's angry. Aren't you ever afraid it runs in the family?*

So far, Ed had found Anthony's presence enormously helpful and stabilizing. Just now it kept him from putting his head down on the table and bawling like a baby.

After breakfast, the parade of witnesses assembled on the front porch. Ed stood watching his grandmother lock and try the door as the rest went down to the car. She took his arm and said as they descended, "Grandpa's proud of his brave boys today." He'd been trying his best all morning to only half listen to her. Really thinking about some of the stuff she was shoveling at them could be dangerous, but this one was hard to shrug off. His religious convictions had pretty much burned themselves out by now – one's head has room for only so many demons. He would have preferred an afterlife, but it seemed unlikely. Yet, as his grandmother invoked her dead husband, Ed did indeed feel watched. His cosmic observer looked on with suspicious apprehension, however, not pride.

Uncle Jack's Buick would have afforded the group more room, but Ed's father preferred to drive, and Ed thought he knew why. At least that much of this wild swirling day could be controlled. The quintet positioned themselves in the Studebaker. In the front seat, one set of Sheffield brothers considered the most practical route to the courthouse. The brothers in the back seat declined the pencil and tablet proffered by their grandmother. They shared a single unspoken thought – no games of hangman today. Louisa Sheffield always remained silent when men plotted navigation. She expected no less of her grandsons.

As for Ed, the arcane mysteries of Chicago's geography held no distractions. His mind was free to wander, and it did. Was there any good to be wrested from this situation, he wondered, and if so, how was he to bring it about? Was it really a foregone conclusion that his mother's freedom would be taken from her? Could he and Anthony, by careful testimony, prevent that from happening? Could the others be right? Was it necessary to confine her, for her own sake as well as theirs? Was there really the prospect of danger if things went on as they were, or was that a wicked misrepresentation to prevent further embarrassment and inconvenience? If that were all, then it was criminal to even think of hiding his mother away and robbing her of her independence.

On the other hand, if, as they kept insisting, she could truly be helped in an institution, wasn't he wrong to oppose that? Wouldn't he be, in fact, harming her, in a misguided attempt to protect her? But even if that were true, how could he ever face her again if he spoke against her? Would she ever forgive him if she knew he had? How could a son ever be the instrument of his mother's incarceration? How could he do that and live with himself – or live at all? But if? But if? And the cycle began again, unending and unresolved. He simply didn't know, and not knowing, what was he to say to Anthony? Yet if he said nothing, he remained the useless non-brother he had always been, "and always will be!"

The other occupants of the car were looking at him. The last four words had escaped him out loud. "A prayer," he lied. They appeared to believe him, but he would make every effort to do nothing strange for the rest of the morning.

At the courthouse, they sat together in the midst of bored strangers watchful for clues as to what had brought the Sheffields among them. Ed was determined they would get none, and said little. The strangers were equally guarded. Other than their faces, the featureless room offered no distractions. Under other circumstances, he would have been limp with tedium, but even after an hour had passed, Ed remained coiled at the edge of his bench.

He thought continually about his impending testimony and about Anthony's. He had deluded himself that, as minors, their opinions would not be sought. Now that the damaging potential of their interviews had sunk in, he needed to talk to his brother in a way that wasn't possible here.

Things had been said last night that could lead Anthony to think Ed wanted him to lie or at least withhold information, and perhaps he did. Ed knew that when each of them was born, there followed a serious and worrisome decline in their mother's health. Both labors had been long and difficult, necessitating extended stays in the hospital. There had been a mental toll as well. His father had told him that when his mother finally came home with him, she had refused food so long she developed malnutrition and had to be forced to eat. Hadn't she wanted them? Had their deliveries been so gruesome and painful she resented them? But that made no sense given the loving, creative, untiring mother she had been to them as children… at least to him. Ed realized that Anthony had been too young at the time of the separation to have his brother's warm memories of how perfect things—and she—had been at first. Ed was afraid, in fact, that for Anthony "mother" was an ill-defined composite of both Frances and Louisa Sheffield. In the middle of the night, Ed had said to Anthony, "Mom had an awful time when each of us was born."

"I know all about it, Eddie," said Anthony. "Aunt Paulina talks about her with Grandma like I'm not in the room. She says, 'Some women should never have children.'" Anthony was so good with people's voices it was spooky.

Shortly before noon, the brothers were conducted down a long corridor and placed in separate but adjoining rooms. Ed wondered if the sounds of his interview would bleed through to Anthony and vice versa. He needed to know. He could hear nothing and decided to make an experiment. He stood up, pulled out a desk drawer as far as he could without dislodging it and slammed it shut with full force. If Anthony could hear it, he might make a noise in return. Even if he didn't, he would know before he began that he could be overheard. No sound came from the room beyond. Ed tried something louder. He drew back his foot and gave the desk a resounding kick. Still nothing. Perhaps the rooms were soundproof. He caught his reflection in the glass of a framed picture of a former governor, one who had not yet served time, and it brought him up short. What was he trying to do? Intimidate his brother? To what purpose? If he wasn't sure what he wanted Anthony to say, how in the world was Anthony supposed to figure it out and oblige him?

Ed patted the desk apologetically and slumped into a chair beside it. Anthony would say what he would say and might even be saying it now. Ed's concern must be his own responses. Sinister questions reared and darted at him with mock innocence.

"So, what is it like, living with your mother?"

"Offhand, can you recall any little incident that might shed some light on your mother's stability?"

"Does anything come to mind?"

Come to mind! he thought, *You betcha! Easiest thing in the world, not like getting it to leave. Step right up for The Amazing World of Mom! Here's a door marked 'Holiday Fun.' Let's see what's behind it. See Mom work in the kitchen all day making Thanksgiving dinner.*

It smells delicious. See Mom bring it to the table. Hear Dad make a harmless remark. See Mom dash the turkey to the floor. See Shorty and Anthony shut up. See Dad clean up the mess. Hear Mom cry.

The next door says 'Payday Blues.' Let's take a peek. See Dad enter apartment with worried look. Hear Dad explain: less time this week, less pay, same bills. Hear Dad make harmless comment. See Mom take Dad's billfold, run to bathroom and tear up money. See week's pay flushed down toilet. Hear Mom cry. Hear Dad cry. See Shorty and Anthony shut up.

But there were other doors of a quite different nature that Ed knew must be included. Behind every one of them stood a little boy who felt he owned all the world worth owning. A beautiful woman sits brushing his hair long beyond all need, just because he likes it. Or she guides him through the wild forests of Avalon Park, like a Celtic Scheherazade, spinning out a thousand and one tales of the gypsies who hide at the end of the wood, where he must never go. There were people enough lined up to tell the squalid tales of a woman in pain, driven to extremes. Shouldn't there be at least one witness to the tales of sunlight and smiles and magic, just as real and relevant to the case? And who if not he? It ought to be simple. What, Ed asked himself, would a sane normal man do? But he couldn't begin to guess, because he was none of those things. He might as well be an alien creature fallen to Earth, trying to interpret human behavior. He had battled tears all morning, and now they came.

"Good afternoon, Edmond." The door had opened, and a young woman with a briefcase looked at him with interest as she crossed the room. He hadn't expected a woman, but this was good. Perhaps she would be more understanding. She seemed young for her job, not too young, but like someone who had skipped grades. She was quietly pretty, with pale blue eyes that were not unkind but measuring. *She'll know if I'm lying*, he thought. It was not clear that she would care, but she would know.

The woman seated herself at the desk, unbuckled the briefcase, and extracted a folder with two typed words on the cover. Even upside down, his mother's name was recognizeable.

"We ran late this morning," said the woman.

So many lunatics these days, thought Ed, but then it became clear she was offering an apology, not calling attention to how busy and important she was.

"Your family was kept waiting a long time; you must be getting hungry by now."

"No, ma'am, we had pancakes this morning."

"Good." She nodded, and Ed thought, *I've had court-approved pancakes.*

"I'm Mrs. Lightner. I'll try not to keep you any longer than necessary." She opened the folder and scanned several pages in silence.

She has to refresh her memory, he thought. *Her briefcase is bulging with other files. She barely knows who we are.*

Mrs. Lightner looked up. "Before we begin, Edmond, I need to tell you that what we say will be tape recorded, if you don't object. It's the most accurate way of documenting what is said."

Ed had never thought of himself as someone who had the right to object to things. He was seldom confident his opinions were correct, and objecting required a gift for self-assertion he had never developed. This had cost him more than he knew. "I'm afraid I do object, Mrs. Lightner." Bad enough that he might say something he'd regret later, but for anyone to be able to listen to him do it over and over? Unbearable! They could jolly well find another means of documenting this session. Ed braced for a battle, but Mrs. Lightner simply said, "Just as you wish," and took out a pen. *Pay attention*, he told himself. *There's a lesson here.*

To start with, the questions were factual, innocuous, and safe. It was like being coaxed bit by bit into a cold lake. First the toes, next the ankles. Gradually, Mrs. Lightner grew more pointed. Had his mother threatened Ed or his brother? Never. Had she subjected them to physical violence? He couldn't remember her even raising her voice to them. It was still easy to answer. Still possible.

Then it came at him. Had he observed acts of violence toward anyone else? His lips pressed together tightly, but now that the question had been put, even silence would be incriminating. The fact that he hadn't snapped out this answer like the rest had probably told her what she was trying to find out. Flapping about in Ed's mind, while he struggled to look calm and ordinary, were images of a fairly recent incident. His father had taken them all to Jackson Park, and the day had gone well until the drive back to the apartment. They had rented a rowboat, and the four of them had eaten his mother's peculiar sandwiches of butter and lettuce out on the lagoon. They were seldom all together anymore, and when they were, Ed had given up trying to figure out what it meant. Still, it had been pleasant. Dad had rowed them around, and everyone had been singing. Then, as they drove out of the park, his mother's voice took on the reckless edge that signaled she might leave the land of the reasonable and spiral into unprovoked rage at his father at any moment.

He wished his father would drive faster because if he could drop them off at the apartment and get away before it happened – it wouldn't. Just as they neared the big statue of the golden lady, a league baseball rolled out from under the front seat. Ed saw his mother pick it up and examine it, but surely… In a flash, she threw it at his father's head as he drove. Violence? Yes. Endangerment? Clearly. Must he now divulge it? He sat there imprisoning the unhappy images for a few seconds more.

Someone tapped at the door, and Mrs. Lightner said, "Think

about it for a moment, Edmund. I'll be right back." She opened the door and stepped into the hall.

Ed opened his mouth and drew a breath. His eyes fell on his mother's open file. If he were careful, he could slide it right side up, glance at it, and move it back exactly as Mrs. Lightner left it. He had to see it. He swung it around and quickly spun it back, but the damage had been done. He had seen words not meant for his eyes and now they would never leave him: EXHIBITS SYMPTOMS CONSISTENT WITH ACUTE PARANOID SCHIZOPHRENIA.

They had already made up their minds! She would be taken away from him.

When Mrs. Lightner returned, he told her, "I've nothing to say that will help you. I can't ... discuss her."

The pale blue eyes took a reading of him. "I understand, Edmund. You can go now."

He got halfway to the door, turned back to her and said, "She's my mother." Mrs. Lightner nodded and closed the file.

Anthony was waiting for him in the hall. He got up from a bench, came over, and stood close to Ed. Neither of them knew what to say. Together, they moved as far from the interview rooms as was possible without being seen through the large circles of glass in the courtroom door.

"Are they in there?" Ed asked.

"Mm-hmm." Anthony nodded.

"Why didn't you go on in?"

Anthony shrugged.

"Have they brought her in yet?"

"No," said Anthony. "Are you hungry?"

"No," said Ed. "What have you got?"

Anthony extended a bag of Cheetos.

Ed laughed grimly. "It's always Cheetos whenever something

really crappy is going on. Remember those four-hour bus rides to St. Luke's for our checkups? Grandma always gave us Cheetos. It must be in case you don't realize how crappy things have gotten. You eat the Cheetos and then you get it." Ed's voice was growing loud. Anthony glanced around to see if anyone was looking at them. "If they send me to the chair," Ed went on, "first they'll give me Cheetos."

Anthony apologized, "They're all I've got." He started to put the bag in his pocket.

"No, wait." Ed stuffed several in his mouth.

"What'd they ask you in there?" Anthony said quietly.

"I guess they ask us all the same things ... pretty much."

"What'd you tell them?" asked Anthony, looking as if he really wanted to know.

Ed shook his head. "I didn't tell them anything."

Anthony got no farther than, "I just –" when Ed grabbed him by the plat of his shirt and twisted it, saying, "I don't want to hear it! Don't ever tell me! Understand?" He walked to the courtroom door, leaving Anthony to ponder the novel experience of being threatened by his brother.

Ed peered through the glass and recognized his relatives from behind. They sat two thirds of the way to the front. He was about to step away when his grandmother turned around, spotted him, and waved him to a space on the bench beside her. Anthony stood at his shoulder. "I'm sorry," said Ed.

"We'd better go in," said Anthony, "or Grandma will come out and get us."

More hearings and conferences with lawyers were going on than Ed could keep track of. He didn't see how the bailiffs could sort it all out, but they did. Everything was happening in plain sight, but you could only hear what was said if you were called up and stood close.

Twice, his father was called up, and Uncle Jack went with him. Ed had no doubt about the eventual outcome, but each time Anthony asked, "What's happening?" only to be told that there were a lot of formalities and not to worry.

Suddenly, Anthony tugged at Ed's sleeve and whispered, "She's here!" From a side entrance, a matron had brought their mother out. Ed winced and thought, *Her freedom's already gone.* It was agony to sit and watch her vulnerable confusion, but they weren't permitted to go to her. The room was large and they sat in separate sections, but he could see that she had dressed for them in his favorite outfit, blue and white. When she located them, her face brightened. *Oh, don't,* Ed thought, *don't smile for us. You don't have to smile for anybody now.* He tried to match her expression but feared it was only a grimace. *She won't let us see her fear,* he thought. *She's the bravest one here. Are you proud of her too, Grandpa?* Ed was frantic that she'd see him as part of this conspiracy. He fidgeted and tried to think of ways to signal his dissent.

They were called up again, this time everyone, including his mother. The words of the judge and the lawyers were a blur to him, but he knew what was happening. Anthony, on the other hand, was paying strict attention. Ed saw his brother's face crumple and knew it was all over.

The others stepped away, and he and Anthony were permitted to say goodbye to her. She might have been a hostess at a garden party, gracious, smiling, solicitous for the comfort of her guests. Nothing in her demeanor betrayed the pathetic, hideous reality of her situation.

Standing in front of her, even "goodbye" seemed too harsh an acknowledgement of her future. Ed stared, incapable of echoing her smile, and said, "I love you, Mom. I'll think of you every single day."

"Think of Anthony too," she amended. No hug or kiss was exchanged. It wasn't their style and would have been an acknowledgment of what was happening. She squeezed his arm and was taken from them. He stood watching until the side door closed and obliterated her.

❦

Wedged tightly between his brother and his grandmother in the back seat of the Studebaker, Ed found the physical contact inescapable and loathsome. As his grandmother began to pat his hand, he shrank himself to a height of two inches and hid in the pit of his stomach, far from her reach. A crowd of thoughts and impressions jostled each other for his attention, and he felt it must be so for the other occupants of the car. None of them could wait to be away from this place, and his father drove, not recklessly but faster than his custom. All the windows were down, and the shoosh of the breeze would have discouraged conversation, had any of them been so inclined. Only his grandmother felt the need to speak, but her remarks required no answer and received none.

"I'm proud of all my boys today. You did the right thing, all of you. You did your duty. It's best for us, best for everyone. You'll see. We'll live in peace and be a real family now. You'll see." She stopped, not because she was through, but because she saw young Edmond's lips moving as he stared intently at the onrushing traffic. "That's it, son," her words resumed, as did the hand patting. "Say a prayer. We need one now. He hears our prayers, and He answers them. You'll see."

Close enough to hear the prayer, Anthony shuddered as his brother whispered over and over, "Hit us. Hit us now."

CHAPTER 8

JUMPING SHIP

Chicago: May 1957

"Tell me again, Edmond. Take me through it one more time. Why are we here? Why are you doing this? I just want to hear you say it. I just want you to hear yourself saying it." Helen Teichman crossed her legs, took a long drag on her cigarette, and directed the smoke away from him in a slow, upward stream. She was a prolific and stylish smoker, and except for her coughing, Ed always enjoyed the display.

Waving away smoke that was nowhere near him, the young man beside her chimed in. "Mom's right, Ed. God, there's a sentence I never expected to utter, but what the hell are you thinking?"

"I just…" Ed shrugged. "I just need to make a change."

"You've ruled out joining the circus, then?" She was trying to make him feel ridiculous, but Ed knew it was kindly meant and grinned at her sadly.

"I would make a good clown, wouldn't I?"

"Well, at least then you could get us free passes, but this…" Her left hand splayed open in dismissal.

They were in the vast Chicago Armory, which served as induction center for much of the Midwest. The three of them had retreated to a small, doorless anteroom to escape the jostle and din of the immense hall immediately beyond them. It was easier for them to hear each other now, but they were frequently interrupted as strangers poked in to look for missing companions or out of boredom – just to look.

"Why now, Edmond? Right in the middle of college?" Mrs. Teichman continued. Ed was happy to have Miles and his mother here with him, grateful they had come, his last links to the life he was leaving behind. But he squirmed under their inquisition and wished they would talk about anything else. How could he explain to them what he still struggled to explain to himself? He was not fully convinced that leaving this way was the right thing to do. All he knew for sure was that staying was the wrong thing. But the Teichmans wanted more.

The sudden intrusion of a voice, a high-pitched and uninhibited buzz saw, bought him time. "'Scuse me all. Ah'm Alton Spraag. Just lookin' around." The startled trio turned to confront an apparition quite beyond their collective experience, a towering, severely undertoothed stringbean of a young man, whose enormous ears and thunderstruck thatch of hair competed for their attention. "So much to see around this place. So minny people! Any of y'all gettin' on that train to Fort Leonard Wood?"

Ed slowly raised his hand.

"Well then, you'n ah might jus' get to be friends. Ah'm Alton Spraag, if I didn' already say so." His name seemed to have acquired more syllables this time around. Alton's exuberant tone and rising pitch conveyed his boundless joy at being in sole possession of such an enviable identity.

"Edmond Sheffield," Ed said quietly. Had he summoned his birth name as a barrier? He hoped not.

'Well, that's a name and a half, but I'll remember," and with that, Alton Spraag vanished.

Everyone spoke at once: "It seems you won't lack for interesting companions." "What do you think happened to his teeth?" "You're a damn fool, Eddie."

Though they were more than capable of adding to Ed's distress, it would have been impossible for Miles or his mother to offend him. Each of the Teichmans had amassed such credit with him in the last six years that he could not conceive of either of them exhausting it.

When Ed met Miles, they were both fourteen. Ed had begun to

think he would live out his days without encountering that elusive creature who was not just an agreeable acquaintance, not just a casual chum, but a real friend, a secret sharer who actively sought his company. He had also begun to believe that he would only be accepted or even tolerated by his peers, to the extent that he kept his thoughts to himself and spoke and behaved like some ill-fitting generic of youth. He didn't find this easy to do, nor did he always think it worthwhile, but at times he felt it absolutely necessary. He wasn't wonderful at mirroring the young people around him – just good enough to scrape by – but more than good enough to feel cheesy and depressed about it afterward.

Meeting Miles in high school changed all of this. For once, the cryptic humor, the aesthetic appetites, the collector's glee confronting the riches of language, all the qualities he had grown used to suppressing lest they put him at social risk were recognized, encouraged, and celebrated. Opinions on every conceivable subject were discussed at school, exchanged over the phone, written down on endless hierarchical lists of the best and worst of everything, and most deliciously of all, aired at the home of Helen Teichman, where children were meant to be heard as well as seen.

Divorce from a popular architect had left Helen disenchanted but solvent. To Miles's friends—and he had many—his mother was generous with her hospitality, her time, and most importantly, her esteem. Once her son chose a companion, this person became, by definition, someone of substance, someone to be taken seriously, nurtured, and supported. In a permanent cloud of Helen's cigarette smoke, Miles and Ed, among others, were chauffeured about Chicago to a dizzying array of diversions including tennis courts, television broadcasts, and political debates. Curiously, at the latter, Ed, who had never held a political thought in his head, discovered his convictions and found them diametrically opposed to those of the conservative Teichmans. Far from putting him off, this led to spirited discussions in which their attempts at persuasion forced him to clarify and sharpen his own positions.

As a member of this exhilarating circle, Ed was more deeply touched by her confidence in him than Mrs. Teichman would ever know. If anyone could persuade him that he would amount to something, it was she. But no one could. Twelve years at the Sheffield's had convinced him of the opposite – that *something* was just what he'd never amount to.

Through Miles, Ed had been introduced to a small band of kindred spirits, most of whom wrote for *The Shoreline,* the school paper. They found him funny, and he soon experienced the heady treat of seeing himself regularly in print. Like Miles, everyone in this group was clearly going places and assumed the same of Ed. He knew better and held his breath when they shared their plans for the future. He savored these friendships more keenly for doubting they would survive graduation. In Miles's case, Ed had so far been proved wrong. Miles attended a top school out of state. Ed commuted to an inexpensive urban branch college while working evenings and weekends at a large drugstore. The Teichmans kept up the contact more aggressively than Ed did. They continued to behave as though there were not the slightest difference in the prospects of the two boys. They had yet to find him out and despair of him, though Ed couldn't shake the idea that somewhere a meter was ticking away and that this army escapade would speed the process.

"Don't you think it's time," said Mrs. Teichman, "that you let your family in on this caper? You're not really going to bolt without a word to them?"

"No... I'm just waiting until..."

"Until it's too late for them to stop you? I think you're safely past that point."

"Well, yes, that." Ed surveyed the floor. " I'm just trying to decide the best way to put it."

"The *best* way?" Mrs. Teichman rolled her eyes. "Lord, protect us from our offspring. Do you really imagine there's a best way? There isn't even a decent way to put it. Edmond, I'm not comfortable at all with this plan. I drove you here so we could try to talk you out of it, and so you wouldn't be alone if we couldn't. I'm pleased, flattered even, that you chose us to confide in, but if you go without speaking to your family, they'll feel I've betrayed them, and they'll never forgive me."

"They wouldn't blame you."

"Please call them now, Edmond."

Ed sighed and stood up. "Okay."

When he had left the room, Miles pantomimed banging his head against the wall and said, "Gaaaaa!" Massaging his straw-colored hair with his fist, he stared earnestly at his mother. "Will they talk him out of it?"

"You know them better than I do. It's gone so far. I really thought by now one of us would have changed his mind and we'd be driving him back to the Sheffields."

"Me too," said Miles, "but he's so stubborn tonight. He's usually pretty malleable."

"Yes, almost to a fault. At times, I've wondered if he weren't almost a little too..." She trailed off.

"Easily led?"

"No, and what have you been trying to lead him into? No, I think the word I was looking for is accommodating."

And as they spoke, Ed stood down a corridor at a stand of pay phones, attempting to accommodate Alton Spraag.

"Hey there, Edmun Sheffeel. Did I get it right?"

"Close enough, Alton."

"You gonna call home?"

"Yes, but I'm not in a hurry. Would you like to call home yourself?"

"Yes, indeed, I'd like that a lot."

"Well, you go first, then." Ed held out the receiver.

"Woodn' do the slightest bit of good."

"No one's home now?"

"Oh they's probably all home. No place else to be in Gullem this time a night."

"Well then…?"

"No telephone."

"There's no phone at your house?"

"No phone in Gullem. Go call your sweetheart, Edmun."

Ed's face was pasted with a fat smile. This unearthly boy, with the mistaken but enchanting notion that Ed had a sweetheart, was someone to keep close. Ed told him, "Thank you," and stepped to the phone. Drawing up the receiver, he held it away from his ear, and with his other hand, pressed down the cradle. He needed the privacy of a booth to collect his thoughts, but the Armory offered only the exposure of an open half cubicle. He looked over his shoulder and saw Alton sitting cross-legged on the floor only a few feet away.

"Ah'm not lisnen." Alton smiled and put his hands over his ears. Ed couldn't bring himself to say, "This is rather private," but Alton read his expression and scooted further on without getting up. Ed turned away and dropped the coin. As his finger tugged and released the circles of the dial, the letters and digits of his home number seemed to spring out at him, large, loud, and red. He stopped mid way at '5' and replaced the receiver. He wasn't ready. He would never be. He dialed again. Until he released the final '7', nothing was broken; everything could be undone. He took a deep breath with his mouth shut tightly and plucked his finger from the dial, locking in the '7' and making the connection. His grandmother answered on the second ring.

"Hello?" Her voice was out of place in this official setting. It pulled him into the connection and focused him.

"Hello, listen, Gramma, this is Ed."

"Of course it is. I know your voice. Are you working late? We're keeping dinner."

"Don't do that. Go ahead and eat. I won't be home."

"Where are you, son? You sound strange."

"Umm…"

"What's all that racket? It's hard to hear you."

"Is Daddy there? I need to speak to him."

"Are you in trouble, son?"

"No!" *Yes*, he thought. "I just need to tell him something."

Ed heard her call out to his father. "It's Edmond. He wants to talk to you. He's acting strange." He grimaced and thought, *Now there's a helpful intro.*

His father's voice came through. "How's it going, buddy?"

"Fine, nev-." He stopped himself. "Never better" was grotesque under the circumstances.

"What's going on?"

"Well, I've… uh…"

"Is everything okay, Shorty?" These days, in deference to Ed's tightly gripped adulthood, his father kept "Shorty" in reserve only for emergency use. Like an extinguisher, its appearance evoked both reassurance and alarm.

"I've joined the army, Dad."

Silence, then, "Have you now?" More silence. "You're serious."

"Yes, I'm serious. I'm at the induction center."

"Just like that? Out of the blue?" Like someone who's had sand kicked in his face, his father's voice was now grainy and higher pitched, and he gulped at his words.

"It's not out of the blue," said Ed. " I've given it a lot of thought."

"But not much conversation."

"I didn't want you to talk me out of it."

"Could I have?"

"Maybe."

"I doubt it. You seem determined to get away from us. But must you bolt like a bat out of hell? Couldn't we have talked about it? Can't we now?"

"No. I've really, really, really got to make some changes – and I can't do it there!" Ed saw Alton looking at him. He had forgotten about him, about the corridor and the Teichmans just beyond it. He realized he was twisting and squirming and had raised his voice. "I'm sorry, Dad."

"Have you been sworn in? Have you?"

"I'm about to be. There's no time to change it now."

"You've planned this carefully." It was not a question and far from a compliment. Ed could hear his father speaking to his grandmother and possibly Anthony. "He's joined the army." His grandmother's "WHAT!" tore through the phone. "What time will you be home?" his father asked.

"We're shipping out tonight." Waiting for that to sink in, Ed thought, *God, kiddo, you could club seals.*

"Aww, Shorty. This just gets better and better. This isn't worthy of you… Look, where are you exactly? We'll all drive down and… say goodbye. I don't like you alone there with no one to see you off"

"There isn't time, and I won't be, Dad. The Teichmans drove me down." No sooner had he said it than he realized its barbed implication.

"The Teichmans. I see."

Ed was writhing. He couldn't trust himself to speak without

doing further harm. He had to end this. He caught Alton's eye and motioned him over. "Dad, I love you. I'll write as soon as I get there. It's in Missouri. What's that, Alton? Dad, the ceremony's starting. I've got to get off."

Alton yelled out, "Hurry up, Edmun. They're callin' for us!"

"Wait – Shorty – "

"I love you, Dad, goodbye." Ed hung up, out of breath.

Alton smiled and asked eagerly, "How'd I do?"

"You were perfect."

"This is just how it'll be in the trenches," said Alton, throwing his arm over Ed's shoulder. A dazed Ed just nodded as they walked off. Alton delivered him back to the Teichmans and discreetly evaporated.

"You look dreadful," said Mrs. Teichman. "Come sit down." She patted the seat beside her, and Ed sank into it. "You've let them know?"

"I did. You were right to make me."

"It wasn't so bad now was it?" She rubbed his hand.

"It was worse. It was awful. They hate me now."

Mrs. Teichman burst out laughing and pulled him close. "It's constitutionally impossible, Edmond. A parent can't hate his child, whatever the provocation." She smiled at Miles and said, "Believe me, I know."

"Ma!" yelped Miles. "I've never given you a moment's provocation." He frowned as she arched her eyebrows and kept smiling. "I'm the model child, for Christ's sake. I have testimonials."

"You're the model student. It's not the same." She turned back to Ed. "If you feel that badly about it, just get up and walk out of here with us. We'll have you home in no time, and they'll be thrilled you changed your mind."

"I can't," he said, firmly but miserably. "It's not my mind I've got to change, it's everything else… everything."

"Oh my, Edmond." She smoothed his hair. "Time takes care of that by itself. You don't need an army."

A sergeant called out from the entrance, "All inductees report for swearing in!"

Ed started to say, "I've got – " but was hugged by both mother and son. Disentangling himself, he babbled his thanks and reassurances that he would write and would miss them. And then he stepped away. The Teichmans followed him out at a distance to watch the ceremony. Young men spilled from every orifice of the building and massed in the center of the stadium.

"He's being swallowed up, Ma," said Miles.

"Yes, he is."

They lost sight of Ed but stood watching.

"So, Ma, when was I hateful? Was I ever hateful?"

She squeezed his hand.

"Let me drive us back. Please?"

She shook her head. "You'll speed. My nerves have had enough for one day."

"Well, you know what they say, Ma. Death drives a slow car."

"Hush, dear, they're starting."

When the Armory was cleared of well wishers, Alton and Ed got their first taste of two military specialties: regimentation and lack of privacy. They stood, naked, clutching their clothes, in an endless line of men edging toward a set of—presumably—medical examiners, including a middle-aged woman who wore the grim expression of a health inspector in a restaurant kitchen where the meat has gone off. As Alton approached, she snapped, "Young man, the army has a good deal to teach you about regular bathing." Ed smarted at the insult to his new buddy, but Alton swung around and muttered, "In

Gullem, we don't allow no ladies this ugly." The boys bade an abrupt goodbye to modesty as they were poked, prodded, probed, and publicly explored in a most thorough and vigorous manner.

On the train to Missouri, Alton could not contain his excitement. "Ah've only heard about it, but now, Ah'm on a train!" Ed, of course, gave him the window seat, but Alton bounded out frequently, racing up and down the aisles in giddy discovery. At one point, Ed heard him exclaim from the end of the car, "Beds on a train! There's beds on this train!" Whatever the general public might have made of the scene, on a troop train crammed with new recruits it went largely unremarked. Most of this evening's passengers were deep in their own thoughts, as was Ed.

He had done something. He had taken steps. He had made a decision, and because of it, he would not have to make another for the next three years. By surrendering his freedom, he had secured it. He was free from worrying about how to finance the rest of his college education – if rest there was to be. He was free to self-destruct, or lose his mind if that were his destiny, but he would lose it anonymously on a military post, far from the prying eyes of the Sheffields. He would not be handled as they had handled his mother. He could drift as fate would have him, without being judged by those he cared about. He cared about them still, however, and as the train bore him away, he slumped under the weight of how badly he had served them today.

Alton thumped down beside him. "Whatcha thinkin' about?"

"I guess I'm picturing what this is going to be like for me."

"Ah know! You jus can't help it, can ya? Ah've got it all pitchered out too, Edmun, an it's gonna be swell. It's like a big adventure, sometimes fightin' in the mud, but sometimes all cleaned up in hansome uniforms and paradin' around and – and – " There was ever so much more as Alton's scenario spun on, concluding at last with a triumphal return to Gullem. It made Ed smile and look forward to a tour of duty with this chirping stork at his side.

The army, however, had other plans for Alton Spraag. He would indeed learn, quickly and brutally, the importance of regular bathing. His bunkmates would see to that. The army would put a few pounds on him, fix his teeth, and at the end of basic training, spit him out and send him back to Gullem in less than triumph. But tonight, as the lights dimmed, the future could be as shiny as Alton wished.

Conversations ebbed, and much of the car was asleep, or trying to be. Ed took out a pad and began to sketch. After a while, he felt the pressure of Alton's shoulder against his, as his companion craned to see the accumulated sketches.

"Whatcha doin'? You got balloons by the people's heads with words in 'em. It looks like the funny papers."

"It is, in a way."

Alton leaned closer and pointed. "Who's that guy above the buildin'?"

"That's the Blue Leopard."

"Mmmm." Alton nodded. "Life jus gets more amazin' all the time." He sat back and burrowed into his seat. "Read it to me, Edmun. Would ya?"

Ed spoke quietly so as not to awaken nearby sleepers. "He was at one with the night . . ."

CHAPTER 9

THE RETURN OF THE BLUE LEOPARD

Manhattan: June, 1957

He was at one with the night. The cobalt blue of his cape could not be distinguished from the evening sky. Stars splashed above him, and he felt the familiar nocturnal sharpening of his senses. From his perch above the penthouse skylight, he watched her move about in the room below. She paused before a round, blue mirror to consider her hair, gently extruding it this way and that, coaxing it upward from her bare shoulders and confining it with a lacquered clip.

He smiled, unseen, as she drifted beneath him, extending a cream white arm to pet the sheaf of midnight irises which always heralded his return. He smiled again as she sat and smoothed her ebony gown with the unhurried gestures that gave him such pleasure. From the night that eerie painting brought them together, Manning Nugent had had a year to observe Kitty Brent and found nothing about her that did not give him pleasure.

The redress of injustice took him to all corners of the earth, but nowhere had he found a better audience for his drollery or a better partner for his ardor than Kitty. They met on his return from Ceylon, where he'd so deftly resolved the matter he chose to call "The Ivory Tower of Death." Walking to his apartment, he had passed "Misfortune's Corner," his name for the location of a rapid succession of unprofitable enterprises. In his absence, a newcomer, Kitty Brent Galleries, had dared the curse. Nearing it, Manning muttered, "Better luck, Miss Brent, whoever you are."

Passing the window, he stopped in his tracks, arrested by a large, peculiar painting. It appeared to be no more than a pleasing depiction of dense jungle foliage; yet wherever the leaves parted, the dark between them held the suggestion of a powerful presence beyond them, unseen, unrepresented, yet overwhelmingly there. As he continued to stare, the vertical slashes of vegetation became a cage, though whether for the beast or the viewer, he could not say. The illusory effect held him, and he could not discern how the artist had managed it. Perhaps his own jet-lagged brain was the conjuror. He had to know.

A young woman with her back to him was already turning out lights, preparing to close. Manning spoke from the doorway, "That picture in the window, what is it called? Who is the artist?"

She turned. "You startled me. What picture would that be?" She didn't look startled. She looked calm and confident and utterly lovely.

Manning lowered his voice. "The great cat... I mean..."

Interest lit her eyes, and her businesslike smile softened into something more genuine. "No, that's it. The title is The Great Cat."

Manning nodded and strode to the counter that separated them. "Who did it? What are you asking for it?" He could barely keep from losing all bargaining power by adding, "I must have it!"

"I 'did' it." She enunciated to mock him, but warmly, "and it wasn't for sale."

Her smile pushed him to say, "Wasn't, but is?"

"I'd begun to think it a failure – inaccessible, too personal. No one before ever sensed the beast."

"Sensed it?" he blurted, "I saw it. It stalked me."

The girl leaned forward on the counter, cupping her elbows and eyeing him intently.

"It is for sale then?" he demanded. "You'll sell it to me?"

Her head was now cocked, and her right hand languidly invaded her hair. "It seems I must."

There were questions to be asked. He said nothing. He needed to let those four enchanting words of hers echo and swell and fill the room,

She didn't move or look away. He knew he should say something and quickly, but he had waited too long and his silence confided too much. Yet, she was silent too. Silence had, in fact, become a third presence in the room, and with each new increment, it bound them together more tightly until at last, no reasonable act remained except a kiss.

The year since then had been the happiest of Manning's life, which had previously resembled a beaded string of dangerous adventures. Now, he had a reason to build space between his crusades, and (except for his larks with Taponto) Kitty filled it all. He had trusted her with his heart almost immediately, and now, tiring of subterfuge, he was about to trust her with his secret as well. This was a singular evening. Before the night was over, Kitty Brent would know that when Manning Nugent held her in his arms, she was the lover of the Blue Leopard as well.

Soundlessly, he undid a metal grip on the skylight and eased into the opening. He hovered a moment to prolong the descent into Kitty's sanctuary that would change their lives forever. Poised to lower and reveal himself, he was choked with affection and desire. He needed Kitty, and he needed to disclose to her all he had hidden so well from the rest of the world. She had earned the right to know, and he could no longer bear what it cost him to deceive her. Surely, even Vivator would understand this and approve.

Vivator! Why, on this sweetest, most tranquil of evenings, did he suddenly feel the warning spirit of his dead mentor? Something was wrong, and it wasn't his decision to lay bare to Kitty his secret identity. Suspended in mid-air, he surveyed the scene below him and found the answer in a corner left in darkness by the placement of the lamps. Unknown to Kitty, a second pair of eyes lay in wait, following her every move.

She was crossing to a corridor that led to her bedroom. Manning let her exit and waited for the crouching figure to stir. A maddening stillness possessed the room as Kitty's footsteps receded on the parquet. A door closed. Nothing... then, tentatively, a dark figure emerged from behind a sofa. The Blue Leopard plunged to seize it and found himself grappling with a powerful opponent swathed in black, with only hands and eyes uncovered. Furiously they thrashed about on the floor. Desperate to wrest himself free, the large, muscular stranger had the strength to prolong the struggle, but there was no escape from the Blue Leopard's savage attack. Soon, the intruder was pinned and held immobile. Manning lunged for the mask, tore it away with his teeth and was startled at what he saw. "A Conniption!" he gasped. Roused by the noise, Kitty ran into the room, distracting Manning just long enough for the prowler to break free and dart for the door.

A dazed Kitty gaped at the carnage as the Blue Leopard tore past her, saying, "I'll be right back, darling." He wasn't, and when the gentleman in the cobalt blue cape returned, it was somewhat sheepishly and without his prey. A vase had been dashed to the floor in the skirmish, and Kitty sat holding a lapful of damp irises.

"Manning?" she asked quietly.

"Hmmm. Can I say 'no' and just leave?"

"Manning, is there anything you'd like to tell me?"

He sat beside her and took her hand. "I guess I've got some 'splainin' to do."

He was a good 'splainer". His confession was not, as it turned out, a complete surprise. Kitty was no one's fool, and coincidences had begun to accumulate. Though young, she was well schooled in—and rather drawn to—life's complexities. Too discreet to put the question, she had hoped instead that, if her suspicions were correct, the answer would come unbidden as a sign of trust, a gift. Tonight, the gift had come, not so much presented as hurled in her direction, on the run. Still, it had *come, and it was warmly received.*

What followed, long into the night, was one of those mutual burrowings to a deeper level of couplehood that make it worthwhile to fall in love in the first place and provide compensation for what may come later. Manning was, in turn, relieved, grateful, excited, and spilling over with effusions of what was in store for the people they had just become. Kitty was honored, reassuring, romantic, and seductively amused, more or less in that order, with some repetition. No incident in their relationship was too small or unimportant to be explored and re-examined for its possible bearing on tonight's revelations. Figuratively and literally, the Blue Leopard was unmasked and remasked over and over, now with happy chatter, now with tearful concern until every question and ramification had been posed, revisited, and exhausted. The courtship which had begun in silence had found its voice.

Then, just as sleep seemed a possibility, the erotic ironies of the great disclosure dawned on them both and were given prolonged and pleasurable attention. The only thing to which the blissful pair did less than justice was the violence and danger that triggered their newfound intimacy. Not until morning did Kitty survey the den and call out, "He doesn't seem to have gotten anything."

Manning sat up in bed and looked thoughtful. Suddenly, he exclaimed, "My God! What a fool I am!" He threw off the sheet, bolted from the bed and raced into the den. His eyes went everywhere.

"Nothing's missing," said Kitty.

Manning looked at her miserably and pressed his finger to his lips. He held out his left palm and, with his right hand, made a gesture of writing. Without a word, Kitty opened the drawer of an end table and handed him pen and paper. Manning scribbled rapidly and handed her a sheet which read: "Nothing's missing because something has been added. We may have spent the night broadcasting dangerous information to the one man in the world who won't hesitate to use it against us. Your lover is an idiot."

The Blue Leopard costume still lay atop the canopy of Kitty's ample bed, where it had been flung at an exuberant juncture in the evening's discourse. Kitty stared in bewilderment as her unadorned paramour prowled the den, leaping and probing every inch of the walls and furniture. Finally, he stood up from behind a sofa, smiling and raising aloft a tiny transmitter. "It's all right," he announced. "I interrupted the brute before he was able to install it."

"Who on earth was he, and what have I done to be spied about?"

Spied upon, thought Manning, who wouldn't dream of correcting his beloved. "I have some ideas about that," he said. "Let me slip into something less comfortable, and I'll try to puzzle it out over breakfast."

Their breakfast took place, as it often did, at the Polka Dot Pantry, owned by Kitty's breezy friend, Trixie Prescott. Trixie was infamous for the eccentricity of her wardrobe, whose colors ranged throughout the rainbow, but whose design never varied. Whatever the hue, the entire ensemble – frock, hat, gloves, scarf, shoes, and bag were always patterned in polka dot. Once, early on, Manning gently broached the subject of fashion fatigue. "Trixie, do you ever get the urge to kick over the traces and wear something different?"

"You read me like a book, Noojie," (Trixie had an inexhaustible store of pet names for her friends. Manning thought his fell especially wide of the mark.) "I'd be bored stiff wearing the same kinda stuff every day. You won't see me in dots this size for a month." As if anything had been explained, Manning nodded, "Ahh," and abandoned the topic forever.

The Polka Dot Pantry was one of the reasons Manning continued to base his operations in Manhattan. Its unorthodox menu had yet to let him down. If he fancied hot Ralston and pumpernickel toast at three in the morning after a rigorous night of battling iniquity, he could find it at Trixie's emporium. This morning, his choice was crunchy bagels, laden with cream cheese, lox, and red onion. It was accompanied by the "bottomless Cuppa Dot," the robust, aromatic coffee for which the café was famous since Manning had put Trixie on to its Arabian supplier.

Kitty and Manning sipped in silence until the waitress moved away from the booth. "I may have overreacted this morning," said Manning. "I took the intrusion personally because the burglar belongs to an ancient sect I had dealings with as a child. The man who killed my parents is the only one who could have brought them here. Understandably, I assumed this was about me, but the more I think about it..."

Kitty leaned forward as if to peer into his mind.

"I mean," Manning went on, "He hasn't seen me since I was eight. He wouldn't know what I look like, and he has no reason to think I'm still alive." Manning took up Kitty's hand and squeezed it reassuringly. "As a matter of fact, great pains were taken to convince him otherwise."

Manning smiled. "I'm not big on coincidence, but this just may be one, and a whopper. I was afraid at first that what he might have learned could put me into his hands again, but it's more likely he was after something else entirely. If I can find out what, and quickly, that could put him into mine."

He had yet to let go of her hand, and now he began to stroke it. "The problem is..." His face scrunched into a grimace. "I don't want you to be frightened, but the more you know, the safer you'll be."

Her eyes widened. "Then it's me he's after? This fiend?"

"No! Don't imagine that," he said emphatically, as he imagined just that. "It's something you have, or information you may not even realize you possess, or that someone you know has. Those parties you give with all those movers and shakers in attendance – that device would have let him be a fly on the wall. It would put me to sleep, but who knows what he'd hoped to overhear?"

"It seems farfetched," she mused, "but that thug really was there, wasn't he? And if he didn't come to steal?" She looked dubious but *fearful. He had never seen her lose her composure before.* To Manning, her steady, even self-possession was one of her most attractive features. Watching her lose it, he learned that, in Kitty, unsteadiness was equally attractive. She needed him, and he had never loved her more.

The lox arrived, and Manning tore into them, eating and talking with equal enthusiasm. Kitty smiled in silence until Manning bit off a chunk of salmon large enough to permit interruption.

"You're my beamish boy again."

"Habbemp I beeb?"

"Don't talk with your mouth full. I merely mean, it's nice to see you like this. You're very handsome when you're serious, but I've missed cute."

Vivator, in his wisdom, had taught Manning that compliments, while seldom to be trusted, are, if kindly given, to be enjoyed without protest. Manning blushed and kept on chewing.

Kitty continued, "See if you can be both when you take me to the fundraiser."

"Must I? I mean, must I go?"

"There's no must, but I like to show you off."

Manning winced.

"Oh, never mind. I won't drag you there if you'd really hate it. Vincent can take me. He'll be there, and I think he'd like to. He's been so helpful and generous. I almost owe it to him."

"Vincent again? He pops up a lot lately."

Trixie refreshed their Cuppas and teased him. "You should be jealous, Noojie. Vincent's quite dashing, mysterious even, and that moustache!"

Kitty shook her head. "My darling isn't jealous. We don't play games like that, but I think he is curious."

"I am, a bit. He shows up out of the blue, and suddenly he's Mr. Save the Arts, throwing donations at you like bouquets. What's his game? What's his name, for that matter? I don't even know his last name?"

"Time you did." Kitty dug into her purse and placed a stylish business card before him. As Manning examined it, the blood drained from his head. A quietly elegant font spelled out "V. Dictor, Arabian Import Export."

"I think I'd better take you after all," Manning said quietly.

It was not the cute Manning who walked Kitty home. His hands jammed into his pockets, he spoke little, just enough to convince her that his mind was not elsewhere, though it was. The business card had seized it and dragged it back to a place of caution and dread where it had not dwelled for many years – a place he had begun to hope it would never go again.

It could still be coincidence.

No, it could not.

He had to see this V. Dictor face to face; then he would know. But the knowledge would be double edged. He didn't resemble the child Vindictor had tormented so many years ago; but the time and distance which had obscured him from the attention of his nemesis had also lulled Manning into an illusion of safety. Vivator had protected him with a new identity, but as Manning approached adulthood, the specters of his past seemed remote, their former intensity bleached by the glare of his success as a crime fighter. The urge to honor his parents and become himself again grew irresistible, and he yielded to it. He was Manning Nugent once more. Now, it appeared this sentimental impulse had placed a target on his back... unless...

He had to know, but did Kitty? Was she safer in ignorance or armed with the truth? He would decide later. The Beaux Arts Ball was less than a week away, but, as Hamlet observed, there was an interim and it was his. He prayed he'd make better use of it than the Dane had done.

To Manning, indecision was as unwelcome as it was unfamiliar. He had to clear his head and quickly. A bit of serenity wouldn't go amiss either. He knew where to find both, and it was not in Manhattan.

"Kitty, I'm going away – just for a bit. I'll be back in plenty of time for the benefit."

He could see she hadn't expected this.

"Don't worry. It's terribly important, or I wouldn't think of leaving you alone right now. I'll speed back to you like a demon, but in the meantime, you've got to stay at Trixie's. Promise me!"

"But – ," She strained to think of something which wouldn't sound like pleading. "What if they come back to install the bug?"

"It's not likely, now that they know we expect it. But, actually, it might be to our advantage if they do. We could feed them just what we want them to think."

He drew her close. "No, Kitts, this is one time I can better protect you from a distance."

Argument was futile. She gave herself up to his fierce parting embrace.

⁂

That afternoon, half a world away, Manning went first in search of serenity. "Howzabout a bath, old friend?" Darting atop the elephant's broad back, he headed Taponto toward the river, where two adult imps, man and beast, cavorted with mindless, luxurious abandon until sunset.

Darkness found him closeted deep in the jungle with a smiling, turbaned gentleman, some forty years his senior. "It doesn't become me to say this, Manning, but I am pleased your life is no longer so blissfully untroubled." The older man nestled a cigarette into a long holder, dragged a wooden match across a Parisian striker, held the flame steady, and drew the smoke thirstily past his lips. "It's good, once again, to have you feel the need of my peculiar services."

"You embarrass me, Dr. Rabiz. I miss your company even when I don't require your services, and I've never thought of them as peculiar. Exotic, yes, and rather wondrous."

A thin white cloud escaped the doctor's lips, slowly curling upward and dissipating. "I know things; that much is true."

A deep and singular trust had developed between the two men since Manning had fled Arabia as a child. Dr. Rabiz had known Vivator and had, in fact, chosen the family with whom the boy would be deposited. While medicine had been Rabiz's ostensible profession in Paris, Manning was soon permitted to observe that international intrigue was the man's specialty - his passion. That this passion continued in his retirement was about to prove most useful.

"Then, this Vincent Dictor," said Manning, "Is it as I suspect?"

Dr. Rabiz set aside his cigarette and fixed Manning with a level gaze.

"It is all of that, and perhaps far worse."

Manning steeled himself for whatever he was about to hear, but the hairs on the back of his neck stirred with apprehension.

"From the time you first appeared to me, as Marius, it seemed a good idea to track the whereabouts and activities of this most interesting brother of Vivator, lest he make himself of further nuisance. The effort has proved endlessly fascinating. He is, indeed, as they say, a man of many hats."

Dr. Rabiz proceeded to detail a rapacious but clandestine career of financial exploitation that left few unsavory avenues unexplored. Blackmail, drug and weapons trafficking, slavery, all had at one time or another been stepping stones in the anonymous but profitable ascent of Manning's old nemesis.

"His fortunes ebb and flow, and when they contract, he retreats to his blindly devout power base, The Conniptions."

Manning nodded and leaned forward, searching the doctor's face with earnest attention. "And now?"

"My surmise is this. Though they serve him well, Vindictor's attitude toward his people is one of increasing contempt. Having tasted acceptance in Europe as a faux philanthropist, he no longer stoops to dirty his hands in the old ways. His new enterprises are more costly, however, with many more palms to grease. He is feeling a pinch and needs a vast new stake."

Rabiz paused, and Manning seized the conversation excitedly. "Yes, of course. He's fastened on Kitty to use her connections to –"

The doctor slowly shook his head. "You misconstrue the situation – to your peril. Your lover's network of donors would not begin to satisfy this devil's ambitions. He courts her, yes, but she has only one contact of interest to him."

Silence filled the room, and as Manning absorbed the doctor's words and knowing look, the young man's face reflected the full range of their implications. At last he spoke.

"It's me you mean – and so he knows. But how do I fit into his schemes except as an overmatched adversary?"

Rabiz smiled indulgently. "My dear young friend! Your innocence is so appealing – and so dangerous. You sit on untold wealth, and yet it does not rule you. You tap it but seldom, and then sparingly, most often in the cause of the oppressed. You live as Vivator would have wished, forgetting for the most part that it is there. But it IS there – vast, silent, glittering, and all consuming to the fiend of whom we speak. His ignorance of its location drives him to the brink of madness and to you."

"The sapphire caves," whispered Manning.

"The sapphire caves," echoed the good doctor.

As simple as that. The idea passed from the older man to the younger, and in transit, as so many times in the past, acquired the weight and solidity of a certainty, washing over him like cold, sobering *water. His head was clear.*

Rabiz broke the tension with a laugh and tousled Manning's hair. "Ah, my pensive Marius, life would petrify without the occasional calamity, would it not?"

Manning smiled grimly. "Don't you think I've had my fair share?"

"What I think is that, without an interesting problem, my gato azul would be bored to death, as would I."

Manning's smile widened, acknowledging that it was so.

"Now you must strategize, and you've never been able to do that on an empty stomach."

Rabiz clapped his hands, and a caftaned servant materialized.

"What would you say to a tagine?" the doctor inquired.

"I'd say, 'Come here, you luscious thing, and let me eat you up.'" It was an old game between them, especially welcome in this perilous circumstance.

"Yes, but no meat tonight, and no strong drink – nothing to dull our senses. Only lovely vegetables and bulgar, some preserved lemons, harissa, and mint tea. Brain food!"

At a wave of the hand from Dr. Rabiz, the servant bowed and withdrew. Manning's head rotated slowly and turned back, letting his eyes graze and caress the sensuous fabrics that softened the walls and ceiling of this comforting hideaway, He sighed deeply and appreciatively.

"I haven't been afraid in such a long time." His voice was low, inaudible beyond the room. "But I'm afraid now, doctor. I don't know if I'm up to this. I work at mastering my gifts, but it's a pampered American boy at work. Vindictor absorbs the dark, ancient arts as easily as breathing. He's steeped in them; they're his second skin."

Dr. Rabiz retied the sash of his smoking robe and smoothed its silken folds across his knee.

"Vindictor was not born a Conniption," he said. "He was, like you, like me, a clever boy, an apt pupil. If you are to succeed in this, you must demystify him. There is nothing innately magical about any of us." But the doctor's good intentions could not penetrate the unbending disbelief in Manning's gaze. Rabiz pressed on. "Well, yes, I cannot, should not overlook those gifts of which you speak. But consider then which gifts are truly prodigious – the hypnotic carnival tricks of a charismatic huckster – or the transformative powers bequeathed you by a force at whose true nature I cannot presume to guess?"

Manning stared at the carpet. "One of his carnival tricks made me what I am."

"Ach! Such sniveling. You deserve a slap, but I could never lay harsh hands on you. When Omar brings our supper, shall I have him slap you repeatedly, as that unworthy utterance deserves? He is having a dull day and would enjoy it."

"No, thank you."

The hand now laid on Manning's shoulder was anything but harsh. "Vindictor took a terrified child and made him believe he was a leopard cub. Vivator gave that child the chance for a courageous leap of faith. But it was the boy's heart, strength, and cunning that made you what you are. With nothing beyond Vindictor's contribution, you might easily be a coat today, draped about the shoulders of an undeserving dowager."

Manning raised his head and met the eyes of his friend. "You pour confidence into me, as always, but when I leave this room…"

"Don't leave it. Use it. Inhale it. Wrap it around you as battle dress – especially this corner."

Rabiz stood up, seized a lamp, and illuminated a design of gold thread previously obscured. Manning came to him and knelt to scrutinize the subtle tapestry.

Drawing in a breath, he exclaimed, "It looks as if I'd drawn it myself!"

"You did. In those early days in Paris, you missed your beloved

Taponto so much that you drew the two of you over and over. One day, I absconded with my favorite version. The beast is groomed as if in a salon. He is being simultaneously brushed, bathed, dressed, and ridden, and all the figures are you."

"It's badly done," murmured Manning, "Yet you saved it, and went to this expense."

"As to that, it's precious to me."

The drapes parted, and Omar entered bearing a tray with their steaming, fragrant repast.

"How I've longed for preserved lemons," said Manning as he tore into the meal.

Rabiz watched his guest with pleasure and observed, "Indeed, there are few things in life which a little lemon can't enhance."

Manning wondered, not for the first time, if one of life's dishes the good doctor would like served up with lemon were Manning himself. There had never been the slightest word or touch, nothing untoward, but for years, Manning had sensed in Rabiz's perception of him a sadness, a longing to be more to the young man than an avuncular advisor. The doctor's feelings for him distressed Manning only in that they were not returned. He was certain the doctor, even primed by wine or the hookah, would never reveal his desires. He was less certain of how he would behave should this happen. He only knew he would never humiliate this kind, wise man who had been of so much help to him in the past and was, this night, about to be still more.

When Omar cleared away their supper, slapping no one, the strategizing commenced in earnest.

"Does Vindictor know you are aware of him? Do you at least start with the advantage of his uncertainty?"

"Hard to say," replied Manning. "It was dark, and the Conniption thug may be confused as to what happened, but can anything ever *really be kept secret from that man?"*

"It can. You meet him shortly. The best course is to feign ignorance of his identity. Call him Vincent. Shake his repellent hand with enthusiasm. Wax warm with praise of his efforts for Miss Brent's cause. It won't hurt to act a bit of the foppish fool as well. Could you do that? Can my little crime fighter act?"

"Well, I've seen The Mark of Zorro."

"Ah yes." Rabiz smiled. "The inestimable Mr. Power." Then he turned serious. "I cannot caution you too strongly about one thing, Manning. Whatever he suspects or doesn't, your only safety is in public places. He will not risk anything at the ball, for example, but you must never be alone with him."

Manning nodded gloomily. "I've understood that from the start."

"And you do realize," he grasped his young friend's shoulders, "I can't bear to put it this way, but it must end in death – his or yours."

Manning's reply was morose. "I guess I— No, of course I realized it, but this was never what I wanted. I only sought to get away from him. He is Vivator's brother, his twin."

"Oh, I think we can say all such niceties ended when this devil stooped to fratricide."

"I was a reckless idiot to reclaim my name! All the trouble the two of you took – can you forgive me?"

Rabiz sank back in his chair. "Well, it's true that if Marius had remained Marius, we would now be having a more amusing conversation, but you chose to honor your parents. I understand the impulse and would never reproach you. It is you who must forgive yourself. We cannot undo what is done, and we waste our spirit in trying."

Manning said quietly, "Thank you."

The two men spoke for hours, plotting contingencies, likelihoods, dangers, and risks. At last, Manning stood up to take his leave.

"So much is unknowable, but I always leave you stronger than I came."

Rabiz rose, smiling. "The corrupt old man, pitted against the courageous youth, pure of heart. I know where I must put my money."

Manning laughed. "Not all of it, I hope. Keep some aside for robes and tobacco – and lemons"

Dr. Rabiz put out his hand but was drawn close and hugged tightly. With that, Manning darted into the jungle and was gone.

⁂

In Manning's absence, events had not stood still. At Trixie's, he found, to his dismay, that Kitty had agreed to let Victor escort her to the ball.

"Don't be cross with me. It's not that I didn't trust you to be here. It's just that he's been so good and so persistent."

Manning could well imagine the persistence. He felt like a father whose child, drawn to the pretty colors, reaches for a poisonous snake.

Kitty went on, coaxingly,"We both know you'd have a miserable evening."

Not as miserable as the one shaping up. His mind raced, but his steady demeanor betrayed nothing. "You're right, of course. Will you always spoil me like this?"

Kitty looked him up and down. "Probably."

"Then throw your things together. Let's go home," home being Kitty's place. Whatever Vindictor's grand plan, the ball was its centerpiece. That he would strike before then made little sense. On this, both he and Dr. Rabiz were agreed.

The moment Kitty closed the door between them, Manning called out to Trixie and drew her aside.

"Trix, will you help me in a little conspiracy? A nice one?"

"Oooh, I love conspiracies, and there hasn't been one in the longest time, Noojie."

"Kitty can't know."

Trixie clapped her hands and rubbed them together. "Marvelous! I'll be dumb as a stone."

"But smart, too," cautioned Manning. "We've both got to be smart for this to work."

She sat down beside him, enthralled.

"Are you going to the ball?" he asked.

"Are you kidding? I've redone my costume twice."

"You've got a date, of course."

"Yeah," she said, without enthusiasm.

"Not a heartthrob?"

She shook her head. "Huh uh, just a way of getting there. He's kind of a pill, but he's crazy about stuff like this."

"Can I persuade you to break his heart and go with me instead?"

"Yeah," she said, easily, "for a price."

"Name it."

"Let me make your costume."

Dear God, he thought. "Sure," he said, reflecting on the steep and bitter cost of protecting those we love.

The following day, Manning appeared, as commanded, in Trixie's sanctorum, an impressively organized workroom, replete with chromatic rainbows of fabric and all the tools, he supposed, of a professional couturier. Trixie approached him garlanded with a tape measure and bearing rolls of what looked like butcher's wrap and a disturbing number of pins.

"Well, get outta that stuff, will ya? I gotta measure." She bristled at Manning's momentary hesitation. "Getcha clothes off, Noojie. We're in New York. It's 1957 for chrissake. You can keep your skivvies on."

Just as he disrobed, they were interrupted by a brusque, insistent banging which Trixie seemed to recognize. She clutched Manning's arm and whispered, "Oh Lord, it's Thirsty!"

Manning stared at her, baffled. "It? Thirsty for what? Our blood?"

"Thurston," she hissed, "The pill. You gotta be my cousin."

The banging ticked up in volume and speed.

"Your cousin? Can't we just toss it a goat through the transom?"

"Hey," she snapped, "this is your conspiracy." He was beginning to wonder.

She opened the door to reveal a tall, slim, petulant man whose many-buttoned coat was fastened clear to his throat. He barged past her with an authority that suggested barging was his usual form of entry.

Manning tried for modesty with an improvised shield of butcher paper as Thurston committed him to memory. "Your cousin? Pah! I knew he'd look like this."

"They all do, darlin'. My family is truly blessed."

Feeling like an ill-wrapped side of beef, Manning clutched at the paper with one hand, and held out the other. "How do you do, Mr. Thurston."

"Yes, right. It's Thurston Biveen, actually. How do you do, Mr...?"

Manning glanced to Trixie for guidance but received only a sheepish shrug.

"Prescott, of course. Norbert Prescott."

Thirsty's pique, momentarily outflanked by the demands of etiquette and civility, now regrouped. "Well, I'm not saying what I believe and what I don't believe about any of this because your cousin, if she is your cousin, is capable of just about anything and more. Which of course you know, if she is your cousin. Although you could know that, I suppose, even if she's really something else."

The others looked at him innocently. He shook his head and raised his voice. "In any case, I can only say, to Prescotts real and alleged, I think it's a mean turn of events."

Trixie patted his hand. "Now, darlin', family must come first, *don'cha* think?"

"Well, yes. Yes, I do. You have me there." She had mollified him enough to steer him to the door. He reached for the knob, then spun back around. "Don't think I'm going to sit at home, missy. I'm not losing out on the highlight of the season. I'll be there and with an enviable companion."

"We look forward to it, Mr. Biveen," Manning said cheerfully.

"Yes, yes, we do, darlin'," Trixie chirped, pressing the door tight behind him. As snappish Biveen footsteps echoed down the hall, she unwrapped her newest relative. "You've got this all crinkled, and – Norbert!!??"

"You can't use my real name at the ball, not even once, all night long. That's crucial. We'll just be Norbert," he grinned, "And Beatrix."

She rolled her eyes. "Must we?"

"Yes, darlin'. It's my conspiracy."

Two hours later, Manning was back at Kitty's, stretched out on her divan. Kitty herself was nestled with her back against it, on the floor. Manning's left hand dangled, playing idly in her hair. His right held the business card which had first set off the alarms in his head that had yet to be stilled.

"You're strange today, Buster," she said softly.

"It can make you strange, waiting for the other shoe to drop."

She twisted her head to look up at him. "The first shoe was the break-in?"

"Yes. It's hard to preempt what you can't see coming at you. I feel like things are sliding out of my control, faster by the minute, and here I sit, well, lie."

He held the card above his head. "There's no address on this card of Vincent's. He must live somewhere, have an office somewhere. There's nothing here but a phone number."

Kitty examined the card and furrowed her brow. "That number is the Plaza. That's where Mavis Throckton told me she reaches him. I guess he manages things from there."

But not everything, *thought Manning*. If one or both of us is to be lured or abducted somewhere, it's damn well not going to be the Plaza. Somewhere in this city, Vindictor is preparing the scene of his trap – but where?

"Vincent's so thorough about everything," said Kitty. "It's funny about his card."

"Yeah, funny," Manning agreed.

The inhabitants and staff of the Plaza hotel went about their tasks, their pleasures, and their intrigues that day and night, blissfully unaware that their every unguarded word and gesture were fair game to an unseen observer moving ceaselessly among them. Vindictor did indeed have a suite there, which Manning took the precaution of entering invisibly, and even then only with room service or housekeeping, lest Vindictor had some means of detecting a presence. For his pains, Manning gleaned nothing beyond insights into the dining habits of Conniptions abroad. It was not until he returned to his own apartment that it struck him his reconnaissance had not been in vain.

He spent less time here now than before he met Kitty, but this was still his aerie of solace and renewal. Everywhere they roamed, his eyes fell on the comforting realia of his life, tastes, and travels, a diverse array that nourished and contented him.

Suddenly, he sat bolt upright. "Of course! The devil. There is no office because there is no business. There is no lair because he doesn't need one. Whatever wretched scene is to play out – my interrogation, my slaughter – it will happen here."

Manning's interim, as if sucked away by a malevolent vacuum, had vanished. The night of the Beaux Arts Ball was upon him. Trixie had asked him to come early to give her time to make any needed adjustments to his outfit. In dismay at his enforced servitude as mannequin to a lunatic designer, Manning hadn't even bothered to inquire as to the nature of his costume. He called out to Trixie, who was fetching it from the workroom. "Who am I? You didn't tell me?"

"Not who. What. We're sort of a matched pair. We're going as a couple of big spotted cats. Leopards."

"No! I can't wear it," he cried out, thunderstruck. Had Trixie been one of Vindictor's minions, she couldn't have picked a more dangerous outfit. All chance of anonymity in the crowd was lost. Trixie's choice would be a bull's-eye on his back, arrogantly riveting Vindictor's attention. Why had Manning waited until now to learn her intentions?

"Whaddya mean you can't wear it? You haven't even seen it," she said drawing closer. "It's really cute – and I've slaved over these things, so don't tell me no. Here, stick your arms out and step into it."

He would do that much. She was offended. But he would go no further. Their lives could not be put at risk for her creative vanity.

She pushed him toward a full length mirror. He peered through his mask and burst out laughing. Staring back at him was a square headed, pointy eared, yellow monstrosity, spattered from head to paw with polka dots of every size and color. He looked as much like the Blue Leopard as jelly beans in a blizzard. It was the damndest thing he'd ever seen. He would wear it.

⁂

The cabbie they flagged down was unfazed by their get-ups. What would it take to faze a New York taxi driver, Manning wondered, as Trixie chattered happily beside him.

"I knew you'd like it, once you had it on," she said, teasing him with his yellow, spotted tail.

Their cab entered a long line of vehicles pulling up to the main entrance of the Hotel Tantamount to disgorge a merry stream of masqued revelers. For the occasion, a silver carpet had been laid down to guide them from the curb to the ticket takers stationed just outside the sprawling Tropadoro Room. If there was a theme to this year's festivities other than "Fork over your cash and strut," it was not immediately evident to Manning. As they entered the glittering, high ceilinged room, he saw, amid a riot of color and spangle, a formidable menagerie of other animals, but harlequins and historical figures could also be spotted, as well as Marilyn Monroes of sundry genders, and even a trapezoid.

Trixie tugged at his pelt. "Do conspirators dance?"

"Tonight they do," said Manning, easing her away from the alcoved tables and into the mottled throng. There was still room to move about if one were purposeful, and Manning jockeyed Trixie around most artfully in search of Kitty and Vindictor. The orchestra, heavy on brass and sax, finished "Old Cape Cod" and was halfway through "My Heart Reminds Me" when he spotted a lovely masked bareback rider, sans horse. There was no mistaking the figure he had so often and so recently embraced. The sight of her companion produced an instant chemical reaction that threw off his rhythm.

Unmasked, perhaps a dozen yards away, was the mirror image of a face he had loved and trusted with all his being. Yet this face was suavely opaque, cruel, and unspeakably chilling. Vindictor's choice of costume was, under the circumstances, all too apt: ringmaster, replete with top hat and whip.

"What is it, Honey?"

"Nothing, Trixie. I just caught a glimpse of Kitty."

"Oh, where? Where?" Her head bobbed to see.

"It doesn't matter. She doesn't need to know I'm here."

"Manning?" She squeezed his arm.

"Remember," he shushed her, "no names tonight."

"It's funny. I never call you that anyway."

"I know."

"It just seemed like I should." All playfulness had drained from her manner. "Honey, you're not here just to spy on her with that Vincent are you? I was only teasin' you about that. You don't need to worry about him in the least."

"I don't. Not in the way you think."

This flip, brassy girl was genuinely concerned about him, and he found it endearing.

"You ever gonna tell me about it?"

"All about it – when it's over. For now, let's keep on dancing."

"You're a puzzle. I like puzzles."

Now he needed to find the Conniptions. Vindictor would keep them close at hand. From his observations at the Plaza, Manning believed there were no more than two of them – but where? They wouldn't be dancing, obviously, nor in conversation with anyone but each other. Not likely they'd be doing that either. They'd be more use to Vindictor in separate parts of the room, perhaps at the exits? All he had to do was find two giant wallflowers. Would Vindictor have gotten them up in fancy dress?

He steered Trixie smoothly around the floor, smiling as he remembered his lessons in the cave with Vivator. He scanned the perimeter, and – yes! One giant lurked beside a potted palm. On the other side of the room, another stood behind a fountain spraying champagne. Motionless and formidable, there was no mistaking them for anything but someone's security, and it wasn't the Hotel Tantamount. Dr. Rabiz had surmised correctly about Vindictor's dismissive view of his Conniption aides. Their costumes were an insulting but unperceived private joke – schoolboy knee britches and dunce caps.

Trixie tapped his shoulder. "Dance me closer to the trapezoid."

"What an outfit!" said Manning. "I give it 'A' for originality."

"It's Thirsty. I knew what he'd be wearing. I wanna find out who he brought."

"Ah yes, the enviable companion."

They neared the gyrating geometric pair, and Manning asked, "So you'd have been the circle?"

"Yeah. This is nicer."

Only the eyes of the enviable companion could be detected as they swung by. The rest of her charms were concealed by a large, wired circle of lavender crepe. Manning lingered nearby long enough for them to hear the trapezoid say, "Get ready, Mother. I'm going to dip." The giggling leopards whirled briskly away in the hope they'd not given offense.

The end of the number segued into a drum roll. Dancers found their tables, and a tall hawk-nosed figure in a peacock cape strode toward the bandstand. Maestro Bunny Landers took the mike. "Ladies and gentlemen, I give you this evening's mistress of charm and charity, the marvelous Mavis Throckton."

In a creepily comfortable tone suggesting familiarity with microphones from the cradle on, Mavis Throckton thanked the crowd for their presence and generosity and informed them of the considerable amount by which this year's efforts had outstripped 1956.

"At this time, I'd like to give my particular thanks to the man and the woman netting the greatest number of new contributors. Our prom king and queen, if you will, Kitty Brent and Vincent Dictor. Stand up. Where are you?" A spotlight sought out the honorees to a ripple of applause.

"It's like we're back in high school," said Trixie as Manning looked on in stony silence.

But Mavis had only begun. "Get up here, you two. It seems only fitting that you lead off the next dance, and what better song for the occasion than the theme from that romantic new picture, "Band of Angels," because that's what all of you are tonight, my band of angels."

"Band of something," muttered Manning as the orchestra swelled and Bunny crooned, "I was alone. I had nobody to love…" Vindictor led Kitty to the center of the ballroom floor. He drew her close. He placed his hand a distance down her spine, north of wolfish, but just. A low, involuntary grunt escaped Manning as he watched them glide and sway. The smiling crowd was clearly charmed by a display that Manning alone found loathsome and obscene. He was able to contain himself only by the realization that although Vindictor's hands were on Kitty, his mind was not. He wheeled her this way and that, as if offering her to the throng, while his eyes darted everywhere, scanning the sea of benign, approving faces, searching for that one discordant reaction which would betray its owner, searching for Manning.

It took effort now for Manning to restrain the beast who shared his body, the beast whose direct, primal urges longed to course through him and find expression in a swift, savage act. His hands remained on the table, perspiring but still. His expression was placid, unchanging. Vindictor's restless gaze continued its probe, but no corner of the room yielded a clue. Soon, other dancers would join and obscure the waltzing honorees. Vindictor became more aggressive. He leaned in closer. He bent Kitty back. He nuzzled her neck.

"Noojie!" Trixie cried out, staring down at their glass table where thin streaks of red trailed up to ten deep, clawlike gouges, just beyond Manning's hands. Vindictor's eyes whirled toward the sound and met Manning's. The masquerade was over.

The band struck up the second chorus, and from all sides of the room, couples took the floor. Straining to see, Manning could make out a bewildered Kitty being hustled away by Vindictor who signaled commands to the hulking Conniptions.

Trixie was in tears and clutched at Manning's hand. "I'm so sorry. I'm such an idiot."

He snatched his hand away, but said, as gently as he could manage,

"Not your fault at all, but you mustn't follow me. Promise!" Hers was a face seldom visited by a serious expression, certainly not of the sort she wore as her escort vanished into the crowd.

Kitty scrambled to make sense of whatever was developing around her. She was outside now, in the alley, her arm still in Vincent's as a limousine with opaque windows pulled up beside them. The door opened, and he attempted to usher her in.

"Vincent, what's going on?"

His smile was warm, reassuring. His voice was playful. "It's a secret." He pressed her hand. "Something happened to me, out there on the dance floor with you in my arms. I find I just can't wait to reveal my little surprise." Gently but firmly, he had eased her into the car, which pulled away as they spoke. "Ignore my aides, Kitty." Vindictor indicated the two large men guarding a basket on the seat facing them. "They are trained to ignore us and well paid to do so. Above a certain wage bracket, privacy and security coexist quite nicely."

"But, the Ball, the committee?"

"La belle Mavis thrives in the limelight. She's delighted to be rid of us."

"Mavis is in on this?"

"The impeccable hostess seeks only the pleasure of her guests," he said enigmatically.

"I've left my wrap, Vincent."

He unfastened his cloak and slipped it about her. "Everything I have looks better on you, my dear," he purred. "Everything."

Kitty laughed uncomfortably. "You're a dreadful flirt, Vincent."

"And here I thought I was being rather a good one." He had the air of one about to spring a delicious joke.

"All right now, just where is this big surprise?" she demanded.

He scrunched down and looked up at her like a mischievous little boy. "It's just a little one, teeny."

"Behave yourself." His high spirits had begun to unnerve and exasperate her.

"As you wish. Actually, it's at your place," he confided, "or it will be, shortly after we arrive."

She eyed him quizzically, "Who delivers anything at this time of night?"

"It's more in the nature of a visit, from a most welcome visitor."

She shook her head. "You're certainly a man of mystery."

He gave her the smallest of nods and stroked her hand.

As Manning burst into the alley, the limousine turned the corner at the far end. It was child's play to catch up to it, but for a time he merely hovered high above it. Kitty was safe for the moment; it was bracing to part the cool air at this speed, and oh, it was good to fly. This was no time, however, for the familiar intoxication of aerial rapture. Uncertain of Vindictor's destination, it was best to descend, match his velocity to the car, and sink to it, gently and invisibly. Wherever they were heading, he could most easily enter it with them.

They stopped outside Kitty's building, and their casual conversation assured him that Vindictor had yet to make his intentions known. Manning gave thought to simply spiriting her away from them, but he knew that would only buy them time. The words of Dr. Rabiz rang in his ears. "It can only end with a death – his or yours."

The close quarters of the elevator called for the finesse of a circus aerialist. He hovered mere inches above their heads, nauseated by Vindictor's oily repartee. How could Kitty think anything was remotely normal, anything but a burgeoning nightmare, flanked as they were by two gigantic Conniptions, so tall that their dunce caps were now bent over their brows by the ceiling of the lift. Was she in innocent ignorance of the danger? Did she suppose Vindictor's goons were lugging a picnic basket with chilled wine? What was in that damned basket anyway? Or was she feigning calm to stall for time until he arrived? He wasn't sure. He wasn't even sure which state of mind was safest for her.

The door to Kitty's apartment swung open, but she paused to caution them. "I really wasn't expecting guests." The delay enabled him to enter before them, the better to station himself strategically. Had the clever girl planned it so, or did she still see this 'Vincent' as her kindly, if not quite disinterested, benefactor? He longed to signal his presence to her, but this deadly farce had to play out just a little longer.

Vindictor settled into a wing chair facing the windows. He had chosen, as Manning anticipated, the nearest approximation to a throne on the premises. Did he expect the Blue Leopard to come crashing through from out of the skies? Had he chosen more wisely, Manning would not now be standing just inches behind him. He wanted to snap the fiend's neck and be done with it, but he had to consider the Conniptions, still standing on either side of Kitty who looked up at them uncertainly.

"Wouldn't your aides like to sit down?" she asked.

"They are accustomed to stand, my dear." Vindictor smiled brightly. "So useful at cocktail parties."

She slid away toward the bar. "Well, if that's what this is, what can I offer them – and you?"

At the merest flick of Vindictor's eyes, the Conniptions moved just close enough to her to stay Manning's hands.

"We are all fine, just as we are," said Vindictor. His eyes fell on an old 78 record Manning had recently brought over. He took it from the coffee table and extended it to Kitty. "Perhaps some music while we wait. This looks amusing."

"If you like, but have we long to wait?"

"I doubt that very much."

The tone arm descended and regaled them with Fats Waller's

"Pantin' in the Panther Room."

This is for my benefit, *thought Manning. He knows I'm here.*

And it was so.

"Dear boy, don't you recognize your cue when you hear it?" Vindictor spoke in the world weary tones of an ancient vampire, for whom no surprises are left. "It's time to reveal yourself. Time to renew old acquaintance while that can still be done at a civilized level."

Kitty gasped as Manning responded to the implied threat to her. He materialized as Trixie's abstract leopard. Vindictor burst out laughing and clapped his hands together in glee. "You," he sputtered with laughter, "you exceed all expectations! You have brass, my boy. I remember these absurd rags. You came quite close on the dance floor, and I never guessed. You wore this to mock me, I take it."

Manning's words almost stuck in his throat, so strange was it to address this monster for the first time in so many years. "It was chosen for me."

Manning had not moved from behind the chair. Vindictor turned fully around, looking up at him. "Have you missed me, Manning? Was it exhausting making all those decisions for yourself, when they used to be made by that little voice in your head – mine?"

Kitty stared at them, silent and terrified. He had to reassure her. "To miss you, I would have had to think about you. I didn't."

"Liar." The word poured out like syrup, intimate and over familiar, meant to intimidate. Vindictor attempted to rise from the chair, but Manning's hands were quick and strong, forcing him back down. "It seems we are at an impasse," Vindictor remained cheerful, "but it only seems that way." At his nod, the powerful Conniptions seized Kitty. "A broken flower would still be – in its way – a thing of beauty, but…"

An instant with any of the three of them off his guard was all Manning needed, and it would come. In the meantime, he would let Vindictor lull himself by playing general, grand puppet master, or whatever title his smug fantasy granted him. All the better if he believed Manning's resources exhausted. "Your move, Sir, but let me assist you." He tightened his grip on Vindictor's shoulders enough to administer pain.

"Well, little cat, we will repair to your – what? Cave? Lair? Litter box?"

"Penthouse," said Manning, delivering an even more painful squeeze.

As they left, Vindictor called out, "Otha, don't forget the basket.

Once under Manning's roof, Vindictor became the most appreciative guest ever to cross his threshold. His eyes went everywhere and back again. No detail of the layout or décor escaped his scrutiny.

"Are you looking to rent or buy?" said Manning.

Vindictor ignored him. "Niktor, make Miss Brent comfortable and present our surprise."

The giant deposited Kitty on a sofa, placed the basket at her feet, removed the lid, and withdrew. As Manning saw what emerged from the basket, he knocked Vindictor to the floor and seized his throat. Vindictor gasped out, "Not... a... good...idea... harmless diversion... but only so long as I... focus and... control it."

Years of battling criminal elements had found him in many a tight spot as Manning Nugent, but never as the Blue Leopard. Across the room, Kitty cowered before a cobra. Manning longed to let the leopard enzymes surge through his bloodstream, but the suave fiend had planned things perfectly and, for the moment, Manning felt powerless. He must submit and bide his time. Holding the massed enzymes in check was an unnatural task, and the unfamiliar sensation it caused was making him ill.

"That's better, Manning," Vindictor said mildly. "Believe it or not, you and your enchanting companion may yet survive to tell the tale *of this evening's events."* He motioned to the two Conniptions. They moved to Manning's side and seized his hands. Vindictor smiled impishly. *"Though, to whom you would tell it, why you would want to, and whether you would be believed . . ."* He shrugged, still smiling.

Then he barked out a command. *"Tear off his clothes."* He patted an ancient wound on his arm, and continued, *"This lad has a fondness for concealed weapons."* With brutal efficiency, Manning's costume and underwear were ripped from his body and tossed aside. Utterly naked and exposed, he was lifted to a table where his arms and legs were stretched out from his sides at full length. Vindictor stood, towering over him. The ease and scope of his success made Vindictor playful. *"Does it occur to you, my boy, how perfectly a sketch of this moment would illuminate the word 'vulnerable' in a dictionary?"*

Manning writhed helplessly and gazed up into eyes dilated with triumph and anticipation. *"You lay completely open to me now, every part of your body and your mind."* Vindictor leaned down across the table, pressing his left palm on the cat symbol he had drawn in blood, years before, on Manning's chest. His other hand slipped behind Manning's head, pushing it up slightly and forcing it to the side, facing Kitty. Vindictor's left hand lifted from Manning's chest and swept the length of his naked body in a dismissive gesture. *"Behold your hero, my dear. I wouldn't raise my hopes too high."*

He lowered his face to just inches above Manning's and spoke with quiet and absolute confidence. *"Your father once chose death to telling me what I wanted to know. You do not have that option – or any other. This moment is simplicity itself. You cannot move. You do not need to speak. You have only to try to conceal from me the knowledge I seek. In so doing, you will reveal it to me, and I will pluck it from your mind."*

Dear God, thought Manning, I AM powerless! It's truly over, and the devil has won.

And so he would have, had hubris not egged him on. Vindictor spoke again, "My brother called you his little cat, but you were never his. I marked you, and you were always mine. You cannot resist me. Vivator cannot help you now. Where are the caves of sapphire? Tell me!"

In a flash, the years fell away, and the meaning of Vivator's dying promise was revealed. Manning made his mind a blank slate except for eight words repeating over and over: "I must not think of the ivory box."

"An ivory box!" Vindictor cried out to the Conniptions. "Find it at once. You need not look far; I have seen such a box here tonight, in plain sight." His eyes darted everywhere and soon fixed themselves on the mantle. "We think alike, Manning. You didn't trouble to hide it – nor would I."

His hands still restrained Manning, but only just, as his excitement grew. "Otha! Niktor! Open the box on the mantle and bring me its contents." Obediently, his brutish aides approached the fireplace, lifted the delicately carved lid, and peered into the ivory box.

Manning kept up his mental chant unabated, permitting no other thought to enter his mind. Vindictor's gaze returned to his victim, and he shook his head, smiling. "Poor boy, you may stop the attempt to hide your secret now. It is already mine." But the chanting continued. Vindictor's smile narrowed. "Have I cost you your wits as well as your treasure? This is imbecilic. Why do you still. . ."

His face drained of expression, and he turned to the Conniptions. They had not moved from the mantle. One held a paper filled with Conniption symbols. Both of them regarded Vindictor with the same cold hatred.

"Why do you wait? Otha, Bring me that paper at once!"

Otha pointed a condemning finger at Vindictor. For all Manning had heard from them up to now, the Conniptions might have been mutes, but the voice that now spoke was thunderous.

"ZAR CONNIPT ZAR!"

Vindictor blanched and had time only to cry, "No! No!" before the brutes were upon him. Otha snapped his arms with two sickening cracks, while Niktor disabled his most fearsome weapon, gouging out his eyes as he screamed piteously.

Whatever means Vindictor had used to control the cobra ceased to function. It writhed and reared menacingly as Kitty recoiled in terror. Manning released the dammed up leopard enzymes within him and the leap for the snake begun by the man was completed by a cobalt leopard who fell upon the flaring hood, shredding it with razor sharp talons as Kitty fainted.

She awakened in the arms of her still naked lover, to find they were alone in the penthouse.

"It's all right, my darling. You're safe with me now. They're gone, and they'll never be back."

Kitty trembled as Manning kissed her and stroked her hair. "Can you be sure?" she pleaded. "He was so…" Words failed her.

"He was evil incarnate, but he is utterly vanquished, from beyond the grave, by his brother, my blessed tutor. Poor darling, what you've seen tonight," he murmured.

"I don't know what I've seen tonight! I can't make sense of it. He controlled us all like puppets, even that hideous cobra, but then those goons turned on him. What was on that paper?"

"His death warrant," Manning said solemnly. "He and my tutor were twins, a rare occurrence among the Conniptions. They consider it a sacred blessing that continues while both twins survive. Because of this, there is no outrage in their tribe equal to that of the killing of one twin by the other. Vindictor deliberately caused Vivator's death but had to conceal it at all costs. He didn't know that his brother had time, before he died, to set down the details. Vivator couldn't bring himself to cause his murderer's death, but without my knowing it, he armed me with the power to do so if ever I were in mortal danger from Vindictor."

"What a wise and wonderful man," Kitty sighed.

"His only foolishness," said Manning, "was to blame himself for the death of my parents. He wanted forgiveness when, if anyone besides Vindictor was at fault, it was me for my childish recklessness. Perhaps now at last he will know he is forgiven."

Manning smiled at her. "He taught me everything I know." He nuzzled her neck. "Well... almost."

"I feel overdressed," said Kitty.

"Leave it to me," he whispered. " I'll handle everything."

"I certainly hope so." She drew him close.

Still holding her in his arms, slowly and tenderly, he began to move them upward, like airborne lovers in a Chagall. With most of the room now below them, he purred, "Have you ever made love on the ceiling?"

"Um... not that I can recall."

He peeled off her long gloves and let them slip to the floor.

"You won't be able to say that in the morning."

CHAPTER 10

MERRY WIDOWS ON THE TOWN

Chicago: October, 1957

There had never been any question as to where they would eat. When they were "on the loose," as Maude liked to put it, only one place would do. Their heads poked up into the sunlight from the mine-like recesses of the Van Buren Street station, and the two women walked north without discussion. Reaching Adams, they turned left automatically. Louisa smiled at the reassuring vertical solidity of the Berghoff sign in the distance.

"You look surprised," her companion said indulgently. "It's still there. It always will be."

"Well, it always has been. You know, Maude, it was the first place Pa took me out, all those years ago. We'd just gotten into the city and didn't have two nickels to rub together, but he wouldn't hear of me cooking that first night. He took it into his head that it would be a bad omen for us, and he brought me to the Berghoff." As they paused for the light to change, Louisa went silent, letting the memory wash over her. Stepping into the street, she continued, "It seemed so grand to me then. Nothing like it in Altoona."

"And now?" Maude inquired.

"Oh now, it's like an old shoe -- a grand old shoe you can trust with your bunions."

"Like us." Maude squeezed her friend's arm as they took their places at the end of the line that had formed outside the revolving door of the restaurant. Ahead of them stood about twenty people. "I would have left earlier," said Maude. "I *was* leaving, but Margaret called. I knew it would be her and with nothing to say, but I'm superstitious about not answering the telephone."

"Oh, I don't mind the wait; it's lovely out," said Louisa. "Look, it's moving already."

They were no longer the last in line. Louisa examined the new people behind them. She wondered if they were first timers, just wanting some lunch, unaware of the treats in store for them. No, she decided, newcomers were fidgety. A calm had settled over this couple for whom, like her, the place held memories. Just now, in Louisa's case, the memories were bittersweet, and Maude had brought her here to soften them. Neither of them would mention it, but on this day ten years ago Henry Sheffield, in a fit of coughing, died in the bed they had shared for forty-five years.

The line outside gave way to the line inside, where the waiting area suggested a tastefully appointed cattle pen replete with mellowed wainscoting and stained glass windows. Aspiring diners were twirled through the entrance only to find themselves immediately hemmed against the wall by the guardrail of a stairway that gouged through the center of the floor and led to subterranean restrooms and a bar. Beyond this pit, running the length of the opposite wall, was a narrow, cushioned window seat where a young woman attempted to gentle three jiggly children. Watching her, Louisa thought, "If I had brought the boys here at that age…" Wincing, she pushed the image away, knowing, however, that it would resurface before this day was through.

Four was the magic number for speedy seating, and two pairs of strangers behind Louisa agreed to let hunger trump privacy and were taken to the head of the line. Louisa looked at Maude who shook her head. "Not today," then she laughed and muttered, "or any other." Louisa nodded. At last, the crisp blonde host led them to a corner table in the darker east room and called out, "Otto!" Otto hustled across the room, bearing a pad and pencil. He wore a morning coat over a black apron whose pockets bulged with bills, change, and the tokens with which he would buy their meals from the kitchen. Like all waiters who lasted at Berghoff, Otto, though halted, seemed to vibrate like a large teutonic hummingbird.

"Beer, ladies? It is Oktoberfest."

"Louisa?" The ladies concurred. "By all means, then. Two good beers for us."

"We serve no bad ones." Otto sprang away and bolted through the crowd.

"He doesn't remember us," said Maude.

"No," Louisa replied.

Maude removed her leather handbag from the table and draped its strap over the back of an empty oak chair. It rested there on Louisa's vinyl purse in amiable intimacy. The women, too, were snugly ensconced, and Louisa looked especially comfortable. Maude had put off satisfying her curiosity about a topic that could prove unwelcome to her friend, but now, the moment seemed right.

"I've been wondering, Louisa, did Victor and Winnie bring you something from Saugatuck?"

Louisa nodded.

"You didn't show me anything before we left."

Louisa regarded her blandly. "Didn't I?"

"No, dear, you didn't." Maude sat back in patient silence to play the part of someone whose attention is consumed for the indefinite future with the loosening of an earring.

Clearly out-waited, Louisa shrugged and spoke again. "Oh, it's a serving tray…with sea shells all around the sides…" But the adjustment of the earring remained a work in progress. "The handles are sea shells as well."

"Sounds pretty."

Louisa drew a piece from a stack of rye bread slices. "It's pretty enough, and it does say 'souvenir of Saugatuck.' That's such a help at our age." She laughed and fished with her fork for butter in a dish of ice. "It's just for show. It's not practical. The handles will come off the first time I serve anything but cotton candy."

Maude smiled. "Just the thing for hot tea when the wrong crowd arrives – and the perfect excuse." They both laughed. Maude pressed on. "Did Victor enjoy himself?"

Louisa looked off. "I suppose so. He always does on these occasions."

"And Winnie?" Maude prodded.

Louisa forced her knife down through a cold square of butter. The clatter against the plate echoed loudly in her silence. "You know," she said at last, "I wouldn't go out with a devil like you if you weren't paying." She shook her head. "Where does he find them, Maude?"

An indecorous parade of pungent answers trooped through Maude's mind, but as she looked at her friend of more than forty years, she grew wistful. "Who knows where any of us find someone?" After a beat, she added, "I did like Rachel. She was always nice to me, and she didn't need to be. It's none of my business, but I wish they'd stayed together."

Louisa spoke up sharply. "That wasn't Victor's doing. I'll never forgive Rachel for it." She sighed. "But, Maude, they just keep coming – and going. They get worse and worse. What is he looking for?"

Maude patted Louisa's hand. "You'll always be Victor's best girl."

Louisa gave a start. "Sweet mother of Jesus! Don't lump me in with that pack. It makes me gag to watch them fawn all over me before they figure out I've got nothing to say about their chances."

Maude leaned forward and lowered her voice. "It isn't nice to say this, but why must he marry them? Couldn't he take them to a motel until they're out of his system?"

Louisa looked far from shocked. "Yes," she said thoughtfully, "I'd say Winnie knows her way around a motel." Winnie's good name was spared further abuse only by the arrival of Otto and the beers.

"Ladies?" Otto's pencil, poised baton-like in mid air, made clear that he would brook no delay. The menus lay untouched, but both women's orders were swift and precise. Louisa would have wiener schnitzel with spaetzle and coleslaw. Maude chose sauerbraten with creamed spinach and asked to substitute mashed potatoes for the noodles. The menu expressly forbade such negotiation, but Otto smiled and nodded. To start, the ladies would share a cup of liver dumpling soup. As Otto took up the menus, Maude caught his sleeve and whispered briefly. He nodded and vanished.

"What tricks are you up to now?" asked Louisa.

"You'd be surprised. I'm a regular magician, these days."

They returned to the subject of marriage and honeymoons but in a more general way. It was agreed that expectations in those areas had increased greatly since they had embarked upon them. They considered themselves fortunate to have had husbands who were neither unfaithful nor physically abusive. Both men had been amiable partners and good providers, and what more could reasonably have been asked at the turn of the century? The matrimonial scales had always been tipped a bit in Maude's favor. Louisa was not blind to the fact that Daniel Weaver had been considerably more easygoing and less set in his ways than Henry Sheffield. He had also been luckier with money and smarter about it. Louisa neither resented these discrepancies nor thought them unfair. It was simply what had happened. It would have taken a husband many cuts indeed below her own for her to have entertained the thought of divorce. It would, in fact, have taken someone so wretchedly unsuitable that she would never have married him in the first place.

"People try each other on for size today, Maude. We had a clearer eye for what would work."

"Yes, I'd say so, but we also knew how to train a man to treat us properly."

Louisa smiled and raised her eyebrows. "I don't know about that. Daniel was already housebroken, and I pretty much let Henry have things his own way."

"You trained him, and I was there to watch. I hadn't known you long, and you were still carrying Paulina." Maude waggled her stein of beer playfully. "Remember?"

"Oh that." In the first year of their marriage, when the house was still a single story and the backyard nothing but a dirt lot, Henry was working odd shifts at the openhearth. Gradually, he drifted into the habit of stopping for a pail of beer before coming home. On the night of which Maude spoke, Henry arrived later than usual, accompanied by six of his fellow shift workers, all of them tipsy, though none more than he. "Set it up here, boys," he said, in a loud, festive voice, and a particularly large pail of beer slopped over as it was thumped on the kitchen table. "Louisa, fix the boys something to eat with this," Henry ordered. Louisa remained seated and looked at him in silence for a moment, while the moist hilarity of the company quieted. It dried up completely as the obviously pregnant woman rose, took up the beer pail, and moved to the kitchen door.

"It's a hot night," she said grimly, "you and the boys will be more comfortable in the yard." With that, she was through the door before Henry could stop her, pitching the entire contents of the pail into the dirt.

Louisa chuckled at the memory. "You trained him all right," said Maude. "You trained the whole lot of them. Was he furious the next day?"

"He was mild as a lamb. He seemed to appreciate that I'd made things clear and that I hadn't yelled and fussed at him. In fact, that was the morning he started calling me Mama."

Maude raised her stein in a toast. "Most impressive! I doubt that

Winnie will be that capable with Victor."

"No," Louisa said thoughtfully, "she'll just leave him."

Otto was back, naming each dish as he placed it before them. "Wiener schnitzel under egg, sunny side up."

"Under egg?" Louisa examined the platter. "But I didn't –"

"Something wrong, Mrs.?" Asked Otto.

Louisa looked at her companion. "This is your doing."

Otto despised situations and sensed one in the making. "You don't wish it?"

"I do wish it, Otto," said Louisa, smiling broadly. "I just wasn't expecting it. It's the way my husband would have ordered it if he were still around. He used to say there were very few things that didn't improve under a fried egg."

Otto remarked, "A wise man, Mrs" and fled.

Neither woman was timid of appetite, and the feast was attacked with enthusiasm. When it was dispatched, Maude descended to the ladies room, leaving Louisa to await the arrival of coffee and a heated apple strudel which they would share.

Alone and undistracted, Louisa found herself thinking again of the children gamboling on the window seat and the young mother trying to orchestrate their energy. Her own boys had been full of such energy right up until the trip to Rainbow Beach and the contagion that changed them overnight and forever into serious little men. Jack showed the symptoms first, then Edmond, who slept with him.

In the beginning, Louisa approached their chills complacently. These were summer colds that would run their course quickly and require little more from her than sympathy and lozenges. Then, Jack's fever suggested something more serious, and Dr. Glascoe was sent for. By the time he arrived, a nervous Louisa had scorched her hand on each of her son's foreheads. She rubbed them with ice and made them drink as much water as they would tolerate between spasms of shuddering. By now, she was more than willing to have Dr. Glascoe tell her she had on her hands a double case of measles or chicken pox, or some other manageable childhood nuisance. He told her very little except to watch them closely and that he would return to check on them the next day. When he did, Jack's right leg was swelling, and he had fallen while trying to reach the bathroom. Both boys were crying and clearly in pain.

No one in Louisa's or Henry's families had ever been hospitalized, except for childbirth, and not always then. So it was with unaccustomed anxiety that the couple listened as Dr. Glascoe made arrangements. When it became clear that neither boy was able to walk to the doctor's car, he called for an ambulance. Louisa insisted on riding with them, holding their hands and trying to make an adventure of it for them. She was not permitted to stay the night at their bedside, but she returned by streetcar, early the next morning. The ride was long and strange, and though she was disoriented from apprehension and lack of sleep, she paid strict attention to the progress of the trolley because it involved several transfers.

Louisa couldn't know then how familiar and automatic this eerie journey would become over the next six months, nor that she would be making it on a daily basis. She couldn't know how many of those mornings she would approach the children's ward with her heart in her mouth for fear that one of the boys had not survived the night. As their hold on life grew more fragile, Louisa took to bringing Paulina with her. She was now obsessed with the idea that her daughter must not forget her brothers if the worst should happen.

At the end of six exhausting months, however, Louisa was transported with elation to watch Jack and Edmond limp without assistance down the hospital walkway to their father's car. The limp would be permanent, but the boys were alive. The look in her husband's eyes brought her back to earth in short order. For him, the sentence was reversed. The boys were alive, but their limp would be permanent. They were still his boys, but now they were broken. She prayed they couldn't read their father as well as she had learned to do. She told herself that Henry, like the rest of them, had been put through a grueling ordeal. He was a good man, and his disturbing reaction could be temporary; in which case, she was prepared to forgive it.

Two years later, when little Victor was born whole and healthy, Henry's delight was both unbounded and a bit unsettling. The arrival of the baby reawakened something in him and brought him fully back to life. Louisa was happy for Henry, but she couldn't shake the feeling that something besides his joy and pride had awakened, something cheap and unworthy of him. Victor was to be his real son, his reward for what he had suffered with the others.

It wasn't long before Jack and Edmond smelled it too. The sobering months in the hospital, and their father's grave demeanor after their return, had made serious little old men of them. It had not made them resentful however. Henry, though still kind, was no longer playful and affectionate, but at first, it seemed to the boys that what had frightened and changed them must have frightened and changed him as well. Louisa encouraged this belief, and gradually, they forgot that their father had ever behaved any differently with them. The boys had never been difficult to manage, but now they became quiet and responsible to a degree that Louisa thought peculiar. Except for Paulina, protected by a thick hide of selfish oblivion, the members of the Sheffield household seemed to be mastering an alarmingly humorless maturity. Then, in one swift, devastating stroke, the boys saw Henry's capacity for intimacy and playful abandon reignited by little Victor's arrival. Watching these forgotten treasures lavished on someone else, they missed them keenly. The sight was dangerously instructive. So, their father was not, after all, incapable of warm, demonstrative affection; he merely felt Jack and Edmond undeserving of it. It was a lesson Louisa could not bear to see her sons learn.

Things came to a head that Christmas day. Edmond had not asked for, but dearly wanted, a lustrous red wagon displayed in Goldblatt's window. Henry had placed it, unwrapped, at the edge of the tree. It would be the first thing Edmond would see as he entered the parlor in his pajamas. As Louisa led the boys from the bedroom, she kept glancing at Edmond's face, anticipating the pleasure that was about to flood it. Unfortunately, she had reckoned without Henry, who, unable to restrain himself, had loaded the wagon with unwelcome cargo, little Baby Victor, wearing a red satin bow. Edmond's face was certainly worth watching as it flooded not with pleasure but contempt. He had to be pushed to the wagon, where he said only, "Oh, is it mine then?"

"Of course," said Henry gruffly, "Who else's would it be? But don't move it yet; I want to take a picture of you pulling Baby." Edmond wandered off, leaving Henry to remark, "Not very grateful, is he?"

At that moment, Louisa knew that her love for her husband, which she always imagined increasing with each year they shared, had limits and had reached them. It would never grow beyond what she now felt, and she would have to work at not letting it diminish. Realizing she would also have to work at minimizing Henry's opportunities for making his older sons despise him, she snatched up Baby Victor and put him to bed.

Maude's return caught her by surprise. "Where are you, Louisa? Wallowing in the sweet bye and bye?"

Louisa shook her head to collect herself, and said, "You were gone so long. I must have forgotten where I was for a moment."

"And here I thought you were being so good."

Louisa squinted quizzically.

"About that," Maude gestured toward the untouched strudel in front of her friend.

Louisa glanced down and noticed it for the first time. "Oh." She took up a knife. "Will you trust me to divide it?"

"Of course not, what do you take me for?" Maude passed her a dessert fork. "Let's just eat it. If you can cut a strudel without making an unholy mess, the crust is no good." As they ate in silence, Maude watched Louisa closely and said at last, "You need a diversion."

"I thought I was having one," Louisa replied.

Maude dug into her purse, produced a much-folded page of the *Tribune* and spread it out on the table. "Let's go to a movie."

Louisa, knowing that Maude would want to pay, said, "It's almost too nice a day to spend inside, and there won't be many more of them." Still, Maude had gone to the trouble of clipping out the schedules. Maybe she was looking forward to it. "If there's something you think we'd like though…"

"Let's see…" Maude moved her fingers across the page, and Louisa saw the smile that always preceded impish nonsense. "Here it is! A double feature at the Monroe: *Catman of Paris* and *Valley of the Zombies*." Louisa rolled her eyes and shook her head. "No? Hmmm," Maude resumed the search. "Margaret and Carl liked this one, *The Three Faces of Eve*. It's at the Oriental."

Louisa's eyes narrowed. "You aren't serious?"

"Well, yes. Margaret went on and on about the new girl in it. She plays this pretty young woman with a --." Maude gasped at her own clumsiness. Her hand covered Louisa's and squeezed. "Oh, Lou, forgive me. Frances. What was I thinking?"

"You weren't, dear," Louisa replied in a dead monotone. Then, melted by Maude's stricken look, she added, "It's all right," and smiled. "It's just that, after spending twenty years with a split personality on my doorstep… no, I wouldn't find Miss Eve too entertaining. She has a few too many faces for me right now."

Maude shook her head. "That's all over and done with. You've gotten poor Frances confined, and she can't harm you, or Edmond, or even herself where she is now, thank goodness."

"Everybody says, 'Poor Frances.'"

"I only mean—."

"Oh, I know what you mean." Louisa sighed. "It's what they all mean. But if they had to jump out of her way when one of her 'moods' flared up and pick up the pieces after it roared through, they wouldn't be so quick to say, 'Poor Frances.' They'd say, 'Poor Edmond,' or 'poor anyone in her path.'"

Maude nodded. "And especially, 'Poor Louisa.'"

"Achh!" Louisa waved her hand upward. "I'm not after sympathy. I'm after peace. And now that we seem to have it, I don't even want to hear that wretched woman's name. The damage she's done to us all!" She leaned forward and spoke faster now, almost sputtering. "I don't care if she didn't mean it. I don't care if she couldn't help it. What difference does it make? It got done. To us! To me! To my son!"

Louisa took a long sip of coffee and sat back. "You're right, Maude. It's over and done, and if I say so myself, I can take a bit of the credit for that."

"Of course you can. Even the boys will see it's for the best one day." Maude patted her hand again. "How are they taking it?"

Louisa spooned a bit of sugar into her cup and stirred it idly. "Well, with Anthony, I can't be sure. He doesn't bring it up. He's in his room a lot these days with his puppets, and now he has a guitar. I think he likes the privacy, with his brother gone. I think he'll be all right."

"And young Edmond?"

"When you come right down to it, Maude, I'm not sure I've ever known what he really thought about anything. Except the movies, of course. Do you know, that's what he writes to us about, when he writes at all? His father and I are worried sick about him, and we're dying to know how he's getting on. Frankly, though I've never said anything, I've been afraid he may not make a go of it." Louisa twisted her wedding ring back and forth. "It was a wrench when he went, so unexpectedly, but now, if they send him back, it might be worse for him than if…" she trailed off.

"Louisa," Maude said crisply, "I don't understand you. Why would the army send him back?"

The comment, and its tone, surprised Louisa. "My goodness, you know him, Maude."

"Yes, that's why I ask."

"Well, you must admit, he's just not …" Why couldn't Maude make this easier for her, she wondered. "I don't like to put it this way, but he's not very good at anything. Not anything useful."

"He can always make me laugh when I need to. He beats the pants off of us at canasta. What would you like him to be good at?" Maude had evidently decided to be impossible.

"But in the service…" Louisa fumbled for the right words to express her concern.

"Louisa, it's only the army." Maude laughed. "And Edmond isn't a dunce."

"No, he can be clever enough when he wants to be. That's what makes his letters so aggravating. He knows perfectly well what we want to hear about, and instead, he writes us movie reviews. It's like pulling hen's teeth to get him to talk about the army or Alaska. When I asked him what was the nicest thing about his new post, he wrote that Warner Brothers sends their movies up there months before we see them in the states. Isn't that exasperating?" She paused for a reaction. "You're laughing at me!" she snapped.

"And I'm eating all the strudel. Here." Maude pushed a forkful at Louisa, who opened her mouth and then chewed vigorously. "They still know how to do it," said Louisa, taking another forkful. She patted her lips with a napkin. "Maude, he acts as though he's not even *in* the army."

"Maybe it helps him to do that," Maude said cheerfully. "He's not in summer camp now, or the boy scouts, and if things are rough or unpleasant for him, why would he write about that?"

"So we'd *know*, for heaven's sake," Louisa hissed. "You're as exasperating as he is."

"But suppose he doesn't want you to know? Did you ever think about that?" Maude kept her voice low and intended it to be calming. "This was nobody's decision but his, and he wants to convince you it was a good one."

"I suppose I could suppose that," said Louisa, staring off, "but…" Maude touched her arm. "What are you really worried about?"

Louisa turned back to the table. "He's not very … soldierly."

"You mean… manly?"

Louisa gave an almost imperceptible nod.

Maude sat back and looked at her thoughtfully before she spoke. "Lou, it's been almost six months since Edmond enlisted. He's been at four posts, with four different sets of sergeants. They've had plenty of time to find out whatever there is to find out about him, and he's still there. I think he's going to be just fine."

Otto approached them with the bill which Maude read quickly and handed him enough to include a pleasant tip.

"Thank you, Maude. Thank you for everything." Maude smiled at her contentedly, and started to take up the newspaper. "No, wait," said Louisa. "Look again. The third time will be the charm. What's at the Chicago? They used to have such wonderful stage shows that it didn't matter what was playing. It's close to the Randolph station.

What's there now?"

Maude examined the theater ads and began to chew her lip. She said nothing but rotated the page and pushed it toward Louisa. "What is it?" Maude remained silent. Louisa glanced down at the paper and found the ad near the top of the page. "Judas Priest!" she exclaimed, "*The Man of a Thousand Faces*. It's a consp—" but she dissolved into helpless laughter and was quickly joined by her friend. She attempted to speak several times before they were able to control themselves. "Three strikes and we're out, I guess," she said, still panting. "But look what's on the back of the page. The Fair has skirts for $7.99. That's just across the street."

Before the afternoon was over, the two companions happily wore themselves out exploring not only The Fair, but Three Sisters, Mandel Brothers, Carson's, and Marshall Field's as well. Now, Maude drowsed across from her as they sat in a crowded coach on the Illinois Central. It would not pull out for another five minutes, but because they had been wise and come early, they had found places together.

What a good day it had been. All that needed to be said had been said, and Louisa felt no overwhelming need to keep her eyes open. She patted her purse, which now contained a slice of strudel as a treat for Big Edmond. Through the window, the autumn sunshine bore down on her gently and luxuriously, like an expensive comforter. She felt herself drifting, giving way to a state that was not quite sleep, but in which, as in a dream, she did not possess firm control of her thoughts. Once again, she was back at the Berghoff, settled in on the window seat. The boys were with her, all three of them. Jack and Edmond were crawling through the window, which now gave onto a grassy meadow. Victor was tugging at her sleeve. "Can I go too, Mama?" "Yes, dear, why not? But stay with your brothers." Now Victor was in the meadow too, but he was tapping on the window. "I can't keep up with them, Mama. They're running away. They're running too fast!"

The doors slid shut, unnoticed by Louisa. Gently, the coach bore her out of the station, leaving the dream undisturbed.

CHAPTER 11
CANDY FROM HOME
Central Illinois, November 1957

The building sat off by itself, sprawling behind a formidable iron fence some distance from the highway and clearly unconnected to the surrounding wintry stubble of farmland. Its stones were the color of lead, and it squatted like a monstrous paperweight anchoring the county against the winds that now whipped up. A green two-door Hudson slowed in the distance, hesitated at the turn-off, then left the road and approached the fence. It pulled to a stop just before the main gate, but the motor continued to run. The woman in the passenger seat stubbed out a cigarette but made no move to get out.

"You can turn it off, Art. We're not robbing a bank. I don't need a getaway car waiting for me."

"You might, Sheila." The driver unscrewed the cap on a pint of Old Granddad and held it toward her.

"Put that away. I don't want her to think I had to get soused to come out here." She reached behind her and pulled two packages from the back seat. "And anyway, I want my head clear for this."

"Are you sure about that?"

"Yeah, I think so. But don't kill it all before I get back." She pushed the door open, stepped onto the gravel, and surveyed the edifice before her.

"You can still change your mind, Sheila."

She turned back to the car with an expression that was furrowed but not angry. "No, I can't. Don't be silly. I'm all right, Art. But *look* at it. This place is like Niagara Falls. It lives up to your expectations."

She closed the car door, walked to the gate, and disturbed the latch. Heavy layers of aging iron rasped against each other with a metallic shriek as she tugged upward and pushed the gate open. She thought of Mrs. Geyer, lying frightened and still, as her bedding was adjusted. No matter how careful Sheila tried to be, the slightest movement could plunge the woman back into pain and provoke a reproachful, arthritic moan.

The main entrance stood twenty yards away, at the end of a straight, concrete path. As she neared the door, she felt her steps slowed by an overwhelming mixture of irony and misgiving. This was a building meant for her, not for her sister. It was waiting for her. She could think of half a dozen night-into-morning escapades, any of which would have reserved a padded suite at this involuntary hotel. But there had been no witnesses, none at least in any shape to put three consecutive words together. She slowed almost to a stop, but this was why she had brought Art. The thought of him watching from the car kept her moving. *Take it inside, kiddo,* she thought. *They've got the wrong Foley. You get to leave.*

Five minutes later, she sat fidgeting on a sofa in an alcove of a large room with a great number of windows onto the hallway. Averting her eyes from several other visitations in progress, she picked at a bow that had been summarily separated from one of her packages at the admissions desk.

"Frances is being prepared," said a voice behind the sofa.

"What are they doing, basting her?" Sheila swung around to address the thickset, unflappable attendant behind her. "Look, Bertha—"

"Berta."

"Yeah. Look, I'm a nurse. I have identification with me. I'm Mrs. Sheffield's sister, and the way you dismembered these presents, you know I'm not smuggling in a hacksaw. We'd appreciate a little privacy. You're not going to stand there while we talk, are you?"

"As a nurse, I'm sure you can appreciate our rules."

"Uh huh. And as a fellow medical worker, I'm sure that you can appreciate the concept of professional courtesy."

"I must observe, but I am discreet."

"Yeah, Bertie, I just bet you are." Sheila dug into her purse then, with a casual deftness that would have done credit to a magician's assistant, slid a bill under Berta's right hand. "Let's see how discreet you can be, say, from over there at the backgammon table."

Berta removed her hand from the back of the sofa. "We are always happy to accept donations to the social fund," she said as she withdrew.

Two figures were moving slowly across the room toward the alcove. Sheila didn't realize at first that one of them was Frances. The walk, so hesitant, seemed all wrong. Was it possible that her sister wouldn't recognize her? She wanted to run to them, but, afraid of frightening Frances, she simply stood up and waved.

As they reached the alcove, the attendant chirped, "It's your sister come to see you, Frances."

"Yes, I know who she is, thank you. And isn't she a sight for sore eyes." Frances was smiling.

"I'll be back in an hour, Frances. In the meantime, if you need anything, Berta is right—uh—over there." She touched Sheila's arm and said conspiratorially, "You should know that Frances is making great strides. We're very pleased with her." Sheila's expression made it clear that she had little interest in what pleased the woman and less in the hand on her arm.

The sisters smiled at each other in silence as she retreated.

"So you're making great strides."

"Yes, great big giant galloping strides."

"I'm gonna hug you."

"Why do you announce it?"

"I don't want to startle you."

Frances frowned. "I'm not that easily startled."

"And you never were the huggiest pup in the pack."

"Let's sit down first."

They sat, and Sheila wrapped her in her arms and pressed their cheeks together.

"Oh Frannie!"

"I'm so glad you've come."

Sheila sat back and stared at her intently.

"You look like the devil, Fran. What are they doing to you? Oh, honey, I've made you cry. I only meant—Jesus, I always say the wrong thing. They should have Big Bertha over there remove my tongue. I'm sure she has just the utensil, and I know she'd enjoy the job."

Frances pressed the back of her hands to her eyes. "I'll never get used to combing my hair without a mirror."

Sheila pondered the implications of that as she gathered her packages from a small coffee table and placed them in Frances's lap.

"For me?"

"Well, I know it looks like ten other people rejected them, but we have sweet Bertiepuss over there to thank for that. I must really look dangerous."

"I've always thought so."

Sheila took Frances's hands in hers and squeezed them. "That's more like it kiddo. And you look okay, really. What I said before-- it's just this place and those Dior wraps they've got you all parading around in."

Frances looked down. "Such pretty paper."

"Bloomingdale's. They do a good job."

Frances smiled up at her. "You brought this from New York."

"C'mon. Open it."

Frances set the top of the box on the coffee table and drew apart just enough tissue to reveal the contents: a silk scarf with thick, irregular stripes alternating in white, deep red, gold, and dark chocolate brown. Sheila watched intently as her sister's conflicted reactions did battle. Frances' face contracted in rueful rejection, even as her fingertips skated in sensuous little circles on the material. The scarf was an exhilarating distraction from life as lived within these walls. It was also a dangerous assault on the numbing defenses that made such a life endurable. "It's beautiful," she said but did not remove it from the box.

"Those are great colors for you. The minute I saw it, it said, 'Take me home to Frances.'"

"My New York talking scarf."

"Take it out. Let me see it on you."

Frances looked around the room and then down at her light blue cotton uniform. She pressed the lid firmly back on the box and set it aside. "I would look like a clown."

"Oh you wouldn't!"

"I do like it. I want you to take it with you and put it aside for me. It's not much use to me right now, and pretty things have a way of wandering off. They don't stay here very long."

Sheila moved the box near her purse. "Sure, honey, I'll keep it safe. You'll be looking like a million in it before you can say Jack Robinson. You know, you always were hard to give things to. But open the other package. I guarantee it's something you can use right here, right now, this minute."

Frances smiled at her questioningly.

"In fa—act, " Sheila grinned and took the box away from her.

"Open your mouth and close your eyes,

and you will get a big surprise."

Frances gave a little laugh and did as she was told, while Sheila took something from the box and pushed it past her sister's lips.

"Close your mouth."

"Mmmf" was followed by muffled crunching noises.

"Ohh, Sheil. English toffee from Fannie Mae."

"Enjoy. I'm going to have a piece myself."

"It's so good."

"Jesus, I certainly know how to make you cry these days. Hold still."

Sheila took a tissue from her purse and dabbed at Frances's eyes. Then, steadying her sister's face, she wiped the lips free of smudged chocolate.

They were silent for a moment, then Sheila picked up her purse again. "I know what we need." She pressed a tube of lipstick into Frances's hand and held a compact mirror up to her face. "It may not be a shade you're used to, but a little color works wonders."

Frances drew back from the mirror, then examined its contents with caution. "I'm not used to any shade these days, but I always welcome wonders." Uncapping the lipstick, she stroked it several times with her index finger, then dabbed unsteadily at her upper lip. "Hold it still, Sheila!" The mirror revealed a scarlet smear that quite overran the lip line. The tube fell and rolled between them. She buried her face in her hands.

Sheila forestalled Berta's approach with a shake of her head. She drew Frances close and patted her back until the trembling subsided. "Now honey, I only brought so much Kleenex. Let's see if we can get a handle on this." She pried the hands away from her sister's face, blotted it, and sat her back against the sofa. "Here, I'm the only mirror you need today." She took up the lipstick, wiped away a bit of fuzz from the sofa, and with a few deft, gentle strokes, painted Frances's lips precisely. "There, it's perfect."

"I feel like your old rag doll."

"It's my revenge for all the times you and Nora used to dress me up in Ma's clothes and laugh yourselves silly."

"We didn't think you remembered that." Frances, who had been leaning back rather limply, now straightened and sat up. "Ma's not out there is she? Is anybody else with you?"

"Only Art."

"Art?"

"My new one."

"But what about Leo? I thought it was Leo?"

"Leo? Yeah, well you've been in here a while, Fran. You know me. Blink and you need a new roster. What the hell did happen to Leo? He said he was going back to his wife, I think…going back to someone anyway."

"And now it's Art."

"Well, it wasn't Art right away, but…" Sheila grimaced and flipped her hand as if to shoo away an assortment of unsatisfactory companions. "Yeah, now it's Art."

"How old is Art?"

"Be nice to me, Frances, We drove a long way."

"I'm thankful you did, and I'm thankful it's just you."

"That's what I thought. I guess that's what everybody thought."

"I don't want Mom and Dad to see me here."

"They miss you like crazy, but they're scared."

"I don't blame them. Keep them away, though. Please."

"Easiest thing in the world. They didn't say it, but what they really need is for me to scout the territory and leave out the worst, or break it to them very slowly and gently."

Frances nodded.

"So what *is* the worst? What are they doing to you?"

She said nothing at first, her eyes moving to the left, then to the right, but taking in nothing before her. She seemed, instead, to be scanning the litter of an unseen attic, searching among the trunks for something safe to unpack.

"They ask me a great many questions."

"You look thinner."

"They've noticed too. They like to weigh you here. It seems I forget to eat sometimes."

"They take care of you though? I mean, the things you hear about! People strapped down, shocked with electricity, soaked in… They're not doing anything like…"

Frances looked away and her jaw hardened. "Frances?" Sheila put her hand out and pressed her sister's shoulder. "Frances?" She dropped her hand and sat back. "The bastards."

Without looking back at her, Frances finally began to speak again. "My days are somewhat different now from when I first arrived. All those great strides, I suppose. Now, I'm trusted to behave myself at our social events. There's a movie night, twice a month. The selection committee is quite taken with Abbott and Costello. Oh, and Flicka and her relatives. It turns out that Flicka has a son called Thunderhead."

Sheila regarded her glumly.

"I'm sorry, Sheil. I don't know what to say. When they think you're crazy, they treat you like a crazy person. But the worst? It's not what anyone does to you or what you're denied or the lack of privacy… Though I have to say, I'd give anything to be able to close a bathroom door behind me, lock it, and settle in for a long, steaming hot soak."

Sheila held out the box of toffee, but Frances declined.

"What is it then? If you can talk about it."

"Just this once, I think I can. But if I ever get out of here, I'm going to bury it so deeply that I'll never be able to dig it back up. There'll be no use asking me then." Frances leaned forward, took Sheila's hands in her own, and met her eyes. "The worst thing of all is the others."

"The others?"

Frances gave a sidelong glance over her shoulder. "Them."

For an awful moment, Sheila was uncertain whether her sister meant real people or …. Frances read the fear in her eyes. "The other inmates. There are some desperate souls here, Sheil. They've run so far inside themselves they're never coming back. I've had to lie among them at night while they howl out their terrors. It's an indescribable experience. It happens night after night. All through the day, I know it will soon be coming at me again… that's the worst. I almost can't remember real sleep. It's like trying to close my eyes and rest in a jungle where, all around me, frightened creatures scream out their panic and invite me into it." She squeezed her sister's hand. "In the middle of the night, when I'm least sure of myself and the things around me, there are moments when their view of the world, the others, almost starts to make sense. After a while, it gets harder to resist." She relaxed her grip and sat back. "But I have resisted it. If I ever was mad, they've scared me sane. And now, I've got to get away from this and back to my life."

"You *will* honey. You don't belong here. They've got to see that, and they will. They'll see that you're no more crazy than I am."

As they stared at each other, an impish smile spread across Frances's face, and Sheila brayed with a loud cackle that halted conversations throughout the room. When she composed herself, she lit a cigarette. "Yeah, well, anyway…" She slid the pack toward Frances, who shook her head. "Still no bad habits?"

"I'm saving myself for something really vile."

"You know what all this is, Fran?" She waved her hand in a large arc. "This is dire straits for you. It's when a good person gets knocked to the absolute bottom for a while. You don't deserve it, but when it's over, you're stronger. And what you don't know while it's going on is that nothing else in your life is gonna be that bad. I'm starting to believe that it only happens to good people. I've gotten away with murder, but I've never been in dire straits. I guess that'll come when I finally check out. I'm sure that Hell is dire straits on a pretty lavish scale."

"Were you drinking on the way out here?"

"No, this isn't liquor talking. You remember when we were little and Pop got let go? They put us out of the house, and we all sat in the back of his friend's truck watching them stick our furniture on the street with the neighbors looking on."

"Of course I do."

"Well that was no picnic for any of us, especially Pop, but I think, for Brandon, it was his dire straits. He was just the perfect age to be humiliated right down to his bones. We were sad and scared, but he was angry. 'I won't be poor! I won't!' He said it over and over again. It was like that carrot scene in *Gone with the Wind*, only it hadn't been written yet. And Brandon was right. He cut the cord, went off on his own, and look at what he's made of himself – living high in California. He could buy and sell all of us."

Frances pursed her lips. "So perhaps there's still a chance for me to make something of myself then?"

"Jeez!" Sheila sighed. "It's so easy to rub you the wrong way. I guess I'd be the same in your shoes. I'd be worse. But it's the last thing I want to do. I just don't know what to say to you."

"Yes, you do. Tell me about the children."

"Well, that I can do. When I moved back from New York and told Pop I was coming here, he went to see the Sheffields."

Frances's eyes widened.

"Yeah, it caught me by surprise too, but he was determined to get you some news and we both knew they'd never open the door to me."

Frances was riveted to her words. "What happened?"

"Believe it or not, it went peculiarly well; in fact—wait till you hear this—he's going back to put in some bushes for them and do a little landscaping."

"I'm dreaming all this."

"I know, well anyway, he gets there and nobody answers the bell. But he hears this loud music, so he goes through the gangway out to the back and there's this little band rehearsing in the garage. It's three or four teen-age boys rocking away, and Pop has to push through a half dozen girls dancing around in the alley and flirting their little heads off at these guys. Well the band stops playing when they see Pop, and he says, 'I'm looking for Mrs. Sheffield.' By this time, he's starting to think they've moved, but now, this tall blond kid who's been singing and playing the guitar says, 'Grandpa?' The funny thing is that Pop wasn't sure he'd be recognized cause it's been a few years. He must think there are a lot more one-eyed gardeners running around than there used to be. Anyway, it turns out HE'S the one who doesn't recognize Anthony."

Frances nodded and smiled but said nothing to interrupt the welcome flow of Sheila's words.

"So Anthony takes him inside and gives him some lemonade and asks him what it's like working at the Museum of Science and Industry and all that. The kid is polite; I'll give him that. He made a point of introducing the rest of the band to Pop. They write their own songs, and evidently Senor Antonio made a big hit at a school assembly. It sounds like you've got a rock and roller on your hands… and a schmoozer."

"I wish he were… on my hands."

"Yeah…" Sheila blew out a puff of smoke and picked a bit of tobacco from her tongue.

"They have filters now, Sheil."

"Tried 'em. They don't taste as good. Anyway, pretty soon Old

Lady Sheffield flounces in with some dame named Maude, and it's obvious this is the very last person on earth she wants to find sitting on that damn wicker, swilling her lemonade."

"The second to the last person. And I've never known her to flounce."

"Who's telling this? In my version, she flounces—never takes a friggin' step without a flounce. But Pop and Anthony pull it off really smooth, and before you know it they're all redesigning the front yard,"

"And Shorty?"

"Gone."

Frances voice went up in alarm. "Gone?"

"He's in the army. The Great Lady told Pop he just ran off without telling any of 'em. She can't figure out why, and now she just sits around with a broken heart—except when she's running around with Maudie."

Frances looked away squinting. "I can't figure it out either. He was doing so well at college, the last I… The army. I can't figure it out."

"I can."

Frances looked back at her.

"Maybe your setup here is his dire straits."

"Please… that's enough of your dire straits for now."

Sheila began to gather her things. "It's enough of me for now, too."

"Don't go, Sheila, please. I've seen no one."

"Well I'm back in town and I know the way now, but Art's out there freezing his ass off. If I stay much longer, I'll find his whole frozen corpse, and that would not be good. I don't drive." She stood up, slipped into her coat, and pulled a slip of paper from her pocket. "Oh, I can't leave without giving you this. La Belle Sheffield gave Pop an address to reach Shorty."

"SHE gave it to him?"

"Yeah, he probably could've gotten it from Anthony, but she volunteered it. Evil isn't what it used to be. Anyhow, now you can dash off a letter to him before I get to the car."

Frances folded the address and put it in the pocket of her uniform. "I couldn't do that. He'll never get a letter from me with this return address."

"Frances Cecilia." She shook her head. "Before I go, I'm going to give you one last—"

"I really don't need to be warned, Sheil. Just hug me—as long as you like."

And she did.

"God bless you, Sheil," her sister whispered, and watched her go. Berta's hand touched her arm. "Shall we go back now, Frances?"

Trailing down the corridor after Berta, the box of toffees dangling from her hand like a child's bear, she thought how sweet it would be to hear herself addressed as Mrs. Sheffield.

※

Art had little stomach to contemplate the mysteries beyond the door from which Sheila now emerged. He'd been facing away from it for quite some time, and it was only the squeak and thudding of the gate latch that turned him around from the featureless landscape he had committed to memory. She pulled open the door, pitched the scarf box into the back seat, and sank into her own. He covered her shaking hand and squeezed, then he extended both his handkerchief and the bottle. "Judas Priest, Art! I don't know which I need first."

"Was she very bad?"

"No, she was just Frances, like always, except the fire had gone out of her. And she was sad as all get out." She took a swallow of the whiskey, capped it, and blotted at her eyes. "I swear I would feel better right now if she had been a gibbering idiot or a raving maniac, but she was just Frances, and that's what made it so awful."

She uncapped the bottle again. "I'm telling you, Art, it must have taken some pretty fancy paperwork to put her there and keep her there. Too bad you're not a lawyer."

"Is she asking for a lawyer?"

"Didn't say a word about it. And she doesn't seem angry about anything that's happened. I'd be furious. So would she in the old days, but now she's as calm as you please. I wouldn't put it past them to have her drugged to the gills on something, but she didn't seem like that either. It's like they performed some kind of 'temper-ectomy.' She used to have a pip."

He turned on the ignition. "Let's get out of here, Sheila. Some food will make you feel better, and we passed a roadhouse about half an hour from here." He switched on the headlights and eased the car almost up to the highway.

"I'm glad you didn't kill it all." She took another swallow. "It's wrong, Art. It's terribly, terribly wrong."

He halted the car and turned to her. "Honey, don't torment yourself with this. You just don't know. You were only with her for an hour, and she's your sister. She's going to behave with you. This is the twentieth century. They don't put people away for—"

The blaze of her stare singed off his words like stray pinfeathers. After another swallow, she turned away from him, rested her head against the window, and moaned to no one in particular, "God, it's hell breaking in a new one."

CHAPTER 12
DREAM CAR
Fort Richardson, Alaska: January, 1958

Mid-Sunday torpor settled comfortably but firmly over Fort Rich. To all appearances, none of the bodies strewn about the M.P. dayroom would ever move again. A kinescope of *Lassie* flickered in silence from a television in the corner. Seen in the states weeks ago, like all but the local broadcasts, it had made its way slowly through the mails to Alaska. No one in the room had the curiosity to turn up the volume or the energy to shut it off.

Ed Sheffield's half-open eyes were pointed balefully in the direction of the small screen. He had not loved the Lassie films as a child, but they had never made him squirm in misery. Was he so changed as an adult? No, it wasn't him, and it wasn't the dog either. There was still a kind of mournful dignity about Lassie herself, when she wasn't barking. It was the humans who were different, simpering inanely on all sides of the poor beast. Once, the regal collie's circle had numbered such chums as Donald Crisp, Elizabeth Taylor, Peter Lawford, and Roddy McDowall, stylish and restrained, with soulful eyes to match Lassie's own, and rich, plummy accents, but now…

The indolent silence in the room was broken by a vigorous rattling of the *Anchorage Times* and a thick, gritty voice from behind it. "Sheffield! You got any money?"

"Some. Are you short, Joe?"

The newspaper lowered to reveal the large, squarish face and the dark features of Private Joseph Terrapino. "What an easy mark! You gotta stop that, Sheffield." He rested the paper on his ample lap. "It's not a loan I need; it's a partner with some cash."

"There's a difference?"

"You're getting to be a wise-ass, Sheffield. It's not becoming, not becoming at all."

There had been, in Ed's life, a small handful of people he thought perfectly cast in their own skins, and Joe Terrapino was one of them. To Ed, it was as though they had strayed from the silver screen, more comfortable with themselves, more at home in their lives than the great masses of humanity around them. "Normal" was what they chose it to be, and never was a care given to fitting in. They had nothing in common with each other: not age or sex, or social condition. Only in their effect on Ed did they become a discernible group. He was drawn to them and warmed by the absence of struggle in their behavior. It seemed to Ed that, like most people, he continually bruised and chafed against the contours of his life; whereas, a few, like Joe, had streamlined themselves to flow smoothly with whatever went on around them. In doing so, they made themselves uncommonly interesting and agreeable to observe. Joe, for example, though large and thick, could move with a dancer's speed and grace, where you might expect him to lumber. Physically and temperamentally, he made Ed think of Jackie Gleason—an unprepossessing exterior masking vast reserves of wit, strength, and finesse.

"Listen, Sheffield, and learn." The paper rattled again, and the large head disappeared behind it. "Two door 1949 Pontiac, good condition, for sale by owner, three hundred dollars." The paper lowered. "Do we know anyone who could profit from this information?" Joe leaned toward Ed and flexed his mighty forest of eyebrows.

"I don't have three hundred dollars."

"No one in this fucking company has three hundred dollars," the powerful voice rumbled back quietly, "but there are *two* of us, and it won't *be* three hundred. No car that's been bouncing on these roads since 1949 is in good condition or anything near it. This guy will come down when we wave cash in front of him, and he sees that we know what's what." Joe leaned in closer. "Now, do you have at your disposal the grand sum of, say, *one* hundred dollars?"

Ed's face was fast scrunching into a refusal. "Yes, but I was –"

An upraised, bearlike hand silenced him. "I always choose my partners carefully. You've justified my confidence in you."

"But Joe, when it comes to cars, except for their looks, I *don't* know what's up or down or sideways."

Joe expelled a massive sigh and massaged his forehead. "I'm not proud to admit it, but on that score, we're in the same boat." The boat, judging from Ed's expression, was springing leaks, and heading for the bottom. "But there's no problem here," Joe boomed. "You forget where we are – a minute's walk from an entire motor pool of talent to advise us. They're sitting around right now with their thumbs up their asses, dreaming about the last time they impressed somebody like us with what they know."

"I guess… if one of them would go with us and look it over…"

"Right." Joe nodded. "Good idea." He relaxed and abandoned his pitchman's intensity. "You know, back in Brooklyn, I never really needed a car to get around. I always wanted one though, and here –"

"What color is it?" Ed asked with a tone of concern.

"What difference does *that* make?"

They looked at each other in surprise. It was puzzling to discover they were not merely from different states but different planets. Joe reexamined the ad, and when his eyes edged back up over the paper, they lacked their usual, easy confidence. "Green?"

"That could be a nice color for a Pontiac."

"Then you're with me in this venture!" Joe's face lit up, and he stuck out his hand to seal the pact.

"No, wait… I don't know. I have to think about this. I'm not very spontaneous with money."

"And a good thing too, or you wouldn't have the hundred." Joe spoke slowly to give each word its maximum impact. "But you *do*, and, for once, so do I." He leaned in closer. "The planets are in alignment, but we have to act quickly." The words came faster now. "All over Anchorage, lowlifes who just got paid are reading this same ad." He gripped Ed by the shoulders. "What'd they tell you about this place before they sent you up here? I'll bet they said it was 'God's Country.'"

"As a matter of fact, they did."

"Well, have you seen anything yet but 'God's Army Installations?'"

Ed squinted. "Not really."

"You go to Anchorage?"

"Of course."

"You're from Chicago. The glitter and dazzle of Anchorage sets your pulse racing, doesn't it, Sheffield? Every time you board the bus, that heady anticipation of new excitements!"

Ed couldn't speak for laughing.

"I didn't think so. You go for the same reason I do. It's not Fort Rich, and for a little while, we're somewhere else—*anywhere* else. But you wouldn't leave home to see it."

"Well, no, but what's that got to do with—"

"What did you hope to see when you shipped out of Fort Gordon?"

"Oh, Joe!" Ed rolled his head around. "Italy! Germany! Korea! All the cycles before us went somewhere really interesting."

"Ok. Ok. But once you *knew* you were coming to Alaska, wasn't there something that you wanted to see?"

"The glaciers."

"So did I. And we will," said Joe. "But we can't do it without a *car*." He gripped Ed by the shoulders, but it was the force of his gaze that pinned the boy in place. "In this God-forsaken wilderness, mobility is freedom. We've got to have wheels, or we're not free men. We must do this, little buddy. You do see that?"

"Yes, Joe."

Ed felt a whopping thump on his back and smiled as he was hustled off to the motor pool.

Joe Terrapino was an astute judge of character, or the lack of it. Ed was fascinated by the uncanny accuracy of Joe's forecasts of human behavior. He had heard him predict, sometimes almost to the quarter hour, just when Florian, the German cook, would hurl a pot at the wall and storm out of the kitchen, cursing through his tears. Joe was seldom wrong about who would be promoted, or put up for soldier of the month. When he silently removed the framed family photo from the top of his footlocker to stow it safely inside, you could hold your breath until a fistfight broke out. He was equally prescient about the interactions of their superiors. His early alert for the tipsy public spat between two warrant officers on New Year's Eve was a D Company legend. Ed had long wondered where *he* stood in Joe's clear-eyed view of base personnel. Encouraged by their impending partnership, he let his curiosity spill over as they made their way to the motor pool.

"Joe?"

"Yeah?"

"I'm not the only one who would've had the money. Why did you pick me?"

Joe's brisk stride came to a halt. "You've always gotta ask one question too many, don'tcha?"

" I'd just like to know."

"You may not like the answer, chum."

Ed couldn't leave it there, though he was beginning to think he should. "No, really. It's okay. Just tell me."

"I know what you want me to say, little buddy, that I'm looking forward to all the jolly times we'll have together in the car." It was written on Ed's face that those were precisely the words he'd hoped to hear. "But think," Joe continued, "How often are we even on the same shift, let alone out for the same sort of evening? Huh-uh, we'll pretty much be driving our separate ways. So as far as companionship, I could just as well be going in on this with Dracula." He started to walk again, and Ed followed.

"Well… what, then?"

"You may not take this as a compliment, but I don't mean it as an insult. I knew I wouldn't have any problems with you."

Nodding, Ed said, "Hmm," and decided he would think about this later.

Just as they reached the motor pool, Ed spoke up again. "What about the glaciers?"

Joe rolled his eyes. "When did I get married and have a kid?"

"You said we'd see the glaciers."

"We *will*. We'll see the glaciers." Joe sighed. "We'll go together." Ed just looked at him. "You have my word on it."

Joe's word was good, Ed knew. "I just wanted to make sure."

"You want a lot for a hundred bucks."

Joe ushered him into the motor pool, and Ed surveyed the scene around him. The mechanics had all removed their thumbs from their asses.

Joe slid seamlessly into conversation with one stranger after another. Ed watched in wonder at a gift he ached to possess. His father had it. His uncles had it, and Ed stood by in wistful envy as it lubricated their lives. Traits sometimes skipped a generation. If Ed had a son, could it resurface? Whenever he imagined his hypothetical child, it was always someone very like himself, flaws and all, someone he could comfort and forewarn. Now, here in the motor pool, a novel and unwelcome prospect presented itself: a glib and facile offspring with no use for the paternal solace and counsel Ed felt uniquely qualified to dispense. Liking such a kid would be work. Ed couldn't let it show. His father never had.

Joe's amiable chatter continued at what might have seemed random to the mechanics, but Ed knew he was sizing them up, seeking a cold, experienced eye to probe for flaws in their intended vehicle. Joe settled on Edwin Kite, a wiry corporal from Tennessee who agreed to drive them in at the end of his shift.

The Pontiac sat waiting for them, a few yards from the owner's trailer. For Ed at least, it was love at first sight. The car looked so solid and normal and full of parts. Brand new feelings gripped him, as powerful as they were peculiar. He understood at last what a great and necessary thing it was to own a car – to drive! It was an essential building block of normalcy and acceptance. It was probably the cornerstone. He'd never imagined it was possible to feel such things for an inanimate object. Others had owned it before, and it had done their bidding because it had no choice. Now it would be Ed's, its best owner ever. He would fill its tank and inflate its tires. He would read manuals and perform regular maintenance (well, he would see that somebody performed it). This car would want for nothing. It would want to take him places.

He needed to name it, a good green name for a good green car. He would call it Russell, but only in secret, when they were alone together. The naming of cars was not something even for the ears of Joe Terrapino. Ed knew the crazy points likely to attach to such a thing, and he couldn't risk losing the trip to the glaciers. He itched to tear the cardboard "For Sale" sign from behind the wiper blades, but he would control himself and feign disinterest.

As feigners go, however, Ed was less than world class, and the haggling went the worse for it. Despite Edwin Kite's brutal assessment of Russell's condition, the owner had only to glance at Ed's dancing eyes and ill-contained fidgets to know that the boy's departure without the car would have to entail wild horses. They paid $275, and that night Ed slept in Russell's back seat.

～∽～

In the next few weeks, Ed proved as good as his word. Russell was pampered, washed, polished, and engaged in a running, if one-sided, conversation. Except for Ed's two-footed driving and a regrettable habit of dramatic, last second application of the brakes, the car could have had no reasonable complaint.

Ed's tentative grasp of geography kept him tethered within a short radius of main arteries and recognizable landmarks. Most of his excursions had no other purpose but to put him behind the wheel, connected to the unchallengeably competent, certifiably regular network of grown up people who drove cars from one place to another. His ingenuous pleasure on these aimless jaunts never quite sank to his exclaiming "Vroooom, vroooom," but he had no illusions that they were much more elevated than that. He didn't care and always came back smiling.

His confidence grew, and presently he let out his leash to explore less familiar byways, always careful to leave a trail of mental breadcrumbs to retrace his route. One evening at dusk, he was rewarded with an adventure. He scrupulously monitored the pressure in Russell's tires, but, like Joe, he was unaware of the menace implicit in their smooth and threadbare tread. Rounding a curve on a steeply raked hill, the right rear tire pressed down on a jagged piece of rock, exploded, and began to flap. Ed managed to steer the car to the outer rim of the road and got out to assess the damage. He knew the trunk held a jack and a spare tire, but he had never imagined actually using them.

He had seen his father perform the procedure; indeed, at one time or another, he had seen all the male Sheffields except Anthony confronting a blown tire with skill, dispatch, and, save for the odd curse, cool efficiency. He wished he had observed the actions of his ancestors for mechanical instruction instead of exotic entertainment. The scenes were as mystifying as magic shows as he now replayed them in his mind, rummaging for any scraps of useful advice. If he could think like his father and not himself for the next few minutes, things would work out.

It occurred to him that, even though no car had passed him since the blowout, he hadn't much daylight left to him, and a speeding car rounding the turn in the dark could knock him and/or Russell down the hill. He opened the driver's door, fumbled for the right switch, and turned on the blinkers. Opening the trunk, he was relieved to see the spare was inflated. The jack was heavier than it looked, and when he managed to raise the rear fender, the giddy tilt at which Russell perched on the hill was not improved. Only a few feet of workspace existed before the edge of the road gave way to a steep drop-off. The frozen death of a new recruit, just yards from the post, had impressed upon Ed the atavistic power of the land around him. Alaska gave no second chances to fools and innocents.

Ed weighed the likelihood of the car spilling on top of him and mashing him down the hill. "You wouldn't do that to me would you, Russell?" Removing the hubcap, it pleased him to remember to use it as a container for the lug nuts. They were rusty and stiff but gradually yielded to the pressure of the wrench. It began to seem a real possibility that he would finish without being killed or losing his tools in the dark. When he'd begun, he was thankful no Sheffields were present to witness his ineptitude, but by the time he tapped the hubcap back onto the spare, he wished the entire clan were assembled at the roadside.

He patted Russell's roof and said, "You see, we can count on each other."

Safe inside Russell, Ed invariably felt less alien, and on this delicious evening, he said aloud, "You're going to change things for me!"

And so, before the week was out, Russell did.

Ed was driving back from Anchorage, with replacement tires so thick of tread his fingers sank in up to the knuckles. Three blocks ahead, a large emergency vehicle turned onto the street and bore toward him with wailing alarm and bright, pulsing lights. Trailing in its wake was an M.P. sedan and, as he would soon discover, a change of fortune. As he watched the truck approach, his brain scrambled in an overheated search for the appropriate response to the situation. Buried under layers of jumbled mental clutter, a voice spoke to him from a deep and seldom used corner of his mind. "This is a special event. It calls for a specific action, which all good drivers know. You must perform it at once."

Yes, yes, he thought, *but what, for God's sake?*

The answer, he was grimly certain, could be found in a "Rules of the Road" manual, probably in large boldface. The truck and patrol car were now two blocks away. Should he just slow down? He tried to imagine what his father would do. Should he come to a stop? But if that weren't right, what about the cars behind him? If only they were in front of him. He could follow their example and seem as calm and wise as you please. He tried to summon up the common sense the Sheffields had always insisted he lacked, but it did not come. If it had ever existed at all, it was now elbowed out of his head by the fevered imaginings that filled it to bursting. He was alone, and the little caravan of judgment was one block away. Urgently, the voice spoke again, "Pull off the road."

The pulsing lights and siren found him sitting at the wheel on the lawn of an elderly woman who peered at him apprehensively through the small gap in her drapes. In the rear view mirror, Ed could see the patrol car deserting the truck and making a U-turn to investigate the more interesting scene on the lawn. "Whatever I was supposed to do," he reflected, "this doesn't seem to be it."

He recognized and was recognized by the M.P. who now approached the car.

"Have some trouble, Sheffield?'

This benign question, delivered with a smile, was maddening in its implications. Perhaps, if Ed had only known his way around an engine, there might have been a painless way out.

"Why yes, Travis, it sounds as though the rear wind grommet is bifurcating the plug fans. Naturally, I left the road at once."

But his imagination, unfueled by even a scrap of factual information, sputtered and died out.

"Actually, Travis, I was just trying to get out of your way."

The interrogator's smile remained, but a shadow of unease furrowed his brow.

"Umm… whaddya talking about?"

"I'm not really sure." Ed sighed as he spotted his audience still rapt behind the drapes.

The M.P. leaned in close and quietly asked, "Been drinkin'?" Ed wished that he had. That would still be trouble but, here on base, a normal, almost predictable kind of trouble. Could he fake it? The soldier had been scanning the interior of the car but now focused solely on Ed. "It don't look like you been drinkin."

Ed threw in the towel. "No, just been stupid."

He knew the M.P. was still making up his mind whether this was covered under the good old boy look-the-other-way-if-he's-in-the-unit code. Ed knew also that there had not been many deposits to his good old boy account, if indeed that account had ever been opened.

Still, the smell of uncertainty hung in the air. He might get a pass.

"Lemme just check your license for a second."

Ed fished a card from his billfold and extended it for inspection. He held his breath.

"No, guy, this is your army driver's permit. I meant your civilian license."

If Ed could freeze the moment here, step out of it, go off and – do what? reinvent himself? A cold breath of reality dispersed the last particles of doubt.

"I don't have it."

Ed was certain he had reached the pit, so it was perversely unpleasant to find it had a tiny, useless guardrail. "You shouldn't leave it in the barracks," said Travis.

"I don't have one." Ed jumped into the pit. "I never did."

Nodding slowly, as though this were the most reasonable answer in the world, Travis handed back the card. "Wait here, Sheffield."

Ed averted his eyes from the conference in the patrol car. It was bad enough to watch people when you thought they were talking about you. When you knew they were, it was a really bad idea. Nor did he let his eyes drift to the house. By now, the old woman must be wild with curiosity. Instead, he treated himself to a tour of Russell's dashboard – the curving numbers on the speedometer that went up to speeds only a demon would attempt, the worrisome heat and fuel gauges he had monitored so nervously, the little orange plastic Indian head he loved to massage. He wondered if he were looking at them all for the last time.

The driver's side door sprawked open, and he heard the M.P. saying, "Slide over, Sheffield. I'll drive you back to the company."

Ed was nervous now, but not because of what had just happened or even what he knew was coming. About that, he was fatalistic and resigned. He had screwed up, and it was only fair that he be made to pay for it somehow. He had been found out, caught at his lifelong pretense that he was normal, that he knew what was going on, what was expected of him. Now he would be exposed. It was what he went to bed each night thankful to have escaped and what he woke up each day dreading. Now it had happened. The question was, had he been found out only in a small way, in which case he must plod on with the rest of the pretense, or would they connect all the dots and find him out completely? Would they realize that this was not just a goofy mistake but a flashing signal of his utter incompetence to function outside the walls of an institution? Would they see that even all the restraints of the army left him with more freedom than he could ever hope to manage? If they saw it, if that had finally come – well, it would be embarrassing at first, but then the weight of pretending would be lifted from him forever, and he could relax. Russell, his faithful green companion, bore him now toward either continued freedom or peace of mind. Whichever, he would face it calmly.

No, it was not the destination that made him nervous but the driver. If a better-looking soldier served at Fort Richardson than Corporal Travis Parsons, Ed had yet to spot him. In Ed's opinion, Army uniforms in general did little to improve anybody's appearance, and M.P. uniforms were especially tricky to bring off. Depending on his build and the shape of his face, an otherwise decent-looking fellow could be rendered quite ridiculous by a brown Eisenhower jacket, a duck-billed cap, bloused boots, and an entire cow's worth of leather gee gaws. It was certainly true in Ed's case, and he knew it. He thought of his M.P. outfit not so much as a uniform but a costume, a clown suit really. Once fully snapped and strapped into it, he shunned mirrors like a vampire, lest his reflection give him the giggles.

Travis Parsons, on the other hand, was a walking recruitment poster. Tricked up in exactly the same gear, he was quite dashing,

Of course, spattered with mud in wrinkled fatigues, he was equally dashing. Ed supposed those crisp blue eyes, that warm easy smile, and the slim but muscled physique would still be dashing in a gunny sack. There would probably be a brisk market among little girls for a book of Travis Parsons paper dolls. Ed could draw it in the loony bin and provide a great variety of wardrobe changes, including the gunny sack.

Because of what happened on the winter bivouac, Ed had been distinctly uncomfortable around Travis ever since. The winter maneuvers were a big deal, and in preparation for them, everybody was issued great piles of equipment: skis, pointed poles, gloves as big as oven mitts, parkas with large fur-fringed hoods, and snowshoes. All of this Ed found strange and therefore interesting. The company was also subjected to a new barrage of training films on winter safety. These he found all too familiar and numbingly repetitious. Like the sermons at Our Lady of Peace, the films drummed out relentlessly the message that Ed's chances of escaping disaster were slim indeed. What the drummers didn't know was that, now and then, Ed considered disaster an interesting, perhaps inevitable alternative.

Throughout D Company, winter bivouac was eagerly looked forward to as a welcome diversion. Even Ed was more focused on the pleasing prospect of a change of scene and routine than on what would normally have gripped his imagination, chilly new opportunities to mess up and humiliate himself.

The operation began in the usual way, clambering onto the back of a crowded truck, jamming yourself against your gear and trying to limit how hard you jostled into the guys on either side of you, or worse yet, across from you. They were driven just far enough so there was no possibility of Ed finding his way back even with breadcrumbs. Then, they were pitched out into the snow for the long trek to their mysterious objective. All at once, Ed experienced the very last thing he had come to expect from the army – great fun.

It was immediately obvious that D Company's collective inexperience with skis and snowshoes would play havoc with forced march efficiency. Patches of ice lurked all about the ground where the trucks had halted, and simply getting feet into equipment now required uncommon finesse if one were to remain vertical and dry. Things might have gone quite differently if the first to take a pratfall had not been Lonnie Millhouse. Lonnie had a mean streak and was gifted at turning someone's chance mistake into a snide, permanent nickname. Ed filed it away as a useful lesson when Lonnie, down on all fours with a face full of snow, laughed loudly at himself before anyone else had the chance. His swift, defensive strike not only removed him as a target but legitimized klutziness, giving everyone else a free pass. What had begun with a modicum of seriousness and caution fast degenerated into an exhibition of military farce to which the Three Stooges would have hesitated to stoop.

For Ed, this was a once-in-a-lifetime opportunity to blunder in public and go scott-free, or better yet, bond with fellow blunderers. Perversely, it turned out to be an immunity he didn't need, though he yearned to save it for future use. Surrounded by Southerners, he was at no disadvantage with the props of winter movement. He was no worse than most and better than many. This was a far cry indeed from his memories of weapons training, where most of the group appeared to have found their baby cribs well stocked with rifles and revolvers.

Ed began to relax and enjoy smashing through the snow on what looked like tennis rackets. Even better was the smooth gliding stride he managed on his skis. He ignored the flatness of the terrain and conjured up Gregory Peck and Ingrid Bergman whooshing toward the brink with the *Spellbound Concerto* swirling around them. He was passing people now and loving it. Over his shoulder, he smiled at Joe who looked like a fur-trimmed and very dignified refrigerator. He reached Lonnie Millhouse and left him in the dust. None of them were equipped with his secret weapon, Miklos Rosza.

He neared Travis and slowed his pace. Travis grinned at him as at an equal. "Beats the shit out of those summer death marches, doesn't it, buddy?"

However casually that 'buddy' had been tossed at Ed, it buzzed through him deliriously, almost throwing him off stride. He grinned back and, careful to drop the 'g', chirped, "Fuckin' A." This was turning out to be the best day he had ever spent in Alaska.

It didn't get worse as it drew to a close. Ten-man tents had been set up, and by the light of a Coleman lantern, Ed watched with an expression of what he hoped would pass for preoccupied disinterest as Travis stretched out on the sleeping bag next to his and removed his boots. The night air outside the tent was seriously cold, but no worse than Ed had felt many times in Chicago. The army seemed confident that the accumulation of body heat in each tent would suffice to prevent stumbling over frozen corpses in the morning. The severity of the weather had turned Sergeant Meehan almost motherly. He told them that while they would probably want to remove a lot of what they were wearing during the night, it was a good idea to keep most of what they took off inside the sleeping bag to stay warm, especially socks and underwear. As Ed zipped up his bag, body heat had yet to work its magic, There wasn't a stitch he was willing to shed.

The last thing he saw before they extinguished the lantern was the arm of Travis Parsons, draped languidly outside the sleeping bag, mere inches from Ed's cheek. Conversations sputtered out in the icy blackness, but the image of that naked hand and wrist illuminated Ed's imagination like a beacon. Only at night, after all talk ceased, did Ed feel connected to his fellow soldiers. In the dark, loneliness rose from them like exhalations, mingling and massing above their heads, so palpable he couldn't doubt they felt it too.

But tonight, there was that arm. Radioactive, it made its precise location known to Ed in the darkness and would not let him sleep. It pulsed in his ear with the promise of contact, wordless but unequivocal acknowledgement of loneliness, real contact which, however brief, would be strong enough to vanquish separateness while it lasted, perhaps beyond. He wanted and needed it. What was to prevent him and Travis from admitting with their fingers that night, in a distant land they hadn't chosen, was a harsh and friendless thing? A warm and kindly prize lay just beyond his face. He had only to unzip his bag a few inches and stretch out his hand. He unzipped his bag a few inches and stretched out his hand. It hovered above Travis's exposed wrist.

But what if Travis misinterpreted the gesture as weakness, perversion, lunacy? And would those really be misinterpretations? What if Travis turned on him, mocked him, and broadcast the incident? This was a military police company, not a conference of philosophers. This was the very outfit where Donald Quibb met his swift and chilling excision, one day offering friendly back rubs, the next day, vanished – shipped out on a section eight, his disappearance acknowledged only in lowered voices: "I always thought so." Ed's hand retreated to the craven security of the sleeping bag.

In this dark, Ed saw nothing. In this silence, he heard nothing. All his senses had taken up residence in his left hand. What if Travis pressed his fingers back – an eloquent sign of understanding? Was Ed's life so perfect or even so satisfactory that he dared not risk a change for the worse? The zipper took a short ride, and Ed's hand reemerged. His fingers uncoiled slowly and with infinite patience. A stealthy advance scout in dangerous territory, Ed's hand began to move, halting when it made contact with Travis's fatigues. With feather light pressure, the backs of Ed's fingers grazed up and down on the sturdy cotton. He paused at the frontier, exhilarated but aware that retreat was still possible. Travis was not one of the barracks dog boys who fell asleep on the way down to the mattress. Possibly he was still awake. An increase of pressure, an advance to bare skin would then be unretractable.

Ed massaged the coarse material a moment more, then held his breath, raised his fingers, moved them out beyond the safety of the sleeve where they remained suspended above Travis's unsuspecting wrist. Ed delayed the descent of his fingers, torturing himself with alternately dire and blissful scenarios. He continued to hover until he heard shifting about in a nearby sleeping bag. Travis might move at any moment, and the wrist would disappear. Ed drew in a full, deep breath and lowered his fingers until they rested on what felt like living, breathing silk. The wrist did not respond. He was filled with a heady but agreeable sensation of speed. He and Travis were soaring aloft in the tent, joined at the wrist… except… There was still nothing to indicate that Travis was actually awake, let alone a participant in the Sheffield aerial circus. The pressure from Ed's fingers might be too slight to register if Travis were already asleep. In the absence of movement, it might seem no more than the accidental collision of shifting slumberers. He had to know.

He slid his knuckles back and forth on the soft space immediately below Travis's open hand. Now there was no going back. He explored the ditch between the two wiry tendons of Travis's wrist. His knuckles climbed the fleshy mounds at the bottom of the hand and nestled into the plush valley of the palm. If only Travis's hand would close on his. It wouldn't even have to squeeze. But there was no response. Ed pressed his fingers to the hollow of the palm, flexing them in timid little circles. Nothing. The tips of his fingers stole upward and explored the calluses at the crest of the palm. Nothing. He rode his fingers gently up Travis's own, halting at the underside of the middle knuckles and stroking softly. *Please press back,* he thought, fiercely trying to will it. *Just for an instant.* He slid his fingers up until his tips touched Travis's, gliding them about, as faintly as he could. It was as far as he dared go, but except for a warmth in the flesh and a discernable pulse, Travis could have been mistaken for a cadaver. Ed withdrew his hand, zipped up his bag, and lay awake for hours pondering the meaning of what hadn't happened.

In the morning, constricted by paranoid embarrassment, he could barely bring himself to look in Travis's direction. Travis's own behavior was unremarkable, neither more nor less friendly than before. The worst moment of the morning came when he observed Travis in conversation with Lonnie Millhouse. Lonnie was sniggering, but that was not unusual. Were they talking about him? Was Travis confiding what would be the last nail in Ed's overstudded coffin?

After a day or two, Ed decided he had been mistaken about the conversation. Lonnie was incapable of passing up an opportunity so ripe for mischief. And there it had remained until today's debacle. Once again, Ed had done himself proud in front of the magnetic Travis Parsons. God only knew what Travis thought of him, and Ed didn't want to. He slumped down in his seat as they drove the last few blocks to Post Command.

In the rear view mirror, Ed could see the M.P. car lagging discreetly behind them. "So," he said, a bit louder than he meant to, "Howzit going with you?"

Travis's smile was noncommittal but calming, the perfect expression for emergency room wear. "Waall... you know how it is."

"Course." Ed was tired of thinking. Even this gibberish was preferable to silence, and they needn't keep it up for long. Travis pulled into the parking lot behind M.P. headquarters and brought

Russell to a smoother stop than he was used to at Ed's hands. Turning to Ed, but retaining the keys, Travis delivered a sentence of concrete that he must have been wanting to unload since the ride began. "Cap'n Knox wants to see you... for a minute." As Ed forced himself up and out from under the words, he weighed them with and without the final phrase. Travis, it seemed, had a future in the diplomatic corps.

Ed sat by himself in a private office behind the dispatch room, awaiting the arrival of Captain Walter Knox. Inspection of the four to twelve shift was in progress, but he could hear little of it through the door. He hoped that meant his impending interview would be just as hard to hear from the other side. With Captain Knox, the conversation would be a vastly different affair than it would with any other officer in charge. Ed showed respect to all his officers, but it was Captain Knox alone with whom it came spontaneously and not compelled by rank. Walter Knox had clearly known real life before joining the army, a life that would resume when he left it. For him, the service was a chapter in that life, and the uniform, essential to the moment, would be packed away with ease, Ed imagined, at chapter's end.

For the others, the uniform was a skin that defined them, never to be shed. They seemed to need the army in order to exist. Lieutenant Santelli, short and portly as a penguin, was the only man on Fort Richardson that Ed was certain looked more ridiculous than he in full military regalia. Warren Santelli's romance with regulation explained the army connotation of 'mickey mouse.' Red-faced Lieutenant Cargill spoke only in obscene metaphors of sports strategy, and Ed marveled at the man's dogged determination to apply them to every situation. Ed longed to hear him attempt a funeral oration. More imposing in manner and appearance was Captain Shropshire. Tall, fit, confident, dignified, not unattractive, and undeniably manly, Lyle Shropshire was just the sort many soldiers would welcome as a leader. To Ed, he seemed as wooden as the native totems, nicely carved, but wooden all the same, and except for the occasional smirk of condescension, utterly humorless. That Captain Shropshire had doubted or questioned himself for a moment was inconceivable.

Ed blew out a sigh of relief that none of these men were about to pass judgment on him. They already had, to the extent that they noticed him at all. He had felt it from each of them in a slight narrowing of the eyes, an unspoken "What's all this? Can we send it back to the factory?" Actually, on one occasion, the words *had* been spoken. It was during barracks inspection, as he lay on his cot pretending to be asleep (an exemption granted those who had just come off the midnight to eight shift). For inspection, your every possession was unlocked and set out in full view in a meticulously prescribed order. His footlocker provoked no comment, nor did the spit shined boots, laced, tied, and lined up under his bed.

Then, his narrow metal clothes cabinet was unlatched, and Ed realized Captain Shropshire was contemplating the non-army issue contents of the top shelf: *The Novels of Jane Austen, Shaw on Music, The Rhetoric* and *The Poetics of Aristotle, A Death in the Family, The Ring Lardner Reader*... Well, so what? Good in fact. Captain Shropshire was no simpleton. What if he found something to his liking, something he remembered fondly? Even better, what if he wanted to borrow something? This could be – then he heard it. "What's all thisss!"

The captain's tone put a torch to the Sheffield Lending Library. Now he heard Sgt. Meehan. "That's just Sheffield – harmless."

"He could use less time on the books and more on the boots, and what the hell is that black sock on his eyes?" Ed had no doubt that if he removed it, he would see the shade of Grandpa Sheffield risen from the grave, nodding in agreement.

"I think it's his version of... um, a sleep mask."

What a thrill to be discussed in the third person. He fantasized tearing it off and roaring at them like a leopard.

"Sleep mask!" Captain Shropshire sniggered and moved on.

No, Lyle Shropshire would not be Ed's inquisitor of choice – not that he cared about such a man's opinion of him. On the other hand, wasn't it going to be even worse when Captain Knox came through that door, a man whose opinion really did matter, a man it troubled Ed to disappoint? Abruptly, the muffled typing and radio chatter grew louder. He stood up and saluted Captain Knox.

"At ease, at ease. Sit down, Sheffield." The officer strode to a large desk that dominated the room. He seemed preoccupied with ridding himself of the clipboard and sheaf of papers he carried. Frowning at the cluttered surface of the desk, he stepped behind it, snatched open a drawer and pitched the clipboard inside.

This afternoon, as always, there was something crisp about Walter Knox, crisp as opposed to starchy. A tall, slim man in his late forties or early fifties, he had begun to show gray at the temples and in his small moustache. Dark eyes peered out above Bogart-like pouches, giving him the appearance of being simultaneously underslept and keenly alert. Clearly a man of considerable education, he seemed at ease discussing anything to which a conversation might turn. That they ever turned to anything beyond sex, sports, or the army was Ed's first clue that Captain Knox was not standard issue. It wasn't long, in fact, before Ed decided that the captain was far sharper than an officer needed to be – in peacetime at least.

Such was the man who now seated himself and turned his attention to the nervous soldier in front of him. "I've been wanting to talk to you, Sheffield. This business this afternoon just pushed it up a little."

Ed twisted the hematite ring on his finger.

"What were you trying to do today, Edmund? Did you think we were getting bored?"

"Sir?"

"You have such interesting vehicular episodes. Did you think it was time to shake us up with another one?"

"Another one, sir?"

"Yes." Captain Knox placed a flat chrome case on the desk and took out a cigarette. "It's not that long ago that I watched from this window as you backed a patrol car into Colonel Tolbert's bumper."

"Oh." Ed's eyes went to the overinformative window. He squirmed as his mind replayed the incident from the captain's point of view. "I'm not always good at backing out in confined spaces, sir."

"How are you with going forward?"

Ed smiled in spite of himself. "Better. I didn't know you knew about that, sir."

"Didn't you wonder why you started getting all gate duty and no patrols?" He pushed the chrome case in Ed's direction.

"Thank you, sir, but I don't trust myself with a cigarette right now. " Ed looked at the uncarpeted floor and shook his head. 'I didn't wonder about that, no. Actually, it was kind of a relief."

"You weren't happy with patrol?"

The lack of irony in the captain's tone relaxed Ed a little. "Well, I liked the company and getting to see all of the post, but gate duty is more, umm, predictable."

"You don't find it monotonous?" The captain's thumb and index finger kept his cigarette close to his lips for quick and frequent puffs.

"It gives me time to think," said Ed.

"And read? Do you read in the gate house?"

Coming from another officer, the question might have seemed a trap..

"You can't – well, I can't enjoy it that way. After a couple of sentences, I have to look up to see that nothing is – amiss. Of course, out there, nothing is ever amiss – or not amiss."

"You're not very happy with any of it then."

Happiness again. What an odd conversation. Ed wondered when the shoes were going to drop. "You don't join the army to be happy. I mean, with all due respect, sir, I don't think most people do that."

"Interesting point. Then why did you?"

So many months into it, Ed still lacked a glib answer. "I wanted to, oh, change things for a while."

"Geographical therapy."

Ed nodded. "That's a good way to put it."

Captain Knox took a last short puff and stubbed out his cigarette. "Getting back to Colonel Tolbert…"

"Can they take the repairs out of my pay? I know I was wrong not to report it."

The officer shook his head. "It was barely a love tap. Five minutes in the motor pool. But, tell me, what is it that you have against the Tolberts?"

"Wh..?" was all that Ed could manage.

"Did you have any idea who that elderly woman was when you roared onto her lawn/'

"Oh, dear Lord, no!"

"Yes, the Colonel's sainted mother, up from Slidell on a visit."

Ed stared again at the polished wood floor.

"You've given her something to talk about back in Louisiana," the captain continued.

"Unfortunately, you've also given us something to talk about."

Without looking up, Ed nodded.

"You admit you're a menace to the highways?"

"Yes, sir."

"And your license?"

Ed forced himself to look at his inquisitor. "The only one I have is my army permit."

"Well, technically, Edmond, you don't even have that right now. It's safe with me." He patted his breast pocket. "How did you drive at home?"

Ed sighed and looked away again. "I never did."

"Then Fort Richardson and the city of Anchorage have been running a sort of unintended driver's training class for you."

"Yes, sir."

The captain lit another cigarette. "What do you think we should do about this, Edmond?"

"I don't know, sir."

"Well, I've given it some thought. I'd have put you on the desk long ago, but you don't type…"

The captain's words came at him now in slow motion, at reduced volume. He strained to focus on them, standing up and moving towards the desk.

"…so I think the best thing, under the circumstances would be to send you over to the stockade for a while."

A barely audible "Yes, sir," followed, then silence. Something was not quite right here. Walter Knox stared at the boy, who stood immobile and didn't even seem to be breathing. Had Sheffield misunderstood him? That didn't seem possible, but what else could explain the zombie-like trance in front of him? What malign force had laid hands on that promising head and cross wired it? And what would it take to unscramble it? At the moment, all he could do was put the boy out of his self-imposed misery, but that needed to be done at once. He leaned across the desk and pressed Ed's shoulder.

"Edmond, " he raised his voice. "I'm sending you to the stockade as a guard." He saw the Adam's apple move and the breathing resume.

"Thank you, sir." The eyes were battling back tears.

"Now go back and sit down. Can you deal with a cigarette now?"

The muffled, snorting response was difficult to interpret, but the boy took a cigarette, put it to his lips, and leaned forward for a light. To Captain Knox, it appeared that Private Sheffield, unready to speak, was trying to puff himself back together. The officer reached inside his jacket, withdrew a small, oblong pamphlet and slid it across the desk.

"Add this to your library."

Ed looked down at "Rules of the Road: Territory of Alaska."

"Terrapino will drive you back. Let him keep the keys until you're legal."

Ed nodded in silence without raising his head.

The captain leaned back in his chair. "My first car was a Plymouth… 1926… two-door …cream colored."

Ed looked up at last. "Cream. I bet it was swell."

CHAPTER 13

AT THE SLAMMER

Fort Richardson, March, 1958

The sheer volume of alcohol consumed by the prison staff took Ed's breath away. His new comrades might be old hands at hoisting, but few of them were concerned about, or even capable of holding their liquor. Within a month of his arrival at the stockade, Ed had witnessed most of them prostrate, sodden, and utterly vulnerable. More tellingly, so had the prisoners.

The prisoners. If for no other reason than their enforced sobriety, Ed feared that they would assess his inadequacies even more shrewdly and swiftly than the staff. Giving orders was not second nature to him, not even tenth, and he did so sparingly. The idea of barking or snarling them, as was commonly done here, seemed only likely to heighten the farcical aspect of his issuing them at all. He could not adopt the prevailing attitude that judgment by the inmates was as unlikely and irrelevant as that of goldfish watching their owners undress. No, Ed knew he was egregiously miscast and took pains to minimize the incongruity of convicts being in *his* charge. He sought to postpone what he foresaw as the inevitable day when one of them simply stood up and said, "No."

Almost miraculously, an incident on his first day as guard bought Ed some time. Guards worked in pairs, both circulating as needed, with the senior-ranking soldier based at the front office and the junior at a desk just outside the individual lockups. Separated from the main dormitory, this was a catchall area for everything from new prisoners and those about to leave to cases that were deemed special. Wilbur Geismann was special on several counts. He yelled out at frequent intervals that he was queer and would service everybody on the staff. He had also attempted suicide.

Ed was partnered with Hap Galbreath, a slim, taciturn southerner nearing the end of a thirty-year career. His calm, seasoned approach lent him a dignity that threw the peccadilloes of his colleagues into sharp relief. He seemed the one man there from whom Ed might actually learn something useful. His insights were served up in unfamiliar regionalisms that Ed found pleasingly exotic. "Pay Geismann no mind," Hap told him on their first shift together. "He'll shut off if you don't take his bait. And he's no dick licker. I can spot 'em. He just wants out and thinks acting nancy will grease his wheels. Probably would if he could get one shrink to believe him."

When Hap left, the unseen Geismann struck up an improbably licentious rant which Ed tried to tune out as he reviewed his situation. "I just have to make it to midnight," he thought. "Nothing is going to happen that Hap hasn't seen before, and if it does, he'll know how to deal with it. He won't expect much of me on my very first shift. I can do this. They're in there, locked up. I'm out here, with the keys. Nothing's going to happen." Immediately, something did.

The crisp tap of footsteps caused Ed to look up and see Hap bearing down on him with a white-strapped coat. "'Psycho-Central' just called. Geismann's going for observation. They want him straight-jacketed. Come on, the ambulance is on the way."

O... kay, thought Ed as he got to his feet and scrambled to keep up with Hap.

Geismann stood two cells in, a small man in his thirties who grew jittery as his eyes went to the jacket. Ed was relieved they weren't confronting a bruiser, but the cell was small. There seemed a good possibility they could all get banged up if Geismann decided to struggle. Ed unlocked the door and slid it aside. Hap stepped past him with the jacket, muttering, "Get behind him. Grab his arms." Ed disobeyed, for he saw what Hap hadn't. Geismann's right hand twitched, and above a line of blood, the fingers clutched a shard of broken glass. With a sudden movement that surprised him as much as the others, Ed's leg shot up, and Geismann doubled over. The makeshift weapon fell at their feet, and Hap said, "Where the hell did he get that?" Ed pointed to the remaining fragment of a glass shield below the bulb in the ceiling. Hap shook his head. "Sweet Genevieve! I should have spotted that." When Geismann was strapped into the jacket, Hap locked eyes with Ed and said, "Thanks, Sheffield."

Ed wished he could stop time and freeze the moment. Through a fluke unlikely to be repeated, he had temporarily won the trust and gratitude of a man he respected. It wouldn't last. It couldn't, could it? After some inevitable screw-up, the scales would fall from Hap's eyes. But for now . . . What people didn't know about you could be so helpful… so wonderful.

A shift log was kept by the senior soldier, brief, sketchy notes mostly, but Hap's were meticulous. Word of the incident spread quickly on both sides of the bars. Ed wasn't entirely displeased, but it made him nervous. He alone knew how uncharacteristic his action had been. He was neither cool-headed nor physically adept. The bar of expectation for him had been raised, accidentally and artificially. Now, when the inevitable fall from grace came, it would be from a greater height. Still, Ed decided it would be ungrateful and rather a waste not to enjoy the reactions around him while they lasted.

Captain Knox took a pretty elastic view of fraternization, and those who found themselves in his quarters were encouraged to speak freely. At the end of his first week at the stockade, Ed sat in the captain's den, beer in hand, with several of the other guards. "Hap tells me you've already distinguished yourself, Sheffield," said the captain, nursing a whiskey.

No sensible reply came to mind, so it was Hap who spoke up. "He saved me from a slice and dice, Captain, and that's the gods' truth. Funny part is, if Geismann had known *why* we were trying to get him into the straight jacket, he'd have leaped into it by himself."

Ed squirmed as Captain Knox leaned forward in his easy chair and fixed him with an amused smile. "So those ju-jitsu classes at Fort Gordon actually come in handy?"

"No room for that stuff, sir," Hap continued gleefully. "Sheffield just kneed 'im in the balls!"

The officer nodded. "Primitive. Brutal. Always a good option. Let's hear it for our young brute." Bottles and glasses were raised as the men chanted, "Brute! Brute! Brute!" Ed was being mocked, but he chose to think there was also some affection in it. He'd take it.

The cadre at the stockade was the smallest subset on post. As such, they knew each other beyond all hope of surprise and to the point of stupefaction. Ed was fresh meat and more welcome for being an unfamiliar cut. Misinterpreting the courtship which now began, he was flattered and failed to see that it sprang less from camaraderie than boredom. There was general agreement that the first order of business was to get the newbie as drunk as possible, get him laid, and observe the results.

Ed, of course, knew none of this as he set out for a night in Anchorage in the company of three eager guides, Jesse Webb, Dale Caulkins, and Earl Sudrow. Though Ed was by now in possession of a valid driver's license, this trio of bon vivants had persuaded him to let Dale drive Russell for the evening. Ed was happily squeezed into the back seat between Jesse and Earl. He was in much faster company than he knew. Jesse and Earl were Dale's rivals for the crown of prison tomcat. Each was good looking in his own way, and had you asked among the men on post, the playing field would be declared pretty level. To women, however, there was no contest.

Slender Jesse was the most dedicated drinker of the three, and though he could disguise his condition for a while, he disliked any challenge that risked prolonging a seduction past his window of performance opportunity. He sought out easy conquests and was undeterred by shortcomings above the neck. Such foreplay as his partners might expect would be, though highly charged, strictly verbal.

Earl was a solidly built oaf. His tightly packed physique was unaccompanied by graces of any other sort. What those ladies who responded to it saw was what they got, roughly and rapidly. Pleasing a partner was not an idea that often crossed either man's mind.

Dale, however, had recognized at age twelve, the value of good word-of-mouth. He was smooth and innovative. That, and above all, his patience, gained him entrance to bedrooms ordinarily closed to men even more physically imposing.

As Russell thundered toward Anchorage, Earl and Jesse busied themselves cheerfully punching Ed and assuring him his money would be no good when they reached town. His high spirits matched their own. Not since his enlistment and seldom before had he had such an attentive audience, so easily captivated by his every remark. As a bonding experience, it was so heady he could scarcely believe his good fortune.

Dale called back over his shoulder, "What's your poison, li'l Sheff?"

"Poison?"

"Booze!" roared Earl.

"Umm… I don't know that I have a favorite yet. Liebfraumilch is nice at Thanksgiving. To tell you the truth—"

Jesse eyed him with a look of warm fascination which Ed, unacquainted with cobras, had never encountered. "Yesss. Tell the truth. That's always best. You're among friends here."

"Well, I mean, sure I've had a beer now and then—"

Jesse nodded agreeably. "Now and then."

"And of course we'd have wine on the holidays..." Earl's enormous grin moved into Ed's peripheral vision. "But I'd probably better stick to something safe – at least until we eat."

Jesse looked thoughtful and said quietly, "Boilermakers. Just the thing to line your stomach."

"Boilermakers!" The group echoed Jesse's choice with resounding accord.

Ed shrugged. "Boilermakers it is then." A whoop went up and fists punched skyward.

"Hey, Sheff?" said Earl. Ed turned and smiled, eager to keep the term in circulation. "When was your last piece of ass?"

"Ohh..." Ed shrugged again, and Jesse muttered, "If ever." Ed looked at him with alarm. Jesse leaned in very close and whispered, "You're a virgin, aren't you?"

"No," Ed sputtered, "I... I..."

"I knew it!" Jesse shouted. Another general whoop went up, louder than the first, and Ed dodged a forest of jabs from all directions.

Dale parked in a vacant lot, and as the four of them walked along, Earl, whose girder-like masculinity would go unquestioned in a ball gown, draped an arm over Ed's shoulder. The hypocrisy of Ed's position in this swaggering band, and his nascent misgivings about them and the purpose of the evening, would have to wait to be dwelt on. Just now, all Ed wanted to do was wallow in the considerable pleasures of being perceived by passers-by as part of this manly group. Better still, he'd be seen as an intimate, favored chum of this prize bull whose casual embrace trumpeted Ed's worth to the world.

They headed for the Hoffbrau, a new place popular for its hearty German food and its big "meet and greet" bar. They bellied up, and Ed detected a ripple of curiosity from several women at nearby tables. The inaugural boilermaker, the first of many, was set before him, and he did as he was told, belting the whiskey back quickly, then dealing with the beer. After the first one, he noticed that, while everyone was drinking steadily, he alone was quaffing the touted boilermaker. Some tardy instinct for self-preservation kicked in, and he disappointed them by reverting to type as a sipper, not a belter. Nonetheless, his exit from the Hoffbrau would be unsteady.

The noise level was high enough to make it difficult to focus on all that his companions were saying, but after a while he heard an exchange that made him wish it were noisier still. Earl inquired of Dale, "So who's the best lay you've had in Alaska?"

Dale needed no time to consider. "Faye. No question," he shot back.

"Yeah." Earl nodded dreamily. "Faye Knox."

A little of Ed's beer spilled out on the bar. "Not Mrs. Knox? Not the captain's wife? You shouldn't joke about her."

"They're not," Jesse said calmly.

Ed spoke excitedly. "We go to his house, Dale. We eat his food. We drink his liquor. He trusts us. You wouldn't…?" He was almost in tears. "You guys are kidding me, right?"

Wrong. Dale put a firm hand on Ed's knee. "Calm down, kiddo. If a man can't handle his wife, she's fair game. Faye Knox is a grown up. Nobody makes her do anything she doesn't want to."

Ed wanted to punch him in the mouth for even using Mrs. Knox's first name. It couldn't be true. It mustn't be true. But the way they were acting, it probably was. He decided to shut up. There was so much to say, but he was still sober enough to know he would only be laughed at. His hosts could not be preached to. They had the moral equivalent of his separate popcorn stomach at the movies. When it came to sex, and God knows what else, they could compartmentalize. Friendship was as shallow as the puddle of his beer the bartender was wiping up, and no one was safe from betrayal. Captain Knox had strong claims on their loyalty and respect. Ed had little or none. He felt exposed and at risk. He wanted the evening over at once, but he feared it wasn't going to be over for a long, long time. He sipped at his whiskey.

Earl and Jesse had a favorite bar that wasn't to be missed, after which, the plan was to drive to the Shimmy Shack and appraise the talents of the local strippers. At Tusker's Keg, Jesse struck sparks with a short, matronly Eskimo woman and wanted to borrow the car keys for a quickie. Dale was annoyed and refused. "God damn Klutch hound! You gotta spoil the party. Just keep it zipped till we get to the Shack."

Jesse moved in close and lowered his voice. "The Shack is iffy. This is a sure thing." He jabbed at Dale's chest for emphasis. "Don't make me waste thisss."

"No," said Dale. "It's not my car. I know you. You'd leave us stranded, you disloyal fuck." Glancing toward Ed, he added, "Think about somebody else for one single time in your whole life."

Jesse grabbed a handful of Dale's shirt. "You stupid shit. I only want to borrow the keys. You won't be stranded because your precious pile of crap car isn't going anywhere. Do I hafta draw you a picture?" Jesse looked at Ed for support. "The kid gets it, dontcha Sheff? And he doesn't mind."

Woozy as he was, Ed got it, and he did mind. Not for the sake of the woman, now wearing Jesse's cap and observing them impassively. The logistics were repulsive, but clearly, the only honor at stake here was Russell's. Ed had already seen bloody fights break out over less than this. He didn't need another one, not on this night that was already spinning out of control. *Welcome to Manland*, he thought and shrugged an okay to Dale. He wondered who would most merit his disgust in the morning, Dale, Jesse, Mrs. Knox, or he himself.

Dale fished for the keys. "Clean up after yourself, Jesse." He closed his fist on the keys and held them back. "She's a runt. How 'bout I just give you the key to the trunk?"

"How 'bout I give you your teeth for a snack?" Jesse snatched the key ring. The woman stood a little way off but well within earshot. When Jesse reached her, Dale called out, "Give our love to Grandma." Jesse swung around, but Earl jumped between them and said, "Just go, Webb, and don't take all night."

"I never do," he chirped and gestured toward the woman with a flourish. "After you, darlin'."

An hour later, they poured Ed into the Shimmy Shack. Earl nudged him in the ribs and said, "They know me here. When you see something you like, I'll put in a good word for ya."

Ed surveyed the premises with bleary eyes and thought, *Sweet mother of mercy! When I see something I like here, put me in a straight jacket and ship me to Psycho Central.* Earl got them a table at the round stage where an alarmingly large set of breasts was violently whipping tassels into a frenzy of what appeared to be fireworks, though Ed had begun to question the reality of his visions several rounds ago. "That must hurt," he said. He hadn't meant it as a joke, but everyone howled. Earl pounded the table and said, "He's killing me."

Ed hadn't known quite what to expect in the way of entertainment at the Shimmy Shack. He knew better than to hope for what he really would have liked, a comely young woman in diaphanous attire, gracefully executing a dance of the seven veils (to Strauss, if the management were really inspired). But he found the surly stomping and clomping that actually took place a bit bewildering. The tough, brassy women strutting and splaying before them could have been MPs. They were like female versions of Earl, without his class and charm.

Starting out tonight, Ed had badly wanted to fit in and had tried hard to do so, but in his current queasy state, faking enthusiasm for this sad, ugly circus was beyond him. Each time he turned away in dismay and embarrassment, someone would point his head back at the spectacle. He knew they were making signs at the performers behind his back because these ladies all made him the prime target of their thrusting gyrations. The dancer who least resembled a stevedore was a sharp-nosed blonde called Yvonne. When Ed saw Dale slip her a bill, he knew he was in for it. Making a beeline for him, she peeled off her brassier and snapped it at him. Then she tousled his hair, grabbed it tightly, and buried his head in her bosom. A roar went around the table and spread throughout the room, accompanied by much pounding and stomping. She released him, and the face he turned to his hosts was wide-eyed and beet red.

Was there to be no merciful end to these grotesque revels? Perhaps if he could focus long enough to manage a display of gratitude, he could beg off and they'd take him home. He would try. "You guys have spent a fortune on me tonight. I'm gonna do something really, really nice for all of you." Then he said, "OOOBLEEAAAHHH!" and vomited on the table.

"Gee, Sheff," said Jesse, "that was mighty swell, but I was hoping for flowers."

"I had him hurling by midnight," said Dale. "Who won the pool?"

"Peeeww," said Earl. "Yvonne just got her titties out of here in time."

Ed said, "I'm so sor –OOOBLEEAAAHHH!"

"So glad we took Sheffield's car, Dale," said Jesse. "Do you think he'll be real nice like I was and clean up after himself?"

"Fuck," said Dale, and they called it a night.

Ed managed to avoid decorating Russell but it was a near thing, and twice they had to pull off the road. He didn't remember swilling great quantities of gasoline and lemon concentrate, but judging by what kept coming up, it seemed he must have.

Back at the stockade, Ed tried to beat a lurching path to the room he shared with Dale and Earl. He was especially anxious not to be seen in his present condition by Hap or any of the prisoners, and he longed for the oblivion of sleep. Jesse, who had his own room, followed them in, which was unusual. Ed had had enough of these companions before whom he had so thoroughly disgraced himself. What more could they wish for? He hoped that he – and they – had seen the last of his retching, since he had already heaved every scrap of food and drink he had consumed this evening, this week, and quite possibly since his arrival at the stockade.

He needed to be horizontal, in silence and darkness, but there they all stood with the lights on. He feared Jesse would keep them talking, but no one was speaking – unless he had gone deaf. Did that happen too, when you drank yourself silly?

He longed to shut the lights off, but it seemed rude to plunge even a group of ill-mannered yahoos into arbitrary darkness. When would they all go away? He closed his eyes and made a wish, but when he opened them they were all still there, beaming at him as though he were their sole source of happiness. He couldn't wait any longer. He stripped in front of them and tried, but failed, to climb into bed. Something was wrong with his feet, or the bed. It wouldn't let him in. He kept trying, but now he could hear them laughing – so he wasn't deaf after all. He slid to the floor in a heap at their feet. Before setting out, they had short sheeted his bed.

Jesse leaned down close to his ear, grinning. "Starched your sheets, dinya?"

"Nooo..." Ed moaned.

"We think yes."

Ed was to be spared nothing. Now these louts knew even that

about him, had known it all evening long. He dragged himself onto the bed and pulled the pillow over his head. It blocked the light, but not their howls of laughter, or Earl saying again, "He just kills me." Ed prayed he had given his last performance. Surely he had nothing left to disgorge but internal organs. Any more of this and he'd have to check the commode for his liver and spleen. All too soon, Ed was compelled to give an encore. This time it seemed only sensible to remain sprawled in the bathroom. Eventually, he heard voices. Dale was asking, "Where's the kid?"

"On the floor in the john," said Earl. " Let him sleep."

"I won't put the light on, but all this beer . . ."

Ed felt himself being straddled by two legs. "Ummphh?"

"Don't jiggle, chum. You don't want to make me miss."

Chum. He was Dale's chum all right, raw chum for shark bait. He cooled his cheek against the porcelain, shut his eyes, and listened to the bold stream echoing just above him. The depth of his humiliation was beyond improvement, even by a urine shampoo from Dale. "You guys were supposed to be my friends."

"If I wasn't your friend, I wouldn't bother to aim." Then Dale bent down and did a very friendly thing indeed. "You think you're all through puking for tonight?" he asked.

Ed moaned, "Oh, I sure hope so." At which feeble assurance, Dale scooped him up and carried him back to bed. He took a small bottle from his locker and set it on a windowsill by Ed's bed.

"You're going to need a hair of the dog in the morning."

Ed sat up. "Never! As god is my witness."

"Oh now, Miss Scarlett," said Dale, "that sounds kinda rash."

"Well, I'm never touching another boilermaker, and I mean it," Ed groaned. "And I'm never, ever trusting you guys again!"

"That's a much better plan. G'night, Li'l Sheff."

So, Ed thought, *It isn't a total loss. There'll be a nickname on my tombstone in the morning.*

⁂

Ed awakened around noon, grateful they had had the decency to stage his debacle on the first night of his off shift. Back on duty two days later, he detected no signs of knowing amusement from Hap or the prisoners. Whatever anyone knew or didn't of his improprieties, the world kept turning and it was business as usual. Ed called roll, collected whatever mail they had written, sent some of them off under guard for work details, sent others to medical or legal appointments, and created busy work for those who remained. Shift after uneventful shift passed without Ed disgracing himself. All credit for this he gave to Captain Knox whose genius had found him a situation of such minimal expectations that even he could meet them.

To Ed's surprise, the next big screw up was not only someone else's, but it was Ed who managed to defuse it and keep it from coming to light. The incident occurred toward the end of Ed's favorite shift, midnight to eight. He liked the long quiet stretches of time to think his thoughts. He liked the intimacy of lowered voice conversations with Hap or the rotating temp guards from other companies. He liked the silent cleansing stillness that settled in after a day of profane clamor. He liked standing at the top of the stairs that led down into the exercise yard and gazing out at that empty space now rendered eerie and theatrical by the night lights, or staring up at a sky filled with alien constellations.

6:00 AM was wake-up, and sleepers caught a break on Ed's shifts. For him, bed was a sacred place, a sanctuary from which an involuntary departure was a barbarous thing indeed. Ed's co-workers, on the other hand, saw themselves as human alarms and strove to be as alarming as possible. Hap was loud, brusque, and no-nonsense. Dale bellowed threats and obscenities. Jesse, except when hung over, employed a collection of party horns and noisemakers. Earl roared out of the darkness like a maniac, banging on cots with a club. Ed, less desirous of inducing coronaries, just switched on the lights and, unless they took too long about it, let the stirrings of some awaken the others.

When they had washed, shaved, and dressed, Ed had to get them into the yard for roll call and exercise. A stoop at the top of the stairs provided a small but ample stage for announcements and demonstrations. Normally, if Ed lagged behind and gave the inmates a moment to mutter and mingle, it was easy enough to form them up when he reached the stoop. If anything, they were more eager than he to have these pre-breakfast calisthenics over and done with. But on this particular morning, they were distracted by something beyond the gates, and Ed had to bark his commands to pry them away. He got the drill started, but those in back kept craning around. He called them to attention, jumped down from the stoop, and made his way quickly to the gate. A few yards outside, at a rather odd angle, Jesse's gray De Soto stood not so much parked as halted. The motor was running, and though he couldn't see a driver, a foot dangled below the open door. Snapping back to the prisoners, Ed called out, "ForWARD!" and marched them as far away from the gate as he could before halting them at attention.

The temp guard in the gatehouse looked too young to be drafted and was clearly eager to make the car and its contents somebody else's problem. "What's going on?" Ed asked him.

"You better take a look," said the kid as he unlocked the gate.

They walked to the car, stepped around the open door, and saw clearly what had been blocked from view. The guard exclaimed, "Whoa!" Ed reached in past the splayed, comatose Jesse, whose pants were around his ankles, and shut off the motor. Slumped naked next to Jesse, was an Eskimo woman considerably younger than Jesse's previous companion.

Ed stared at the guard. "How long has he been out here?" he demanded. "Why didn't you call in?"

The guard squirmed and explained, "Uhhh…"

"Couldn't you at least have shut off the motor and closed the door?"

"Uhhh…" the kid elaborated.

Ed realized he was scaring the boy, and novel though the experience was, he had no wish to prolong it. He himself was all too fluent in "Uhhh."

"Never mind," he said. "No real harm done. I'll take care of this." That unaccustomed phrase and the relief on the boy's face gave Ed a rush. *I WILL take care of this,* he thought and savored the prospect of obliging this undeserving trio in distress. Peering into the back seat of the De Soto, he could see the girl's clothes scattered about. He plucked up the skirt and blouse and, without attempting to dress her, draped them to cover her nakedness. He turned back to the boy. "Just get his pants up. Get him ready to go inside."

The guard's face scrunched into an unspoken, "Do I have to?" Ed cocked his head and raised a loud eyebrow. The boy, unaware that it was not in Ed to write him up, decided he was getting off easy and bent toward Jesse with resigned distaste.

Ed strode across the yard and shouted at the prisoner's backs, "It's gonna rain. Dismissed for breakfast." Inside the mess hall, Hap and the cook looked up at him quizzically. "Don't want them in the yard right now," Ed said tersely. To his considerable satisfaction, they accepted without discussion that he had his reasons. "Be right back," he said to Hap and strolled to the door. Once outside, he ran across the yard, and the guard scrambled to unlock the gate.

"Is he ready?"

"Well, he's dressed, but I wouldn't say he's ready to go anywhere."

The guard was a bit breathless. "He's groggy, but he kept swinging at me. I had to hit him."

"Good," said Ed.

The guard pulled the door open and jumped back to indicate that Jesse was all Ed's. Ed took Jesse's wrist and shook him gently. "Jesse…Jesse, it's me, Sheffield. I know you can hear me. I'm gonna get you inside. Nobody has to know about this if you just stay quiet."

Jesse's eyes opened and regarded Ed with unfocused malevolence.

"But Jesse – " He shook him again, more vigorously. " Jesse, if you get loud or try to swing at me, you're so wasted I can hurt you. We're gonna do this fast and quiet, you understand? Jesse? Do you?" Jesse nodded, and Ed was able to stand him up and drag him across the yard to a side entrance. Once inside his own room, Jesse flopped face down on the bed.

"We've got to get her out of here," said Ed. "Where does she live?"

"Live? Who?"

"That girl, Jesse."

"She live someplace? I dunno." He was fast melting into the bed.

Ed made one more try. "Where did you find her, Jesse?"

The head reared up angrily. "You gonna be the big man? Well, you're not. You figure it out. I gotta sleee . . " He sank back into the pillow. Ed opened Jesse's locker, took out a raincoat, and left the room.

In the mess hall, Hap noted the raincoat and said, "You gonna tell me about this sometime, or is it classified?"

"Classified? Around here?" Ed laughed. "I'll tell you all about it when I get back, if you're interested."

"I'm not. You don't ever need to tell me shit."

Ed got up to leave, smiling at this man he liked more with each shift they shared.

❧

Back at the De Soto, Ed spoke to the sleeping girl, trying to rouse her without touching her. "Miss? Miss? I'm going to drive you home. Will you tell me where you live?" It was useless. The 8:00 to 4:00 shift would soon bring prisoners back into the yard. Ed started the car, drove a discreet distance away, and pulled off the road by a stand of black spruce. He got into the back and searched, even under the seats, for a bag or a purse. "Not that type, I guess." He got back in the driver's seat next to her, draped her with Jesse's raincoat, grabbed the edge of her skirt from beneath it, and dragged it free. She moaned and stirred slightly, but her eyes remained tightly shut. A quick search of the skirt pocket yielded a billfold with an employee ID. This woman of mystery worked at the Matanuska Pride Grocery Market. "No point taking her there in this shape," he decided. "I don't want to get her fired."

Tired as he was, Ed had almost resigned himself to staying with her until she woke up, but when he turned over a photo of a middle aged native couple, he could make out printing on the back. "If you find this, please return to --." He started the car and headed for Anchorage, saying to the still inert figure, "We're on our way, and I bet we have your mother to thank for it."

It took him an hour, and two stops for directions to reach the address on the photo. By that time, the girl was sufficiently clear-headed to dress herself. She was singularly incurious about her unexpected companion, asking only if they had had intercourse. Ed assured her they had not, but to his exasperation, she seemed unconvinced. When he attempted to reclaim Jesse's raincoat, she snatched it up and insisted on keeping it. "This way, I know he'll see me again," she explained. "It's a good raincoat, military."

It took Ed even longer to find the way back to Fort Rich. He turned the radio up loud because by now he was as much in need of sleep as the errant lovebirds. Back at the stockade, he opened Jesse's door quietly and set the car keys on a dresser. Before Ed could leave, Jesse muttered, "So, did you fuck her?"

"Of course not."

Closing the door, he heard Jesse say, "Faggot."

"You're welcome," Ed replied. Heading at last for his own bed, he thought, *Eddie needs some new friends.*

The thick, heavy door to Ed's room was like soundproofing. The click of punctuation it made as it sealed him in was Ed's favorite sound at the stockade. He took a box of stationery into bed with him. The exchange with Jesse had stirred unwanted energy that would keep him awake a while longer. He propped himself up and used his knees as a writing desk.

"*Tardy tidings, esteemed Pop, tardy and uneventful. Nothing new here, I'm afraid. Things plod along here predictably. Your lazy chameleon continues to blend in and keep a low profile. On a good day, they can barely distinguish me from the paint on the walls, so all is well, and not to worry.*

I miss you lots, whole big vacant lots. I'm still not sure I'm entitled to do that, after the way I bolted, but I'm doing it anyway because, whatever I bolted from, you know it wasn't you – not ever.

That's not to say I wish you were here – I wouldn't wish that on anybody. If you were here with me, you'd want me to show you around the place, but that wouldn't work. I'd get us lost, and I wouldn't know what anything was for. You could show me around though. You'd be onto this place in two minutes.

What I'd rather do is take you to the theater on post that's showing "The Big Country." You'd like it. I've already seen it, but William Wyler has stuffed it with so many good bits that it's worth a rewatch. Surprised to hear me praise a western? Me too. But the score and the close-up of wagon wheels hurtling through a deep, narrow canyon pulled me in before the credits were over, and I never got back out. There's a terrific shot of a bloody brawl with the camera pulling back and back until the audience feels like God peering down at the fight from a cosmic distance. Wyler uses the shot to play with our feelings about the characters. Close up, you've got a stake in the outcome and the fight is a serious matter, but the farther back he pulls us, the tinier and more absurd the combatants become. It's so beautifully…"

Ed bit his lips together and considered the ceiling.

",,,detached. "

His search for the precise adjective made him drowsy. Pages slid to the floor, and Ed stretched out to sleep.

CHAPTER 14

NORTHERN BELLES

Fort Richardson: April, 1958

Ed started going into Anchorage more often and alone. He didn't imagine he'd actually make new friends; that was rare under the best of circumstances. But the prospect of at least seeing new faces might lessen the crankiness in which recent events were marinating him. To his surprise, he was soon befriended by two women of whom he would continue to think fondly, long after he left Alaska.

The first of these was the proprietress of what would become Ed's favorite haunt, Tom's Record Shop. If she had a last name, he never discovered it. To her clients, she was Mrs. Tom. A widow in her fifties, she sported a crisp hairdo and personality that made Ed think of bright new pennies. The first time he passed the shop window, he was stopped in his tracks by the display on the right hand wall: Maria Callas, Tito Gobbi, Jussi Bjoerling, and Renata Tebaldi, all in costume, smiling out at him. An entire wall devoted to opera! In Alaska! He was rooted to the spot.

A smoke-textured voice spoke from behind the counter, "Come inside, soldier, if you've nothing better to do."

"Oh, believe me, ma'am, I haven't. And what could be better than this?"

He entered and was still there an hour later, exploring stack after stack, calling out to her frequent exclamations of delight at his discoveries. She knew her music, and though she wasn't native to it, she knew her Alaska. Casually, almost imperceptibly, she reeled him into a kind of ongoing seminar about territorial lore and points of interest. He'd never heard these things spoken of on post, and it seemed an unpromising topic. Courtesy compelled him to listen, but her anecdotes were both inspiring and scandalous. He couldn't get enough of them.

Before he left, he wanted to repay her attentions. He brought a boxed set of *The Barber of Seville* up to the cash register.

"You don't have to buy anything, Eddie." By this time, he had confided his name and a good deal more.

"I want to. I'll listen to this as soon as I get back. And anyway, you're in business."

"Indeed I am, but I know how it is, or how it can be, with my military visitors."

"Do you get many?" It seemed improbable.

"You'd be surprised," she said. "Airmen from Elmendorf, mostly, but some from the army as well. Medics come by."

"I'm an MP." It was out before he could recall it.

"Good for you!" He could have hugged her for her lack of surprise. "You're my first," she added. "Come back anytime, to shop or not."

He did. It was the first place he'd seek out when he came into town. Some days, she'd help him plan how to spend the rest of his time, and some days he'd spend much of it right there in the shop. Ed would ask her about business, which led one day to her telling him she'd bought a small bit of airtime for a radio commercial. She showed him the proposed text and was rewarded with a frown.

"Do you see a mistake?" she asked.

"Oh no, it's quite correct, Mrs. T., it's only…"

"What? Tell me. It doesn't go on 'til next month."

"Well, it's just – I'm not sure it's going to bring people into the shop."

Mrs. Tom frowned back at him for a moment. Then she turned the sheet over and pushed it toward him. Several weeks later, as Ed took lunch in the mess hall, he had the exquisite pleasure of hearing his own words read out for the greater Anchorage area by a deep-voiced announcer. He could have turned to his companions, pointed to the radio and said, "I wrote that." Instead, he just smiled. No one at that table was going to believe him.

It was through Mrs. Tom that Ed met his second benefactress in Anchorage.

"Is there any place nice I could eat?" he asked her one day. "Any place with some atmosphere?"

She was happy to oblige. "There's a spot I like called the Ritz-Venice. It's not cheap, but it won't cost you a fortune either. Tell them I sent you."

In a town Ed had come to think of as his northern wild west, Ritz-Venice struck him as an incongruously seductive moniker for an eatery. After getting directions from Mrs. Tom, he set out for it at once. It was nice in the sense of being clean and tidy, but rather a small, narrow place with one aisle running between two rows of comfortable leather booths in a bearable shade of green. As to atmosphere, it supplied little of its own beyond a couple of deco travel posters. Cozy rather than swank, it boasted a terrific kitchen and an even more terrific waitress, Paulette.

Paulette was uncommonly nice to all, far nicer than someone with her looks needed to be to get generous tips. Ed's self-consciousness about dining alone was obvious to her, and she made it a project to put him at ease. Her manner was quietly conspiratorial. Like all pretty women with a sense of humor about her beauty and its effect on others, she made Ed nervous even as she charmed him. If she stood close to take his order, he smiled for no reason. If she leaned over his shoulder to point out an item on the menu, the skin on his neck tingled. The night she brought him a lobster and tucked a paper bib under his chin, he blushed loudly and held his breath. Paulette's attentions never struck him as flirtatious; if anything, they seemed maternal, but her proximity rendered him clumsy and distracted. Forks clattered to the floor, salt shakers tumbled, and anything on a stem was a goner. This disarray was all the more vexing to Ed as he tried to appear suave and distinguish himself from the general run of warriors on the loose. Had she betrayed irritation at the nuisance and extra work his spastic shyness caused her, he would have understood and forgiven it. Instead, her smiles grew warmer as she wiped and replaced. Thus indulged, Ed came to think of Paulette's stations as safety islands where only good things happened. She continued to enchant him, but he relaxed to the point where crystal could remain upright.

Paulette had about a decade on Ed, but he knew that men in general would find her most alluring. Her customers certainly did. One elderly regular never got through a meal without inquiring, "When's my Polly of the Ritz stepping out with me?" Ed found this tedious, but he couldn't blame the old coot. Whenever Paulette left Ed's table, he tried to think of something interesting to say when she came back. If she were busy, he kept it short, but he kept it.

Sitting in the Ritz-Venice, Ed learned about dining. Putting himself in Paulette's hands, he discovered he liked a great many things that had never graced Louisa Sheffield's table: veal in all its forms, turkey tetrazzini, and spaghetti Caruso. Paulette even managed to pry him away from the Sheffield tribal conviction that meat must be ordered well done. "Honey," she said one day, "Can I say something and you won't think it's out of turn?"

Ed gulped. What was coming? What had he done to disappoint her?

"We've got a really good chef back there. He orders the best cuts he can find, and he'll cook them any way you ask, but – "

"But?"

"But it makes him sad when he has to send them out well done. He says it cooks all the flavor out of them. I'm not saying he's right, but could you, to make him happy just this once, order your steak, say, medium well?"

"Okay," said Ed, "if you think I should."

"I think you should."

Variations of this scene played out over Ed's next few visits to Anchorage, until Paulette was able to ask, "Are you sure you're ready to do this?"

"It's got to be done," Ed said sternly.

"You can still change your mind. No one will think the less of you."

"The time has come. I'm going to do it."

Paulette sped to the kitchen door and gave a thumbs up sign. The beaming chef himself bore the steak to Ed's booth.

"Rare?" said Ed.

"Rare." The chef nodded eagerly.

Paulette turned to a nearby booth and said, "It's rare."

"Rare," echoed the smiling diners.

She coaxed a round of applause as Ed tore into the bloody steak with enthusiasm.

Ed also learned about potables. Early on, still smarting from the boilermaker episode, he asked Paulette, "Could you bring me a cocktail that civilized people drink?"

From her expression, she thought it a jolly request. "I can use my own judgment?"

"It's better than mine."

"Do you like them sweet?" she inquired.

Ed shook his head. "I don't know what I like, but no, I don't think so."

She considered briefly, then nodded. "I'll be back. If you don't like it, we'll try something else."

"I'll try to like it," he called after her.

When she returned, she set before him a small half tumbler of iced yellow-green liquid, topped with a slice of lime. She stepped back and stood waiting with one hand over the other. Ed sipped and found it tart, agreeable, and unthreatening. "Good," he said. "What is it?"

"Vodka gimlet."

He took another sip. "Thank you, this was a good choice." Later, he asked her, "Are these strong? If I have another, will I get – hammered?"

"Do you get hammered easily?"

"It's happened, but I had a lot of help."

She looked at him thoughtfully. "Hammered on two gimlets? Maybe not, but you could get squiffy."

"That sounds nicer."

She looked at the glass, emptied of all but an ice cube. "Mmm. It's still squiffy."

Ed followed her eyes to the glass. "No, I don't even want to get squiffy."

"That's a good boy." She could say things like that without making him squirm. Years later, long after gimlets fell out of fashion, Ed, in a certain mood and a certain type of place, would order one, partly because he liked them and partly to evoke Paulette.

CHAPTER 15

THE FALL

Fort Richardson: May, 1958

"Any mail for me, Val?" Ed peered over the high counter in the front office at the obese chief clerk. An order had once come down for Val Hand to commence a sensible, restricted diet. What had melted away, however, was not Val's girth but the order itself. There was nothing worth knowing about anyone in the company that Val hadn't made it his business to find out and store away for future use. He was as close to being untouchable as anyone on post could be. Ed was convinced Val had searched his room and gone through his things. More than once, he had observed him exiting the rooms of other guards while they were on duty.

"Your *Variety* came, and a letter from that Jewish friend of yours with the big handwriting." Ed wondered if a good rummage through the clerk's desk would reveal a hot plate and a tea kettle. Val stood up and leaned over the counter, clutching Ed's mail just out of reach. In a quiet, low rasp, he confided, "Sodomy charge, admitted late last night." Val's heavy-lidded eyes practically danced in anticipation of a reaction. Ed knew better than to give him one, beyond, "Huh." He snatched his mail and went back to his room thinking, *That's something new.*

Ed had seen sex offenders pass through the gates before, but those had been rapists. Not one had been charged with homosexuality, and he had begun to think no one ever would be. That night, Hap told him that, unlike the business with Geismann, this was the genuine article. "He's a dick licker, and no mistake." How could Hap be so certain so quickly? Ed wondered, but he didn't ask for fear of seeming unduly curious. He could easily have taken a look for himself but instead went straight to bed. This was a prison, after all, not a zoo.

The next morning, he got his first look at Larry Tappen. It took his breath away. There in the cell, looking sheepish and sad, was the most beautiful boy Ed had ever seen in uniform. Honey-yellow hair fell over his pale forehead, and his hands were clasped together tightly on his kneecap, as though to keep it from falling off. His left wrist wore a bandage. He had slashed himself before they brought him in, and Hap warned Ed to keep a sharp eye on him. Ed did so, for a moment, and then said, "Tappen?"

The boy looked up, and Ed was overwhelmed with a need to make him smile. Whatever this kid had done, it shouldn't have landed him here where he was so clearly in over his head and reeling from it. The only words that came to mind were inane, but Ed uttered them as pleasantly and quietly as possible. "Welcome to Devil's Island." The greeting surprised the look of misery on Tappen's face into something like a smile on training wheels.

Tappen nodded. "Makes sense. I'm the devil."

This was tricky. Ed could be misunderstood and make things worse. "Well, even Lucifer needs to… keep up his strength. Eat that breakfast. I'll be back for the tray in a while."

Walking away, Ed heard a constricted voice say, "I'll be here."

Ed walked to the end of the corridor and stood beyond the cells, where he could not be seen. Had he just been unprofessional? The possibility unsettled him. Yet, was anyone ever professional in this place? Ye gods! Hadn't he heard the most hair-curling threats and obscenities bellowed at the inmates – and bellowed back by them? What gnawed most at Ed's composure was not what he'd said but why he'd said it. The smile had, perhaps, made the kid feel better briefly, but seeing the smile had made Ed feel quite a lot better and was continuing to do so.

To varying degrees, he had at times felt sympathy for a prisoner, but it usually took the form of a mild regret that some basically harmless soldier had screwed himself up so stupidly. Ed's behavior at such times did not really alter, for he hoped he treated decently even the inmates who tried to get under his skin. This was going to be different, and he knew it. It bothered him that Tappen was here, that he faced a stretch at a real prison, and that, at best, he'd be dishonorably discharged and sent home to his family in disgrace. Ed didn't care if Hap were right. Whether Tappen were guilty or not, whatever was legitimately in Ed's power to—but where was this going? Ed had no power to improve the kid's lot while he was here, and he had no business to try.

When he closed his door that night, the image of Larry Tappen alone in his cell bled through even the dark sock draped over Ed's eyes. Instinct warned him he had better attempt to control the form this image took. Well, he could at least call the boy's attention to the prison library. It was limited but contained some good stuff, including donations from Ed himself. The kid looked like a reader, a swell reader. "Stop it!" Ed hissed at himself, "Go to sleep!" But now, sleeping or waking, Ed found the landscape of his thoughts quite altered. At any given moment, whatever else he might be doing or saying, a part of his attention was siphoned away, contemplating the handsome, downcast occupant of the third cell in.

Licensed by Hap's encouragement to do so, Ed checked frequently on Tappen. Cautiously monitoring himself at first, he said little, and Tappen spoke only when spoken to. But things were rearranging themselves so quickly inside Ed's head that he couldn't recognize the place. He found himself rehearsing his appearances at Tappen's cell, determined to keep the smiles coming, without... without what? He wasn't sure. Feeling lopsided, he would shake his head at himself in puzzled derision. Ed was used to straining forward toward his days off. They held escape and relief. But all of a sudden, they seemed an intrusive nuisance. Though he batted it away, the reason was obvious. When his time was his own, he had no legitimate reason to look in on Larry Tappen.

Gradually, the cellside exchanges became conversations, driven by Ed's need to understand who Tappen was, what he had done, and why he had done it. In agitated debate with himself, Ed bristled at the idea that this was mere gossip or morbid curiosity at work. He managed to convince himself that the specifics of Larry Tappen's predicament held the key to important philosophic riddles of morality and justice.

Tappen was no chatterbox, but he didn't resent Ed's questions. He came to feel that this peculiar inquisitor, so determined to be helpful, was at least a neutral, unthreatening presence. It passed the time, and sometimes it was close to nice. Ed learned the boy was from Connectcut, had studied piano before being drafted, and was within months of his discharge at the time of his arrest. They spoke of music, of New England, where Ed had never been, and of "Uncle Wiggly in Connecticut," which Tappen had never heard of until Ed put it into his hands.

The day came when Ed could hold back the question no longer. "Did you do what they say you did?"

"Are you wearing a wire?"

At the stricken look on Ed's face, Tappen said, "Hey, Private Sheffield, I'm teasing you."

"I shouldn't have asked." Ed started to leave.

"Wait. It's okay." The boy stood up and came closer to the bars. "Yes, I did it. When everybody was asleep, I crawled into Gilley's bunk and gave him a blow job – or started to. Then these guys came in late. If they hadn't been drunk, they probably wouldn't have thrown the lights on, but they did, and there I was with Gilley's dick in my mouth."

"Wow!" said Ed.

"Yeah. Wow."

"Why did you do it?"

Tappen gaped at Ed as though he had never heard a question so odd. Then his expression changed, and he said, "Oh, you mean, why did I do it then, when I was such a short timer?"

Ed decided it was best to pretend that was what he had meant.

Tappen continued, "We'd been drinking – a lot. Gilley's the closest thing to a friend I've had here. All evening, he'd been acting like – well, I thought he'd like it. And I knew I would. I'd never have had the nerve though, if I hadn't been so drunk."

Ed nodded. Then he said, "But where's Gilley? Didn't they turn him in too?"

"I'm not sure what they saw until Gilley yelled, 'Get this guy off me. He's a cocksucker!'"

"Well – but, how long had you been doing it to him?"

"About ten minutes. I wanted him to enjoy it. I didn't want to rush."

"This is a million kinds of crazy," Ed sputtered. He's your friend. You're doing him this fantastic favor, and *he* turns you in."

Tappen shook his head. "Gilley just panicked. He thought they'd seen us. What was the use of both of us going to jail if he could save himself?"

"What a bastard!"

Tappen shrugged. "I guess I can't blame him."

"I can," said Ed. "He's the reason you're here, where you don't belong. I'd never have –" Ed was mortified. He hadn't just crossed the line of professionalism, he'd pole vaulted over it. Tappen was looking at him in a new way. Was he picturing the night that had changed his life with Ed in Gilley's place? Was he picturing Ed picturing it, even as he struggled not to?

Tappen spoke and broke the alarming spell. "I don't know what's going to happen to me. I'm scared."

Ed grabbed the bars and drew his face close to them. "Nothing's going to happen to you! I know how these things play out," he lied. "You're an embarrassment to them but not a menace. And you're a short timer. They don't want to keep you around. Listen to me, Tappen, they're going to send you home!" He stared at the boy, willing him to believe it.

The skin on Ed's neck prickled. He turned and saw Hap standing at the end of the corridor. Involuntarily, Ed's hands flew back from the bars, and as they did, he realized the movement had brought about his long delayed fall from grace. A quick gesture, nothing more, but no earthquake or avalanche could have done it better. In that instant, he and Hap were sundered and left on opposite sides of an unbridgeable chasm. Across the length of the hallway, Ed searched Hap's face for a merciful sign of surprise or disbelief. He found only calm, implacable disgust. The judgment was final, irreversible.

We each select a few moments in life to fasten on and replay endlessly, twisting them this way and that in the futile attempt to experience a better outcome. In time, Ed came to feel that if he had only stood still, lowered his voice, and continued speaking to Tappen, perhaps… but that wasn't what had happened. Hap never spoke to Ed about it or about anything else if it could be avoided. Since it usually could, their shifts together went on for months in a painful silence to which Ed deferred. He had always taken other people's cues, and Hap's were unmistakable. Ed fervently wished to explain, but at the same time felt it beneath him and feared it would make things worse. In that sense, he knew that the silence which tormented him was also his protection when they were alone together.

When others were present, the torture took a different shape.

Hap became quite vocal around the temp guards from other companies. He spoke at length to people he would previously have ignored, lavishing on them the companionable chatter Ed was denied and longed for. Indirectly but repeatedly Hap insulted Ed in ways that escaped his puzzled new audience. "Dick-lickers" and the perils of working with them became the theme du jour and du soir, ad infinitem.

Ed squirmed and endured these sessions without holding them against Hap because he felt that, from Hap's point of view, these oblique injuries were the reasonable and justified responses to a betrayal. But at last Ed had had enough. In the middle of the night, as half a dozen of them sat in the darkened mess hall over coffee, he interrupted Hap in a voice much larger than necessary. Nodding his head vigorously, he said, "Yes. Working with someone like that must be God-awful. It must be just about the worst thing on earth!" The bleary eyed young guards said nothing and showed no sign they understood the dynamics of the situation. Hap never did it again, but he never broke his silence.

Several months later, when Hap's tour was up, Ed persuaded Val to lend him the skeleton key he always suspected the clerk possessed. He slipped into Hap's room where a neatly packed suitcase lay open on the bed. Carefully, Ed lifted several layers of shirts, and burrowed beneath them to place a small box bought in happier times. It contained a set of black jade cuff links on which silver elephants reared up, raising their trunks for good luck. There was no card, but Hap would know. As he closed the door, Ed hoped he had buried them too deep to be easily found and left behind.

CHAPTER 16

ALTERED STATE

Anchorage: July 7, 1958

Ed thought he'd just go into town and have a quick look around. After pulling three midnight to eight shifts he was tired, but this was no day to waste on Fort Rich. The Alaskan Statehood bill had passed. History was being made, and he wasn't going to sleep through it. He'd needed a couple of hours under the pillow, just enough so he wouldn't drift out of focus once he got to Anchorage, so he asked for a wake up. At 11:00, Donnie Heeringa had kindly looked in on him and kicked the bed.

Now it was noon, and as Ed peered through the lens of his camera, he saw the bus approaching. He probed his pockets to assure himself that he hadn't come off without pad and pen. He'd see how the locals behaved as their territory won the forty-ninth star. He'd see it and snap it and record it. If the festivities didn't amount to much, he'd cut it short and head back for some real sleep. But, in years to come, even if he had to add a few picturesque embellishments to the celebration, he could truthfully say he'd been a part of it.

It was Tom's day for the car, but the weather was good and Ed didn't mind. As a symbol, Russell the Pontiac remained an object of pleasure for him. After all, it was behind the wheel of Russell that Ed had finally earned a real driver's license. But as reliable transportation, Russell was a sometime thing. The bus pulled up, and once aboard it, Ed moved all the way to the back, burrowed into a window seat, and gave in to his drowsiness. It didn't matter. If he fell asleep, they'd put him off when he got to town. Nothing mattered. A day off was a good one, and there were two more coming when this one was done. He let his eyes close. When they opened, it was because he felt the bus rocking from side to side. It was surrounded. Laughing faces pressed in at all the windows. People pounded on the bus, shouting, "Hooray for statehood!"

"Hooray for Alaska!"

"Hooray for us!"

Hooray for anything and everything looked like the order of the day. When Ed managed to battle his way out of the bus, an elderly Eskimo grinned excitedly and pushed a paper cup at him. For a second, Ed thought it was an aggressive attempt at charitable extortion, but the old man rasped, "Drink up, son. It's been a long time comin.'" Ed thought it was early for beer, with only puffed wheat in his stomach, but it seemed ungracious to decline. "Thank you." He found himself swallowing not beer but champagne. Perhaps the festivities would amount to something after all.

He climbed back up on the steps of the bus and aimed his camera at the Eskimo. The old man danced about in the viewfinder, waiving an uncorked bottle. "Could you hold still, sir?" But the man couldn't. "I wish this were a movie camera." They were both laughing now. Ed snapped the shutter but doubted he'd gotten more than a blur.

Still on the steps, he trained the camera down the street but then lowered it to confirm with his eyes alone what the lens asked him to believe. In the space of the first block directly ahead of him, more bodies were moving about, or trying to, than the sum total of all the people he had seen on all the streets he had walked on all of his previous trips to Anchorage combined. The blocks beyond this one promised equally impressive crowds.

Where had they been up to now, this cast of thousands surging through streets he had found quiet, even lonely at times? He needed a higher perch to take it in properly. Could he get up on top of the bus? That didn't seem safe. The rocking had stopped, but a sudden swell of the crowd could pitch him from the roof onto… well, onto the crowd, he supposed. Ed raised the camera, steadied it on the rear view mirror, and took his second shot of the day. The picture would be impressive even if the frame were a bit askew. It might even be better that way. He smiled as he stepped down, but he knew it would be slow going to get as far into town as he now meant to.

"Happy Statehood, soldier!" yelled a red-headed man from the door of a souvenir shop. How did they know? Ed had never been able to figure it out. No matter what he wore, on every trip to Anchorage, some local would call out, "Hey there, soldier!" and then laugh as though Ed had been caught trying to sneak around in disguise. It was written all over him in some way, and it wasn't just him. Everyone in town on pass came back with the same tale. You'd always be spotted and tagged, though it didn't seem to be done with hostility. The town was friendly enough even if you showed up in uniform, which Ed never did. He couldn't wait to get out of it even on post. They didn't much care what you did, unless you were trying to date their daughters, but they just had to let you know they knew. It was a harmless sport for the locals, but mysterious and unnerving.

Ed examined the shop window and laughed out loud. Rows of carved whales, walruses and moose held tiny American flags in their teeth. "Whaddya think, soldier?" asked the shopkeeper. There was no point in telling him that, so Ed said, "I think you'll make money, sir."

The redheaded man surprised him by replying, "Not on you. Not today. Pick something out and it's yours." He seemed sincere, and, not wanting to take advantage, Ed chose a wooden totem figure that was small and inexpensive but nicely done. Ed would have been happy just to pocket the piece, but the man insisted on wrapping it.

"I'll keep this as a memento of this special day," said Ed as he took it. "I'll remember your kindness whenever I look at it."

"Don't mention it soldier. You're in my army now." Ed almost regretted not having worn his uniform. "Would you mind if I took a picture of you outside your shop?" he asked.

"Mind? What are you talking about? Get the sign in it." The man almost knocked Ed down in his eagerness to pose. "And the flags. Make sure you get the flags!"

Ed laughed. "That won't be difficult." As he moved on from the shop, the owner called after him, "I want a copy of that. You're working for me now." *I guess I am*, thought Ed.

He patted the totem for luck and pushed his way into the crowd. He liked to think he'd eluded the clutches of formal religion, but he knew he could still be a patsy at times for magic and superstition. He felt somehow armed and protected by the carving, even as he laughed at himself for doing so. He couldn't shake the good feeling he had about it, and he didn't want to.

The shop owner's kindness was not to be the last such gesture Ed would encounter as he made his slow progress down the street. In fact, as the day wore on, it appeared the merry denizens of Anchorage were in a prodigal mood, determined that his money be useless. They also seemed bent on getting him thoroughly plastered as quickly as possible. Without setting foot in a bar, he was pressed by passers by to toast the occasion with every potable known to man. Those unknown to man were the fate of anyone reckless enough to venture inside a tavern this day. As a point of pride, each watering hole had devised its own unique commemorative cocktail. By the time Ed's palette had been punished with the Statehood Sazarack and the Admission Freeze, he suspected that novelty held a considerably higher priority in these creations than drinkability.

With that standard in mind, Ed would have awarded the prize hands down to the bizarre brew that greeted him in the Penguin Tap. He was almost past the place when a loud, urgent female voice called out, "Shorty! Shorty? Is that you? I thought I'd never see you again!"

Was his mind playing tricks on him? He turned to confront a portly, laughing woman who began a breathless apology. "I didn't mean to blow out your eardrums, but that's my husband, Shorty, in front of you. We got separated in the crush. Isn't this murder?"

"That's okay, Ma'am. I can still hear. I only turned around because people used to call me Shorty too."

"Well, isn't that something. You two Shorties have got to meet," she said. "Hey, Shorty! Oh, it's no use. Just bang my husband on the head, will you? He's a little hard of hearing."

Ed demurred, "Oh, I couldn't do that. He doesn't know me."

"He'll know ya in a minute. Just pop him one," the woman insisted. Ed tapped his name-mate on the shoulder as politely as the situation permitted. The other Shorty, like his wife, was ample of girth and good humor.

"What can I do you for, buddy?"

"Your wife thought she'd lost you, sir," said Ed.

Shorty looked him up and down and said gruffly, "And what? You're my replacement?" The woman had taken hold of Ed's arm.

"Oh no, sir, it's just –"

The woman cut through Ed's embarrassment. "Shorty, meet Shorty."

"You got my wife, Mac. You don't get my name too."

"He's already got it. He's had it for years, and nothing you can do about it," said the woman, racked again with laughter.

"Well, where you from, Shorty, so I can stay the hell outta there?" asked her husband.

"I'm from Chicago, Shorty," said Ed. The whooping laughter of the couple was contagious, and by now, Ed had caught it too. "But please don't stay away on my account. In fact, would the two of you have a drink with me? I'd like to return some of this Anchorage hospitality."

"Whaddya think, Pam? Can we afford to be seen with this mobster?"

"Now just because I'm from –"

Pam cut Ed off again. "He's the one taking the risk, I'd say."

"All right then, against my better judgment," said Shorty. "But this is on us. Might be dangerous to owe Chicago Shorty here a favor."

"Oh, for heaven's sake!" said Ed.

With Pam and Shorty as a flying wedge, it didn't take too long to penetrate the crowded recesses of the Penguin Tap. "I wonder what cock-a-mamie cocktail this joint has dreamed up?" said Shorty as they found a small table and borrowed a third chair from a nearby group of celebrants. Pam moved her thumb back and forth in the direction of a taped sign in magic marker that commanded, "You must have our commemorative Muckluck Martini."

"I always obey signs," said Shorty. Then he yelled at a bartender, "Hey, Jasper, what's in that Muckluck mess?" The question was obviously a popular one, for three people at the bar spun around on their stools and chanted, "Gin, chartreuse, vermouth …" Then they spun back and gestured to the bartender who added, rather ominously, "and a special secret ingredient."

"Hmmmmm," said Ed. Pam too looked dubious, but Shorty decided for the group. "Send three of 'em over here, Jasper."

Ed thought he should try to make conversation. "Have you known Jasper long, Shorty?"

"Never laid eyes on him, but don't he look like a Jasper?"

The trio turned toward the bar and scrutinized the bartender's features judiciously.

Pam nodded. "He does to me."

"I'm not sure," said Ed. "I've never seen one."

"That's just how they look," Shorty growled. "He's lucky I don't call him something worse, like his momma probably named him."

Pam spoke up. "Well, your momma named you Milan, and that's what I'd better call you here so we don't get all confused. It's either that or Shorty One and Shorty Two."

"My mother named me Ed, if that helps any."

"Well, Ed," said Milan, serious for the first time. "This is a great day, with good times coming for all of us up here."

Ed smiled and said, "Welcome aboard, Milan—and Pam, if I may."

Milan thrust out his hand and Ed shook it. Pam leaned forward and kissed Ed's cheek.

"Don't worry, mobster, that kiss has my blessing," said Milan.

"He's a sweet boy, and he deserved a kiss," said Pam. "I'll bet he doesn't get too many, up here alone in the army."

How well she had put it. "No, Ma'am. That was my first."

She patted his hand. "You should give us your address in Illinois. Now that Alaska will be a state, Shorty and I are going to drive through each and every one of the others. It would be nice to know somebody in a few of them."

"I brought a pad; I'll write it down for you," said Ed, digging in his pocket. "But only if it's my treat when you get there."

"Speaking of that," said Milan, "Where are those damn drinks?"

"Here they come," said Ed. "Do you think we'll figure out the special secret ingredient?"

That turned out to be simplicity itself. When the Muckluck Martinis were placed before them, Pam screamed and recoiled, Ed said, "Ye Gods!" and even Milan was abashed. Bobbing forlornly in each briny looking brew was a fish head. The triumph of the Penguin Tap was absolute. The garrulous trio stared in silent disbelief at their macabre refreshments. Then their eyes met, and the table exploded in pent up laughter. It was Milan who spoke first. "You gotta hand it to them."

"Hand it back to them, you mean," said Pam.

Her husband was undeterred. "Well, bottoms up."

"Or gorges," muttered Ed.

"What shall we toast first?" asked Pam. Toasts of all stripes and feathers had been called out since they arrived. Each one was then echoed by most of the room. Milan raised his glass, and the fish head turned its eyes to Ed.

"To statehood!"

"To statehood!" roared the Penguin crowd, as the trio sipped and shuddered.

"To my two Shorties!" Pam called out.

"To my two Shorties!" roared the crowd that by now might as well have been penguins for all the sense they were making.

"It's your turn, Ed," said Pam.

Ed shook his head, gave a quiet laugh and looked off into the distance. Pam was solicitous. "What's wrong, honey? You feeling homesick?"

"Not exactly," Ed replied. "Well, maybe in a weird way, I am. It's just... I don't know. This whole day, everywhere I've gone, someone's treating me to a drink that's crazier than the last one. Just now, I was feeling like I was here under false pretenses. It's not really my kind of day, but then I thought of someone this day was made for, someone who'd love it."

"You're missing someone from home." Pam squeezed Ed's hand.

"Not missing her, but thinking about her, yes."

"Who is it, sweetie?"

"My Aunt Sheila. She'd be perfect for this. She should be here in my place."

"We'll toast her then," said Milan.

"Oh no, that's not –"

Milan stood and addressed the room. "To a great lady who'd love to be here right now. To Aunt Sheila!"

"To Aunt Sheila!" roared the penguins.

"To Saint Sheila!" piped a voice from a corner, "the patron of Anchorage!"

"To Saint Sheila!" the roar went up.

"She's not the patron of Anchorage," snarled a voice across the room, and opinions weighed in on all sides.

"If it ain't her, who is it then?"

"Some damn fish, probably."

"It oughta be Aunt Sheila. She loved Alaska, and Alaska loves her!"

"To Saint Aunt Sheila!"

"To Saint Aunt Sheila!"

Six glassy fish eyes fixed Ed with baleful reproach as his relative's praises thundered about the room. Pam looked at him with concern, but then he smiled. "I wouldn't dare tell her about this," he said sheepishly, "but it's a dirty shame she'll never know."

Outside the Penguin Tap, history continued to be made, and Ed longed to witness it, but he lingered with Pam and Milan. When he returned to the street, he would be alone again for the rest of the day, and he was reluctant to give up the luxury of people to call by name. Before he left, he took a picture of the couple raising aloft their Muckluck Martinis. "Bend down so I can give you a hug," said Pam, and as he headed off, she called out, "Come visit us, sweetie. You've got our address."

Ed had almost made it to the door when a misty-eyed stranger grabbed his elbow and whispered reverently, "We must never forget her, soldier."

"Who, sir?"

"Saint Anshela."

Ed found it harder to get out of the bar than it had been to get in. The crowd he wedged his way back into had thickened and grown, if possible, less inhibited. He managed only a few steps before he was jostled into an older woman whose hair was an especially cheerful shade of copper.

"You almost knocked me down," she chided.

"I'm terribly sorry; it's this mob." In mid apology, he recognized a benefactor. "Mrs. Tom! It's you. Now I'm twice as sorry."

"Who? Oh, Ed." A smile broke through her stern expression. "Isn't this something?"

"Yes," he shouted. "This is funny. I was on my way to your shop."

"It's closed." She too strained to be heard.

"Oh sure," Ed nodded, "on account of the holiday."

"No, on account of the shenanigans. No one but you wants to buy records today."

"That's because they're all buying me drinks." A giggle escaped him.

She eyed him appraisingly. "Yes, I can see that."

"I don't want to buy records either," he said. "I brought my camera with me. I want to take your picture, Mrs. Tom, in front of the shop. Could we go back there for a second?"

A chubby boy of about nine, whose face bore greasepaint stripes of red, white and blue, shoved between them, blatting a trumpet. Mrs. Tom surveyed the scene and shook her head. "That's sweet of you, Ed, but we'd never make it. I'm not sure I'll make it to the corner. I don't want to fight my way back to the shop. If you get there, take a picture with my blessing."

"But it's you that I –"

"Well, just take it right here then." She turned to the window to check her reflection. "Oh no, wait. Not in front of a bar. If you show it back home, they'll think I was some Yukon rummy."

He smiled at her and yelled, "There's a Christian Science reading room in the next block."

"What?"

"There's – oh, never mind."

She squinted at someone in the street and waived. "Conrad! Conrad, over here." Taking the camera from Ed's hand, she said, "Now you can be in it with me. If someone bangs into Conrad, he's so big it won't spoil the picture." A moose of a man materialized beside them. "Conrad, this is my friend, Ed. For some reason, he wants a picture of me, and this is a day to grant wishes." Conrad the great took the camera without a word and moved back against the crowd like a human cowcatcher, sweeping several merrymakers into the street. Ed grinned as Mrs. Tom drew him to her side and put her arm around him. "Just the two of us now, Conrad, none of these liquor signs." Conrad stopped the crowd in its tracks, snapped the picture, returned the camera, and departed as silently as he had come.

"Thank you, Conrad," Ed called after him, "nice to..." but he was gone.

Ed turned to Mrs. Tom. "You know this whole bunch," he said, sweeping his arm out toward the crowd, "and I don't know a soul. Oh, sorry, Ma'am." His gesture had knocked askew the hat of a passing woman who glared as she readjusted it. "Anyway, Mrs. Tom," he continued, "we're shouting ourselves hoarse out here. Will you let me buy you a drink? My money's been no good today, and I'd like to reciprocate."

"You don't need to, Ed. Not with me, or anyone else. Save your money. And stay out of trouble today." She patted his arm. "But thank you all the same. As for me, I've seen enough, and I want to go home."

"At least let me help you through the crowd," he pleaded.

"And knock me down again? Look at yourself. You need more

help than I do, but Happy Statehood, my friend."

"Happy Statehood, Mrs. Tom."

As she pushed through the crowd away from him, he pondered whether it was entirely logical for Alaskans to wish him "Happy Statehood." Logical or not, it pleased him, and he was certainly feeling more Alaskan as the afternoon wore on. He stopped resisting and let the momentum of the crowd move him slowly down the sidewalk. He became a smiling face moving in a sea of smiling faces.

A dark blue shape caught his eye, and Ed realized that he in particular was being smiled at. The crowd bore him along, but the dark blue shape, a hooded sweatshirt, kept pace and the face within it kept smiling at him. The more Ed thought about it, the more certain he was that he had seen this same blue sweatshirt earlier in the day, perhaps several times, without realizing that the smile it held was not the generalized smile of an aimless reveler but one directed specifically and repeatedly at him alone. *I'm being followed*, he thought, *or at least I'm being kept up with, and by a dark blue smiler.*

Before Ed could decide exactly what he thought about this development, the street crowd, flowing at a different speed, swept the dark blue smiler out of sight. Ed kept moving but unsteadily. Mrs. Tom was right; he needed help. He needed food. A steady diet of glacier gimlets and Skagway stingers could only take a man so far. Well, actually, they could take him very far indeed, but not in a direction Ed was sure he wanted to go. If he could make his way to the Hoffbrau, there would be rare roast beef with potent horseradish to clear his head and hot soups to do whatever else needed doing to him. Yes, the Hoffbrau it would be.

The crowd had other plans. Midway in the next block, the giddy tide came to a standstill. The wind seemed to speak with human voices. "Wooooooh!" Then silence, then again, "wooooooh." It was human voices. Heads around him turned to look across the street.

He felt himself edged off the curb, and though he was beginning to distrust his senses, a woman appeared to fly above the heads of the crowd, swept up by another "wooooooh!" "Blanket toss!" a man next to him called out. The Hoffbrau and its healing powers would have to wait a bit. Ed wanted a picture of this phenomenon.

It took some doing and a focused determination not to be pushed back, but after three more startling astral appearances by an elderly Eskimo woman, a burly sergeant, and a small boy who flew especially high, Ed made it close enough to see the giant blanket and the spirited group who gripped its edges. Unfortunately, he found himself almost too close to do justice to the event with his camera. He stepped out from the crowd to avoid being bumped while he framed the shot, but his action was misinterpreted. "Whoa! Hey! Where's my camera? Nooo!" he cried as many hands propelled him onto the blanket. His protests were drowned out by the chanting of a countdown and a thunderous "wooooooh!" as Ed was snapped into space.

The next few seconds went by in slow motion, long enough to permit an arc of varied impressions: fear that he was being separated from his stomach and might soil the blanket… or the crowd; regret that a thief had made off with his camera and its irreplaceable contents; further regret that, as always, he was alone with no friend to share this moment; and gratitude that, however misguidedly, he had been embraced by this warm, wacky mob.

Ed's return to the tautly stretched blanket generated one more small bounce that left him on his hands and knees. A voice called out, "Over here!" and, woozily, he crawled toward it. Two hands gripped his to pull him off, and he found himself face to face with the mysterious blue smiler. It warmed Ed to know that his solo flight had after all been recorded by at least this pair of friendly eyes.

"Come on," said the stranger, familiarly, "let's get out of here."

"Who are you?" Ed asked, in a tone that was clearly not a refusal.

"We'll decide that together."

The stranger's confidence and presumption didn't offend Ed; in fact, they drew him in, and he told himself they would have done so even had he been in a more sober state of mind. The tousled jet black hair peeking out from the hood didn't hurt. Neither did the dark eyes, quick and direct, nor the youthful smile of mischievous intimacy. If this weren't enough, the shade of the sweatshirt looked more like cobalt blue by the second. "I've got your camera, by the way," said the stranger. "I grabbed it for safekeeping. I took a picture of you up there. I hope you don't mind." *It's always been my lucky color,* Ed thought, as he followed him across the lot, away from the crowd.

Falling behind as they neared the sidewalk, Ed called out, "Wait! I'm still catching my breath." The stranger stopped instantly and returned to his side saying, "I'll wait then. I've lost you too often today." The words were unimproveable. Ed just stood there letting them echo in his head, in no hurry to replace them with any of his own. The blue smiler was quite at ease with the stillness and the silence, but at last Ed said, "Well, *that* didn't help me get my breath back. You can't seem to say anything I don't like."

"Hope not."

If handsome is as handsome does, thought Ed, this guy will be an Adonis any minute. Ed spoke again. "What's this all about?"

"Nothing you don't want," the young man answered enigmatically, and then, after a pause, "but everything you do." Ed stared at him questioningly. The possibilities bolting through his mind couldn't be the same ones the stranger intended. Could they?

"Here," said the young man, extending Ed's camera, "Take a picture. It'll last longer."

Ed took four then asked, "What do I call you, until we decide who you are?"

"Tex," he said. "It's not my real name, but I prefer it."

"I don't like my real name either," Ed confessed.

"Tell me." Tex held up his hand. "I swear I won't tease you."

"I still wouldn't want you to hear it. If you can be Tex with no explanation, why can't I just be … Eddie?"

Tex was all assurance. "Because I'm a fixer. I'll do something you'll like with it."

"Nothing can be done with Edmond."

Tex's eyes sparkled. "Give me a hard one next time. In Brazil, you'd be 'Ed-MOON-do.'"

Ed smiled. "You're awfully good Tex, but I'm not in Brazil."

"Except with me, Edmundo."

"I've had enough drinks today to think that's not corny," said Ed, "and I didn't buy a single one. Every bar in town has invented its own gruesome concoction."

"It's a nightmare," Tex agreed. "The Martians have landed, and they're mixing our drinks." He was laughing now. "The worst was the one with –" he snorted, "the fishhead."

"The Muckluck martini. Bleeah! Did they make you try it too?"

"Look," said Tex, putting his hand on Ed's arm, "I don't live far from here, but is there anything else you wanted to see… while you can still see?"

"I wanted to see everything, Tex." Ed liked using the name the boy had given himself, and he planned to do so at every opportunity. It was like touching him, but safer. "I'd better get some food into my stomach though. I was trying to make it to the Hoffbrau, and we're practically there, if that's okay."

Tex looked thoughtful. "That's a good choice for us. They get a pretty diverse crowd." Ed didn't see what that had to do with it, but he was glad Tex approved. He had begun to want to please him.

Tex proved better than Ed had been at snaking through the crowd to some purpose. Gripped tightly at a belt loop, Ed was maneuvered through the front door of the Hoffbrau in less than five minutes. There were no tables or booths to be had, but Tex said, "I know Artie at the bar. You can eat there." Tex settled Ed on the last available stool and stood beside him, which made it easier to talk. Ed wanted to know everything about Tex, but Tex said that would only be clutter at this point and could wait. He acted as though he already knew plenty about Ed. The only thing he asked was when Ed had to report back on base.

"I just came in for the day," said Ed between bites of roast beef. Tex's mouth tightened at the corners. "Although technically, I don't start a shift for another two days."

Tex's corners unclenched, and he drawled, "Technicalities are just… swell."

Ed didn't know what to say to that, so he took another bite of roast beef. Then he said, "I don't usually stay over though."

Tex's eyes swept the room, lingering over the antics of an especially boisterous group halfway across the room. They had hoisted a nervous waitress onto their table to serenade her as she laughed nervously. "You see anything usual around here, Edmundo?"

"No."

"Are you feeling usual?"

Ed grinned. "No, not at all."

"Then you'll stay over."

"I didn't pack anything," said Ed, growing hopeful that all his sensible objections would be swept aside.

"You'll stay over. You won't be much use tonight, but tomorrow …"

Ed's pulse quickened. *There's a tomorrow in all this, too?* he wondered.

Artie motioned Tex to a stool he had managed to clear. Waiting for them as they turned to the bar were two peculiar looking libations. Pearl onions rested at the deep blue bottom of tall, snow-capped glasses topped with tiny American flags. Ed and Tex exchanged wary glances. "What's this, Artie?" asked Tex.

"In honor of the day, my special creation," said Artie with no little pride, "the Artiearctic! You're supposed to say it real fast. It sounds even better that way. Try 'em." Artie beamed and wiggled his eyebrows.

The new friends spoke up simultaneously: "Et tu Artus?" "I'd better not."

"They'll be good for you, troopermen. Blue curacao and vodka, smooth as silk," Artie explained, "a little buried treasure on the bottom and cream on top to line your stomach. They're on the house. Drink up now. Don't insult me."

"You don't have to, Eddie." said Tex.

Ed shrugged. "Well, they are a pretty shade of blue." He reached for the glass, but Artie called out, "Wait for the eel!" and bore down on the beverages with dangling anchovies

"Nooo!" the boys yelled in chorus. Ed was quick enough to snatch and swallow his anchovy.

"Now it won't be authentic," Artie pouted.

"Thank goodness," Ed said as he drew the Artiearctic to his lips. Tex stiffened and shot him a look of apprehension. Ed ignored him and took a swig. "Oh, Artie's your friend," he said through a moustache of cream. "I feel fearless today, and nothing blue will ever hurt me." Tex rolled his eyes.

The Artiearctic soon dispatched the meager shreds of Ed's remaining equilibrium. He smiled excitedly and pointed at the juke box, leaning so precariously toward the rolling swirls of guitar music that Tex reached out to keep him on his stool.

"Steady, Edmundo."

"It's *El Paso!*" said Ed, looking gleefully daffy.

"I'm not really from Texas, Eddie."

"No," Ed laughed, "It's not for you. It's my song… kind of. It was my salary." Tex looked simultaneously puzzled and as though he knew something good came next. "I wrote some commercials for Mrs. Tom's record store." Ed accompanied his words with animated but irrelevant gestures. "It was fun, and it was more fun to hear them on the radio. I would have done it for nothing, but Mrs. Tom made me take an album for it, so I picked *Gunfighter Ballads.*"

Tex nodded. "You like cowboy songs."

"Not especially," Ed corrected, "but *El Paso* is irresistible. It just sweeeeps you away. Oh, rats! I'm so sorry." Artie toweled up the spilled drink and, to Ed's surprise, made him another, this time fully authentic. "I'm not sure I can be trusted with this," Ed said, embarrassed.

"I'm not sure it matters today, kid," Artie replied.

Tex swiveled Ed's stool so they faced each other. "You find this tune irresistible, do you?"

"Yesss, just listen." He gazed at Tex with blurry intensity as Marty Robbins raced once again down into the valley through a hail of bullets to reach the faithless Felina. "You see?"

Tex leaned forward, and Ed felt their knees touching. "The only thing irresistible in this place is…"

Ed broke their eye contact and stared at his shoes, but a smile forced its way onto his face and he knew he must be blushing. Was this really happening to him? And how drunk was he?

"I know what you want, Tex," he said at last, without looking up.

"No big prize for that, soldier. This whole crowd must know it by now."

"It seems crazy, but I really think you want…" Ed chewed his lip.

Tex's gaze was patient, fixed, and attentive. Ed looked down again. "But I could be wrong."

Tex's hands came to rest on Ed's knees and he said, "Having a little trouble in the confidence department?"

Ed nodded. "I've no...," he raised his voice to be heard above the din, "no prior experience along these lines." Tex grinned and said something but still more revelers surged through the door, jostling the crowd and raising the noise level. Ed was thankful he and Tex had stools, but it was getting harder to understand this magnetic new friend, whose conversation grew more important to him with each word.

"What, Tex?"

Tex tried again. "– arming gnats –"

The boisterous mob was robbing Ed of precious treasure. "What?"

Artie yelled into Ed's ear, "He says you're charming the pants off him." Ed swallowed and mouthed, "Thank you," at Artie. He delayed looking back at Tex. This was a moment unlike any he had ever experienced, and he wanted to savor it. Someone extremely agreeable had singled him out in a crowd, pursued him, and now was actually courting him with – with – the word swam sweetly into his head – with blandishments. He was glad he didn't have to say the word out loud. His booze-thickened tongue wouldn't have managed it. The room, or perhaps only his head, was spinning a little. The music had ceased to be random and was now a soundtrack created for this singular occasion. He turned toward Tex and saw to his delight there was no mistake. He was looking into the face of someone who desired him.

Ed was no longer in control of the expressions on his face. "That's a mighty big smile," Tex commented. "I take it I haven't been injudicious?" The sense of well being Ed thought had surely peaked now took a quantum leap. He echoed, "in-ju-di-cious," slowly, sighed and requested, "more, please."

"More pretzels? Not another Artiearctic?"

"No, Tex," Ed said blissfully, "more words like injudicious."

"Why?" asked Tex, smiling indulgently.

"You don't live in an army barracks. You can't know how starved I am for anything…" Ed strained for the precise word.

"Polysyllabic?" offered Tex.

"Ooohh." Ed sipped in a long breath.

"Well, if you're starving…" Tex smiled wickedly. "I guess it's incumbent upon me to feed you."

"In-cum-bent," Ed repeated as if in a trance.

Tex stood up, cupped Ed's ear with his hands and spoke directly into it. "Come home with me now, Edmundo. We will disport ourselves with shameless and reprehensible abandon. Does that sound good to you, you goofy wonder?" Ed's head gave a slow, unequivocal nod but all he could squeak out was, "Yep." As he cautiously made the attempt to dismount the stool without further disgracing himself, he heard Artie say, "Made a friend, didja?" Ed's feet reached the floor without incident, and he stood next to Tex, steadied by the press of the crowd.

"Is the whole world onto me, Tex?" he inquired plaintively.

"Pretty much," said Tex, beaming at him.

"I wish I'd been onto me sooner," Ed said ruefully.

Tex shook his head and said, "I don't."

It took a while for them to push their way to the door, but Ed didn't think it time ill spent, not with the electric current buzzing through his shoulder from Tex's guiding hand. They were welcomed back to the street with a noisy barrage of sky rockets that startled Ed and made him lose his balance. Only Tex's swift intervention prevented a solid meeting of Ed's head and a brick wall. Ed leaned against the wall smiling up ay the crackling rainbow the evening sky had become. "Will you look at that, Tex!" he exclaimed, "and it won't be dark for hours."

Tex's eyes remained on Ed. "Anchorage just can't wait for its fireworks." He smiled and moved closer. "Neither can I, Eddie."

But Ed still needed to babble. "I'll never forget this day," he said excitedly. "The crowds, the spirit, the generosity, getting tossed in the air, the fireworks, and you, Tex. I'll remember this day for the rest of my life."

Tex peeled him from the wall, put an arm over his shoulder, and said, "We'll just go make sure."

CHAPTER 17

FEMME FATALE

Fort Richardson, December 1959

Faye and Walter Knox stood facing each other, a few feet apart beside the fireplace. Pine logs, brought in this morning by new recruits, crackled gently at their feet. The Knoxes were communicating with more candor than was their habit. They had been doing so for some time. Walter's temples throbbed. Faye kept talking, but now, a flatness crept into her tone. Clearly, she felt she had explained herself enough and was losing interest.

"That's how it is, Walter. You'll just have to –"

His hand shot out and slammed across her mouth, rocking her backward.

"Have to what, you fucking bitch!"

He felt a sudden measure of relief and wanted to do it again, perhaps several times. What stayed his hand was the unfamiliar and disturbing expression on her face. He thought he had seen them all, but this was something new. She too wanted him to continue what he had begun. Her look was fearless. It held surprise, yes, but also an alarming intensity of… involvement. It was an invitation, a totally unexpected opportunity for him to rewrite their contract on her terms. All that his previous discretion and forbearance had accomplished was to bore the pants off her, literally. He could have her again. He could probably have her right now, or in a matter of minutes. All he had to do was ride the rush of mindless emotion surging through him and trust the stranger he had become.

He backed away from her, and his upraised arm dropped to his side. They were both breathing heavily.

"That was interesting," she said evenly.

"Don't get your fears up, my dear," he said and walked out into the hall, closing a great many doors behind him.

Now what? The first seconds of a new and utterly uncharted life. He stood still in the hall and looked about uncertainly. The realities of his situation had only begun to sink in. Bereft of someone to turn to with expectations, he was also accountable to no one. In the land of "After Faye," there was nothing that had to be done – and nothing that couldn't be. Only one thing was sure, to impose a philosophy on this great mess that was now his life, he needed a drink.

He went into the den and pulled open the leaded glass doors of the bar cabinet. How many of the bottles before him had Faye poured for her lovers, warming their ardor, heating their imaginations? Darkly glowing liquors mocked him with endless possibilities of the lewd images they must have reflected. Slowly and unwillingly, his eyes made the rounds of the room. His glance fell on pet objects acquired on his travels with Faye: the Turkish ottoman, the colored glass lantern from Morocco. The space was strewn with favorite pieces which, on his most difficult days had brought him comfort, but now revolted him. All was suspect, as though not just Faye but the house itself and every stick of furniture in it, silent, unprotesting witnesses, had betrayed him.

There must be something, one decanter whose contents even she would have realized were too subtle to waste on her dim-witted parade of privates. His fingers moved from shelf to shelf, shoving aside bottle after bottle, repulsed by his suspicions. If nothing here had gone untouched by those who had touched her, it would be more than he could bear. At last, at the back of the top shelf, he found one drink he felt he could trust not to have been an accessory during the fact. He clasped it in both hands, drew it down carefully and clutched it gratefully to his chest. Then he smiled and said aloud, "I've gone mad."

He took up a snifter and poured an inch of the colorless liquid, sighing as he sat down. He smiled again, this time at the glass in his hand. He moved it in little circles for a moment, brought it toward his face, inhaled deeply, then tipped it up to let a little of the liquid spread out across his tongue and reach the back of his throat. He was not calm. All of what had stirred in him, the anger, the disappointment, the disgust, the longing – all of it still swirled and would not quickly come to rest. The law of bodies in motion had not been repealed. But if there were not yet calm, there was clarity – and completion. This was all to the good. His clear vision of the finality of what had just happened would at least keep him from prostrating himself and trying to wheedle back bits and pieces of their former life from Faye. There would be no dignity, no honor for either of them in this situation, but there would be welcome distance and soon..

The doorbell rang. He was now sitting with his eyes closed. He was not eager to open them and see this room again. The bell rang a second time. He heard Faye padding to the door and then voices. In a previous life, he had asked Edmond Sheffield to stop by tonight. Faye spoke to him from the doorway of the den.

"It seems the school of soft Knox is in session again. You didn't tell me."

He opened his eyes. "I must work on my communication skills."

Everything that had once besotted him about this woman was now an abrasion to his spirit.

"I'll make myself scarce," she said.

"Yes, do that." Seeing Edmond approach, he added, "My dear."

Edmond started to enter the room, but Captain Knox stood up, gathered the bottle and another glass and said, "Let's not talk in here." As they crossed to the parlor, Edmond asked about the bottle. "It's Pear William, hence the pear lodged inside it. It's a favorite of mine, but tastes are different. If you don't like it, I'll – well, you can dig around in the bar for something else."

He poured out a tiny amount and offered it to Edmond, who had pulled a rocker up to the coffee table. The boy drained the glass, looked up at Captain Knox, and said, "I think it's wonderful. May I have a little more, sir?"

"Why not?" The captain smiled and poured liberally. "There aren't many secrets around here. You may have heard, I'm transferring to another post."

"Yes, sir. Everybody's going to miss you and your wife."

"Actually, Mrs. Knox will be staying on for a while."

Edmond looked at him for only a split second before nodding and saying, "Sure. Lots of loose ends to tie up when you move."

Good old Sheffield, thought Captain Knox. *No one loses face on his watch.*

"This is a goodbye then?"

"Well, I'm not disappearing at dawn, if that's what you mean, but the transfer is approved and I'd like to wind things up quickly. I didn't want to leave without saying a few things to you, and this evening, we can talk at our leisure. After tonight, there may not be much opportunity."

"Then, I'll propose a toast," said Edmond earnestly." He stood up and raised his glass. "To the best officer the army ever had, or ever will. Long may he prosper!"

After a brief silence, the captain said, "That's even nicer than it would have been a few drinks from now."

Edmond was still standing. "And – and to my mentor."

He wouldn't have thought it possible, but Walter Knox felt his spirits rising slightly and a grim laugh escaped him. "A mentor? Hardly that."

"Oh gosh, yes. I wouldn't know where to begin. I'd have a very different view of the army if not for you – and I'd have had a very different experience of it."

The captain smiled across the coffee table. "So, it hasn't all been . . ."

"No," the boy bubbled on. "All of it was interesting, and some of it was even nice, I mean—"

The captain nodded. 'Good. You weren't this cheerful when you arrived on post."

"Oh, well, then I didn't know what I was doing." Edmond smiled and shrugged. "Not that I really do now, but I was lonesome then, and lonesome people do stupid things."

Captain Knox had taken up a cigarette and was rolling it back and forth in his fingers, unlit. "Mmm. The lonely haven't cornered the market on stupidity. But you've made friends since then."

Edmond grimaced. "Not so much here, and Terrapino left in May, but yes, I've found company."

"Off post?"

"Yes."

"That's best – if you're careful." The captain looked at him most seriously. "Are you careful, Edmond?"

"I've learned to be, sir." Edmond wasn't sure what they were talking about now. Was the captain cautioning him about floosies and social disease, or did the officer suspect Ed's company might be someone like Tex? He really couldn't tell. It didn't matter. He was so comfortable here with this man, comfortable enough to ask, "Was it you, sir, who put me up for Soldier of the Month? I've often wondered. I think it must have been you."

"I might have… then again I might not have. I guess you'll never know."

"It was you. I wish you hadn't."

"Why? It's an honor, Edmond."

"I know, but it made me really nervous, and I never stood a

chance anyway."

"And why is that? You did quite respectably on the military questions, and you were letter perfect on current events."

"That's all verbal. That's not what counts with them. It's your bearing. They can't have a Soldier of the Month going around giving crappy salutes all over the place, and after two and a half years, that's still the only kind I've got."

"Crappy is harsh. I'd call them entertaining. I'm sure it brightened their day."

"Well it darkened mine, and it's the one thing I don't thank you for." He paused and then smiled at the officer. "But there are so many other things that I do thank you for. Look at this. It came in today's mail." He handed Captain Knox a large envelope.

The captain put on his glasses. "The University of Chicago." He looked up at Edmond who was nodding vigorously. "You've been accepted. Congratulations!"

"I'd never have gotten in without you."

"I didn't take your exams, Edmond."

"I wouldn't have taken them either if you hadn't bullied me into it."

"I'm a mentor *and* a bully?"

"Yes, you are. Both. I needed both. You were relentless." Ed's voice thickened. "You had more faith in me than I did."

"This is great news," said the captain. "I'm very pleased but not surprised in the least."

Edmond clinked at the captain's glass with his own. "Merry Christmas, sir, a little early, but –"

"Christmas, yes," the captain said quietly. "You're right; it's almost upon us."

"I wanted to get you something, sir, but I wasn't sure if that would be appropriate."

"It would not have been."

"I wanted to though…"

"There's no regulation against good will, Edmond, not yet."

They spoke on at length, ranging over topics of cosmic consequence and gossamer triviality, from the profound to the profoundly silly. Now and then, they simply sat in amiable silence. Edmond feared it might be the best talk he would ever have with anyone, and he worked at prolonging it but it was not like work. It was like swimming with a current so strong you hardly needed your arms at all.

Edmond Sheffield had been born with a horror of outstaying his welcome. Wherever he went, he strove to anticipate the cues of his host, but tonight there were none. The captain swam with him, and it grew late. With great reluctance, Ed stood up at last to take his leave. They walked to the door and stopped. Captain Knox tugged it open but stood in Ed's path, neither of them eager to conclude what both knew might be their last conversation.

"Now that Joe is back home, what will you do about your car?"

"Dale wants it, sir. He's going to give me $200."

"Handsome!" blurted the captain. "I mean –"

"I thought so too, but he knows I've kept it up."

"You say he's *going* to give it to you? When?"

"Well, Dale asked if he could send me some of it after I get home."

The captain shook his head. "More like all of it?"

Ed lowered his voice. "Maybe."

"You get it all, before you leave, or he doesn't get the car."

The air about them was suddenly perfumed, and Ed felt the pressure of Mrs. Knox's hand on his shoulder as she squeezed past them and out of the doorway. Her outfit was peculiar, an expensive black fur over ski pants and a woolen cap jammed over her long brown hair. She paused at the edge of the steps and turned back to look directly at Ed. In the light of the porch lantern, she seemed so beautiful to him he thought it would hurt to look at her for very long.

"That's good advice my husband is giving you about Dale. If I were you, I'd take it." She turned to go and added over her shoulder, "Don't wait up, Walter."

The two soldiers watched in silence as she strolled unhurriedly to a waiting car, the snow dancing all around her.

CHAPTER 18

PRIZE NIGHT

Chicago: December 25, 1959

The scream dragged him back to the lobby of the Jeffery. Because his body couldn't, Raymond's mind had wandered very far indeed. "God, what now?" he thought as he raced toward the auditorium. "What a Christmas!" Just as he neared the center entrance, a door burst open and clipped him on the forehead. A rumpled, older man flew past him clutching a purse. Surprisingly fleet, the man was almost at the ticket booth before Raymond started after him. *If I can't catch him*, he thought, *can I bamboozle him?* "I've got a gun on your back and I'll use it!" he yelled. To Raymond's surprise, the thief froze and dropped the purse. Raymond sped to retrieve it, but as he bent down, the man, who by now could see the threat was idle, pushed him off balance. Raymond caught him by the legs and wrestled him to the ground. Drunk and unsteady, the man was no match for Raymond, but though he could be kept down, his arms could not be controlled and flailed everywhere. Tightening his embrace and feeling more idiotic by the second, Raymond watched in exasperation as the pocket of his jacket was ripped.

"Jeezuz, Dwight! Can you give me a hand here?" A thin young man stepped dubiously from behind the popcorn counter. He had been regarding the scene with a puckered expression suitable for watching a commode overflow.

"What should I do, Mr. Muzydlo? Do you want me to call the police?"

"I want you to grab his hands, dammit, so I'm not still here on the floor when the feature lets out!"

After several attempts, Dwight gingerly caught the old man's hands together, at which point the trio underwent a change of mood. Raymond grew quiet, the thief went limp, and Dwight became positively exuberant. "Well, we did it, didn't we! What a breath on this guy. What do we do now?"

"Help me get him over to the cleanup closet, and we'll lock him in."

"Should I call the police now?"

"Let's wait a minute on that." Holiday business, already down, was not likely to perk up at this news. Perhaps he could manage something.

A woman in her forties watched them from a doorway to the inner lobby. She had observed the scuffle in silence and spoke only now that it was over. "If you look inside that pocketbook, you'll see a letter to Frances Sheffield."

The thief stopped wriggling and started to cry. Raymond stretched out his hand for the purse and held it up toward the woman who remained quite still in the doorway. Her upraised left arm kept the door back. Her right arm bore a cloth coat, drawn to her chest like a shield.

"No need to check, Ma'am; I'm certain it's yours. If you'll just step back inside 'til we secure this fellow, I'll be right with you. We're terribly sorry about this."

"Don't let him hurt you."

"No, Ma'am. Did he hurt you?"

"No... not really."

"If you'll just step back inside for a moment..."

She looked more serious and alert than frightened. Her coat struck him as inadequate for the weather, as did the striped scarf at her throat, though it was smart and rather pretty. She had probably been so herself once, he thought, watching her walk away.

He returned his attention to the purse snatcher. "Now, junior, let's get you on your feet."

"Yeah," said Dwight. "Move it."

"You're really getting into this, Dwight. Want to take over?"

"No!"

When they had dragged him as far as the closet, Raymond opened the door, tugged at a string to light the small room, and pushed him inside. Bewildered amid the buckets, brooms, mops and absorbent powders, the man braced himself to be hit. "Behave yourself, and this may work out better than you deserve," Raymond told him. "I'm going to lock the door and leave the light on. You're going to be quiet. If you talk or bang on the door or disturb so much as a broom handle, I'll be back to unscrew the light bulb. If I have to open this door before I want to, you'll be arrested. If I don't, you may be anyway, but we'll see. You got it?"

The man nodded. Raymond closed the door on him and locked it. Dwight grinned at Raymond. "He's got it. The mops'll make more noise than he will."

"Go sell some Milk Duds."

"Who to? You want some?"

"I'll be inside."

Raymond had developed manager's eyes. The darkened auditorium was only slightly harder to scan than the lobby. He confronted an essentially empty house. "If you can't do business on Christmas Day, you can't do business at all." How often he had heard that in the trade. The saying still held. People needed to escape their relatives by Christmas afternoon, but these were leaner years and on a bone-chilling night people were less easily torn from their cozy inertia in front of a television screen. It was doubtful there were a hundred spectators scattered about the theater. He spotted her quickly. She sat a few rows from the back, looking at him instead of the screen. What, he wondered, had drawn her out in the cold by herself to his emporium, where tonight the holiday surprise was not free china but drunken felons.

As he eased into the seat beside her, Bing Crosby and Danny Kaye sang out with determined hilarity in a forest of giant snowflakes. Tall chorus girls stalked about in gowns of intense and lurid hues. Raymond spoke quietly, though no one was near them. "I'm sorry the show was spoiled for you, Mrs. Sheffield."

She glanced at the screen. "It comes pre-spoiled. It's not very good. I don't know why you keep bringing it back."

"People like it. They want to hear 'White Christmas.'"

"Then why not show *Holiday Inn?*"

"Well, this is in color."

"Yes, and Vista Vision. When I first went to the movies, we thought we were having a great time without color or sound, let alone Vista Vision."

Raymond snorted. It was the first time he had laughed all day. This was not the conversation he expected to have. It was not the conversation he needed to be having.

"Why don't we go out to the office? I want to try to make this right, and I need to ask you just a few questions."

Out in the lobby, she asked, "Where is that man?" They were close enough to the closet to be overheard, but nothing betrayed the occupant within.

"He's quite secure. You won't be bothered again."

"Wouldn't it be something if any of us could say that for certain?"

The office, not an inch larger than its functions demanded, offered little room to maneuver. A phone and typewriter sat atop a metal desk whose surface was strewn with coin rollers and money wraps. The desk was flanked by two three-tier file cabinets and a combination safe on which rested a wooden stacker bearing labels reading "invoice transmittals," "box office report," and "inventory." Taped to one side of the cabinet was a large calendar, almost entirely covered with departure and arrival times, and much crossing out of names.

The walls were another matter. A collision of framed images from decades of bookings bore mute testimony to the disparate whims of the manager of the moment. Nancy Carroll beamed down sweetly from a *Shopworn Angel* half sheet. Jean Arthur and Cary Grant defined grace under pressure, and a palm tree, in *Only Angels Have Wings*. James Cagney, depending which way you looked, slyly serenaded Ann Sheridan in a *Torrid Zone* one sheet, or exploded in bestial insanity in *White Heat*. The full panoply of slink, from formal attire to contemporary casual, was also represented by Rita Hayworth in *Gilda*, Marilyn Monroe in *Don't Bother to Knock*, and Brigitte Bardot in *And God Created Woman*.

Frances surveyed the contents of the room with an air of interest and approval before taking the small armchair in front of Raymond's desk.

"This won't take long. Can I get you something?"

"A cup of coffee would be a great help, if you could."

He opened the door and called out, "Dwight!"

Rummaging in the stacker, Raymond removed a legal pad, and then installed himself behind the desk.

Dwight poked his head in without knocking and inquired, "Yeah?"

Raymond's look of sad distaste was wasted on him. "Run across to Peter Pan and get us two coffees." He held out a bill.

"But it's cold as a – it's cold out there."

Frances smiled at the boy. "Indeed it is, and going for coffee isn't your job, especially on a night like this. That's all right."

"No, it isn't, Mrs. Sheffield," said Raymond. "Dwight's job, while he has it, is to do whatever the situation requires. He's happy to fetch you a cup of coffee. Aren't you, Dwight?"

Dwight took the bill. "Sure."

"I do appreciate it. Please button up before you go outside." She had lowered the level of his humiliation, and the boy smiled his thanks.

"I will, ma'am."

Ma'am? Raymond would bet money the word had just made its first trip across those lips. The door closed, and he turned back to her. "If you could tell me exactly what happened in there."

Frances leaned forward. "I was aware of him the moment he came in. It looked as though he'd been drinking, and it was obvious he hadn't come for the movie."

"We should never have admitted him." It slipped out as fast as he thought it and couldn't be taken back. But Raymond's luck, missing all day, wandered back in as Frances spoke.

"Oh, I wouldn't go that far. You never can judge a person without – how does it go? – without walking two moons in his moccasins. I remember thinking maybe he just needs somewhere to rest for a while. I didn't see any great harm as long as he didn't sit near me. He didn't at first, but he kept looking around and changing his seat. That's what made me suspicious."

She spoke with a clear, high, pleasing lilt. If Raymond closed his eyes, he could imagine a much younger speaker before him. Yet, though the voice was girlish, it was in no way affected. *A voice worth listening to*, he thought, if he had to hear this.

"It was as if he were seeking the perfect person to bother. I hoped it wasn't me, but after a while, it turned out it was. Each time he changed seats, he came a little closer. Finally, he was close enough to look directly at me. I was quite alarmed, so I clutched my purse with both hands and gave him my fiercest look."

Raymond smiled as he imagined the look. "I wish you had alerted an usher."

"I couldn't see any to alert."

Raymond stopped smiling.

Frances went on. "He knew I was paying attention to him, so he decided to leave. I watched him all the way out the door and kept on watching after it closed. When it seemed to be all right, I turned around. Somehow, he snuck back in when the movie got loud, and the next thing I knew, these two arms were reaching down over me, going straight for my purse."

"You must have been very frightened."

"Well, of course. That's when I screamed, and I'm not a woman who goes around screaming. I had a tight grip on my purse, but he tore it right out of my hands and ran out."

Looking at her, listening to her, Raymond regretted not unscrewing the light bulb in the closet.

"It wasn't just the money, Mr. - " she leaned closer to examine the nametag now listing from his torn pocket at an unreadable angle.

"Ma ZID lo," he enunciated. "Just call me, Raymond." He removed the nametag and tried to reposition it to secure the pocket.

She shook her head. "You'll make it worse. Hold still." Raymond didn't move as she reached across the desk, delicately extracted the tag from his jacket, and surveyed the damage. "No, it needs stitching. Let me see . . ." She unsnapped the clasp on her purse and removed a small cloth pouch from which she produced a needle and a length of thread wound around a cardboard rectangle. Holding the thread toward his jacket, she shook her head again, and fished out another thread in a shade more to her liking. "Just slip it off for a moment," she said, in the reassuring tone one might adopt with a reluctant child.

Raymond squinted at her, making no move to do as she asked.

"You don't want to go around looking like that for the rest of the evening," Frances said pleasantly.

"Mrs. Sheffield, I can't have you - "

"Don't be difficult, Raymond. I'm good and I'm fast, but I can't fix anything while you're still inside that jacket." She held out her hand, and Raymond, still squinting, rose, removed the jacket, and passed it across the desk. "We won't waste time," she said. "Ask your questions while I work." She wet the thread with her tongue, swiftly threaded the needle, and plunged it into the material. "In another life, I might have been a seamstress." A little ruefully, she added, "Who knows? I may yet be in this one."

Raymond was smiling at her now. "The questions can wait a bit. I won't disturb an artist at her work."

"Not much art required here." She bit off the thread end and examined the pocket. "And not much work, really." She handed back the jacket. "This will get you through the night. Your wife can improve it when you get home."

He tugged lightly at the pocket. "She won't need to." *She wouldn't know how,* he thought. "Well, I certainly thank you." He refastened the nametag and slipped on the jacket.

"Umm… So, it wasn't the money you were most concerned about?"

"It wasn't. I had little enough of it with me, and money is just not something to make yourself sick over." She settled back in the chair. "I know how that must sound, as though I've always had plenty and knew where the next batch was coming from. Nothing could be further from the truth, but… well, a woman's pocketbook just isn't like a man's billfold."

"My wife's purse is enough to convince me of that."

"You can joke, but I'm serious. Men think we cart around a drug store and a beauty parlor. I suppose we do, to some extent, but the really important things a woman wants to have with her are little pieces of her life… her family, things that can make you smile unexpectedly when you're searching for something else. Ticket stubs from a special occasion can do that, or a snapshot."

"Or a letter?"

"Yes… or a letter." Her eyes left him, and she contemplated the purse in her lap. She went on, but as though she were thinking aloud. "If you ever found yourself without access to home, to family, even for a little while – and I hope you never do, Raymond – you might begin to understand the trifles that pile up in a woman's purse. When they're taken away…"

Raymond didn't know what to say. He only knew they both needed him to end this uncomfortable silence, and he didn't know how.

The welcome return of Dwight was heralded by an unaccustomed knock.

"Come in, Nanook."

Still swathed in a stocking cap, ear muffs, and a scarf that began at his nose, Dwight set a small paper sack on the desk. "I didn't know how you take it, Ma'am," he said through his muffler, " but there's lots of cream and sugar in the bag." He removed a lid and handed her a tall paper cup.

"Lots is just what I take. You did well, Dwight."

He handed a lidded cup to Raymond and began an elaborate process of unwrapping himself. His employer regarded the boy with silent amusement.

"Now, if there's nothing else, I'll just get back to my counter duties."

"Yes," said Raymond, "an impatient horde has been massing out there in your absence. Where's my change?"

"Oh." Dwight pulled a thick glove out of his coat pocket, dug out the coins, and made an only semi-pouty withdrawal.

"You're not very easy on him, are you?"

"Dwight? Oh it evens out. He's extremely easy on himself."

"I think he admires you."

Raymond laughed out loud, spilling a little of his coffee.

"Well then, let's say he's prepared to admire you – if you're prepared to be admired."

"Oh, I think Dwight has more exotic role models in mind, Mrs. Sheffield."

"We don't realize the impression we make at times. I saw the way he looked at you when you held that man down." She emptied two containers of cream into her cup and stirred it slowly with a wooden stick from the sack. Then she took three long sips with deep breaths in between before setting the cup down and smiling at him. He felt as though he had witnessed a medicinal ritual.

Now it was over. "Raymond, I know you're busy, so - "

But something had changed on his side of the desk. "Don't rush with your coffee. This is an easy night. It shouldn't be, but… and anyway, if we weren't in here sorting this out, I'd be out there, making life miserable for the staff."

She ignored his smile, responding instead to the joylessness behind it. "Christmas *can* be a difficult time."

Uncomfortable, he took up pad and pen. "Do you want to press charges?"

"You'd prefer that I didn't, wouldn't you?"

"What I might prefer doesn't enter into it, Mrs. Sheffield. I hope I haven't given any other impression."

"But it will be easier for you if I don't?"

"My employers are more comfortable with uneventful days, yes, but it's for you alone to decide what's appropriate here. I mean that sincerely."

Frances pursed her mouth and looked beyond him. "He gave me a good scare, and I don't want him scaring someone else, or worse. The responsible thing would be to turn him over to the police."

"Yes, it may. I can do that now." He eased his hand in the direction of the phone.

"Just a minute! I didn't say I feel up to doing the responsible thing. I don't want to go to court. Would I have to?"

"Not necessarily, but possibly, yes."

"I don't even want to see that man again here, let alone in court, and I don't want him to see me."

"It might be avoided." Raymond sought to look thoughtful. "But I can't presume to promise."

"You see my dilemma," said Frances. "I don't want to be responsible for some other woman being accosted, but if I can possibly avoid - "

"Believe me, I understand, and while I meant what I said about not wanting to influence you, it occurs to me there are some things you might want to consider."

"Such as?"

Raymond steepled his hands and tried to look positively omniscient. "Well, for one thing, what happened tonight may have shocked you, but it's not going to shock the police or a judge. From their point of view, it's a pretty minor incident. If this man goes to jail at all, it'll only be for a short time. If this is his first offense, which we have no way of knowing, that might be enough to turn him around, but in any case, whether you pursue this or not, he'll soon be back out on the street to do pretty much whatever he wants."

He sat back to watch his words work. He knew that, after all, he had managed it. *My job description,* he thought, *Manager.*

Frances took another sip. "When you put it that way, I can see I'm not likely to accomplish much by going on with this."

"It's hard to say, of course." He lowered his eyes to the legal pad and fought the beginnings of a smile.

She measured him with a look. "I think you're what my mother used to call a smooth customer, Raymond. Is there at least some way to throw a scare into him and make him think twice before he does this again?"

"I hope that's happening as we speak."

"Where have you got him? You never told me."

"Out of harm's way, I assure you."

"I'm picturing a dungeon," said Frances, "deep in the underground recesses of the Jeffery."

"With moss on the walls."

"When will you let him out?"

"Not until after you've gone," said Raymond. "The Jeffery is sending you home in a taxi tonight."

"Oh my!" She was visibly pleased. "I don't take many taxis these days."

Probably none at all, he thought. "Maybe you should check over your purse to make sure he didn't slip something out."

"A good idea." She poked about and pulled out a change purse, tissue, keys on a dark blue ribbon, more tissue, and an envelope. Feeling his curiosity, she looked up. "It's from my older son. He's in the army. We haven't seen each other in over two years."

"But he writes."

"Yes, but not often, which makes me prize the letters even more when one does come."

"The army keeps you pretty busy."

"You think that's it?"

"It's quite possible. It depends where he's stationed. Everyone's situation is "

She shook her head and cut him off. "I don't think so. No, the fewer the lines you have to read between, the better you get at it. I think he doesn't write because he knows he's gotten himself into a tiresome and inappropriate situation. He made a rash decision, and now he's feeling foolish about it."

"A rash decision?"

"Enlisting. He wasn't called up. He called them. It happened out of the blue and took everyone by surprise."

"You couldn't talk him out of it?"

Her face clouded. "I wasn't around to try."

"You'd have persuaded me," said Raymond. "But you were away?"

Frances nodded. "Mm-hmm." She spoke less to him than to the room in general. "Farther than you can imagine." Her tone was not an invitation to further questions. She rose and gathered her coat from the back of the chair. "I'd better go on."

She examined the posters while he called for a cab.

"It'll be about ten minutes." When he replaced the receiver and turned back to her, she had brightened considerably.

"He'd be surprised to see me here, and envious. Eddie was always crazy about anything to do with the movies. I suppose that's really why I'm here tonight. Most of the time, it's hard to picture what he might be doing, but all week, I've had the feeling that on Christmas he'd be inside some Alaskan movie house. What wouldn't he give to be right where I am now, inside the manager's office? Wait 'til he hears about this."

Raymond chuckled. "No offense, Mrs. Sheffield, but I'm not used to such enthusiasm about my office. You're really going to write your son about this room?"

"I certainly am, and about you too. He'll want to know."

Raymond was grinning now. "And, of course, he'll get right back to you."

"Oh… I've learned not to expect that."

"Uh huh. Do you want my advice?"

"Well..."

But he had her attention. "We accumulate a lot of memorabilia here. It's all supposed to go back to the distributors, but some good stuff slips through the cracks. Pick out something you think he'd like and write him that I've given it to you, but don't tell him what it is. If he's still as keen about all this as you say, you may get a response by return mail."

"I really might. If anything, he's only gotten worse over the years."

"What were his favorites?"

"There was almost nothing he didn't like."

"Westerns?"

"Oddly, no."

Raymond drew a large box from a file cabinet and spread out an array of old lobby cards across the desk.

"This is kind of you. It's hard to know... His taste as a child was always a little...surprising. I'll just pick one at random. I'm sure he'd be thrilled with any – oh my! I remember – this one would be perfect, if you can spare it." She held up an image from *The Postman Always Rings Twice*, John Garfield in swimming trunks, emerging from the sea, with his arms full of Lana Turner. Frances was beaming. "He was nine years old and determined to see this. It was playing here, as a matter of fact. I remember it so well. It was adults only, and even if it hadn't been, there was no way in the world I was going to – I mean, he was nine years old, for heaven's sake. But you would have thought we had shot his dog. Oh, he could give lessons in sulking."

"Can Dwight enroll? He won't want to miss that."

She tried to frown, but settled for, "Oh now, it's Christmas." She looked again at the lobby card. "Ed will think this is marvelous."

"Then it's yours, but he's not to get it until you've had a proper letter." He put a stiff piece of cardboard behind it and stuffed it into a manila envelope. Then, he unlocked the center desk drawer and took out several cards. "I'm putting in a couple of passes. Our friend will never be back. I'm going to introduce him to the staff before I put him out."

He opened the door, and they stepped out into the lobby. Passing two ushers deep in conversation, Raymond hissed, "Get back inside the auditorium. I'll want to talk to you." As they neared the candy counter, Dwight whipped out a rag and began to polish the glass with great flourishes.

"Good night," said Frances, "and thank you again."

"Anytime Ma'am. We want you to think of this place as your home away from home."

"Like you do?" said Raymond.

They moved past the stub box into the outer lobby. Raymond stepped to the side of the ticket booth and peered out onto 71st Street. "The cab should be here any minute."

"You don't need to wait with me."

"You'll offend me, Mrs. Sheffield."

"Well then, I'm happy for the company."

He kept watch. "What a night. It's like color hasn't been invented yet."

"Raymond?"

"Yes?"

"I hope you're not always as unhappy as you seem tonight."

He looked at her but said nothing.

"Now I really have offended you."

He shook his head.

"Will you come outside with me, just for a moment?" She took his arm and led him through the door nearest them. "I know it's cold. I won't keep you long." She stepped toward the Jeffery curb and beckoned him after her. "Come all the way out from under the marquee and look up."

He moved beside her, and felt her gloved hand on his arm.

"You looked out, Raymond, and saw a lonely street, gray and deserted, but anyone alone on this street sees what we're seeing now." She directed his gaze upward. "Look. Slim lines of pink neon, cascading down around those great white letters blinking JEFFERY." As she became more animated, it was she, not the sign, that he chose to watch. "Silent fireworks, my son used to call it. He loved theater signs, and yours especially. When that sign goes off at night, the street does become the bleak affair you saw from inside, but while it shines..." The lights pulsed and rippled busily as she spoke. "It's an explosion of light and color that distracts us from everything around it, and, for a moment at least, it raises our spirits."

A Checker cab slid up beside them, Raymond opened the door for her, tapped on the window, and handed several bills to the driver.

"Go back inside, Raymond, before you freeze, but think about what I said sometimes."

"Goodbye, Mrs. Sheffield. Take care of yourself."

He closed the door and watched the taxi pull away, its windows suffused with reflected pink neon.

Shivering, he strode inside, stopping to polish his knuckles and assess the lobby.

"C'mon with me, Dwight. Let's spring the Prisoner of Zenda."

As they reached the closet, the boy tugged at his sleeve. "Mr. Muzydlo?"

"Mmhmm."

"Before you open the door, who's Zenda?"

Raymond looked at Dwight, looked at the door, put the keys back in his pocket, and sat down on a red velveteen bench. Patting the bench beside him, he said, "Siddown, kid. I'm gonna tell you all about it."

CHAPTER 19
A LOONEY TUNE
Chicago, August, 1960

They lay facing each other beneath a single sheet, just far enough apart to keep their noses from bumping. The boy nearest the window flinched as the other put out his hand and gently grazed the dark bluish bruise just below his companion's left eye.

"I won't hurt you."

"It's still sore."

"How did you do that? Were you in a fight?"

"It was no fight. It was a frigging massacre."

"Somebody you…met?"

"No. I've been in some dumb scenes, but that hasn't happened yet." He pressed the back of his finger against his lips, as if to dam the flow of words, then let it drop. "My father."

They continued to face each other in silence for a few seconds more, then the boy nearest the door raised up on his elbow, leaned over, and kissed the bruise.

"What was he mad about?"

"I never know. He doesn't do it much when he's sober." He examined the sheet and smoothed it. "I don't know. It's not any one thing. I'm just a great disappointment to him in general. Sometimes it bothers him more than others."

The other boy rolled on top of him and slid his arms beneath him.

"You're anything but a disappointment to me, Dwight, and I'm the only one here. Disappoint me again, pleeez, sir."

Dwight grinned. "Really?"

His partner cupped his head and licked an ear. "Oh yes, little apricot ears!"

"Eddie, half the time I don't know what the heck you're talking about."

"Is that a *big* problem?"

Dwight blushed. "No, because the rest of the time you make me feel like a real hotshot."

"You are a real hotshot. I merely point it out. There's nobody here to dispute it."

Dwight closed his arms around Ed and pulled him tighter. "Say it again, Eddie."

"Hotshot! Hotshot! Hot—" A door slammed. Dwight shot up rigid with a look of panic.

"You home? You in there, Dwight?" a voice called loudly.

"Yeah, Dad." Dwight moved like lightning. Ed found himself shoved toward the window, covered with a pillow and blankets. His mouth was stopped by the tight grip of Dwight's hand. By the time the bedroom door opened, Dwight was propped against him facing it.

"They didn't show up, so I knocked off early. What are you doing in bed? You look really strange. Stranger than usual."

Dwight spoke rapidly as his father approached the bed. " I don't feel good. It's my stomach. I've got cramps. I thought maybe if I could sleep—"

"You don't look good. All right, take it easy."

Ed held his breath and heard the man walk back to the door. "Listen, kid, about

last night; I know I flew off the handle. You just get me so goddam mad sometimes."

"I'm sorry." Beneath the covers, Ed frowned and thought, "*Why?*"

"Let's forget about it," said the older man.

Ed was smothering. He thought of the underwater sequence

in *Ziegfeld Follies*, where he had almost turned blue trying not to breathe until Esther Williams did. The door closed. He silently filled his lungs and stared at Dwight who leaned in close and spoke in the merest whisper.

"I'm so sorry. He wasn't supposed to be back for hours. You've got to get out of here."

Ed matched his hushed tones. "I'm not the only one who needs to get out of here."

They were almost miming. "I do, sometimes, when it gets bad."

"Where do you go?"

"My boss lets me sleep at his place."

"Does he fool around with you?"

"No, it's not like that." He kept looking nervously over his shoulder.

"Can't you lock it?"

"I wouldn't dare."

Ed slipped his arms around him, but Dwight did not relax. They sat motionless until Dwight said, "There. He's got the television on. He'll leave us alone."

Dwight leaned his head against Ed, his tension abating, though he continued to whisper. "Anyway, no, Raymond, my boss, is married. At first his wife wasn't thrilled about me sleeping over, but now when it happens, she fixes great breakfasts for me. She says she wants to fatten me up."

Ed turned Dwight toward him and squeezed him tightly. "Don't you let her do it."

"Why?"

"Because you look like this big wonderful rabbit, tall and slim. I've always wanted to find someone who looked like a rabbit. I won't let them turn you into a panda."

Dwight backed off. "What do you want someone who looks like

a rabbit for?"

"This, of course." Ed pushed him down and smothered his face with his own while Dwight wriggled beneath him.

When Dwight stopped moving, Ed sat up and heard a barely spoken, "You're a great kisser, Eddie."

"Yes, and who knew?" Ed raised his eyebrows. "Maybe it just seems like I am because your father is lurking on the other side of the door, ready to bash our heads in."

"No, that would have been a great kiss even if nobody was ready to bash our heads in."

"See, you *can* laugh."

"I guess," said Dwight, "but it's no joke. He's nuts, really nuts."

"I never whispered this much in church," Ed observed.

"I know. It's kind of – hot."

"Mm-hmm."

Ed took Dwight's face in his hands and kissed him again.

"I don't want to move, Eddie."

"Neither do I. Let's not. I was in the M.P.'s. They taught me jujitsu."

" Listen, if my father comes back in here, you'll think he invented jujitsu. I don't want him to hit you too. I can't believe I'm saying this, but please put some clothes on."

"O.K." Ed stood up and looked around for his briefs. He froze as a voice boomed in from the hall.

"Hey, Miss America! You still awake? What did you do with the TV log?"

Ed flattened on the floor and had only just slid under the bed when the door opened.

"Uhh, I was asleep. I think it's in the drawer in the end table. I'm tired, Dad. I really feel lousy."

"All right. I won't bother you again."

Ed waited until Dwight patted the edge of the bed before he

eased his head out from under it. Dwight's head was leaning over to meet it. Ed smiled up at him. "You were quite convincing."

"Ya gotta be, in this business."

Slowly, Ed eased himself out from under the bed, and as he did, Dwight crab-walked over him matching his motions until he lay on top of Ed, in the middle of the floor. They said nothing for a moment and felt each other breathe. Dwight pressed his forehead into Ed's and rotated it, like a cat, whispering, "Stay. Go. Stay. Go. Stay. Stay."

Ed pressed back and crossed his eyes, smiling. At last, he whispered, " How am I going to get out of here?"

Dwight pointed to the window.

"I said I was an M.P. I didn't say I was Spiderman."

"There's a fire escape."

Ed pulled Dwight's head to him. "I missed this ear."

They broke apart, stood up, and pulled on their briefs and pants. Each taking one side of the window, they eased it up, pausing at any slight noise it made. Ed gathered up his socks, shoes, and shirt.

"Can your father see the fire escape?"

"No."

"Then step out with me."

Dwight followed him over the sill, shirtless and barefoot.

"You can really see from up here!" said Ed. "What is this, the sixth floor? I lost count on the walk up."

"We're on five."

"It's high enough." Ed stepped to the railing. "Look at that! You can see the towers of the Avalon in the sunset! I've never seen it from this height... not exactly."

Looking back, he saw that Dwight was sitting against the wall of the building. He joined him, and their shoulders touched.

Dwight leaned into him. "I've slept out here when it was really hot. Nobody ever looks up."

Ed slid his arm around him. "Your father doesn't know about you, obviously."

Dwight shook his head. "Huh-uh. And he *won't*, as long as I'm here."

"How long will *that* be?"

"It's not as easy as you think." Dwight's face set into a pouty frown. "My job doesn't pay much, and I'm not exactly skilled labor."

"How old are you?"

"It's rude to ask. Don't you know that?"

"I'm sorry." Ed kissed his cheek, "but it's not just curiosity."

"Aw, I'm sorry too. I think you're the least rude person I ever met... I'm nineteen."

"It's time to move out, Dwight."

"I'm telling you, it's not so easy. Don't judge by today. I can handle things. I mean, he'd be all by himself. I'm used to it, really."

Ed shook his head. "You shouldn't be."

"Well, you should talk. You're still living at home, I bet. Isn't that why we couldn't go to your place?" But then Dwight dropped his defensive tone. "Or is there somebody you didn't tell me about?"

"There almost was," said Ed. *There should have been*, he thought.

"What went wrong?" asked Dwight.

Ed leaned back, remembering. "It was too soon. He said I was a work in progress." After a second, he added, "Bad timing... bad geography." He shook his head and with some effort forced Tex from the overcrowded fire escape.

He smiled at Dwight. "There's no one. There really isn't. I'm still with my relatives because I just got out of the army. But I assure you, that's a very temporary situation. Besides, nobody's beating me up."

"It sounds different when *you* talk about it."

"Easiest thing in the world, telling other people what to do with their lives."

"Except that you're right."

"Don't be scared." Ed knew he was saying it to both of them. "Maybe I can help you figure it out."

"If you could do that Eddie..." Dwight pressed close, and Ed felt tears on his neck. They were silent for a bit, then Dwight spoke again, "I wish we had hours and hours here, Eddie, but it's just minutes... they feel like seconds."

"Let's make 'em count. What? Whaaat? Why are you smiling?"

"We're out here, but I'm really back there in bed with you."

"Yeah..."

Dwight nuzzled Ed's shoulder and said, "I didn't know it could be so nice ... afterward."

"In my limited experience," said Ed, " there hasn't been much afterward."

Dwight's eyes grew wide, and he raised his voice. "Egg ZACKly! They just—"

Ed put his finger to his lips. " I don't want to get tossed off this balcony, and I'm getting good at this whispering. I *like* it. I'm barely speaking, and someone is really paying attention."

Dwight grimaced. "Oh Eddie, don't mess with me."

Ed scrunched his eyebrows. "I'm new to this; I don't think I'd know *how* to mess with you."

Dwight's baby face tightened into a bitter, unattractive smirk. "Queers are born knowing how to mess with each other."

Dwight was Ed's junior, though not by much, still Ed knew that, in this particular arena, Dwight was more experienced. Gradually, Ed had grown used to giving more weight to opinions from outside his own questionable head (except, of course, in matters of aesthetics, where he bowed to no one). Where human behavior was concerned, he had no more confidence in his judgment than the Sheffields did. But if Dwight were right, if this new world opening to him was really that cruel, that ugly, (even if at the moment he seemed to have the upper hand)... no, he would not believe it until he had to.

Dwight's expression softened as he watched Ed's debate with himself play out in silence. "Eddie, it's just.... well.... I like you, but I know we don't have too much in common. So, please don't lie to me or say more than you mean."

Ed stroked Dwight's hair. "I'm impatient too. I know I should just enjoy whatever happens, but I can't wait for the big love affair to begin, and I know that's a really stupid and dangerous way to behave."

"I don't think you'd be telling me that if you thought *we* could have a big love affair."

"Dwight, you have no idea how little I know about how to act or what to say to people I'm attracted to—or even what to think about them. But I promise I'll be as honest with you as I know how."

"Then tell me, honestly, when you go down this fire escape, I'm not ever going to see you again, am I?"

"Of course you are! You're my lucky rabbit." He pulled Dwight to him and kept their cheeks together as they spoke. "Did you think I was going to vanish without giving you my number?"

"Well, it's all been kinda odd. I wasn't sure."

"Dwight, I swear I'm beginning to think that odd is all there is. Climb inside and find a piece of paper." But in the very act of trying to persuade him they had a future together, Ed felt the undertow of Dwight's need and fear begin to pull him away. Why had Dwight raised the question so soon, forcing Ed to consider it? Had he done this before, not realizing the effect it could have - was having - on his prospects with someone? If this were Dwight's m.o, Ed could understand his companion's shrunken expectations. Ed didn't want to think about all that they mightn't have in common—not yet—certainly not while their ideas of sexual pleasure were so harmonious. But sex you could have by yourself. Lord knew, Ed had perfected that to a high art in the most uncongenial environments. With Dwight, there was more than sex. There was intimacy. You couldn't get that on your own. Ed craved it, and Dwight was terrific at it. Why was Dwight making him picture spending their lives together when it was so obvious Ed was dying to spend the night?

More than anything, Ed didn't want to join the parade of louses marching in and out of Dwight's life, but when it came to relationships, he had only his daydreams to draw on. Life had yet to present a diagram that seemed especially helpful. Captain and Mrs. Knox? His own parents? Uncle Vic and the Victorines? Did everything have to be decided immediately? Would it be so horrible if he and Dwight practiced a little, 'til they knew what they actually had? If he wasn't sure, was it kinder to do what Dwight feared and leave now rather than later? "I won't hurt him," Ed whispered to no one in particular, yet, he wondered, was it possible for Dwight to find a way to use him to hurt himself?

Did romance always arrive swathed in daunting layers of complexity? Ed hoped that love, when it came, would be simpler. It would not come tonight.

What if it never came? Grim pickings indeed if at the end your private life amounted to no more than a parade of ill-fitting adventures. It disturbed Ed that when Dwight turned around he would have no idea how much and how quickly their situation had altered. A process of disengagement, as gentle and imperceptible as Ed could make it, had already begun.

Easing cautiously over the windowsill, Dwight felt his back being massaged. There was nothing to write on, and he couldn't leave the bedroom—what to do…? He slid his calendar from the nail, tore a strip from April, and handed it through the window with a ballpoint.

Ed printed carefully.

"Hurry up, I'm scared," Dwight hissed at him.

"Here, call me. It's my grandparents' place, so it's no use to us. I'm trying to find a really cheap apartment that won't depress the hell out of me."

"We could go back to Rainbow Beach where you found me."

"How do I get hold of you? I guess you don't want me calling here."

"Yikes, no! Just come to the Jeffery. I'm there all the time at night," and then, almost before the words were jittered out, he was fast inside. For Dwight, desire had been elbowed aside by fear of his father, a fear that would keep him company until Ed moved out of sight.

He started down the steps and then, certain that he was well below the window, he sat down. As quietly as he could, he pulled on his socks and slid into his shoes. The eyes that he knew were peering by now from the side of the shade could not see him, but it was just as well not to alarm those little apricot ears with squeaking iron. Easing his arms into his shirtsleeves, he scanned the sea of rooftops for the towers of the Avalon. Pale shards of pink and amber played about the domes. *Cobalt blue*, he thought. Only someone in a cape of cobalt blue, long stored in moth balls, could sort out the mess in the apartment above him. Was it even worth it to try?

Still…

Piano music settled on him from above. Dwight had turned on the radio. Notes swelled and receded in short dramatic bursts, strutting with portent. Ed had just time to recognize the theme from *The Apartment* before Dwight reconsidered and it was gone.

There was something raw and touching for Ed in the behavior of anyone observed unaware. Their innocent exposure evoked Ed's protective instincts as Dwight's did now. Ed imagined him moving about in the small bedroom and was seized by the urge to embrace him out of his fidgets. If only – but what was it?

If only it didn't bother him that Dwight drew so much of his identity from being gay. Ed knew he had no right to blame him. He had done the same thing at first. The shock of discovery is dizzying and fraught with promise. Ed felt at the time he'd been granted a handle on an otherwise unmanageable world. Without realizing it, he'd gone through life holding his breath. Then, let in on this staggering secret, he could finally exhale.

It was the child's thrill of escape he had known fleeing the foyer at his mother's apartment, or racing down the Sheffield steps, but better... much better. Without change, just as he was, there were people to desire him, hidden and waiting in the most unexpected situations. All he need do was show up and be recognized.

He had stumbled upon a club with its own language and signals. Its membership was small but found everywhere, probably even on Mars, eager to welcome him into its rituals. It was frustrating in its unpredictability, but it could teach him who he was – or so he had thought.

Initially, the prospect of large numbers of others who felt as he did was most encouraging and agreeable, but he soon found that his sense of fraternal identity diminished proportionately as the membership around him increased. A mutual interest in men did not, in itself, make for good company. It was not battalions of buddies he needed in order to find himself. Just one, the right one, would do nicely.

Ed had but two regrets about his sexuality, that he had denied it as long as he had, and that it didn't explain him to himself as he hoped it might. It was, in fact, merely the latest in a series of misleading markers the world used to read him. As purveyors of reliable information about him, the labels Sheffield, Foley, Irish, Catholic, Caucasian, American, even male (and he would once have added "screw-up") were on a par with gift t-shirts worn by tourists' children.

Whoever he was, it was represented no better by this newest logo, "Gay," than by any of its predecessors. He was not, in any deeply important way, any of those things. They were accidental, not chosen but imposed upon him. Some of them came with social discount coupons, but none were worth bragging about.

Perhaps, unlike Manning Nugent, Ed would never learn his secret identity. Perhaps it didn't exist, and if these labels were stripped away, nothing would remain. Ed considered the darkly interesting destination toward which his train of thought now sped.

After a moment, he shook as if warding off a chill and let a grin take slow possession of his features. Beneath the labels, something did remain, peculiar and specific, even if he couldn't give it a name. It was selfish, lazy, and silly, but earnestly well intentioned, benevolent, optimistic, and amusing. It had sustained him in the past, kept his demons at bay, and would continue to do so in the future. It was there for the right person to sniff out and enjoy, but whether or not that ever happened, it was there. It was who he was, and he liked it.

He sat squinting into the distance for a few moments as shadows extinguished the last of the light on the towers. How different everything looked to him now. Alaska had sent him back with a gift of sorts, a new pair of eyes. He hadn't opened them or even suspected he had them, until he reached the Sheffield house. He assumed he was returning to an unchanged world, whose door he dreaded to reopen, but when he did, he saw little behind it that had remained the same. If he had gone to Mars or grown a second head, they could not have received him with greater curiosity, enthusiasm, and—most gratifying of all—adult civility. For almost two decades, he had been to them - what? Their budding indigent, their apprentice lunatic, their most dependable guarantor of shame and disappointment. Now, abruptly, he was treated as someone with his own agenda of reasonable plans and wishes. Didn't they realize it was still the same person who stood before them, no better, no worse, just a little older? Had Mrs. Teichman been right? Had he been a fool chasing after change and distance, when all he needed was just to wait, the one thing he did best in the world? He couldn't accept that; it trivialized his three-year army odyssey and would involve too much banging of his head against the wall, though the irony of it appealed to him.

Still, if he *had* changed, the Sheffields had had no time to take that in before launching on their pleasantly unsettling courtship of him. The biggest surprise in that regard was Uncle Victor. He kept taking Ed aside and trying to draw him into conversation with an air of camaraderie that Ed would once have cherished but now found quite resistible. If they would never be buddies, however, they had reached an accord to their mutual advantage. Victor used his connections at Sears to get Ed a job with hours flexible enough to accommodate a college schedule. Ed discreetly kept his uncle supplied with sacks of the White Castles that Victor's watchful new wife, Corrinne, denounced as unhealthy. Ed considered it a pretty even exchange.

Victor had been right about one thing. The sturdy machinery of the normal world could easily have ground Ed up and spit him out, and he knew it. What his uncle had neglected to mention was the inefficiency of that machine and the random nature of its operations. Disaster would always be out there as a possibility, but it was not the inevitable outcome Ed had grown up believing in. There were chinks and gaps that, with a little luck, he could slip through. Scattered here and there were pockets of kindness and even boredom with relentless regularity that worked in his favor when he could find them. He would need luck and resourcefulness, but so did the certifiably normal, who, Ed had learned, could also tumble into the machinery.

He squirmed and stood up. If he sat any longer on the fire escape, the pattern of its rungs would be branded on his bottom. He began his descent on tip-toe, though by now, Dwight would think him long gone. Ed had expected the amorous romp to last well into the evening, but now he had time on his hands and time these days was especially golden. The brief interim before his classes began was his alone, to be spent however, wherever, and with whomever he chose. He felt deliciously free and hopeful. He would "make 'em count."

He reached the bottom rung and stepped onto the sidewalk. Halfway down the block waited a car so ugly that Joe Terrapino would have shaken his head in disbelief: an elderly, orange Chevrolet, with sagging muffler and fenders flaked with rust. Manning Nugent would not have set foot in it, but the price had been right, and so far it had taken Ed where he wanted to go. He started it up and pondered the best possible thing to be doing with his evening. Several blocks later, he pulled to the curb, got out, and entered a phone booth. Depositing a dime, he looked at the slip of paper he had fished from his wallet, and dialed.

The throaty voice that answered had grown huskier than he remembered. "Hi, this is Ed. I wonder if I could... yes, how are you?... Of course I recognized your voice... You didn't?... A University of Chicago accent? I'm not sure I know what that would sound like... oh, I see, just like me... Well, I don't see how they could have spoiled me already; I don't even start classes until... aw jeez, could you just put Mom on, please?... Hi, thank goodness! Look, do you want to get out of there for a while and cool off? The Clark has a couple of Conrad Veidt movies tonight and I'd... I know, I know, we'll have to keep a sharp lookout." The Clark Theater, unfortunately, was one place where the audience might actually live up to his mother's old fears. It was also the only place where such fare as *The Thief of Baghdad* and *Escape* could be found.

"We could eat at The Casbah or outside at Café Azteca; they won't be crowded on a weeknight... I know, but we're worth it. Tomorrow

I'll just open a can of tuna… Well, I'm only a few blocks away, but I can dawdle. Can we make a quick getaway, though? Aunt Sheila's spoiling for a fight… Good. Okay, twenty minutes, then." He'd give her forty-five.

Then they would hurtle through the night along the lake in a decrepit car, eat strange food, and disappear into the ramshackle darkness of a theater where he might have to keep the audience at bay.

What bliss!

ACKNOWLEDGEMENTS

Fierce thanks go to Karen Jackson Grote, my editor, whose delight in the Blue Leopard led to his having two chapters of his own. Already, I miss our debates over each semicolon and conjunction.

Safe Inside could easily have been abandoned if not for the encouragement of my tiny band of faithful work-in-progress readers: Steve King, Johnnie Putman, Donna Kivland, Kay Moore, Katy Ahearn, Hannah Frisch, and Laurane Carnivale. Chapters came at them in chaotic order, often after epochal time lapses; yet, they asked for more, and so I finished.

Without Loyal Griffin, manager of the former Avalon Theater, (now the New Regal), this book would have depended too much on frayed and distant memories. This sympathetic and indulgent gentleman let me graze the vast and still shimmering interiors of the Avalon, sketching and sighing for hours. My childhood recollections had not exaggerated the exotic charms of this pleasure dome one bit.

Apologies to Kathy Pilja, my typist, now half blind from deciphering my decorative but only semi-scrutable longhand, amid a thicket of cross-outs and arrows.

Thanks also to Julie Bennett Lefkow who made me realize the need for a "Bungalow Blues" to kick start the narrative.

Darin Klatt's inspired rendering of the Blue Leopard comic book cover gives me a shiver of pleasure each time I look at it. He captures precisely Shorty's intentions and the mood of the piece.

Warmest appreciation to Rick Kaempfer and David Stern for believing in me and guiding me through this process safely and gently.

Finally, boundless love and gratitude to my mother and father, the sources of anything good, creative, funny, or worthwhile in me or this book.

SAFE INSIDE
A Memoir

is available at:
www.eckhartzpress.com

ECKHARTZ
PRESS

Also available on Eckhartz Press:

- *The Living Wills* by Rick Kaempfer & Brendan Sullivan
- *Records Truly is My Middle Name* by John Records Landecker & Rick Kaempfer
- *The Balding Handbook* by David Stern
- *A Reluctant Immigrant* by Felizitas Sudendorf
- *Back In the Game* by Rich King
- *The Daly News* by Joel Daly
- *Best Seat in the House* by Bruce Bohrer
- *Cheeseland* by Randy Richardson
- *Lost in the Ivy* by Randy Richardson
- *Life Behind the Camera* by Chuck Quinzio
- *Down at the Golden Coin* by Kim Strickland
- *Father Knows Nothing* by Rick Kaempfer
- *Truffle Hunt* by Brent Petersen
- *Hugh Hefner's Last Funeral and other True Tales of Love and Death in Chicago* by Pat Colander
- *Patty and the Stump,* Tim Clue and Spike Manton
- *Out the Door!,* M.L. Collins
- *In Small Boxes,* Ann Wilson
- *Rantings of a Bitter Childless Woman,* Jeanne Bellezzo
- *Monkey in the Middle,* Dobie Maxwell